Gendered Lives

Communication,

Gender,

and Culture

Gendered Lives

Communication,

Gender,

and Culture

JULIA T. WOOD

The University of North Carolina,
Chapel Hill

WADSWORTH PUBLISHING COMPANY
Belmont, California
A Division of Wadsworth, Inc.

COMMUNICATIONS EDITOR: Holly Allen
ASSISTANT EDITOR: Kathy Hartlove
EDITORIAL ASSISTANT: Joshua King
PRODUCTION EDITOR: Deborah Cogan
DESIGNER: Ann Butler
PRINT BUYER: Barbara Britton
PERMISSIONS EDITOR: Jeanne Bosschart
COPY EDITOR: Melissa Andrews
COMPOSITOR: Thompson Type
COVER DESIGN: Cassandra Chu Design
PRINTER: Malloy Lithographing, Inc.

I(T)P˜

International Thomson Publishing
The trademark ITP is used under license

2 3 4 5 6 7 8 9 10—98 97 96 95 94

Printed in the United States of America

Library of Congress Cataloging-in-Publication Data

Wood, Julia T.
    Gendered lives: communication, gender, and culture / Julia T. Wood.
        p.   cm.
    Includes bibliographical references and index.
    ISBN 0-534-20316-7
    1. Sex role.   2. Communication—Sex differences.   3. Gender identity.   I. Title.
HQ1075.W69   1993
305.3—dc20   93-3780

This book is dedicated to:

Emma Goldman, Elizabeth Cady Stanton, Susan B. Anthony, Sojourner Truth, Charlotte Perkins Gilman, Frederick Douglass, and other women and men who began the conversation about gender in this country;

and to:

Betty Friedan, Ella Baker, Marilyn French, Evelyn Fox Keller, bell hooks, Sandra Harding, Warren Farrell, Nancy Chodorow, Susan Faludi, Karlyn Campbell, Mary Daly, and other women and men who have kept cultural dialogue focused on issues of gender;

and to:

Cam McDonald, Michelle Wood Wilco, Keenan Bingman Cox, Daniel Wood Wilco, and other boys and girls whose voices will shape the next generation's understanding of women and men, masculinity and femininity, and the nature of gender in our society.

JULIA T. WOOD completed her doctoral studies at age 24 and joined the Department of Communication at the University of North Carolina at Chapel Hill. She is now a professor within that department, where she teaches courses and conducts research on gender and communication, feminist theory, and interaction in close, personal relationships. During her academic career, she has authored or coauthored seven books and edited three others. In addition, she has published more than 40 articles and chapters in books, presented numerous professional papers, and edits one of the major journals in the communication field.

Professor Wood lives with her husband, who is also on the faculty at the University of North Carolina; her cat, Scrambles; and Madhi-the-wonder-dog. When not engaged in academic pursuits, she enjoys traveling to countries like Nepal and Mexico, baking, and having conversations with friends, family and students.

Contents

ix

PART THREE

Gendered Communication in Practice 177

Acknowledgments

One of the most gratifying aspects of writing a book is the opportunity to thank those who have offered support, insight, and advice. I am indebted to many people for assisting me in writing *Gendered Lives*. First and foremost are my students. The undergraduate women and men in my classes are unfailing sources of education for me. Their questions and ideas, their willingness to challenge some of my notions, and their generosity in sharing their perceptions and experiences punctuate the pages that follow — sometimes in obvious ways, sometimes subtly, but always there.

My thinking about gender also reflects my interaction with many graduate students. In classes and conversations, we have collaborated to teach each other about intersections among communication, gender, and culture. Among the graduate students who have influenced my thinking are Lisa Lenze, Stephanie Sedberry, Michelle Violanti, Chris Inman, Eileen Dordek, Sharon Varallo, Chuck Grant, Houston Spencer, Richard Danek, Michele Mason, Debbie Lee, Brooke Baker, Linda Bourne, Deborah Austin, Lisa Hobbes, Andrea Wagner, Helena Economo, and Heidi Hamilton.

I am fortunate to be part of a department and a campus that support research and teaching about gender. My colleagues in the Department of Speech Communication have inspired new questions and helped me rethink familiar ones. Cori Dauber, Beverly Long, Soyini Madison, and Della Pollock in particular have enlarged my understandings of how gender is embodied and expressed in diverse ways, and Bill Balthrop in his role as chair has been especially generous in providing me with research assistance. I am also grateful to Chris Inman, also known as "Sherlock," for his careful and efficient research assistance during the writing of this book.

Until I wrote *Gendered Lives*, which is my ninth book, I was convinced that editors do not see their job as supporting authors actively. Holly Allen either never learned that rule of being an editor or she chose to disregard it. From our first discussions in the fall of 1991 through the development and publication of this book 2 years later, Holly was a constant source of enthusiasm, support, advice, and encouragement. She facilitated my work at every turn. Whatever strengths this book has result in substantial measure from her active collaboration. Among the many ways in which Holly supported this project was her selection of reviewers for preliminary drafts. The book as it now appears is substantially improved from former drafts, largely as a result of careful and considerate comments and suggestions from the following individuals: Sandra Albrecht, University of Kansas; Victoria DeFrancisco, University of Northern Iowa; Bonnie Dow, University of Cincinnati; Valerie Downs, California State University, Long Beach; Larry Lance, University of North Carolina at Charlotte; Suzanne McCorkle, Boise State University; Edward Schiappa, Purdue University; Patricia Sullivan, State University of New York, the College at New Paltz.

And, of course, always, I acknowledge my partner in work, love, mischief, and life: Robbie Cox. He consoles me when writing doesn't go well and cheers me when it does; he tolerates my preoccupation with projects like *Gendered Lives* even when they detract from our time together; and he provides me with a living model of the limitless possibilities for growth and change in humans and their relationships.

JULIA T. WOOD
The University of North Carolina
August 1993

Gendered Lives

Communication,

Gender,

and Culture

INTRODUCTION

Most textbooks open by discussing the area of study, but I'd like to launch our relationship a bit differently. I think you're entitled to know something about the person behind the words you're being asked to read, so I want to introduce myself.

Although we tend to think books are impersonal sources of information, this is an illusion. Like anything humans create, books reflect the experiences and identities of those who compose them. Authors influence books when we decide to include certain topics and to disregard others, to rely on particular theories that shape how information is presented, and to include some groups of issues and people and exclude others. Choices about content, writing style, and theoretical stance shape the content and the overall meaning a book has. This doesn't mean books are not informative or reliable, but it does mean they reflect authors' points of view. Like all books, *Gendered Lives* is personal. By telling you a little about who I am, what I believe, and why I wrote this book, I am inviting you to recognize that what you read is a human construction — not impersonal, objective information.

Who I Am

Let's start with some simple demographic information. I am a Caucasian, heterosexual, middle-class woman, who has been in a committed relationship for over 20 years. Yet, if you think about it, this information isn't really "simple" at all, since it implies a great deal about my identity and my perspective on life. For instance, I am obviously privileged in many ways — my race, class, and sexual orientation are approved by mainstream Western culture. I am also socially disadvantaged by my sex, since women are less valued than men in Western culture. I did not earn the privileges conferred by my skin, sexual orientation, and class, nor did I earn the inequities that come with being female in America. That is the nature of privilege and inequity — they are unearned. They do not reflect the achievements, efforts, or failings of individuals who enjoy and suffer them.

The Social Construction of Inequality

To speak of being privileged in some ways and diminished in others does not mean I take either for granted. The fact that my sex makes me vulnerable to job discrimination, violence, dismissal, and exploitation is not something I accept as unchangeable. In fact, one reason I wrote this book is that we *can* bring about changes in our society. I also do not accept my privileges unreflectively. Our society constructs inequality by assigning different value to various skin colors, genders, sexual orientations, and classes. The realization that my personal and professional life are contoured by whether I fit what our culture arbitrarily designates as "superior" makes me keenly aware that sex, gender, race, sexual orientation, and class profoundly influence individuals' knowledge, experience, and possibilities.

If we don't want to be limited to the horizons of our social position, we can try to learn about the experiences, feelings, and views of people in other social positions — the anger and hurt gay men and lesbians experience in a society that defines heterosexuality as normal; the resentment that heterosexual white men sometimes feel toward efforts to instigate changes that might reduce some of the privileges they enjoy; the frustration women experience in knowing they cannot venture out at night without risking assault; what it means to be a person of color in a sea of whiteness. Yet, we should not delude ourselves into thinking we understand fully the lives of others who are unlike us. Sensitivity and earnest efforts to understand are important, yet they cannot yield genuine insight into the daily reality of others' lives. We need to respect others as the authorities on their experiences.

What we can do is stretch ourselves to realize that our feelings, identity, values, and perspectives are not those of everyone. Mine, like yours, are shaped by the standpoint in a culture that uses personal qualities to define normal, superior, and inferior. Realizing the limits of our personal standpoint encourages us to learn from people whose standpoints differ from our own. We do this by respecting the difference of their lives and by recognizing that only they can define the meanings of their experiences, feelings, hopes, problems, and needs. We cannot speak for them, cannot appropriate their voices as our own. But to listen is to learn, and to learn is to broaden our appreciation of the range of human experiences and possibilities.

In addition, realizing that inequality is socially constructed empowers us to resist personal participation in sustaining it. We have choice in whether to accept our culture's designations of who is valuable and who is not, who is normal and who abnormal. We don't have to treat white skin, heterosexuality, maleness, and middle class as standard, or right. Instead, we may challenge social views that proclaim arbitrary values for differences and that limit human opportunities.

This book reflects my belief that inequities are socially constructed and are harmful to all of us—those our culture defines as good as well as those it labels inferior. Three features distinguish this book and support the views I discussed above. First, I include discussion of diverse classes, ethnicities, races, and sexual orientations whenever research is available. Unfortunately, what I can include is constrained by the limited study of people outside what our society designates as the norm. Regrettably, there simply is not enough research from a communication perspective on the range of human nature. I hope *Gendered Lives* better reflects the diversity of human beings than many current books.

A second feature of this book is language designed to include all readers. I will use terms like *he and she, women and men,* and *feminine and masculine,* in preference to *he, mankind,* and *men.* Yet, inclusive language means more than including women. It also means using language that recognizes other groups our culture has marginalized. For instance, I refer to individuals in intimate relationships as *partners* rather than *spouses.* The term *spouse* excludes lesbians and gay men, since our society denies gays and lesbians the legal, material, and interpersonal legitimacy accorded to heterosexuals. My use of inclusive language is not merely an effort to be "politically correct." Rather, it reflects my unwillingness to contribute to sustaining inequities, even in subtle ways. If I use exclusive language like *spouses,* then I participate in oppressing those whose commitments our society refuses to recognize.

A third way in which *Gendered Lives* reflects awareness of my own limited standpoint and my respect for those whose standpoints differ is in the narratives that punctuate this book. In the pages that follow, you'll meet a lot of students—

some like you, some quite different. In my course on gender and communication, students keep a journal in which they write about issues that arise in our class conversations. Many of my students were kind enough to give me permission to include their ideas in this book. I've tried to return their generosity by including a range of individuals and viewpoints, including ones with which I personally disagree. I have refrained from evaluating or interpreting their ideas, since the students speak clearly and eloquently, and I don't want to muffle their voices with my analysis. You'll encounter their narratives unedited, so you may mull them over on their own terms.

Feminism — Feminisms

Finally, in introducing myself to you, I inform you that I am a feminist. My students tell me this is the new "f word," and most reject that term when describing themselves. Yet, when we talk, we often discover we agree on most issues but disagree about what feminism means. There's good reason for this. First, feminism is not one single belief or stance, but many. Chapter 4 discusses a variety of feminist positions as well as different stances within men's movements. Most people's impressions of feminism have been shaped by how media have portrayed feminism and feminist movements. Beginning with the *inaccurate* report in the 1960s that feminists burned bras (which did not occur then), media have consistently misrepresented feminists as man-hating, tough, shrill extremists. Yet, that stereotype fails to fit many women and men who define themselves as feminists. Like me, many feminists have good relationships with both women and men, and most are generous and compassionate as well as vocal in challenging inequities in our society. Common to most feminists are recognition that women have been unfairly devalued and marginalized and a commitment to changing this.

I define feminism as an active commitment to equality and respect for life. For me, this includes respecting all people, as well as nonhuman forms of life and the earth itself. Simply put, my feminism means I am against oppression, whether it be oppression of women, men, lesbians, African-Americans, Jewish individuals, gay men, elderly people, children, animals, or our planet. I don't accept oppression and domination as worthy human values, and I don't believe differences must be ranked on a continuum of good and bad. I believe there are better, more humane and enriching ways to live, and I am convinced we can be part of bringing these alternatives into existence. That is the essence of feminism as I define it for myself. During the course of reading this book, you will encounter varied versions of feminism, which should shatter the myth that it is a single thing and should invite you to consider where to position yourself among diverse viewpoints.

Feminism is not something that just happens. It is an achievement and a process. For me it began in the 1970s when a friend first introduced me to some readings that made me aware of discrimination against women. My initial response to this knowledge was denial—I tried to rationalize inequities or repress them, perhaps because recognizing them would be too painful. When denial failed to work, I entered an angry phase. I was bitter about my growing understanding of ways women, including me, were treated. This anger led me to strike out, sometimes at inappropriate targets. It was a deep anger directed both toward discrimination against women and toward myself for having been ignorant of it for so long. The angry and embittered phase was necessary for me to absorb what I was learning, but it could not lead me forward in any constructive sense.

Finally, I transformed the anger into an abiding commitment to be part of change, not so much for myself as for the next generation. I want our society to be more fair, more respectful of differences, and more affirming of individuals than historically it has been. Years later when I began to study gender issues, I learned that the path I had traveled to achieve my feminist identity is not uncommon: Denial, anger, and transformation to constructive commitment are stages many individuals undergo as they dislodge themselves from one identity and understanding of how the world operates and form alternate ones.

Becoming Aware

You may be unsettled as you read this book and discuss gender, culture, and communication in your course. If you are a woman, you may find it disturbing to learn the extent to which Western culture discounts your experiences and limits your opportunities. I also realize a number of women reading this book have been raped, abused by relatives, sexually harassed, and/or battered; some of you are bulimic or anorexic; some have suffered job discrimination. Reading *Gendered Lives* is likely to stir up issues like these in your personal life. If you don't wish to deal with these, then you may wish to forego or delay study in this area. If, however, you are ready to wrestle with serious personal matters, then this book should help you understand more about why issues in your life are not only personal but also political. They reflect widespread cultural biases that marginalize women, condone violence and aggression, and promote inequities.

If you are a man, you may become more aware of the unearned privileges conferred on you just because of your sex, and you may feel uneasy about some of your attitudes and actions. You may find it uncomfortable to focus on social expectations of masculinity that pressure you to perform, succeed, win, be self-sufficient, repress feelings, and maintain control. If you are white and straight, you may also feel on the spot, since this book and the class explore how a society that names white, heterosexual men as superior oppresses women, minorities, gays, lesbians, and anyone else outside of that narrow category. This is not a personal indictment of you or other individual men. It's important for all of us—men and women alike—to distinguish between individual men and inequities that arise from cultural evaluation of men and masculine ways as superior. This book does not suggest that individual men are bad, oppressive, or discriminating — some are, some are not. The point is that a culture that constructs inequality on the basis of sex, skin color, sexual orientation, and other factors diminishes all of us. It limits our appreciation of human diversity by falsely defining a very restricted zone of what is good, normal, and worthy of respect. Regardless of whether you are privileged or oppressed by social evaluations of what is normal and good, studying gender, communication, and culture may be unsettling. If you find this material triggers too much stress, then you might find it helpful to talk with your instructor or to visit the counseling center at your school. Professionals should be able to assist you in using stress as a path to personal growth.

▄▄▄ Why I Wrote This Book

Writing a book is a major commitment that makes sense only if an author believes in her or his message. I invested the time and energy to write *Gendered Lives* because I believe change is needed and possible and understanding empowers individuals to act as agents of change.

Change is needed. In the chapters that follow, you'll learn about the extent to which our society creates inequities by defining men, white skin, middle- and upper-class status, and heterosexuality as superior to women, colored skin, lower-class and lesbian and gay orientations. I hope to make you more aware of the impact of these inequities on the psychological, interpersonal, professional, economic, and material circumstances of people's lives. Is it right, for instance, that 50 to 75% of women working outside of the home experience sexual harassment in their jobs? Is there any way to justify the fact that a woman is battered by her intimate partner every 12 seconds, every day in the United States, or that four women die from battering each day? Is it acceptable that the longer males stay in school the higher their esteem and desire to achieve, and the longer females attend school the lower their esteem and desire to achieve, even though boys and girls enter school with equal self-esteem and motivation to achieve? Is there any legitimate basis for a white woman's being paid 72 cents for every dollar a white man makes, while minority women are paid even less?

If you were unaware of these issues and you think they should be changed, then read on. Becoming aware of the ways in which our culture establishes and communicates inequities is necessary, but that alone does not lead to progress. In fact, concentrating exclusively on what is wrong tends to depress us and paralyze impulses toward reform. Awareness of gender inequities must be coupled with belief that change is possible. A bit of historical perspective should convince us of this. Until 1920, women were not allowed to vote — they had no voice in the government and laws that affected them. They also had no access to university educations, could not own property if they married, and were barred from partic-ipating in many professions. Since 1972, schools receiving federal funds have been required not to discriminate against women. When my mother had a child in 1958, her employer dismissed her because he believed that a mother should not be actively engaged in brokering stocks. She had no voice and no legal recourse. We now have laws to protect women against unfair employment practices. In the last decade, sexual harassment has been named and brought to public awareness, and in February of 1992, courts ruled that victims of sexual harassment may sue institutions for compensatory as well as punitive damages.

Paralleling these changes in laws are substantial transformations in how we view ourselves and each other as women and men. Our culture formerly defined women as too frail and delicate for hard manual or intellectual work. Today women pursue careers in business, construction, science, education, politics, and the military. Despite lingering barriers, they are doing things and defining them-selves in ways not previously possible for women in America. Men, too, have changed. At the turn of the century, our society defined manliness in terms of physical strength and bravery. Following the Industrial Revolution, the ability to earn a good salary became the social standard of manliness. Today many men are challenging social definitions of men as income producers and demanding greater opportunities to participate in family life and personal relationships. You have options for what you will do and who you will be that were not available to your parents. Recognizing that views of gender have evolved fuels our conviction that further changes can be realized.

▨ Communication as the Fulcrum of Change

Change comes about through communication, which is the heart of social life and social evolution. Through communication we identify and challenge cur-rent cultural views that constrain individuals and create inequities. We also rely on communication to define alternatives to the status quo and persuade others to share our visions. At all levels of social change we find human communication. Speeches by women like Elizabeth Cady Stanton in 1848 galvanized support for the women's rights movement that was instrumental in enfranchising women. Public discourse sparks and guides collective efforts at political reform. Yet, other kinds of communication also instigate change. Perhaps you talk with a friend about gender inequities and your friend is influenced to alter her or his percep-tions. Maybe a teacher discusses sexual harassment with a class and a student is empowered to bring charges against a man who has been harassing her. You talk with your father about ways in which current leave policies disadvantage working mothers, and he persuades his company to revise its policies. Wherever there is change, we find communication. Through your public, social, and interpersonal communication, you are a powerful agent of change—someone who can bring about transformations in yourself and the society in which we jointly participate.

A key foundation for effective change is information. Before you can define what needs to be different, you must first know what exists now and what it implies. To be a credible catalyst for change, you must be informed about gender inequities and how they are created and sustained by communication within our culture. You must understand how conventional views of masculinity and femininity lead to inequities, how they reflect cultural values, and how institutional, social, and personal communication sustains the status quo. In addition, you should consider diverse perspectives on gender issues, rather than assuming there is one, single "truth." Reading *Gendered Lives* and taking this course should make you more informed about issues and a range of viewpoints on them. In addition, it should enhance your awareness of the pivotal role of communication in sustaining and altering existing cultural patterns. Then you can make informed choices about what you believe and about what identity you wish to fashion for yourself. Some of you will want to change your identity and how you view gender. Others of you may be entirely satisfied with your identity and/or with traditional gender arrangements in our culture. Either stance is grounded if it is an *informed* choice, but no choice is wise if it is not based on information, discussion, and serious reflection.

The Challenge of Studying Communication, Gender, and Culture

Studying communication, gender, and culture requires courage, because it involves us in unsettling questions about our culture and our personal identities. It forces us to think seriously about how our society defines gender and what that means for our personal lives, safety, relationships, and professional opportunities. We have to be willing to consider new ideas openly and to risk values and identities that are familiar to us. Further, with awareness comes responsibility. Once we are informed about gender and communication, we can no longer sit back passively as if this is not our concern. It is our concern both because it affects each of us directly and because we are part of a collective world. Thus, how we act—or fail to act—influences our shared culture.

Because studying communication, gender, and culture is unsettling, it is not easy. Yet, it can be very worthwhile. By questioning constructed inequality, we empower ourselves to do more than reproduce the cultural patterns we inherited. By involving ourselves in communication that enlarges others' awareness and revises cultural practices, we assume active roles in creating personal and collective lives that are more fair, more humane, and infinitely more enriching than what might otherwise be possible. That is the goal of *Gendered Lives*.

𝒟iscussion Questions

1. The author states that books do not present objective information. Do you agree or disagree? If books aren't neutral and unbiased, how do we know what to believe and what to do with ideas in books? Could an objective, neutral book be written?

2. The author explains who she is and how that affects what she has written. What is your image of the author based on the information she provided? How does that image affect your perceptions of the book? How do you think her identity shaped her thinking about issues of communication, gender, and culture?

3. What is your own standpoint, or position? Using the author's self-description as a guideline, define yourself and discuss how your identity influenced your choice to take this course, as well as how it may affect your perceptions of topics in the book and the course.

4. How have you been privileged and disadvantaged by your membership in various groups designated by our society? How have your privileges and disadvantages affected your opportunities, knowledge of issues, interests, abilities, goals, and so on?

5. If each of us is informed and constrained by our unique standpoint, to what extent is it possible to understand others? Can someone who is white, in the upper socioeconomic class, heterosexual, and Protestant really understand the experiences of a Hispanic man, a Latina, a gay person?

6. The author explains why she will use language that is as inclusive as possible. Is this a good idea? What do you think of modifying language to reduce exclusion? Is *partner* preferable to *spouse*? Is *he or she* better than *he*? Does language make a difference in how we think?

7. Write out *your* definition of feminism. What does it mean to you? What differences has it made and can it make in your personal life and the society? When you've completed this course, review this definition to see if it still expresses what feminism means to you.

8. The author discusses change as one of her goals in writing *Gendered Lives*. What changes do you think are most needed in our society? How are these related to issues of communication, gender, and culture?

PART I

Conceptual Foundations

CHAPTER ONE

The Study of Communication, Gender, and Culture

Not long ago, I mentioned to a friend that I was writing a textbook about communication, gender, and culture. In amazement, she asked, "How could you write a whole book on such a limited topic? And are many students really interested in a course in that?" I was as surprised by her questions as she was by my project. In response, I explained that gender and communication courses are among the most rapidly expanding areas of study in college and university curricula. Many campuses, like mine, cannot meet the high student demand for enrollment in these classes. I also assured my friend that there is more than enough research on gender and communication to fill *several* books!

This chapter introduces communication, gender, and culture as an area of study. After discussing how studying relationships among gender, communication, and culture can empower you personally and professionally, we will look at the key concepts that form the framework of this book. This should provide us with a common vocabulary for the chapters that follow.

Communication, Gender, and Culture as an Area of Study

Two reasons explain skyrocketing enrollments in gender and communication courses: (1) expanding knowledge about intersections among gender, communication, and society and (2) student interest.

Knowledge of Gender, Communication, and Culture

Had you attended college even a decade ago it's unlikely you would find a textbook like this one. Classes that explore various aspects of gender have become widespread only in recent years. Before this, research on gender and communication was limited and offered no extensive understanding of how both interact with culture. During the last 20 years, an explosion of interdisciplinary scholarship has generated rich insight into how gender is created and sustained through communication within cultures. Courses informed by this substantial scholarship are especially stimulating because they reflect multiple, complementary perspectives of diverse disciplines. This research illuminates patterns in women's and men's communication, why their communication styles and goals sometimes differ, and how their communication tends to be perceived by others in settings ranging from personal to professional. In short, we now know a great deal about how cultural structures and practices create and sustain understandings of gender and how these engender the identities of individuals.

Student Interest

A second reason for rising enrollment in courses in gender and communication is students' interest in the subject. Because all students communicate constantly and all are women or men, gender and communication are ongoing and important dimensions of everyday life. Differences between women's and men's communication show up when heterosexual intimate partners try to work through problems using distinct styles of conflict management, when male and female co-workers have different preferences for how to lead a meeting, and when female and male political candidates say similar things but the public evaluates them differently. In these areas, as well as others, gender affects how we interact with others, and social views of gender influence how women and men are perceived. Given the constancy of gender and communication in our lives, it is little wonder students seek courses to help them be more effective in interacting with women and men.

The Value of Studying Communication, Gender, and Culture

Learning about relationships among communication, gender, and culture serves three important goals. First, it will enhance your appreciation of complex ways in which communication, gender, and culture interact. Reading this book should increase your understanding of the extent to which cultural values and habits influence your views of masculinity and femininity. In addition, you will become more aware of ways in which cultural expectations of gender are communicated to you in your daily life. In turn, this should expand your insight into how your own communication affirms or challenges prevailing cultural prescriptions for gender. This enables you to be reflective and active as you craft your personal identity and participate in cultural conversations about gender.

Second, studying communication, gender, and culture should enhance your effectiveness as a communicator. Once you understand how culture shapes gender and gender shapes communication, you'll find you listen more perceptively to what others say. By extension, learning about differences in how women and men communicate should enlarge your ability to appreciate the distinct validity of diverse communication styles. This allows you to interact more constructively and insightfully with others whose ways of communicating may differ from your own.

A third value of studying gender, communication, and culture is to expand your options as a communicator. Most people who haven't studied this material are restricted to a single style of interacting. We stay limited if we don't recognize and understand varied ways to communicate. On the other hand, when we learn about alternative styles and develop skill in communicating in multiple ways, we expand our choices for being effective in diverse situations with a variety of people. A broad and flexible repertoire of communication skills is especially important today, since we are a global community in which diversity is a constant. Effective participation in contemporary life demands that we understand varied individuals with whom we interact and that we develop options for how we communicate.

▨ The Meaning of Gender in a Transitional Era

These days we hear a lot about problems between the sexes and about "the gender gap." We're told that men and women misunderstand each other and don't speak the same language. Talk shows feature guests who discuss "women who love too much" and whether women should have active roles in combat duty. In magazines we read about the "new fathers" who are actively involved with their children. Men are often confused when women want to continue talking after an issue is settled; women become frustrated when men seem not to listen or respond to what they say. What men and women expect of each other and themselves is no longer clear.

Confusing Attitudes

If you are like most people who have been socialized in America in the past 20 or so years, then you have a number of attitudes about gender and what it means. You probably do not subscribe to your grandparents' ideals of manhood and womanhood, which rigidly distinguished men as breadwinners from women as homemakers. It is likely that you think both women and men should be able to pursue careers and both should be involved in homemaking and child care. You probably have taken classes taught by women and men, and some of each were quite good while others were not so interesting. You are not surprised when a woman knows something about car maintenance or a man prepares a good meal. These experiences and your attitudes about them depart from those of former generations. Americans as a whole have enlarged their perspectives on women's and men's roles and abilities.

Yet, if you're like most of your peers, there are also a number of gender issues about which you are confused. Many people believe women should have equal opportunities in public and work life, but they think women should not be involved in actual combat during wars. We might think women should not be

MICHAEL

The other day in class we were talking about whether women should be in war. I'm really uncomfortable with where I stand on this, since I *think* one way but I *feel* another. I do think women should have to serve just as much as men do. I've never thought it was right that they didn't have to fight. And I think women are just as competent as men at most things, and could probably be good soldiers. But then when I think about my mom or my sister or my girlfriend being in the trenches, having to kill other people, maybe being a prisoner who is tortured and assaulted, I just feel that's wrong. It doesn't seem right for women to be involved in killing when they're the ones who give life. Then, too, I want to protect my girlfriend and sister and mom from the ugliness and danger of war. But then this other part of me says "Hey, guy, you know that kind of protectiveness is a form of chauvinism." I just don't know where I stand on this except that I'm glad I don't have to decide whether to send women into combat!

judged primarily by appearances but should be recognized for their intellectual, personal, and career capabilities. Yet the cosmetics industry makes a billion dollars a year because American women still pursue the ideal of beauty and because American men still regard attractiveness as very important in women (Wolf, 1991). Although a majority of young adults believe both parents should participate in childrearing, most people also assume the mother, not the father, should take time off from a career to be with a child during the early years of life (Hochschild, 1989). You may believe women are as effective as men in management, yet you're still more comfortable with a man as your supervisor.

When we grapple with issues like these, we discover that our attitudes are less than clear even to ourselves. On one level many of us think women and men are equal in all important respects; yet, on another level where deeply ingrained values and beliefs reside, we have some very traditional feelings and views. The conflict in our own attitudes and values—the clash between ideals of two distinct eras—makes us unsure of what we *really* believe and of who we *really* are. This reminds us that we live in a transitional time in which we no longer embrace former views of men and women, yet we haven't become comfortable with alternative images of the sexes. This makes our lives and our relationships interesting, unsettled, and sometimes very frustrating!

Differences Between Women and Men

Are women and men really as different as pop psychologists would have us believe? Certainly between the sexes there are some important differences that we need to understand. There is also a great deal of variation within the sexes, with regard to diverse experiences, sexual orientations, races, and classes. And there

MANDY W.

Sometimes I think my boyfriend is from another planet. It just doesn't seem possible we grew up in the same world when we can be so different. Just last night, when I said I'd like to talk about our relationship, he did the standard male thing—rolled his eyes and groaned, "Oh, no, what's wrong *now?*" Why does something have to be wrong to talk about a relationship? He just doesn't seem to enjoy thinking about us and looking at how we behave with each other. He says it's boring. But I think talking about our relationship is fascinating, and it makes me feel closer when we do it. Like I said, different planets.

are a great many similarities between women and men — ways that the two sexes are more alike than different.

Because there are similarities between the sexes and variations within each one, it is difficult to come up with language for discussing general differences in communication patterns. Terms like *women* and *men* are troublesome because they imply a sameness across all women and all men. When we say, "Women's communication is more personal than men's," the statement is true of most, but not all, women and most, but not all, men. Certainly not all women engage in personal talk and not all men avoid it. Thinking and speaking as if all women are alike and all men are alike is referred to as **essentializing**,* the tendency to reduce either sex to certain essential characteristics. When we essentialize, we distort by implying that all members of a sex are alike in basic respects and that they are distinct from the other sex in these respects (Spelman, 1988; Young, 1992). Essentializing obscures the range of characteristics possessed by individual women and men and conceals differences among members of each sex. In this book we will discuss generalizations about women and men, but this does not imply any essential, universal qualities possessed by all members of a sex. We'll also take time to notice exceptions to generalizations about gender.

To think constructively about differences and similarities, we need to understand what gender and sex are, how they are influenced by the culture in which we live, and how communication reflects, expresses, and re-creates gender in our everyday lives. In *Gendered Lives*, we'll consider different images of masculinity and femininity and explore why such diverse views exist and what practical implications they have. To explore this, we'll need to consider more than gender alone. We will also want to examine both how communication creates our gender identity and how we use communication to express our masculinity or femininity in interaction with others. A third focus of our attention will be culture, since gender is embedded within culture and reflects the values and assumptions of the larger society. To begin our study, we need some preliminary definitions of the central concepts in this book: gender, culture, and communication.

▓ Relationships Among Gender, Culture, and Communication

When once asked to discuss a particular aspect of nature, John Muir, who founded the Sierra Club, said he could not discuss any single part of the natural world in isolation. He noted that each part is "hitched to the universe," meaning it is connected to all other parts of nature. Gender, culture, and communication

---

*Boldfaced terms appear in the Glossary at the end of the book.

are interlinked, and they are hitched to the whole universe. Because this is so, we cannot study any one of them without understanding a good deal about the other two. What gender means depends heavily on cultural values and practices; the ways a culture defines masculinity and femininity lead to expectations about how individual women and men should act and communicate; and how individuals communicate establishes meanings of gender that, in turn, influence cultural views. Clearly, gender, culture, and communication interact in elaborate, ongoing patterns. Each of these three concepts is complex, so we will clarify them in the following sections. This will allow us to share common meanings and vocabulary in the chapters that follow.

Gender and Sex

Although you sometimes hear *gender* and *sex* used interchangeably, the two concepts have very distinct meanings. Sex is a designation based on biology, while gender is socially and psychologically constructed. Each of us has some qualities that our culture labels feminine and some it defines as masculine. How much of each set we have indicates our psychological sex, or gender. Sometimes the two go together so that men are masculine and women are feminine. In other cases, a male is more feminine than most men, or a woman is more masculine than the majority of women. Psychological sex, or gender, refers to how an individual sees himself or herself in terms of masculine and feminine tendencies. In many respects, your gender represents an area of potential choice for you, since you can change it more easily than your sex. Because sex is the less complex concept, we'll explain it first, then discuss gender.

Sex.　**Sex** is classified by biological characteristics. Our society uses genetic and biological qualities to define whether a person is male or female. Designation of sex is usually based on external genitalia (penis and testes in males, clitoris and vagina in females) and internal sex organs (ovaries and uterus in females, prostate in males). The genitalia and internal sex organs, in turn, are determined by chromosomes, which program how a fetus develops. Of the 23 pairs of chromosomes that direct human development, only one pair affects sexuality. The chromosome pair that determines sex usually has two chromosomes, and one of these is always an X. The presence or absence of a Y chromosome determines whether a fetus will develop into what we recognize as male or female. Thus, an XX creates female sex, while an XY creates male sex. Genetic research (Gordon, 1983) indicates that the X chromosome has a more complex molecular structure, which may be why males, who usually have only a single X chromosome, are more vulnerable to a number of X-linked recessive conditions.

You might have noticed that I qualified discussion of genetic determination of sex by using words like *usually* and *typically*. That's because there are occasional departures from the standard XX or XY structure. Some sex chromosomes are XO, XXX, XXY, or XYY. As long as there is a single Y chromosome, a fetus will develop into what we label male, although he may differ in some respects from males with the more standard XY pattern.

Sex is also influenced by hormones, another biological factor. Even before birth, hormones affect us. Beginning only 7 weeks after conception, hormones influence sexual differentiation in the fetus. They determine the development of internal sex organs, which control reproductive capacities. In most cases, biology works smoothly so that the hormones direct development of female or male reproductive organs that are in line with external genitalia. Occasionally, however, something goes awry and sexuality is ambiguous or mixed, with the result that a person has some biological characteristics of each sex. People whose internal and external genitalia are inconsistent are called hermaphrodites, a condition usually caused by irregularities in hormones during the early stages of pregnancy.

When pregnancy proceeds normally, fetuses with a Y chromosome are bathed in androgens that ensure development of male sex organs, and fetuses without a Y chromosome receive relatively little androgen, so female sex organs develop. In some cases, however, a pregnant woman does not produce the hormones conducive to normal sexual development of a fetus. More typically, when normal hormones are not present, it is due to outside intervention. Hormones may be administered externally, as when doctors give a synthetic form of progesterone to lessen the likelihood of miscarriage. Because this stimulates male sex organs to develop, a genetically female fetus (XX) that is exposed to excessive progesterone (progestin is the synthetic form) may develop male genitalia. The opposite is also true: If a male fetus is deprived of progesterone during the critical period of sexual differentiation, his male genitalia may not develop and he will appear physically female (Money, 1986).

The influence of hormones does not end with birth. They continue to affect our development by determining whether we will menstruate, how much body hair we will have and where it will grow, how muscular we will be, and so forth. Because male fetuses receive heavier amounts of hormones, they become sensitized to hormonal influence. Researchers currently think this may be why males are more sensitive than females to hormonal activity, especially during puberty (Jacklin, 1989).

Because research on biological sexuality is still relatively new, there are many questions for which we lack conclusive answers. For instance, among scientists there is divided opinion about whether sex hormones affect sexual preference (Adler, 1990; Money, 1988) and cognitive abilities (Adler, 1989; Bleier, 1986). Also, there is controversy over whether high levels of testosterone result in aggression and violence. It will be a long time before we unravel these mysteries, as well as others surrounding sex chromosomes and hormones.

What we do know with confidence is that however strong the influence of biology may be, it seldom, if ever, determines behaviors. It *influences* behavior in greater or lesser amounts, but it doesn't *determine* behavior, personality, and so on. There is general consensus among researchers that environment is at least as great an influence on human development as biology, and a majority of researchers conclude environment is the stronger of the two factors in influencing what we think, feel, and do. Awareness of environment in shaping our identities moves us into discussion of a second concept: gender.

Gender.   **Gender** is a considerably more complex concept than sex. There is nothing a person does to acquire her or his sex. It is a classification based on genetic givens and one that is enduring. Gender, however, is neither innate nor necessarily stable. It is acquired through interaction in a social world, and it changes over time. One way to understand gender is to think of it as what we learn about sex. We are born male or female — a classification based on biology — but we learn to be masculine and feminine. Gender is a social construction that varies across cultures, over time within a given culture, and in relation to the other gender. We'll elaborate this definition in our discussion.

Gender is a social, symbolic creation. The meaning of gender grows out of a society's values, beliefs, and preferred ways of organizing collective life. A culture constructs and sustains meanings of gender by investing biological sex with social significance. Consider current meanings of masculinity and femininity in America. To be masculine is to be strong, ambitious, successful, rational, and emotionally controlled. Although these requirements are perhaps less rigid than they were in earlier eras, they remain largely intact. Those we consider "real men" still don't cry or need others to help them; "real men" are successful and powerful in their professional and public lives.

Femininity in the 1990s is also relatively consistent with earlier views, although there is increasing latitude in what is considered appropriate for women. To be feminine is to be attractive, deferential, unaggressive, emotional, nurturing, and concerned with people and relationships. Those who embody the cultural definition of femininity still don't outdo men (especially their mates), disregard others' feelings, or put their needs ahead of others. Also, "real women" still look good (preferably very pretty and/or sexy), adore children, and care about homemaking. For all of the changes in our views of women and men, the basic blueprint remains relatively constant (Cancian, 1989; Riessman, 1990; Wood, 1993a).

Gender is learned by individuals. Socially endorsed views of masculinity and femininity are taught to individuals through a variety of cultural means. From infancy on, we are encouraged to conform to the gender that society prescribes for us. Young girls are often cautioned "Don't be selfish — share with others," "Be careful — don't hurt yourself," and "Don't get messy." They are praised for looking pretty, expressing emotions, and being nice to others. Young boys, in contrast, are more likely to be admonished "Don't be a sissy," "Go after what you want," and "Don't cry." Usually they are reinforced for strength, independence, and

BISHETTA

I remember when I was very little, maybe 5 or so. My brother and I were playing outside in the garden and mom saw us. Both of us were coated with dirt—our clothes, our skin, everything. Mom came up to the edge of the garden and shouted "Bishetta, you get out of that garden right now. Just look at you. Now what do you think folks will think of a dirty little girl? You don't want people to think you're not a lady, do you?" She didn't say a word to my brother, who was just as dirty.

BOB

What I always thought was unfair in my family was the way my folks responded to failures my sisters and I had. Like once she tried out for cheerleader and she was not picked. So Maryellen was all crying and upset and mom was telling her that it was okay and that she was a good person and everyone knew that and that winning wasn't everything. And when dad came home he said the same things—telling her she was okay even if she wasn't picked. But when I didn't make the junior varsity football team, dad went bonkers! He asked me what had gone wrong. I told him nothing, that other guys were just better than I had been. But he'd have none of that. He told me I couldn't give up and had to work harder and he expected me to make the team next season. He even offered to hire a coach for me. It just wasn't okay for me not to succeed.

success, particularly in competitive arenas. When socialization is effective in teaching us to adopt the gender society prescribes for our sex, biological males learn to be masculine and biological females become feminine.

So far we've focused on how individuals learn gender, yet gender is not a strictly personal quality. Rather, it is a complex set of interrelated cultural ideas that stipulate the social *meaning* of sex. Because social definitions of gender permeate public and private life, we see them as normal, natural, and right. When the practices and structures that make up social life constantly represent women and men in particular ways, it is difficult to imagine that masculinity and femininity could be defined differently. Later chapters show how a range of institutional structures and communicative processes sustain social views of masculinity and femininity.

The fact that the social meanings of gender are taught to us should not mislead us to believe society exercises a one-way influence on our identities. Cultural views do not endure without support from individuals. In fact, they tend to reflect the values and beliefs of a great many people. As each new member of a society is born, she or he receives prior generations' views of many things, including gender, as a birthright. The cultural script is composed before we are born, and it is communicated to us through family, peers, teachers, media, and so forth.

Yet we are not merely the recipients of cultural meanings; we also influence them (West & Zimmerman, 1987). In our choices to accept cultural prescriptions or to reject them, we affect the meanings our society endorses. Those individuals who internalize cultural prescriptions for gender reinforce traditional views by behaving in ways that support prevailing ideas about masculinity and femininity. Other people, who reject conventional prescriptions and step outside of social meanings for gender, often provoke changes in cultural expectations. In the early part of the last century, for instance, many women challenged social views that asserted women were not entitled to vote or pursue higher education. In voicing their objections through marches, organizing, and political action, these suffragists departed from conventional expectations of women as quiet and unassertive (Simon & Danziger, 1991). In defying their era's definition of women, these individuals transformed social views of women and the rights to which they are entitled.

Meanings of gender are also changed by communication less public and less collective than social movements (Rakow, 1986). Role models, for instance, provide individuals with visible alternatives to traditional views. Two of my colleagues have infants, whom they sometimes bring to the office. When students see a female professor teaching with her baby nearby and when they confer with a male faculty member while he rocks his baby, the students encounter an alternative definition of professionalism — one that recognizes that men and women can be professionals and parents simultaneously. Concrete embodiments of alternatives to conventional roles create new possibilities for our own lives. We also influence ideas about gender as we interact casually with friends. When one woman encourages another to be more assertive and to confront her supervisor about problems, she may instigate change in what her friend sees as appropriate behavior for women. Similarly, when one man tells another that time with his family is a top priority, his friend has to rethink and perhaps change his own views of men's roles. As these examples indicate, there is a reciprocal relationship between individual communication and cultural views of gender: Each influences the other in an ongoing spiral that creates and re-creates the meaning of masculinity and femininity.

To realize how arbitrary meanings of gender are, we need only consider varying ways different cultures define masculinity and femininity. Many years ago anthropologist Margaret Mead (1935/1968) reported three distinctive gender patterns in New Guinea societies she studied. Among Arapesh people, both women and men conform closely to what we consider feminine behavior. Both are passive, peaceful, and deferential, and both nurture others, especially young children. The Mundugumor tribe socializes both women and men to be aggressive, independent, and competitive. Mothers are not nurturant and spend very little time with newborn babies, but instead wean them early. Within the Tchambuli society, genders are the converse of current ones in America: Women are domineering and sexually aggressive, while men are considered delicate and are taught to wear decorative clothes and curl their hair so that they will be attractive to women.

In some cultures, a person's gender is considered changeable (Kessler & McKenna, 1978), so someone born male may choose to live and be regarded as female, and vice versa. In other societies, notably some Native American groups, more than two genders are recognized and celebrated (Garbarino, 1976; Olien, 1978). Individuals who have qualities of multiple genders are highly esteemed. I personally realized the arbitrariness of gender definitions in America when I spent some time living with Tamang villagers in the hill country of Nepal. I discovered that both women and men did what we consider gender-specific tasks. For instance, men do much of the cooking and child care, and they seem especially nurturing and gentle with young children. Women also do these things, as well as engaging in heavy manual labor and working as porters carrying 70+ pounds of trekking gear for Western travelers.

Even within a single culture, the meaning of gender varies over time. Views of gender in America were not always as distinct as they are today. Prior to the Industrial Revolution, family and work life were intertwined for most people (Ryan, 1979). Thus, men and women participated in the labor of raising crops or running businesses, and both were involved in homemaking and childrearing. Affection and expressiveness were considered normal and natural in men as well as in women (Degler, 1980); industriousness and strength were attractive in women just as they were in men (Cancian, 1989; Douglas, 1977). During that era, both women and men were expected to show initiative and caring.

The Industrial Revolution gave birth to factories and to paid labor outside of the home as a primary way of making a living. With this came a division of life into separate spheres of work and home. As men took jobs away from home, women increasingly assumed responsibility for family life. Consequently, femininity was redefined as being nurturant, dependent on men for income, focused on relationships, and able to make a good home. Masculinity was also redefined to mean emotional reserve, ambition, success at work, and, especially, ability to provide income (Cancian, 1989).

As another example of how meanings of gender change, consider how ideals of beauty for women have varied over time in America. In the 1950s, Marilyn Monroe was widely considered the most beautiful, most sexy woman alive. Yet, by today's standards of excessive slimness in women, Marilyn Monroe would be considered fat! As these examples indicate, what we take for granted as masculine and feminine is really quite arbitrary. Meanings of gender vary across cultures and over time in any given society.

We should also realize that gender is a relational concept, since femininity and masculinity make sense in relation to each other. Our society defines femininity in contrast to masculinity, and masculinity as a counterpoint to femininity. As meanings of one gender change, so do meanings for the other. For instance, when social views of masculinity stressed physical strength and endurance, femininity was defined by physical weakness and dependence on men's strengths. Perhaps you've read in older novels about women's fainting spells and the "vapors" they kept nearby to bring them out of faints. With the Industrial Revolution, sheer physical strength was no longer as important to survival, so masculinity was redefined as intellectual ability and success in earning income. Simultaneously, women's fainting spells seemed virtually to disappear as did their former acumen at business and family finances. In part, this happened because society relied less on physical strength to distinguish between women and men.

Today in America, many women are reclaiming ambition and intelligence as qualities consistent with femininity, and they are exercising these in careers and civic and social involvements. As women become more assertive and active in public life than their foremothers, many men change their roles as well. Some men are learning skills in homemaking and child care that formerly were regarded as "women's work," and many are discovering the special nature of dual-career relationships in which partners have equal power and status. These illustrations remind us that the way one gender is defined influences expectations of the other; consequently, our views of femininity and masculinity constantly interact.

Let's summarize this extended discussion of gender. We have noted that gender is a social, symbolic category that reflects the meanings a society confers on biological sex. These meanings are communicated through structures and practices of cultural life that pervade our daily existence, creating the illusion that they are the natural, normal ways for women and men to be. Yet, we've also seen that what gender means varies across cultures and over time in a particular culture, and how we conceive each gender is related to our views of the other. This reminds us that even though what our society defines as feminine and masculine may seem natural to us, there is nothing necessary about any particular meaning given to gender. By extension, this insight suggests we have more choice than we sometimes realize in how we define ourselves and each other as men and women.

Culture

A **culture** consists of structures and practices that uphold a particular social order by legitimizing certain values, expectations, meanings, and patterns of behavior (Weedon, 1987). To explore this idea, it may be helpful to consider how our culture creates and sustains one of its most basic values, democracy, and then examine how it upholds meanings of gender.

Our republic places a high value on representation, participation, and equality of opportunity and rights. Although inequity and inequality still persist in America, they are less pronounced than in less democratic cultures. Social structures, or institutions, reflect democratic values and seek to ensure they are enacted. We have a Congress to "represent the will of the people," and we have open voting in which each person's ballot is equal to that of everyone else's. Social structures such as laws protect freedom of speech and equality of rights and opportunities for all citizens. To make sure all citizens are represented, our judicial system guarantees everyone the right to counsel, regardless of whether she or he can pay for it. Schools cannot exclude students on the basis of age, race, sex, national origin, or other criteria, because we want to furnish educational opportunities for all citizens.

Normative practices of our culture also reflect its democratic values. We have "open meetings" so that policy-making can be understood and influenced by those not charged to do it. Most businesses have complaint departments so that consumers have a place to air grievances and receive a hearing. Lobbying, protesting, and striking are protected activities by which people may dissent from the will of those in power. And those in power are subject to recall or impeachment, should enough people object to them and their activities. Thus, we see that many of our society's structures and practices reflect and sustain democratic values.

Now consider how meanings of gender are reflected in and promoted by social structures and practices. One of the primary practices that structures society is discourse, or communication (Weedon, 1987). Surrounding us is communication that announces social images of gender and seeks to persuade us these are natural, correct ways for men and women to be and to behave. We open a magazine and see a beautiful, sexy woman waiting on a man who looks successful and in charge; we turn on our television and watch a prime-time program in which a husband tells of a big business coup while his wife prepares dinner for them; the commercials interspersed in the show depict women cleaning toilet bowls and kitchen floors and men going for the gusto after a pickup game of basketball; we go to dinner and our server presents the check to the man; we meet with a group of people on a volunteer project and one of the men assumes leadership; a working woman receives maternity leave, but her husband cannot get paternity leave. Each of these practices communicates our society's views of men and women and the "proper" roles of each.

Consider additional examples of cultural practices that uphold gendered meanings. The custom whereby a woman gives up her name and takes her husband's on marriage, although no longer universal, still prevails. It carries forward the message that a woman is defined by her relationship to a man, rather than by her individual identity. Within families, too, numerous practices reinforce social views of gender. Parents routinely allow sons greater freedom and behavioral latitude than they grant daughters, a practice that encourages males to be independent and females not to be. Daughters, much more than sons, are taught to do housework and care for younger siblings, thus reinforcing the idea that women are supposed to be concerned with home and family. These and other practices we take for granted support social prescriptions for gender and provide guidelines for how we are supposed to live as individual men and women.

Socially endorsed meanings are also communicated through structures such as institutions, which serve to announce, reflect, and perpetuate gendered cultural views. Because gender is important in our society, our institutions uphold preferred meanings and encourage individuals to conform to what is collectively endorsed as "appropriate" masculine and feminine behavior. Schools, for instance, are institutions that reinforce cultural prescriptions for gender. Research has shown that teachers tend to encourage dependence, quietness, and deference and frown on assertiveness in female students. Contrast this with the finding that teachers generally reward independence, self-assertion, and activity in boys (Krupnick, 1985; Sadker & Sadker, 1984). Further, studies consistently report that teachers are more likely to encourage academic achievement in male students than in female students and that both teachers and guidance counselors tend to foster career ambitiousness in male students but discourage it in female students (Sandler & Hall, 1986; Wood & Lenze, 1991a). Thus, schools are institutions that reinforce the feminine prescription for low achievement and deference and the masculine prescription for aggression and ambition.

Another institution that upholds gender ideology is the judicial system. The view of women as sexual objects is supported in many states by legal codes, which do not allow a wife to sue her husband for rape, since intercourse is regarded as a "husband's right" (Russell, 1982). Men's rights are abridged by judicial views of women as the primary caretakers of children, which are expressed in the presumption that women should have custody of children if divorce occurs. Thus, it is extremely difficult for fathers to gain child custody, even when they might be the better parents and/or have better situations for raising children.

Through its structures and practices, especially communication practices, societies create and sustain perspectives on what is normal and right. We are saturated with these culturally legitimized viewpoints, which punctuate our lives at every turn. Because messages that reinforce cultural views of gender pervade our daily lives, most of us seldom pause to reflect on whether they are as "natural" as they have come to seem. Like the air we breathe, they are so continuously around us that we tend to take them for granted and not question them. Learning to reflect on cultural prescriptions for gender (and other matters) empowers you as an individual. It increases your freedom to choose your own courses of action and identity by enlarging your awareness of the arbitrary and not always desirable nature of cultural expectations.

Communication

The third major term we want to define is **communication**. In another book (Wood, 1992a, p. 12), I noted that scholars have proposed well over 100 different definitions of communication. This suggests that communication is very complex and difficult to define. Still, we need some working understanding of what communication is if we are to study how it interacts with gender and culture. *Communication is a dynamic, systemic process in which meanings are created and reflected in human interaction with symbols* (Wood, 1992a). This rather complicated definition can be understood by focusing on one part of it at a time.

Communication is a dynamic process.   Central to understanding communication is recognizing it as a highly dynamic process. This means that it constantly changes, evolves, and moves ever onward. Because communication is a process, there are no definite beginnings or endings of communicative interactions. Suppose a friend drops by while you're reading this chapter and asks what you are doing. "Reading about gender, communication, and culture," you reply. Your friend then says, "Oh, you mean about how men and women talk differently." You respond, "Not exactly — you see, gender isn't just whether you're male or female, but it's the meaning culture attaches to your sex." Did this interaction begin with your friend's question, or with your instructor's assignment of the reading, or with other experiences that led you to enroll in this class? Think also about when this communication ends. Does it stop when your friend leaves? Maybe not. What the two of you talk about may influence what you think and do later, so the influence, or effect, of your communication continues beyond the immediate encounter. All communication is like this: It is an ongoing, dynamic process without clear beginnings and endings.

Communication is systemic.   All communication occurs in particular situations, or systems, that influence what and how we communicate and especially what meanings we attach to messages. For example, assume you observe the

T E R E S A   L .

The stuff we talked about in class last time about contexts of communication helped me understand something that happens a lot. I really hate it when people call me "girl." I mean, I'm an adult, and that means I am a woman, not a little girl. People don't call 22-year-old guys "boys," do they? So it grates on me when folks say that. Except it doesn't bother me when older folks like my grandfather call me a girl. I think that doesn't irritate me, because I know that "girl" means something different to him and he's of a different generation. I can't really expect someone 66 years old to understand this issue and to change a whole lifetime's habit. So I know he doesn't mean it as an insult, and I don't take it as one. But if a 20- or 30-year-old calls me "girl," I'll call them on it!

following interaction. In an office building where you are waiting for an appointment, you see a middle-aged man walk to the secretary's desk and put his arm around her shoulders and say, "You really do drive me crazy when you wear that outfit." She doesn't look up from her work but responds, "You're crazy all the time, regardless of what I'm wearing." How would you interpret this interaction? Is it an instance of sexual harassment? Are they co-workers who are comfortable joking about sexuality with each other? Is he perhaps not an employee but her friend, husband, or a man she dates? The only reasonable conclusion to draw is that we cannot tell what is happening or what it means to the communicators because we don't understand the systems within which this interaction takes place.

When we say communication is systemic, we mean more than that its contexts affect meaning. As John Muir said, each part of communication is "hitched to the universe." As a system, all aspects of communication are interlinked and interactive. Who is speaking affects what is said and what it means. In the foregoing example, the secretary would probably attach different meanings to the message "You drive me crazy when you wear that outfit" if it was said by a friend or by a co-worker with a reputation for hassling women. Communication is also influenced by how we feel: When we're low, we're more likely to be irritated and short than when we feel good. If you were just assaulted by lewd remarks from construction workers, you might take offense at a comment that ordinarily wouldn't bother you. The time of day and place of interaction may also affect what is communicated and how our words and actions are interpreted.

The largest system affecting communication is our culture, which is the context within which all of our interactions take place. As we saw in the preceding section, all societies have norms about gender—routine ways of regarding and treating men and women—and these change over time. Thirty years ago it would have been rude for a man not to open a car door for his date and not to stand when a woman entered a room. Today most people would not regard either as rude or ungentlemanly. Even a decade ago, sexual harassment was largely un-named and not considered cause for grievance or legal action (Wood, 1992b). Today, however, laws and policies prohibit sexual harassment, and employees may bring charges against harassers. The same behavior now means something differ-ent, and it may have different results than it did 10 years ago. The systems—situation, time, people, culture, and so on—within which communication occurs interact so that each part affects all others and what they mean.

Communication has two levels of meaning.   Perhaps you noticed that our definition of communication referred to meaning*s*, not just a single meaning. What communication means depends on the individuals engaged in it. In addi-tion, all communication has two levels, or dimensions, of meaning. Years ago a group of clinical psychologists (Watzlawick, Beavin, & Jackson, 1967) noted that all communication has both a **content** and a **relationship level of meaning**.

The content level of a message is its literal meaning. If Ellen says to her partner, Ed, "It's your turn to fix dinner tonight," the content level of her message is a rule about sharing cooking and a reminder of whose turn it is. The content level also indicates what response is expected to follow from a message. In this case, both Ellen and Ed may assume he will get busy working on dinner. The content level of meaning involves a literal message and implies what response is appropriate.

The relationship level of a message is not so obvious. It defines the relation-ship between communicators by defining each person's identity and indicating who they are in relation to one another. In our example, Ellen seems to be defining the relationship as an equal one in which each partner does half of the cooking. The relational level of meaning in her comment also suggests that she regards it as her prerogative to remind her partner when it's his turn. Ed could respond by saying, "I don't feel like cooking. You do it tonight." Here the content level is again clear. He is describing how he feels and suggesting this implies he will not cook. On the relationship level, however, he may be arguing about the power balance between him and Ellen. He is refusing to accept her reminder that it's his turn to cook. If she agrees and fixes dinner, then she accepts Ed's definition of the relationship as not exactly equal; she affirms his right not to take his turn at k.p. duty and his prerogative to tell her to cook.

The relationship level of meaning is the primary one that reflects and influ-ences how people feel about each other. It underlies and serves as a context for the content level of meaning, because it tells us how to interpret the literal mes-sage. Perhaps when Ed says he doesn't feel like fixing dinner he uses a teasing tone and grins, in which case the relationship level of meaning is that Ellen should not take the content level seriously because he's joking. If, however, he makes his statement in a belligerent voice and glares at her, the relationship level of meaning is that he does mean the content level. Relationship levels of meaning tell us how to interpret content meaning and how communicators see themselves in relation to one another.

Relationship levels of meaning are particularly important when we try to understand some of the patterns of communication between genders. A good example is interruptions. Research has shown that men tend to interrupt women more than women interrupt men when interruptions are used to change topics (Baird, 1976; Brandt, 1980; Kramer, 1974). The content level of an interruption is simply whatever is said. The more important meaning is usually on the relationship level, which declares that a man has the right to interrupt a woman, dismiss her topic, and initiate his own. If he interrupts and she does not protest, they agree to let him control the conversation. If she does object, then the two may wind up in extended negotiations over how to define their relationship. We speak of meaning*s* in communication, because all messages have two levels of meaning.

Meanings are created through human interaction with symbols. This premise suggests two final important understandings about communication. First, it calls our attention to the fact that humans are symbol-using creatures (Blumer, 1969; Cassirer, 1978; Wood, 1992a). Symbols are abstract, arbitrary, and ambiguous ways of representing phenomena. For example, ♀ and ♂ are symbols for women and men, respectively. Words are also symbols, so *woman* and *man* are symbols of particular physical beings. Humans rely on symbols to communicate, and that is largely responsible for their distinction from other creatures. In contrast, animals think and interact on a concrete, nonsymbolic level. A snarl is an unambiguous warning one dog gives to another; there is nothing abstract or uncertain about the action. The other dog doesn't need to reflect on what the snarl means. No real thinking need occur for the two animals to understand each other through their concrete behaviors.

Because human communication is symbolic, it requires mediation, or thought. Rather than reacting in automatic or instinctive ways to communication, we usually reflect on what was said and what it means before we respond. Symbols require thought to be interpreted. Symbols are also ambiguous, which means what they mean is less than clear-cut. Recall our earlier example in which a man tells a secretary, "Your outfit drives me crazy." To interpret what he said, she has to think about their relationship, what she knows about him, and what has occurred in their prior interactions. After thinking about all of these things, she'll decide whether his comment was a joke in poor taste, a compliment, sexual harassment, or a flirtatious show of interest from someone with whom she is romantically involved. Sometimes people interpret what we say in a manner other than what we intended because symbols are so abstract that more than one meaning is plausible.

The second implication of the premise that we create meanings through interaction with symbols is that the significance of communication is not in words themselves. Instead, humans *create* meanings in the process of communicating with one another. Our verbal and nonverbal behaviors are not simply neutral expressions of thoughts but imply values and judgments. This implies that how we express ourselves influences how we and others feel about what we communicate. "You're a feminist" can create distinctive impressions depending on whether the inflection is one suggesting interest, shock, disdain, or admiration. Calling a woman "aggressive" conjures up a different impression than calling her "assertive." A man who interacts lovingly with his child could be described as either "nurturing" or "soft," and the two descriptions suggest quite distinct meanings. People differ in how they interpret identical messages. One woman is insulted when a man opens a door, while another considers it rude if a man doesn't hold a door for her. One person finds it entirely appropriate for a woman manager to give orders, but another employee thinks she's acting unfeminine. The meaning of communication depends on much more than verbal and nonverbal behavior; it also entails interpretations of what is communicated.

The fact that symbols are abstract, ambiguous, and arbitrary makes it impossible to think of meaning as inhering within symbols themselves. Each of us constructs an interpretation of communication by drawing on our past experiences, our knowledge of the people with whom we are interacting, and other factors in a communication system that influence our interpretations. Because the meaning we attach to communication is heavily influenced by our personal experiences, values, thoughts, and feelings, we inevitably project ourselves onto messages to interpret what they mean. This certainly makes communication interesting and often very confusing and frustrating. Differences in how we interpret messages are the source of much misunderstanding between people. However, you can become a more effective communicator if you keep in mind that people do differ in how they perceive and interpret communication. Reminding yourself of this should prompt you to ask for clarification of what another person means rather than assuming your interpretation is "correct." Similarly, we should check with others more often than we sometimes do to see how they are interpreting our verbal and nonverbal communication.

𝒮ummary

In this chapter we began to explore the nature of communication, gender, and culture. Because each of us is a gendered being, it's important to understand what gender means and how we can be more effective in our communicative interactions within a culture that is also gendered. The primary focus of this chapter was introducing the three central concepts that form the focus of *Gendered Lives*: gender, culture, and communication.

Gender, we saw, is a social, symbolic system through which a culture attaches significance to biological sex. Gender is something individuals learn, yet because it is constructed by cultures, it is more than an individual quality. Instead, it is a whole system of social meanings that specify what is associated with men and women in a given society at a particular time. We also noted that meanings of gender vary over time and across cultures. Finally, we found that gender is relational, since femininity and masculinity gain much of their meaning from the fact that our society juxtaposes them.

The second key term, *culture*, refers to structures and practices, particularly communicative ones, through which a society announces and sustains its values. Gender is a particularly significant issue in our culture, so there are abundant structures and practices that serve to reinforce our society's prescriptions for women's and men's identities and behaviors. To understand what gender means and how meanings of gender change, we must explore cultural values and the institutions and activities through which those are expressed and promoted.

Finally, we defined *communication* as a dynamic, systemic process in which meanings are created and reflected in human interaction with symbols. In examining the dimensions of this definition, we emphasized the fact that communication is a symbolic activity, which implies that it requires reflection and that meanings are variable and constructed, rather than inherent in symbols themselves. We also saw that communication can be understood only within its contexts, including the especially important system of culture.

What we have covered in this chapter provides a foundation so that we may go forward to examine ways in which individuals learn gender, the differences and similarities in feminine and masculine communication, and a range of ways in which gendered communication and identities punctuate our lives.

*D*iscussion Questions

1. Why are you taking this course? What about this era accounts for growing student interest in communication, gender, and culture? What do you hope to learn about issues and yourself as a result of taking this course?

2. How different do you think men and women are? Drawing on your experiences as a man or woman and your knowledge of both sexes, do you think men and women are more like each other (with a few differences) or more different from each other (with a few similarities)?

3. The author discusses generational changes in attitudes about gender. How are your views of women and men, gays and lesbians, minority and majority peoples

different from those of your parents and grandparents? How do you think the next generation's views about communication, gender, and culture may differ from yours?

4. Why are communication, gender, and culture intimately interwoven? How do cultural beliefs shape communication and gender? How does gender shape communication and culture? How does communication influence gender and culture?

5. Think about your sex and your gender. Deciding which sex you are won't be difficult. Identifying your gender, however, is more complicated. How closely do you conform to society's views of masculinity and femininity? Do you have what our culture defines as masculine and feminine qualities in yourself?

6. Think about how you learned gender. Can you recall early interactions in your life when you understood that others defined you as a girl or boy? Did you receive clear messages about what being a girl or boy meant in terms of what you were expected to think, act, and be?

7. What are current cultural prescriptions for femininity and masculinity? As a class, discuss what society today defines as masculine and feminine and write the ideas on a blackboard. How comfortable are you with current views of masculinity and femininity? Which ones do you find restrictive? Are you doing anything to change them in society's view and/or to resist them in defining your own personal identity?

8. The author notes that gender isn't the same across cultures, and she points out that even the idea of only two genders isn't universal. If you could define gender for the whole society, how would you define it? Use your imagination; be creative. How many genders would there be, and what would each one mean in your ideal vision?

9. The author claims that gender is relational. What would feminine mean without the idea of masculine? What would masculinity mean if there were no femininity? How do changes in social definitions of one gender affect the other one?

10. The author notes that social practices produce and reproduce understandings of gender. How do current practices in the United States inscribe views of masculinity and femininity?

11. How do the two levels of communication pertain to messages about gender? Bring a couple of ads for products for women and men to class and discuss the content and relational levels of meaning in them. Do you find that messages about gender occur more on the relational level of meaning than on the content level? What does this imply?

$\mathcal{T}$heoretical Approaches to Gender Development

By age 5 or earlier, children know which sex they are, and they understand basic expectations our society has of masculinity and femininity. How does this happen? Does biology dictate that females become feminine and males become masculine? Do we learn from parents and others how to be masculine and feminine? Does the culture as a whole influence our gender development? Are masculinity and femininity cultivated in an infant's relationship with his or her primary caregiver? Is gender changeable? These are the questions we will explore in this chapter as we consider different theories about how individuals become gendered.

Theories in Everyday Life

Although we sometimes think theories are removed from the real world, actually they are part of our everyday lives. A **theory** is simply a way to describe, explain, and predict relationships among phenomena. Each of us has many theories, and we use them to guide our attitudes and actions and to predict others' behavior. Even though theories are not always conscious, they still shape our conduct and expectations.

Most of us have theories of gender that we rely on to make sense of men's and women's behaviors. For instance, assume you know Kevin and Carlene, who are 11-year-old twins. In many ways they are alike, yet they also differ. Carlene is more articulate than Kevin, and she tends to think in more synthetic, creative, and integrative ways. Kevin is better at solving analytic problems, especially mathematical ones. He also has more developed muscles, although he and Carlene spend equal time in athletics. How you explain the differences between these twins reflects your implicit theory of gender.

If you subscribe to biological theory, you would note that different cognitive strengths result from differential hemispheric specialization in male and female brains. You might also reason that Kevin's greater muscle development results from androgens, which encourage musculature, while estrogen programs the body to develop more fat and soft tissue.

Then again, perhaps you think there is another reason for the differences between Kevin and Carlene. Knowing that researchers have shown that teachers and parents tend to encourage analytic problem solving in boys and creative thinking in girls, you might explain the twins' different cognitive skills as the result of learning and reinforcement. The same explanation might be advanced for disparity in their muscle development, since you could reason that Kevin is probably more encouraged and rewarded for strength than is Carlene.

A third way to explain differences is to point out the likelihood that each twin identifies with same-sex role models. If so, we would predict that Kevin will imitate the behaviors he sees in a man or men he chooses as models—physical strength and logical thinking. Identifying herself with one or more women, Carlene is more likely to emulate feminine models.

These are only three of many ways we could explain the differences between Kevin and Carlene. Each represents a particular theoretical viewpoint—a way of understanding the relationship between gender and people's behaviors and abilities. None of the three is clearly right or even more right than the others. Each viewpoint makes sense, yet each is limited, which suggests that an adequate explanation may involve several theories. It's important to realize that theories do more than provide explanations. They also have impact on our attitudes and behaviors.

Our theories about gender affect our thoughts and behaviors. How we explain the twins' differences is likely to influence how we treat them. If you think the differences in muscle development are determined by biology, then you probably would not push Carlene to work out more in order to cultivate muscles. On the other hand, if you think differences result from learning and role models, you well might encourage Carlene to develop her muscles and Kevin to think more integratively and creatively. If you believe women have a "natural maternal instinct" (biological theory), then you might not expect fathers to be equal caretakers. A different set of expectations would arise if you theorize that women are taught to be nurturant and that men can learn this too. If you think males are more aggressive because of their higher levels of testosterone, then you are apt to tolerate rowdiness in boys and men and to discourage it in girls and women. The theories you hold consciously or otherwise influence how you see yourself as a woman or man, what you expect of women and men generally, and what kinds of changes you attempt to bring about in gendered behavior. Because the theories we hold do affect our perceptions, behaviors, and expectations, it's important to examine them carefully. That is the goal of this chapter.

Theoretical Approaches to Gender

A number of explanations for gender development exist, and most regard communication as central to the process. Because theories attempt to explain only selected dimensions of gender, they are not in competition with one another to produce *the* definitive explanation of gender. Instead, theories complement one another by sharpening our awareness of different ways in which communication, gender, and culture interact. Thus, as we survey alternative theoretical approaches, the goal is not to pick the *best* or *right* one. Instead, we want to identify the limitations and appreciate the particular insights each theory yields into the mysteries of gender development. Taken together, the theories we will discuss provide a richly layered account of the gendering process and the critical role of communication in it.

Theories about gender development and gender behavior can be classified into three types: ones that focus on biological bases of gender, ones that emphasize interpersonal origins of gender, and ones that concentrate on cultural influences on gender development. Within these broad categories, there are a number of specific theories that offer insight into factors and processes that contribute to gendering individuals. As we discuss these, you will probably notice both how they differ in focus and how they work together to create an overall understanding of gender development.

Biological Bases of Gender

Perhaps the first attempt to explain general differences between women and men was **biological theory**. Specifically, this approach maintains that biological characteristics of the sexes are the basis of gender differences. Biologically based theories focus on how X and Y chromosomes and the hormonal activities they activate influence a range of individual qualities from body features to thinking and moods.

Although in recent years biological explanations of gender have been increasingly overshadowed by theories that emphasize socialization, it would be unwise to discount biological factors altogether. While the jury is still out on some of the connections theorized between biology and gender, existing research does demonstrate some biological and genetic issues that influence gender development.

The role of hormonal activity in behavior is a primary focus of biological theories of gender. Sex hormones affect development of the brain as well as the body. For instance, estrogen, the primary female hormone, causes women's bodies to produce "good" cholesterol and to make blood vessels more flexible than those of men (Shapiro, 1990). Estrogen also strengthens the immunological system, making women generally less susceptible to immune disorders and more resistant to infections and viruses. Thus, it is not surprising that men are more vulnerable to physical problems than are women from fetal stage throughout life (Jacklin, 1989). A third biological feature that estrogen bestows on women is greater deposits of fat around the breasts and hips to provide protection for a fetus during pregnancy. There is also some preliminary support for the claim that estrogen impedes liver functioning so that women process alcohol more slowly than men and, thus, may react quickly to alcoholic consumption (Lang, 1991).

LUANNE

When I was in high school, I wanted to play football. My folks were really cool about it, since they'd always told me being a girl didn't mean I couldn't do anything I wanted to. But the school coach vetoed the idea. I appealed his decision to the principal as sex discrimination (my mother's a lawyer), and we had a meeting. The coach said girls couldn't play football as well as guys because girls are less muscular, weigh less, and have less dense bodies to absorb the force of momentum. He said this means girls can be hurt more than guys by tackles and stuff. He also said that girls have smaller heads and necks, which is a problem in head-to-head contact on the field. My dad said the coach was talking in generalizations, and he should judge my ability by me as an individual. But the coach's arguments convinced the principal, and I didn't get to play just because women's bodies are generally less equipped for contact sports.

Male sex hormones also have some documented effects, as well as some controversial possible influences. After surveying an extensive amount of research on sex hormones, Carol Tavris (1992, p. 151) concluded that men, like women, have a hormonal cycle, and, again like women, men's hormones affect their behavior. Males who behave delinquently, use drugs, engage in violence and abusiveness, and have conduct disorders tend to be at their cycle's peak level of testosterone, the primary male hormone. A recent study of 1,706 men from 39 to 70 years old found that men with higher levels of testosterone had personalities researchers described as "dominant with some aggressive behavior" ("Study Links High Testosterone," 1991, p. 8-A). Higher levels of testosterone were linked to jockeying for power, attempts to influence or dominate others, and expressions of anger. Another study ("Study Links Men's Cognitive Abilities," 1991) reported that fluctuations of testosterone affect men's cognitive functioning so that men have better spatial abilities at low points in their hormonal cycle. A second male hormone, androgen, has also been linked to aggressiveness and even an instinct for killing in animals ("Male Hormone," 1991). Whether these findings also apply to humans remains open to question.

Another focus of biological theories of difference is brain structure and development, which appears to be linked to sex. Research indicates that although both women and men use both lobes of the brain, each sex tends to specialize in one. Men generally have greater development of the left lobe of the brain, which controls linear, conventionally logical thought; sequential information; and abstract, analytic thinking. Specializing in the right lobe, women tend to have greater aptitude for imaginative and artistic activity; holistic, intuitive thinking; and some visual and spatial tasks (Hartlage, 1980; Lesak, 1976; Walsh, 1978).

Linking the two lobes of the brain is a bundle of nerves and connecting tissues called the corpus callosum, and women generally have greater ability to use this structure. Thus, it may be that women are more able to cross from one lobe to another and to access the distinct capacities of both. It is tempting to see in these reports indisputable evidence of the force of biology, but a very recent study suggests this conclusion is not warranted. M. Hines (1992) found that within the corpus callosum there is a thick, rounded fold of connecting tissues, which she labeled the splenium. Her preliminary work indicates women have thicker spleniums, which may account for their greater verbal abilities. However, Hines cautions us not to interpret this as demonstrating innate difference due to biology. She stresses that the splenium changes as a result of experience, which implies we can develop it by using it, just as we use exercise to develop other muscles in our bodies.

Research on brain development also suggests there may be differences between the brains of heterosexuals and gays. The National Academy of Sciences (Elias, 1992) recently reported that sexual preference may be strongly influenced by biology. Examinations of brains revealed that a band of fibers called the anterior commissure, which is part of the tissues connecting brain lobes, is significantly larger in gay men than in heterosexual men or women. The researchers hypothesize that prenatal hormones may influence development of the anterior commissure.

In summary, biological theories of gender attribute masculine and feminine qualities and abilities to genetics and biology. Specifically, it appears that chromosomes and hormones affect brain development, physiology, thinking, and behavior. A value of this theory is identification of ways in which our choices are influenced by innate and relatively stable factors. Yet, biological theories tell us only about physiological and genetic qualities of men and women *in general*. They don't necessarily describe individual men and women. Some men may have less testosterone and be less aggressive than men in general, while some women, like Luanne (see her commentary on p. 38), may have the mental and physical qualities necessary to play football.

Although virtually no researchers dispute the influence of biology on gender, there is substantial controversy about *how* strong and how immutable biological forces are. Those who hold an extreme version of biological theory maintain that our chromosomes and other biological factors program, or determine, masculine and feminine behavior. A greater number of researchers, like Hines in reporting on the splenium, argue that biology is substantially edited by environmental factors. By extension, many claim that biology is most accurately understood as an influence, not a determinant of gender. To consider how environmental forces may mitigate biological endowments, we turn to theories of interpersonal and cultural influences on gender.

Interpersonal Influences on Gender

A number of theorists have focused on interpersonal factors that influence development of masculinity and femininity. From their work, two major theoretical views have emerged to explain how individuals become gendered. Psychodynamic theory emphasizes interpersonal relationships within the family that affect a child's sense of identity, particularly his or her gender. Psychological theories stress learning and role modeling between children and a variety of other people, including parents. We'll introduce both theories here and pursue them in greater detail in subsequent chapters.

Psychodynamic views of gender development. Originally advanced by Sigmund Freud (1957), **psychodynamic theories** focus on family dynamics that influence individuals' development of gender identity. More recent work has refined psychodynamic theory to compensate for some of Freud's blind spots, particularly his misunderstanding of women's development (Chodorow, 1978, 1989; Gilligan, 1982; Miller, 1986; Surrey, 1983).

Object-relations theory, one of the most widely endorsed branches of psychodynamic thinking, claims that relationships are central to the development of human personality and, specifically, gender identity. According to this theory, early relationships are the primary basis of our sense of identity. For most children, the single most important early relationship is with the primary caretaker, typically the mother. That relationship is thought to be the most fundamental influence on how an infant comes to define herself or himself and on how she or he understands interactions with others.

Psychoanalytic theorists think that development of a sense of self and a gender identity occurs as an infant internalizes others around him or her. So, for example, infants who are lovingly nurtured by a mother tend to incorporate the mother's view into their own sense of self, and they regard themselves as valuable and worthy. In addition, the mother's tendencies to nurture, be attentive, express affection, and so forth are internalized so that the child develops these capacities as part of herself or himself. Internalizing others is not merely acquiring roles; instead, it creates the basic structure of the psyche — the core self.

Psychoanalytic theory explains the development of masculine or feminine identity as the result of different kinds of relationships that typically exist between mothers and children of both sexes. According to N. J. Chodorow (1989, p. 6), one of the most widely respected psychoanalytic theorists, the key to understanding how family psychodynamics create gender lies in realizing "that we are all mothered by women, . . . [and] women rather than men have primary parenting responsibilities." Because the mother herself is gendered, she forms distinct relationships with sons and daughters. Consequently, male and female infants follow different developmental paths, depending on the specific relationship they have with a mother.

Between a mother and daughter there is a fundamental likeness, which encourages a close identification between them. Mothers generally interact more with daughters and keep them physically and psychologically closer than sons. In addition, mothers tend to be more nurturing and to talk more about personal and relationship topics with daughters than with sons. This intense closeness allows an infant girl to import her mother into herself in so basic a way that her mother becomes quite literally a part of her own self. Because this internalization occurs at a very early age, a girl's first efforts to define her own identity are infused by the relationship with her mother. The fact that girls typically define their identity *within a relationship* may account for women's typical attentiveness to relationships (Surrey, 1983).

The relationship between a mother and son typically departs from that between mother and daughter. Because they do not share a sex, full identification

JENNIFER

I remember when Marilyn was born. She was our second; the first was Bobby. From the moment Marilyn entered our lives, I felt connected to her in a way I never had to my son. I love Bobby just as much, but the connection is different. When I look at Marilyn I sometimes feel there is a circle connecting us — a kind of a private union so that we are one and no one else can enter the bond we have. I encourage Marilyn to be with me and do things with me, whereas I let Bobby go off on his own a lot more. It's just a different kind of connection — almost a fusion between Marilyn and me.

is not possible. Theorists (Chodorow, 1978; Miller, 1986; Surrey, 1983) suggest that infant boys recognize in a primitive way that they differ from their mothers. More important, mothers realize the difference, and they reflect it in their interactions with their sons. In general, mothers encourage more and earlier independence in sons than in daughters, and they interact less closely with sons. Also, mothers are more likely to discuss impersonal topics with sons and to talk less about personal and relationship matters. Thus, mothers tend to encourage autonomy in sons at very early ages.

How do young boys formulate their gender identities? Because they cannot define it through the relationship with their mothers as daughters typically do, boys pursue a different path. To establish his identity, a boy must differentiate himself from his mother — declare himself unlike her. Some psychoanalytic theorists argue that boys actually negate and reject their mothers in order to define an independent self. The idea that a boy must renounce his mother to establish masculine identity underlies the puberty rites in many cultures. To enter into manhood, boys are required to repudiate their mothers and, with them, the female world (French, 1992, p. 15; Gaylin, 1992). Whether a boy rejects his mother or merely differentiates from her, becoming independent of others is central to a boy's initial sense of self. Distancing himself from others and defining himself apart from them becomes a fundamental anchor of masculine identity.

Identity, of course, is not static and fixed completely in the early years of life. The initial self that we construct out of primary relationships continues to grow and change throughout life as we interact with others and revise our sense of who we are. Yet, object-relations theorists maintain that the identity formed in infancy is fundamental. They see it as the foundation on which later views of the self are erected. Thus, while identity clearly evolves, it does so on a foundation laid in infancy.

According to psychodynamic theorists, as infants mature, they carry with them the basic identity formed in the pivotal first relationship with their mothers. Thus, as girls become women, they elaborate their identity in connections with others, and relationships tend to figure prominently in their values and lives. As boys grow into men, they too elaborate the essential identity formed in infancy, making independence central to their values and lives. This major difference in self-definition suggests that close relationships may mean quite different things to masculine and feminine persons. For someone who is feminine, intimate relationships may be a source of security and comfort, and they may affirm her (or his) view of self as connected with others. In contrast, someone with a masculine orientation may feel that relationships stifle the independence essential to selfhood and security (Gilligan, 1982; Rubin, 1985; Wood & Lenze, 1991b).

A primary value of this theory of gender development is that it highlights the importance of relationships in creating and sustaining human identity. Thus, this perspective offers us insight into the role that connections with others play in cultivating gender. Whether or not we agree with the extent of influence psychodynamic theorists accord to relationships, their insights into this area are important to overall understandings of gender. As we will discover later in this chapter, a number of other scholars, who represent distinct theoretical schools of thought, also focus on relationships.

Psychological theories.   Psychological theories also focus on interpersonal bases of gender, but they do not emphasize intrapsychic processes as do psychodynamic explanations. Instead, psychological theories of gender highlight the role of communication in individual learning and cognitive development as the genesis of gender.

Social learning theory, developed by W. Mischel (1966) and others (Bandura & Walters, 1963; Lynn, 1969), claims that individuals learn to be masculine and feminine (among other things) through communication and observation. Children notice how others interact and imitate the communication they see on television and in parents, peers, and others. Because young children aren't very discriminating in what they imitate, they are likely to mimic almost anything that catches their eyes or ears. However, other people will reward only some of a child's behaviors, and those behaviors that are reinforced tend to be repeated. Thus, social learning suggests that others' communication teaches children what gender behaviors are appropriate for them. Because children prefer rewards to punishments or neutral responses, they are likely to conform to what others approve (Condry & Condry, 1976; Frieze, Parsons, Johnson, Ruble, & Zellman, 1978).

Social learning theory does not regard biological sex as the basis of gender identity. Instead, it argues that children learn gender by imitating others and

D E R R I C K

O ver break I was visiting my sister's family, and her little boy attached himself to me. Wherever I went, he was my shadow. Whatever I did, he copied. At one point I was dribbling a basketball out in the driveway and Derrick got it and started dribbling. I egged him on, saying "Atta boy! What a star!" and stuff like that, and he just grinned real big. The more I made over him for playing with the ball, the harder he played. It was really weird to see how much influence I had over him.

continuing to imitate those behaviors that bring them positive communication from others. Young girls tend to be rewarded when they are deferential, considerate, quiet, loving, emotionally expressive, and obedient — all qualities associated with femininity. They tend to get less positive responses if they are boisterous, independent, unconcerned with others, or competitive — qualities associated with masculinity. As parents and others reinforce in girls what is considered feminine and discourage behaviors and attitudes that are masculine, they shape little girls into femininity. Similarly, as parents communicate approval to boys for behaving in masculine ways and curb them for acting feminine — for instance, for crying — they influence little boys to become masculine. Researchers have shown that parents emphasize social abilities in young girls (Beckwith, 1972; Clarke-Stewart, 1973) and physical independence in young boys (Cherry & Lewis, 1978).

You may have sensed that social learning theory views children as relatively passive in the learning process. It suggests they more or less absorb a gender in response to external stimuli such as rewards and punishments from parents and other important people in their worlds. Social learning theory also suggests that the reinforcement process continues throughout life with messages that reinforce femininity in women and masculinity in men.

Cognitive development theories also focus on how individuals learn from interaction with others to define themselves, including their gender. Unlike social learning theory, however, this approach assumes children play an active role in developing their own identities. Researchers claim that children use others to define themselves, because they are motivated by an *internal* desire to be competent, which includes knowing how to act feminine or masculine in Western culture.

Within this school of thought, theorists like Lawrence Kohlberg (1958), Jean Piaget (1932, 1965), and Carol Gilligan and her associates (1982, 1988) have offered models of how children develop gendered views of themselves, relationships, and moral orientations. Central to the development of identity is communication, which is the primary way kids learn what is considered feminine and masculine, as well as the principal means by which they practice their own gender behaviors. Work in this area suggests that children go through several stages in developing gender identities. From birth until about 24 to 30 months, they search others' communication for labels to apply to themselves. When they hear others call them a "girl" or "boy," or when others respond by saying "That's not very appropriate for a little lady/man," they learn labels for themselves. Then begins a stage of active imitation, in which children use their rudimentary understanding of gender to play roles and engage in communication and other behaviors they think go with the gender labels they give themselves.

A key developmental juncture occurs very early in life, by age 3 according to most experts on human development. At this point, a child develops **gender constancy**, which is the understanding that gender is relatively unchanging. They see being feminine or masculine as a fixed aspect of their identity—it is inevitable and unvarying. Given this, say cognitive developmental theorists, children develop a high internal motivation to learn how to be competent at the gender that they realize is enduring. Boys and girls now devote themselves to identifying behaviors and attitudes others consider masculine and feminine and to learning to enact those for their gender. Same-sex models become extremely important as gauges whereby young children figure out what range of behaviors, attitudes, and feelings goes with their gender. If mommy is identified as the same gender as a little girl, then whatever mommy does and is communicates information about feminine gender. Likewise, little boys study their fathers and other important males in their world to learn what counts as masculine. Actively using others as models allows children to mold themselves into the gender their culture expects of them.

As children mature, they continue to seek same-sex role models to become competent at being masculine and feminine. Perhaps you, like many adolescents, studied teen magazines and watched movies and television to figure out how to be successful as a boy or girl. Everything from how to style your hair and do the latest dances to how to feel about various things is learned, and often what is considered appropriate differs for the genders. It's feminine to squeal or scream at the sight of bugs or mice, but boys who do so are quickly labeled "sissies." It's acceptable—if not pleasant to everyone—for adolescent males to belch, but any teenage girl who belched would be criticized.

In studying how senses of morality and relationships develop, Gilligan (1982, 1988) theorized that females learn to value connections with others, to communicate care and responsiveness, and to preserve relationships. According to developmental theory (Kohlberg, 1958), males are more likely to value autonomy and to communicate in ways that preserve their independence from others.

Each has learned what is appropriate for her or his gender, and each guides her or his own communication to be consistent with social prescriptions for gender.

In summary, psychological theories focus on how individuals learn gender through interpersonal communication. Whether you think children are more or less active in the learning process, it's clear from this perspective that others' communication both teaches lessons about gender and provides models of how to enact masculinity and femininity. Once gender constancy is established, most children strive for communication, attitudes, goals, and self-presentations consistent with the gender they consider theirs. Throughout life, people enter into interpersonal relationships in which they continue to learn about gender from how others communicate.

Cultural and Communication Contributions to Gender

Perhaps the largest number of theorists believe gender is best understood through a cultural perspective. Scholars in this area do not dispute biological and psychological factors but assume that these reflect the larger influence of culture. The ways that mothers, fathers, and other models for children behave, for instance, embody socially approved views of masculinity and femininity. Thus, interpersonal influences on gender are part of a broad system of cultural views and values. Because it incorporates other theories, the cultural perspective is a particularly comprehensive approach to understanding the development of gender and what it means in any society at a specific time.

Of the many cultural contributions to knowledge about gender, we will focus on three. First, we'll look at findings from anthropology to discover what cross-cultural research tells us about gender. Next, we will explore symbolic interactionism, which concentrates on how cultural values get into individuals so that most of us adopt the identities our culture designates as appropriate for our gender. Finally, we'll look at standpoint theory, which is a recent approach that augments the insights of symbolic interactionism and anthropology.

Anthropology.   Anyone who has traveled outside of the United States knows you learn not only about those countries but also about your own. When confronted with different values and ways of doing things in a foreign culture, you see the norms of your own society in a new and usually clearer light. This holds true of gender. Our recognition of gendered identities and the meaning of gender in America is enhanced by considering what it means elsewhere.

In Chapter 1, I mentioned the pioneering anthropological work of Margaret Mead (1935/1968), in which she discovered distinct meanings of gender in three different societies. One reversed what is considered masculine and feminine in our culture, one encouraged extremes of what we consider masculine in both sexes, and the third promoted what we regard as feminine in men and women. This provided an early clue to the arbitrary nature of gender by demonstrating that different cultures create quite distinctive gender arrangements and identities.

Much work has followed that of Margaret Mead. C. G. O'Kelly and L. S. Carney (1986) analyze the gender arrangements and assumptions characteristic of different kinds of cultures. In foraging, or hunter-gatherer, societies there is the least gender division and, therefore, the greatest equality between women and men. Horticultural and pastoral societies tend also to be egalitarian, although less so than purely foraging cultures. Agrarian peoples generally have a pronounced system of gender stratification in which women are subordinate to men in status and rights. Finally, industrial-capitalist societies like ours distinguish sharply between the genders and confer different value on women and men.

This overview of diverse forms of social life suggests that the more technologically complex and advanced a culture is, the more stratification it creates to divide people by gender, as well as by other factors such as race and class. With technological advancement comes competition, and this lays a foundation for inequality, since some people will have more than others of whatever is valued by a culture. One of the arrangements that capitalism encourages is a division between public and private realms of life and the placement of women in the private, or domestic, sphere. Because public life is considered more important, this arrangement fosters subordination of women. Further, as O'Kelly and Carney point out (p. 315), those who are "isolated in the domestic sphere and cut off from participation in political, economic, and social institutions . . . [become] less powerful," so the system perpetuates the inequality on which it is based. Even today in America there persists an association of women with home and family, and men with work and public life (Cancian, 1989; Fox-Genovese, 1991; Okin, 1989; Wood, 1993c).

Further evidence of the cultural nature of gender comes from work by B. Whiting and C. Edwards (1973). They studied gender identities in children from 3 to 11 years old in three cultures. What they found was that nurturing inclinations and skills we associate with femininity are taught to whomever a society labels caregivers. One African group is structured so that young boys are responsible for taking care of babies. In this society, unlike our own, young boys are actually *more* nurturant than young girls.

Perhaps the most important lesson we can draw from anthropological studies is that cultures profoundly shape gender identity. Amazingly few gender differences have been found across a range of societies, and the ones that have been documented tend to be very small (Adler, 1991). For instance, both boys and girls in most cultures show tendencies to nurture and to be aggressive. What usually differs is the extent to which these qualities are encouraged in each gender by particular cultures.

Symbolic interactionism.   Cultural perspectives on gender also inform us about the intricacies of gender arrangements within our own society. George Herbert Mead, often called "the father of **symbolic interactionism**," developed a very broad theory that holds that individuals learn to participate competently in their society and to share its values through communication (symbolic interaction) with others. His theory covers socialization in general and can be applied specifically to how we learn gender through interaction with others.

According to Mead, awareness of personal identity arises out of communication with others who pass on the values and expectations of a society. Because newborns do not enter the world with a sense of self as distinct from the world, they learn from others how to see themselves. As parents and others interact with children, they literally tell them who they are. A child is described as big or dainty, delicate or tough, active or quiet, and so on. With each label, others offer the child a self-image, and children internalize others' views to arrive at their own understandings of who they are. Communication is the central process whereby we gain a sense of who we are. From the moment of birth, we engage in interaction with others, especially parents, who tell us who we are, what is appropriate for us, and what is unacceptable.

Gender is one of the primary aspects of identity that we learn through conversations with others. Within Western society, gender is extremely important and is tied to the social order as a whole (Fox-Genovese, 1991; Janeway, 1971; Miller, 1986; Riessman, 1990; Wood & Lenze, 1991b). Research has shown that views of gender are communicated by parents through their responses to children (Chodorow, 1978, 1989; Safilios-Rothschild, 1979; Shapiro, 1990), through play activities with peers (Maltz & Borker, 1982), and through teachers' interactions with students (Sandler & Hall, 1986; Wood & Lenze, 1991b). The intensity of focus on gender may explain why this is one of the very first clear senses of self that children develop. Before they know their nationality, religion, or social status, most children develop gender constancy and see themselves as gendered beings.

Let's look more closely at exactly how cultures communicate norms and expectations for gender to children. The process occurs as others define them by sex or gender and as those others link gender to particular activities and feelings. "You are mommy's helper in the kitchen," mothers may say to daughters, a label that defines young girls as both connected to their mothers and appropriately involved in domestic activities. This and similar labels encourage young girls to define themselves through helping activities and care for others. When young boys carry in packages after shopping, parents often praise them by saying, "You're such a strong little man." This defines the child as a man and links strength with manhood and praise. At school, young girls are likely to be reprimanded for roughnecking as a teacher tells them, "That's not very ladylike." Boys engaged in similar mischief more often hear the teacher say with some amusement, "You boys really are rowdy today." In play with peers, gender messages continue. When a young girl tries to tell a boy what to do, she may be told, "You can't boss me around. You're just a girl." Girls who fail to share their toys or show consideration to others may be told, "You're not being nice," yet this is considerably less likely to be said to young boys. Thus, children learn what is expected of them and how that is related to being masculine or feminine. Gender is so basic to a conception of self that E. Fox-Genovese (1991, p. 120) claims, "To be an 'I' at all means to be gendered." Beginning with birth, infants interact with others who respond to them as gendered. As others communicate our gender to us, we learn to define ourselves that way and to understand that our gender has major implications for what we are expected to do and be.

Symbolic interactionism makes it clear that the process of defining a personal self is inevitably a social process, which reflects the views of others we have incorporated into our own perspectives. Our thinking about ourselves never occurs from some absolutely personal, idiosyncratic perspective, but from the viewpoints of others and the cultural values they embody (Wood, 1993b). Having studied the process by which we learn to conceive of ourselves, George Herbert Mead was able to answer his question, How is it that society gets into individuals? His conclusion was that through communication with others, we learn who we are and what that means in the culture into which we were born.

An important contribution to a cultural theory of gender is the concept of **role** and, specifically, how our society defines roles for women and men. A role is a set of expected behaviors and the values associated with them. In an insightful analysis, Elizabeth Janeway (1971) discussed two dimensions of roles. First, roles are external to individuals, because a society defines them in general ways that transcend particular individuals. Roles are assigned to individuals by the society as a whole. Thus, for each of us there are certain roles we are expected to fulfill.

Within our culture, roles for gender are one of the primary ways that social life is classified. Women are still regarded as caretakers (Wood, 1993c), and they are expected to provide the majority of care for infants, elderly relatives, and others who are sick or disabled. If a child is sick, the mother is generally expected to take off time from work or other activities to care for the child (Hewlett, 1986, 1991; Hochschild, 1989; Okin, 1989). If a parent or in-law needs help, it is the daughter or daughter-in-law who is expected to, and who does generally, provide the help, regardless of the costs to her personal and professional life (Aronson, 1992; Wood, 1993c). Even in the working world, the feminine role is evident. Women remain disproportionately represented in service sectors and human relations divisions of companies, while men are moved into executive positions. Women are still asked to take care of social activities on the job, but men in equivalent positions are seldom expected to do this.

There are masculine roles too. Men are still regarded as the primary breadwinners for families. This is perhaps the most central aspect of present-day views of "being a man." Thus, it is seen as more acceptable for a woman than a man

M A R K

I see how gender roles work in my own family. My mother works full-time, and she's still the one who fixes all the meals and does all the shopping and most of the housework. Both she and dad seem to accept that as the way things are supposed to be. Last year her mother had a stroke, and since then mom's been doing another job — taking care of her mother. Every day she goes by to see how grandma is, and she shops for her and cleans her house as well as ours. My dad has told her she's doing too much, and it's clearly taking a toll on mom. But I don't think she feels she can do less. And it doesn't seem to have occurred to dad that he could do more to help. When I asked her why she was doing so much, she told me grandma expected her help and needed it, and she felt that way too. I don't know how long mom can keep taking care of everybody else without breaking down herself.

not to have a job. Many young women today regard a career as an option, something they may or may not do, or might do for a while and then take time off to raise a family. Very few young men regard working as optional. To fulfill the masculine role successfully, a man must work and bring in an income; the feminine role does not require this.

Not only are roles assigned by society, but their value is defined as well. Within Western culture, the feminine role remains subordinate to the masculine role. Men are still regarded as the "heads of families," even if their wives earn more than they do. Men are more often seen as leaders and given opportunities to lead than are women. Further, the work that men do is more highly regarded by the society than is the work assigned to women. Janeway noted that the roles assigned to women — caring for families, keeping a home, and so on — have low prestige in our culture. Jean Baker Miller (1986, p. 61) agreed, noting that "in our culture 'serving others' is for losers, it is low-level stuff. Yet serving others is a basic principle around which women's lives are organized." Society teaches women to accept the role of supporting, taking care of, and responding to others. Yet that is a role clearly devalued in America. Competing and succeeding in work life and public affairs is the primary role assigned to men, and to that role high prestige is attached.

A second important dimension of role is that it is internalized. For social specifications of behaviors to be effective, individuals must internalize them. They must accept them internally as part of who they are. As Mead pointed out, by communicating with others we discover how they see us, and we learn how to see ourselves. At very young ages, girls understand that they are supposed to be nice, put others' needs ahead of their own, and be nurturing, while boys understand that they are supposed to take command and assert themselves. As we take cultural scripts for gender inside of ourselves, we learn not only that there are different roles for men and women but also that unequal values are assigned to them. This can be very frustrating for those who are encouraged to conform to a role that will not be esteemed.

Symbolic interactionism clarifies the ways in which gender reflects meanings widely endorsed by a culture. While gender is clearly influenced by family psychodynamics, learning, and cognitive development in interpersonal settings, those relational contexts themselves are part of a larger society whose values they echo and perpetuate. Symbolic interactionism underlines the fact that gender is socially created and sustained through communication that teaches us to define ourselves as gendered and to adopt the roles that society prescribes for us.

Standpoint theory.   A final contribution from the cultural perspective is **standpoint theory** (Collins, 1986; Harding 1991; Ruddick, 1989), which offers insights into how a person's location within a culture shapes his or her life. Standpoint theory focuses on how gender, race, and class influence the circumstances of individuals' lives, especially their positions in society and the kinds of experiences those positions foster. To symbolic interactionism's emphasis on how we are socialized into a common social world, standpoint theory adds that the common social world consists of very different positions within social hierarchies. We may all understand that our culture defines people by class and race and values those differently; yet each of us experiences only being in a certain race and class. The particular standpoint that an individual has in a society guides what she or he knows, feels, and does and directs an individual's understanding of social life as a whole.

Although modern theorists have developed standpoint theory, it began some time ago with George Wilhelm Friedrich Hegel's reflections on the institution of slavery. Hegel (1807), a prominent 19th-century German philosopher, noted that society as a whole recognized that slavery existed, but that the nature of that institution was perceived quite differently depending on whether one's position was that of master or slave. From this insight, Hegel reasoned that in any society where power relationships exist, there can be no single perspective, no "correct" understanding of social life. Each person sees society only as it appears from the perspective of his or her social group, and every perspective is limited. All views are partial because each reflects only a particular standpoint within a culture stratified by power.

A particularly important implication of standpoint theory is that while all perspectives on social life are limited, some are more limited than others. Sandra

Harding (1991, p. 59) argues that those in positions of high power have a vested interest in preserving their place in the hierarchy, so their views of social life are more distorted than the views of persons who gain little or nothing from existing power relationships. Another reason that those in groups labeled subordinate may have fuller understandings is that they have to understand both their own perspective and the viewpoints of persons who have more power. To survive, subjugated persons have to understand people with power, but the reverse is not true. From this it follows that marginalized groups have unique insights into the nature and workings of a society. Women, minorities, gays and lesbians, people of lower socioeconomic class, and others who are outside of the cultural center may see the society from a perspective that is less distorted, less biased, and more layered than those who occupy more central standpoints. Marginalized perspectives can inform all of us about how our society operates.

According to standpoint theory, different social groups like women and men develop particular skills, attitudes, ways of thinking, and understandings of life as a result of their standpoint within society. Patricia Hill Collins (1986) used standpoint theory to show that black women scholars have special insights into Western culture because of their dual standpoints as "outsiders within," that is, as members of a minority group (African-Americans) who hold membership in majority institutions (higher education).

Another application of standpoint logic came from Sara Ruddick's (1989) study of mothers. She claims that the demands of their role lead mothers to develop what she calls "maternal thinking," which consists of values, priorities, and understandings of relationships that are specifically promoted by the process of taking care of young children. Ruddick argues that what we often assume is a "maternal instinct" that comes naturally to women is actually a set of attitudes and behaviors that arise out of women's location in domestic, caregiving roles.

K I M

My mother never finished college, but she sure understands the standpoint theory we talked about. The thing she drilled into us as kids was "Don't ever judge someone until you've been in their shoes." She said that all the time, and I still hear it in my head whenever I start to judge somebody who's different than I am. I think there's a lot to this idea, since the situations people are in do affect how they think and what they are like, and if you haven't been in a situation, you can't judge somebody who has. You can't even understand them really.

Interesting proof of this idea came from two other researchers who studied men in caregiving roles. In her research on single fathers, Barbara Risman (1989) found that men who are primary parents are more nurturing, attentive to others' needs, patient, and emotionally expressive than are men in general and as much so as women. Another study (Kaye & Applegate, 1990) found that men who care for elderly people enlarge their capacities for nurturing.

Standpoint research also calls into question the extent to which biology influences gendered behavior. When we discussed biological theory earlier in this chapter, I noted findings ("Study Links Men's Cognitive Abilities," 1991) that men's testosterone level seemed to affect their aggressiveness and their ability to perform certain cognitive tasks. Yet those findings have to be qualified by noting that men in higher socioeconomic classes did not display more aggression when their testosterone was high. This suggests that their standpoint in society included socialization that taught them it is inappropriate to behave aggressively. Violence and aggression are more tolerated, and sometimes encouraged, in lower socioeconomic classes than in higher ones. The upper-class men in the study had learned from their standpoint as members of a particular class that destructiveness and physical force are not acceptable, and this shaped how they acted. Even when their testosterone rose, they had learned not to react by being violent and aggressive.

In summary, the cultural perspective broadens our understandings by demonstrating that gender is not merely a quality of individuals. Instead, it entails social expectations that define meaning of sex and that are systematically taught to individuals. Cultural views of gender reflect three related research traditions. From anthropology we gain insight into the arbitrary and variable nature of gender by seeing how variably it is defined in diverse cultures. Symbolic interactionist theory offers an understanding of culture as a whole and the key role of communication in socializing new members into the understandings and values of a common social world. Finally, standpoint theory adds the important realization that individuals' positions within a society influence how they see social life and how they define their roles, activities, priorities, and feelings. This is a particularly important point, since Western culture is decisively stratified by gender, race, and class. Women and men typically occupy different standpoints in our society, which profoundly influence how they understand and act in the world as well as how they define themselves.

*S*ummary

In this chapter, we have considered different theories that offer explanations of relationships among communication, gender, and culture. Rather than asking which is *the right theory*, we have tried to discover how each viewpoint contributes to overall understandings of how gender develops. By weaving together the different theories' focus on individual, interpersonal, and cultural influences, we gain a powerful appreciation of the complex origins of gender identity. The cultural perspective seems broadest, since it incorporates interpersonal and biological theories yet also goes beyond their foci. The remainder of this book reflects the view that gender (not sex) is culturally constructed and that the meanings a culture assigns to femininity and masculinity are expressed and sustained through communication. Adopting this broad perspective allows us to include, but not be restricted to, theories with less explanatory power.

We are born as sexed beings — biologically male or female. What sex means and what it implies for participation in life, however, are matters of social convention that are communicated to us. Various societies attach different meanings to masculinity and femininity, so what it means depends on the society in which one lives and the particular position one occupies in that society. The meanings a given culture establishes for gender are passed on to individuals through communication. Families, schools, peers, and others teach children the cultural dictates of gender. Thus, in the process of becoming socialized, we internalize gendered identities that shape how we understand the common life of a culture and our own places, opportunities, and priorities within it. The crux of the gendering process, as we have seen, is communication, through which we learn others' views of masculinity and femininity and usually import those inside ourselves.

With this theoretical background, we are now ready to consider contexts in which gender is formed and communicated, as well as ways in which individuals accept or resist cultural directives for masculinity and femininity. The next chapter builds on this one by probing in greater detail the ways in which communication develops individuals' gender identities. In later chapters, we will consider how communication within rhetorical movements redefines socially shared views of men and women and how gender influences and is influenced by particular communication situations.

$\mathcal{D}$iscussion Questions

1. The author asserts that theories are not abstract and unrelated to our everyday lives. Do you agree or disagree? Why?

2. What are your theories about gender as you begin this course? Do you tend to think gender is influenced more by biology, society, or interpersonal relationships? How do your implicit theories affect your own actions and your interpretations of other people's attitudes and behaviors?

3. What are the implications of research indicating that men have hormonal cycles that affect their moods and behaviors? Women's hormonal cycles have long been used to justify not trusting women's judgment and excluding them from important roles in decision making. If men too are influenced by their hormones, should we distrust their judgment and actions?

4. Think about your relationship with your parents. How were your connections to your father and mother different? How were they similar? How did sex and gender influence each relationship? If you have siblings of the other sex, were their relationships with your parents different from yours?

5. Can you recall when gender constancy was fixed for you? Do you remember a point in your early years when you knew you were a boy or a girl and realized that wasn't going to change? How did this affect your thinking about yourself and life?

6. The author summarizes work indicating that the more technologically complex a society is, the more tightly it stratifies people by gender, race, and class. Why do you think this is so? Why is social stratification useful to a culture, and why is it more likely in complex cultures?

7. Standpoint theory maintains that where a person is located in a society has effects on what she or he can know and be. Do you agree or disagree? How has your gender affected your standpoint in society? In turn, how has your standpoint affected how you see yourself, others, and social life? As a man or a woman, what do you think you understand particularly well? About what do you not have much insight? Relate this to standpoint theory.

PART II

Creating Gendered Identities

$\mathscr{T}$he Origins and Implications of Gendered Identities

If you woke up tomorrow and found you had changed into the opposite sex, how would your life be different?

Before beginning this chapter, write out a one- or two-paragraph response to this question. Resist the temptation to skip this, and take a few moments to think seriously about how being the other sex would really change your life.

Karl Marx is famous for saying, "Give me a child until age 5 and he will be mine forever." In this comment, Marx expressed a central insight about human nature: The experiences during the early years of life profoundly influence individuals' identities. Although we continue to evolve throughout our lives, foundations of our personalities, values, attitudes, and perspectives are established through communication during the formative years between birth and age 5. What happens then has enduring implications for how we define ourselves and how we interact with others.

In this chapter, we focus on the ways in which gender is communicated to infants and children during the early years of life and what that implies for our identities as adults. You will recall that Chapter 2 introduced interpersonal and cultural theories to explain how society communicates its views of gender to individuals. Now we will explore in greater depth the communicative processes by which children come to learn and internalize society's views of gender and how these views then affect their lives. As George Herbert Mead (1934) pointed out, children learn social values through communicating with others, who introduce them to the definitions, meanings, and values of the culture. Having learned these, the majority of women and men then embody them in their own communication, thereby reproducing existing social views of gender.

To launch our discussion, we will first consider the necessarily social human self. By this I mean that we will examine how individual identities are inevitably created through interactions with others. We will then focus on communication from parents, teachers, and peers, all of whom participate in the process of teaching children the cultural code. Exploring the content and patterns of communication clarifies how interaction genders boys and girls so that most adopt, respectively, masculine or feminine identities. Finally, we will trace the implications of gendering processes by considering how they are reflected in contemporary college students' views of what it means to be masculine or feminine in North America today. By understanding the origins and implications of gender roles, we should gain clearer insight into our own identities — and perhaps options to them.

▬ Talked into Humanity

We are born into a gendered society. We enter a social world that emphasizes masculinity and femininity. From the pink and blue blankets hospitals frequently use to swaddle newborns, to parents' distinct interactions with boys and girls, gender messages besiege infants from the moment of birth. Key players in the gender drama are parents, teachers, and peers, each of whom contributes to imparting cultural expectations and prescriptions to newcomers in the society so that they may understand and, thus, participate in a common social world.

Communication is a primary agent of socialization. Through interaction with others, children learn about the society into which they were born. They discern social norms, values, and expectations, and they apply these to themselves. As they do so, children form a sense of who they are — an identity that reflects how others see and act toward them. Because this process relies on interaction with others, the identity an individual claims for herself or himself is also necessarily a social one that arises out of our communication in relationships.

The Social Self

According to Mead, we have no self at birth. Instead, we develop an identity through communication with others who are significant to us. Newborn infants experience themselves as blurred with the rest of their environment. To develop awareness of personal identity, a baby interacts with family members and others who are part of a larger social world. These interactions facilitate two processes central to developing a personal identity: conceiving the self-as-object and monitoring.

Self-as-object.   By the term **self-as-object,** Mead did not mean that individuals take a detached view of themselves, nor that they objectify themselves. Rather, he was pointing out that humans are distinct from all other sentient creatures in their ability to reflect on themselves. We are unique in the capacity to be simultaneously the subjects and objects of our own thinking. We are able to stand outside of ourselves in order to perceive, describe, and evaluate our own activities, much as we would those of others. For instance, we say "I am attractive," "I am strong," "I ought to take care of my sick parent," and "I'm overweight." Our ability to self-reflect enables us to define ourselves and exercise some choice over who we will become.

How we think about ourselves inevitably reflects the views of us that others have communicated. In ongoing interactions, children discover how others see them. At first, others' views of us are external, but gradually, they are internalized into ways we see ourselves. Because our sense of identity begins outside of ourselves, it is infused with the values, meanings, and understandings of a larger society. Mead (1934, pp. 150–161), in fact, insisted that we can *experience self only after experiencing others.* Because gender is one of the most basic and important categories of identity in our society, it is a major focus of others' perceptions of us and of their communication to and about us. The emphasis others place on assigning gender to children explains why this is one of the first clear senses of self that we develop. If you reflected on the question posed at the beginning of this chapter, you have some idea of how central gender identity is to your sense of who you are. Trying to imagine yourself as the other sex is extremely difficult, because gender is a primary facet of our identities.

Monitoring.   Because we learn to take the self as an object, we are able to **monitor** ourselves, which means we observe and regulate our attitudes and behaviors (Wood, 1992a, p. 80). We use symbols, usually language, to define who we are (son, student, mother, attorney, kind, independent, and so on). Monitoring is an internal process people use to keep themselves within the external norms and expectations of society. Mead spoke of *internal dialogues* to indicate that monitoring happens inside of us, but it involves the perspectives of others we have imported into our own thinking. Thus, in our private self-talk, we engage in a dialogue with the social world. As we do so, we remind ourselves what we are supposed to think, do, and feel in various situations—that is, we tell ourselves what the social codes stipulate as "appropriate" (Wood, 1993b). For instance, a 5-year-old girl might think "I want to go play in the yard" and then monitor that wish by repeating something she has heard from her mother: "but nice girls don't get dirty." The little girl voice's and the mother's voice engage in an internal dialogue through which the child decides what to do.

Because we reflect on ourselves from the perspectives of others, we monitor our own actions and feelings from the viewpoint of our society as others have communicated it to us. Through internal dialogues, we keep ourselves attuned to the social perspective and use that to guide how we think, act, feel, and define ourselves. With this background on the process by which identity reflects social meanings, we may now consider in more depth how communication from families, peers, and teachers contributes to forming gender identities.

▇ Gendering Communication

The different theories introduced in Chapter 2 offer us a variety of insights into how children discover social meanings of gender and integrate these into their identities. By interweaving these theories, we may understand in some depth how families, teachers, and peers shape development of gender identity in children.

Gendering Communication in the Family

The family is a primary source of gender identity. Through both overt, deliberate instruction and subtle, unconscious communication, families contribute in major ways to the formation of gender identity. To understand how families gender children, we will focus on two dimensions of communication between parents and children. First, we will elaborate on the largely unconscious process of internalizing gender, which was introduced in Chapter 2. Second, we will examine more overt ways in which children learn gender from parents. Parents' beliefs about gender influence how they interact with sons and daughters, what expectations they communicate to each, and how they themselves serve as gender models for children. Taken together, the unconscious and conscious processes call our attention to the fundamental importance of parent-child communication in creating gendered identities.

Unconscious processes: Identification and internalization.   Even skeptics of psychoanalytic theory generally admit that the conscious level of human communication does not fully explain human personality, including gender identity. Insight into unobservable yet very important unconscious dynamics comes primarily from psychoanalytic theories. The basic principle of psychoanalytic theories is that core personality is shaped by family relationships in the early years of life.

Sigmund Freud is famous for claiming "anatomy is destiny," by which he meant that biology, particularly genitals, determines with which parent a child will identify. According to Freud, at an early age children of both sexes focus on the penis. Boys are motivated to identify with their fathers, who also have penises, while girls recognize their similarity with mothers, who lack the coveted organ. Freud theorized that girls regard their mothers as responsible for their lack of a penis, while boys view their fathers as having the power to castrate them and deprive them of their penis.

By identifying with their same-sex parent, each child aligns himself or herself with one perceived as responsible for the possession or absence of a penis in the hope of gaining that person's protection. Freud argued that boys' fear of castration is more formidable than girls' penis envy, so males develop stronger and more intense gender identities. Following identification with the same-sex parent, children internalize the gendered behaviors and attitudes of their primary models. Interesting as Freud's theory is, there has been little empirical support for it, and some studies indicate that at least parts of the theory are not valid (Basow, 1992; Pleck, 1981; Williams, 1973).

Lack of support for Freud's ideas, along with the growing realization that he misrepresented female development, led to alternative explanations of the psychic bases of gender. Newer theories reject Freud's assertion that anatomy is destiny and his claim that females are preoccupied with penis envy. According to more recent thinkers (Chodorow, 1978, 1989; Goldner, Penn, Sheinberg, & Walker, 1990; Miller, 1986), females do not literally want a penis. What they may envy is what the penis symbolizes—the privilege and power our society bestows on males.

EILEEN

I don't buy this stuff about penis envy. I've never envied my brother his penis. I remember when we were both little, we took baths together sometimes, and I saw that he was made differently than I was. I thought it looked strange, but I didn't want it myself. But I do remember being jealous of him, or of the freedoms my parents allowed him but not me. They let him go off all day long to play, but I had to stay in the yard unless my mother was with me. He could play rough and get dirty, but I'd get a real fussin' if I did it. I remember wishing I was a boy so that I could do all of the fun things, but I didn't wish I had a penis. Definitely not.

Although current psychoanalytic theorists reject some of Freud's ideas, they agree with his fundamental claim that family psychodynamics are critical to the formation of gender identity. During the earliest stage of life, children of both sexes are in a similar state of "infantile dependence" (Chodorow, 1989, p. 47) in which they depend on and identify with the person who takes care of them. Almost invariably this is a woman, usually the mother. This implies that children of both sexes typically form their first primary identification with an adult woman.

Yet common identification with a female does not mean boys and girls pursue similar developmental paths. Because mothers and daughters have a sameness that mothers and sons do not, boys and girls form distinct relationships with their mothers. Mothers tend to identify with daughters more closely than with sons, they seem to experience daughters more as part of themselves, and they encourage daughters to feel connected to them (Apter, 1990; Chodorow, 1989; Fliess, 1961). With sons, mothers are inclined to emphasize the difference between them and to encourage sons to differentiate from them. Through a variety of verbal and nonverbal communications, mothers fortify identification with daughters and curb it with sons.

According to psychodynamic theory, around age 3, male and female development diverges dramatically. You'll recall that this is the stage at which gender constancy is secured so that children realize gender is an unchanging, continuous part of their identity (Kohlberg, 1966; Money & Ehrhardt, 1972). For girls, development proceeds along the path initially established—identification with the mother. Through concrete, daily interactions with her mother, a daughter continues to crystallize her sense of self within the original primary relationship.

To develop masculine gender identity, however, boys must sever the early identification with the mother and replace it with an identification with a male, often the father. This process is complicated by the fact that fathers are generally less physically present in boys' everyday lives and often are emotionally remote as well (Keen, 1991; Slater, 1961; Winch, 1962). The gender model with which boys

MARY KAYE

helped mom a lot with cooking and cleaning when I was little. I used to really enjoy that, because it made me feel like an adult. I remember thinking "I'm just like mommy" when I'd be cleaning or doing stuff in the kitchen. I wanted to be like her, and doing what she did made me feel we were the same.

identify is usually more abstract and removed from their daily lives than the one for girls. Because boys typically lack a concrete, personal relationship with the person whom they are supposed to become like (Mitscherlich, 1970), masculine gender is elusive and difficult to grasp. This may help explain why boys typically define their masculinity predominantly in negative terms—it is being not feminine, not like mother. This can be accomplished by repressing the original identification with mothers and denying anything feminine in themselves. By extension, this may be the source of boys' tendencies to devalue whatever is feminine in general ("Ugh, girls are icky"), a pattern not paralleled by girls' views of masculinity. D. G. Brown's (1956) early studies, as well as more recent work (Burton & Whiting, 1961; Chodorow, 1989; Gaylin, 1992; Miller, 1986), suggest boys may feel compelled to disparage what is feminine in order to assure themselves that they are truly masculine, an identity that is less accessible than femininity because of the remoteness of fathers in many homes.

As development continues, girls are encouraged to be "mommy's helper" and to interact constantly with a single, specific person. However, around age 5, boys begin to roam from home to find companions. Boys' development typically occurs in larger groups with temporary and changing memberships; for girls, it unfolds within a continuing, personal relationship with an individual (Jay, 1969). These different contexts and relationships socialize boys to focus on achievement and independence and girls to emphasize nurturance and relatedness (Barry, Bacon, & Child, 1957; Chodorow, 1989; Gilligan, 1982; Miller, 1986).

REGGIE

I was really confused as a kid. My father left us before I was even a year old, so I didn't know him at all. My mom worked all day and was too tired to date or anything else, so there wasn't a man around. I tried to help mom, but she'd tell me I didn't have to do this stuff because I was "her little man." I used to watch mom doing stuff around the house and I'd think, "That's not what I'm supposed to do," but I had a lot of trouble figuring out what it was that I *was* supposed to do. I just knew it wasn't girl stuff. Then I got a big brother through a program at school. He was 17, and he spent most every Saturday with me and sometimes some time after school during the week. Michael was great. He'd let me hang out with him, and he'd show me how to do stuff like play ball and use tools to make things. Finally I had a sense of what I was supposed to be like and what I should do. Michael really helped me figure out who I was.

Early experiences do more than provide behavioral training consistent with gender; they also shape core identity. By engaging in distinctive kinds of family relationships, boys and girls unconsciously internalize different roles into their fundamental sense of selfhood. Chodorow (1989, p. 57) suggests that because girls develop feminine identity within personal, ongoing relationships, as they mature they continue to seek close relationships with particular individuals and to prioritize personal communication with others. Throughout life, women in general rely on communication in close relationships to learn about themselves and nurture connections with others (Chodorow, 1989; Gilligan, 1982). Because boys separate from their initial relationship with mothers in order to form masculine identities, and because they tend to interact in temporary groups with changing members, they learn to define themselves through independence and to maintain a "safe" distance between themselves and others. They tend to engage more in doing things than in personal communication with others. For example, if you observe young children, you're likely to notice that girls typically engage in conversation or talk-oriented games (for example, playing house), while boys usually favor activities that require little verbal interaction (for example, baseball).

The different styles typical of males and females—whether as children or adults—have been described as *agentic* and *communal*, respectively (Bakan, 1966, 1968). Explaining these differences, Bakan (1966, p. 15) wrote that agency and communion

> characterize two fundamental modalities in the existence of living forms. . . .
> Agency manifests itself in self-protection, self-assertion, and self-expansion;
> communion manifests itself in the sense of being at one with other organ-
> isms. Agency manifests itself in the formation of separations; communion
> in the lack of separations. Agency manifests itself in isolation, aliena-
> tion, and aloneness; communion in contact, openness, and union. Agency
> manifests itself in the urge to master; communion in noncontractual
> cooperation.

While others have used different terms, Bakan's association of agency with masculine identity and communion with feminine identity is widely accepted by clinicians and researchers. Various studies (Belenky, Clinchy, Goldberger, & Tarule, 1986; Carlson, 1971; Cohen, 1969; Gilligan, 1982; Gilligan & Pollack, 1988; Gutman, 1965; Thompson & Walker, 1989) confirm the generalizations that femininity is generally relationally oriented while masculinity pivots more centrally on independence. It's important to understand that these are generalizations about gender, not sex. Women as well as men with masculine inclinations value independence and prefer distance from others, and men as well as women with feminine orientations place a premium on relationships and interpersonal closeness. How is identity formation affected when men, not women, are primary caregivers? Research on this is just beginning, but it might encourage a more relational, communal identity in male children, since they could define themselves within the first relationship with another male.

Ego boundaries. Concurrent with the process of constructing gender identity is a second intrapsychic development: formation of **ego boundaries** (Chodorow, 1989; Surrey, 1983). Ego boundaries define the point at which an individual stops and the rest of the world begins. They distinguish the self—more or less distinctly—from everyone and everything else. Because they are linked to gender identity and evolve concurrently with it, masculine and feminine ego boundaries tend to differ. Individuals who develop feminine gender identity, which emphasizes interrelatedness with others, tend to have relatively thin or permeable ego boundaries. Because girls are encouraged to identify with mothers and not to differentiate, they often do not perceive clear-cut or absolute lines between themselves and others.

The relatively thin ego boundaries cultivated in females may partially explain why they tend to be more empathic—to sense the feelings of those close to them and to experience those feelings as nearly their own. It may also explain why women, more than men, sometimes become so involved with others that they neglect their own needs. Finally, this may shed light on the feminine tendency to feel responsible for others and for situations that are not one's own doing. When the lines between self and other are blurred, it's hard to tell what *your* responsibilities and *your* needs are. To the extent that others merge with yourself, helping them is helping you. This may be related to a tendency toward co-dependency, which is a major new focus of research and therapy.

Masculine gender identity is premised on differentiating from a female caregiver and defining self as "not like her." It makes sense, then, that masculine individuals tend to have relatively thick or rigid ego boundaries. They generally have a definite sense of where they stop and others begin, and they are less likely to experience others' feelings as their own. The thicker ego boundaries encouraged in masculine socialization help us understand why later in life men generally keep some distance from others and, especially, from other people's problems. Rigid ego boundaries also suggest why men in general are unlikely to take responsibility for other people and situations, and why they tend not to experience another's feelings as their own. Contrary to some accusations, people with masculine identities are not necessarily unconcerned about others; instead, it is more likely that men generally experience others' feelings as separate from their own.

Interested in the implications of ego boundary development for adults, Ernest Hartmann (1991) has studied the nature and function of internal ego boundaries in his clinical practice. He explains that people with thick boundaries have "a very solid, separate sense of self [which] implies not becoming overinvolved and can also imply being careful, not becoming involved with anyone rapidly" (p. 36). He goes on to note that "people with thin boundaries may become

VINCE

My girlfriend is so strange about her friends. Like the other night I went by her apartment and she was all upset and crying. When I asked her what was wrong she told me Linda, her best friend, had just been dumped by her boyfriend. I said she acted like it was her who'd broken up, not Linda, and she didn't need to be so upset. She got even more upset and said it felt like her; couldn't I understand what Linda was going through? I said I could, but that *she* wasn't going through it; Linda was. She told me it was the same thing because when you're really close to somebody else you hurt when they hurt. It didn't make sense to me, but maybe this theory of ego boundaries is what that's all about.

rapidly and deeply involved with others and may lose themselves in relationships" (p. 37). After measuring ego boundaries of nearly 1,000 people, Hartmann concluded that there are "clear-cut differences between men and women. . . . Overall, women scored significantly thinner than men—thinner by about twenty points, or 8% of the overall score" (p. 117). He also found that women tend to be comfortable feeling connected to others, sensing that their lives are interwoven with those close to them, and they may be uneasy with too much autonomy.

Men, on the other hand, tend to feel most secure when autonomy and self-sufficiency are high, and they may feel suffocated in relationships that are extremely close. This may explain why women typically want more togetherness than men find comfortable and men tend to desire more separation than women enjoy. Some theorists (Rubin, 1985; Schaef, 1981) see the genders' distinctive preferences for closeness as a reason why women create more emotionally intense same-sex friendships than do men. With other women, they find the kind of intimate, personal connection they value. These patterns, which are particularly evident in adult life, have their roots in childhood socialization processes.

In noting the influence of early communication on adult gender identity, we don't want to repeat Freud's fallacy of thinking that anatomy is destiny. Important as childhood socialization is, we should remind ourselves it is not an absolute determinant of adult personality. Gender, like other important aspects of ourselves, is not fixed by age 5 and then constant and unchanging throughout the rest of our lives. Our understanding of gender and of our personal gender identity changes over time as we experience different situations and diverse people who

BONITA

You asked us to think about whether we ever got the message that males are more valued than females. I know I did. I guess I got it in a lot of ways, but one really stands out. I remember when I was 9 my mother was pregnant for the third time. When she went into labor, daddy took her to the hospital with me and my sister. We all sat in the waiting room while they took mom down the hall. Later the doctor came in and went to my father. I still remember his exact words. He said, "I'm sorry Mr. Chavis, it's another girl. Guess you'll have to try again."

embody alternative versions of masculinity and femininity and who communicate how they see us.

Summing up the ways in which family communication in the early years of life unconsciously shapes gender identity, Chodorow (1978, p. 169) states, "The basic feminine sense of self is connected to the world, the basic masculine sense of self is separate." These differences are not merely in behaviors and attitudes but are rooted in the basic psyche, which is formed through early, primary relationships in the family and which shape identity in enduring ways. To discover how children build on the basic intrapsychic structure, we will now discuss what and how they learn about gender through communication with others.

Parental attitudes about gender. Communication from parents frequently reinforces the unconscious bases of gender identity we have examined. Children learn gender roles through rewards and punishments they receive for various behaviors and through observing and modeling others of their gender. Typically, girls are encouraged to be communal through communication that reinforces cooperation, helpfulness, nurturance, and other behaviors consistent with social meanings of femininity. In boys, agentic tendencies are promoted by rewarding them for behaving competitively, independently, and assertively. In addition, children learn about gender by watching parents, who themselves usually embody cultural views of masculinity and femininity. Children observe what mothers and fathers do, using parents as models for themselves.

One understanding of gender that most children learn through early communication is that males are generally more valued than females. According to Basow (1992, p. 129), "Nearly everywhere in the world, most couples prefer male children to female children," a preference that is communicated, indirectly or directly, to children. In fact, preference for males is so strong that in some cultures female fetuses are aborted and female infants are killed immediately after birth (French, 1992; Steinbacher & Holmes, 1987; Williamson, 1976). That males are routinely more valued may explain why many young girls wish they could be boys — they understand that their parents and the culture as a whole regard males more highly than females.

Parents' attitudes toward sons and daughters often reflect gender stereotypes more than responses to their particular children. Social scientists have shown that labeling a baby male or female affects how parents perceive and respond to it. In one study, within just 24 hours of birth parents were responding to their babies in terms of gender stereotypes (Rubin, Provenzano, & Luria, 1974). Although male and female babies were matched for size, weight, and level of activity, parents described boys with words such as *strong, hardy, big, active,* and *alert.* Parents of equally large and active girls described their daughters with adjectives such as *small, dainty, quiet,* and *delicate.* More recent experiments show the persistence of parental tendencies to gender stereotype children (Delk, Madden, Livingston, & Ryan, 1986; Stern & Karraker, 1989).

Parental stereotypes affect children's development. Qualities that are expected and promoted are more likely to be woven into children's behavioral repertoires than are those that are not expected and/or are discouraged. Parents have been shown to act toward children on the basis of gender labels. In general, boys are treated more roughly and encouraged to be more aggressive, whereas girls are treated gently and urged to be emotional and physically reserved (Antill, 1987). One study found that parental gender stereotypes prompt parents to expect boys to excel at math and science but do not expect or encourage this in girls (Eccles, 1989). Another recent report (National Public Radio, 1992) noted that parents praise sons more than daughters for accomplishments, a pattern that encourages boys to aim for achievement and to tie their successes to what they are able to do. Finally, researchers (Fagot, Hagan, Leinbach, & Kronsberg, 1985) report that parents respond more approvingly to assertiveness in sons than in daughters and react more positively to interpersonal and social skills in daughters than in sons.

Parental communication about gender. In addition to guiding parents' responses to children's behaviors, gender stereotypes are communicated by the toys and clothes parents give children and the chores they assign to them. Despite evidence that rigid gender socialization restricts children's development (Morrow, 1990), many parents continue to select toys and clothes that are gender specific. Recently, a group of researchers surveyed the rooms of 120 boys and girls who were under 2 years old (Pomerleau, Bolduc, Malcuit, & Cossette, 1990). They found girls' rooms were populated by dolls and children's furniture, and the color pink was prominent. Boys' rooms most often were decorated in the colors blue, red, and white, and in them were various vehicles, tools, and sports gear.

Further investigations have shown that many parents actively discourage their children's interest in toys and games that are associated with the other sex (Antill, 1987; Fagot, 1978; Lytton & Romney, 1991). For instance, boys may be persuaded not to play house or to cook, and girls may be dissuaded from engaging in vigorous, competitive games. Different types of toys and activities promote distinct kinds of thinking and interaction. More "feminine" toys like dolls encourage quiet, nurturing interaction with another, physical closeness, and verbal communication. More typically "masculine" toys such as sporting equipment and train sets promote independent and/or competitive activities that require little verbal interaction. Because the toys children play with can affect how they think and interact, some researchers caution parents not to limit children to toys for one sex (Basow, 1992; Fagot, 1985).

Another way parents communicate gender expectations is through the household chores they assign to sons and daughters. As early as age 6, many children are given responsibilities that reflect their parents' gender expectations. As you might expect, domestic duties such as cleaning and cooking are most often designated for girls, and more active chores such as outdoor work, painting, and simple repairs are assigned to boys (Burns & Homel, 1989; Goodnow, 1988; McHale, Bartko, Crouter, & Perry-Jenkins, 1990). There are several implications of differential responsibilities delegated to girls and boys. First, like toys, various tasks encourage particular types of thinking and activity. Domestic chores emphasize taking care of others and taking responsibility for them (cleaning their clothes, shopping for their needs, and so on), while maintenance jobs encourage independent activity and emphasize taking care of things rather than people. Domestic chores also tend to occur in small, interior spaces, whereas maintenance chores are frequently done in open spaces.

In general, boys are more rigidly gender socialized than girls. This is more true of Caucasian than African-American families, since the latter tend to socialize children of both sexes toward autonomy and nurturing of children (Bardewell, Cochran, & Walker, 1986; Hale-Benson, 1986). It's much more acceptable for girls to be "tomboys" than for boys to play house or cuddle dolls. Similarly, it's considered more suitable for girls to be strong than for boys to cry, for girls to act independently than for boys to need others, and for girls to touch and show tenderness toward other girls than for boys to demonstrate closeness to male peers.

These differential gender latitudes are evident in how parents communicate with sons and daughters. Sons tend to receive more encouragement to conform to masculinity and more rewards for doing so than daughters receive for femininity. In addition, boys are more directly and strongly discouraged from any feminine inclinations than girls are from masculine behaviors and interests. It's also been shown that fathers are more insistent on gender-stereotyped toys and activities, especially for sons, than are mothers (Caldera, Huston, & O'Brien, 1989; Fagot & Leinbach, 1987; Lamb, 1986). The overall picture is that boys are more intensively and rigidly pushed to become masculine than girls are to become feminine.

Why are boys more vigorously socialized into gender, especially by fathers? Some researchers believe this pattern reflects cultural and parental preferences for males and a general valuing of masculinity (Feinman, 1984) with the corresponding devaluation of femininity (French, 1992; Miller, 1986). It would make sense that boys would be encouraged to become what the culture esteems, while girls would not be so strongly urged to become something less valued. It's also possible that being masculine is more difficult than being feminine, since the former requires repressing human feelings and needs (Maccoby & Jacklin, 1974; Pleck, 1981). If so, then stronger socialization would be required to overcome natural inclinations.

Parental modeling.   Another way parents communicate gender is through modeling masculinity and femininity and male-female relationships. Parents are powerful models for gender — they are perhaps the single most visible, constantly present examples of how to be a man and a woman. We have already discussed children's tendencies to identify with their same-sex parents. As a daughter identifies with her mother, she begins imitating her mother to become feminine herself. Boys use mothers as a negative example of what they are *not* supposed to be and do (Chodorow, 1989). In addition, boys look to fathers for a definition of masculinity; a father is his son's primary model of manhood, one he emulates in his own efforts to become masculine.

Children also learn about gender by watching who does what in their families. By observing parents, children gain understanding of the roles socially prescribed for females and males. One particularly striking example of gender roles that children learn from parents involves mothers' and fathers' responsibility for child care. Research consistently shows that mothers invest considerably more time and more constancy in taking care of children than do fathers (Hochschild, 1989; Okin, 1989; Riessman, 1990). Even when both parents hold full-time jobs outside of the home, only about 20% of husbands do half of the child care and homemaking chores (Hochschild, 1989). Further, mothers and fathers engage in different kinds of child care. Mothers do the constant day-in, day-out activities of feeding, bathing, dressing, supervising, and so forth. Fathers more typically engage in occasional activities and ones that are more enjoyable for both children and parents, such as playing games or taking weekly trips to the bagel shop or zoo (Burns & Homel, 1989; Hochschild, 1989). Given this, it's not surprising that most children turn to their mothers when they need help or comforting and to

D A V I D

> I never thought about why I thought dad was so much more fun than mom, but what we're studying now makes sense. We used to wait for dad to come home, because he'd always spend a half hour or so before dinner playing with us — tossing a ball or working with the trains or whatever. Mom never did that. Now I can see that she was really doing more for us all of the time — fixing our meals, buying us clothes, taking care of our doctor's appointments, and just generally being there for us. Maybe it's because dad was around less of the time that he was more special to us. Anyway, he was the one we looked forward to playing with.

their fathers when they want to play. Fathers are the preferred playmates (Thompson & Walker, 1989). Learning these gender roles through observing parental models prepares children to reproduce the roles in their own lives as they grow into adulthood.

Fathers appear to be particularly important in shaping gender in children. As we noted earlier, fathers generally have more rigid ideas about gender roles, and they enforce them on children more intensely. This is particularly so with sons, whom fathers encourage to do what the society defines as masculine activities and to avoid ones regarded as feminine. Interestingly, young girls use both parents as models, but boys tend to rely almost exclusively on their fathers or other males (Basow, 1992). Further, the extent to which fathers themselves hold strong gender stereotypes affects the attitudes about gender that children develop. Children of fathers with traditional gender beliefs tend to be conservative and hold rigid gender stereotypes themselves. They also seem to have more narrow views of what males and females can do (Fagot & Leinbach, 1989). Conversely, children of androgynous parents tend to have more androgynous and flexible attitudes themselves (Sedney, 1987).

In summary, parents play a major role in shaping children's understandings of gender in general and their own gender in particular. Through unconscious identification and internalization of gender to more overt learning from communication of parents and modeling, most children's initial views of masculinity and femininity reflect their parents' attitudes, behaviors, and interactions. Of course, parents are not the sole influence on gender development. We now will look at two other sources of communication about gender: teachers and peers.

Teachers' Communication

Like families, schools are primary agents of gender socialization. One of the most striking and continuing ways teachers communicate cultural views of gender is through unequal attention to male and female students. Starting with kindergarten and continuing through college and graduate school, teachers give more time, effort, and attention to male students than to female ones. They do this in a number of ways. They generally praise boys' contributions more lavishly than those of girls (Epperson, 1988; Hall & Sandler, 1982), call more frequently on males (Hall & Sandler, 1982; Sadker & Sadker, 1986), and recognize males' achievements more than those of females (Hall & Sandler, 1982; Spender, 1989; Wood & Lenze, 1991a). Further, teachers routinely discuss academic work and career ambitions with boys but are less generous in the academic counseling they provide to girls (Hall & Sandler, 1982, 1984; Spender, 1989). Taken together, these differential behaviors reinforce the societal message that males are more important than females.

Another way teachers communicate gender is by encouraging and discouraging gender stereotypical behaviors in male and female students. Consistent with cultural views of femininity, teachers reward female students for being quiet, obedient, and cooperative. Equally consistent with cultural views of masculinity, teachers reward male students for accomplishments, assertion, and dominance in classrooms (Hall & Sandler, 1982; Sadker & Sadker, 1986). While teachers tend to accept answers that boys shout out, they routinely reprimand female students for "speaking out of turn." Responses like these communicate to children that boys are expected to assert themselves, and girls are supposed to be quiet and polite.

Teacher expectations are particularly striking in their effects on African-American students. When they begin school, African-American girls tend to be active, ambitious, and independent, results of their familial socialization, but teachers encourage them to be more nurturing and less autonomous. By age 10, these girls have often learned that independence and achievement are not rewarded. To gain teachers' approval, many African-American girls become more passive and more dependent ("Study of Black Females," 1985). Many teachers also communicate low expectations of African-American males. More than their white peers, African-American males are disproportionately targets of teacher disapproval and unfavorable treatment (Grant, 1985). Even when actual behaviors are controlled, teachers generally perceive African-American males as more disruptive and less intellectually able than white males or females of either race (Ross & Jackson, 1991). When these attitudes infect the everyday life of schools, it's small wonder that African-Americans' academic motivation often declines the longer they stay in school and that they drop out in high numbers. This is another illustration of relationships between gender and race oppression.

Are there differences in male and female teachers' gender stereotypical expectations and behaviors? At least at higher education levels, there seem to be rather consistent differences. Female university and college professors, compared with their male counterparts, tend to be less biased against female students, are more able to recognize females' contributions and intellectual talents, and are more generous in giving them academic and career encouragement. In general, female students participate more actively and more equally with their male peers in classes taught by women than in ones instructed by men. Unfortunately, substantial influence on gender identity has taken place by the time a student enters college. Further, while female faculty may be less likely to gender stereotype students, they remain scarce in higher education, so there are fewer women with whom to take classes. Research also indicates that differences in teachers parallel those found in parents, with male teachers tending to have stronger, more rigid gender stereotypes than female teachers (Fagot, 1981; Weiler, 1988).

Existing evidence suggests many teachers have gender stereotypes, which they communicate to students through their expectations, responses, and distinct interaction with males and females. The fact that male students generally receive substantially more recognition, encouragement, and academic counseling than females makes the classroom a "chilly climate" for girls and women, who are often not expected to excel and are not encouraged to learn skills of assertion and independent problem solving. Given the differential treatment male and female students receive, it's hardly surprising that males' self-esteem rises the longer they stay in school, while females' self-esteem and expectations of achievement decrease the longer they stay in school (Astin, 1977). Because school has such a powerful impact on self-concept and opportunities in life, we will consider gendered education in depth in Chapter 8.

Communication with Peers

Finally, let's consider the ways in which communication with peers influences gender identity. The power attributed to "peer pressure" is no myth. Once children begin interacting with other children, peers exercise strong influence on attitudes and identities. Acceptance by peers is higher when children conform to gender stereotypes (Martin, 1989), and this is especially true for boys (Fagot, 1984). Males are much more insistent that boys do boy things than females are that girls do girl things, which continues the more rigid gender socialization imposed on males.

Looking back on your own experiences, you can probably confirm the lesser tolerance for boys to engage in feminine activities than for girls to engage in masculine ones. Most young girls, in fact, do play rough sports, but boys generally don't engage in playing house, for instance. Those who do are likely to hear the cardinal insult for a young boy: "You're a sissy!" Peers communicate gender expectations for aggressiveness and passivity, although once again there is greater acceptance of girls who deviate from feminine prescriptions for passivity than for boys who don't "measure up" to the rules for masculinity (Maccoby & Jacklin, 1987). Peers make it quite clear that boys are supposed to act like boys, which means, above all, they must not show any signs of femininity. Once again, this reinforces the cultural message that masculine is more valuable than feminine: Boys may *not* act feminine, but girls may act masculine.

The kinds of interaction between girls and boys differ in ways that further gender identities. In an early study, D. N. Maltz and R. Borker (1982) found that the games typically played by girls encourage cooperation, inclusion, and inter-personal communication. In contrast, boys' games promote competitiveness, in-dividual achievement, and a focus on goals. More recently, developmental psy-chologists ("How Boys and Girls," 1992) confirmed these patterns, noting that boys teach each other to be controlling and competitive, while girls teach each other to be cooperative and kind. Thus, informal interaction with peers reiterates parents' and teachers' gender lessons.

Although peers are important to both sexes, they seem more critical to boys' development of gender identity (Maccoby & Jacklin, 1987). Male bonding tends to occur in adolescence and is extremely important in reinforcing and refining masculine identity (Gaylin, 1992; Raphael, 1988; Rubin, 1985; Wood & Inman, 1993). Males' greater reliance on peers for gender identity may reflect the differ-ence in parental same-sex models available to boys and girls. In most families the mother is more constantly present in the home than the father, so a female child can learn how to be feminine within an ongoing, continuous relationship with another person. Because fathers tend to be more physically and psychologically removed from family life, they are less available as concrete models. Young boys may need to find other tangible examples of masculinity in order to define their own identities.

In summary, peers contribute in major ways to creating our gendered iden-tities. They communicate expectations and establish rules that determine who is part of the "in group" and who is not. Because peer acceptance is extremely important in the first two decades of life, fitting in with friends and chums is a cornerstone of esteem. Thus, children and adolescents generally do what is nec-essary to gain the approval and acceptance of their companions. This is a source of considerable frustration to many parents who try to eliminate stereotypes in how they raise their children, only to find that peers quickly and effectively undo their efforts. From ages 5 to the early 20s, peers typically have influence at least equal to that of families, and this influence seems particularly pronounced in encouraging gender stereotypical attitudes, behaviors, and identities (Huston, 1985; Martin, 1989).

We have now considered how various individuals contribute to gendering our identities and how different theories provide insight into this process. Becoming gendered usually entails maternal caretaking during the initial years of life and the kinds of identification and the development of ego boundaries promoted by that caretaking. Further gendering of identity occurs as children interact with parents, peers, and teachers who communicate cultural expectations of masculinity and femininity. In concert, these sources define cultural views of gender and talk individuals into masculine and feminine identities, which guide how they think, act, and feel.

The players in the gender drama we have discussed do not fully explain the persistence of gendered identities throughout our lives. The gender socialization begun in early years is sustained and reinforced by other cultural influences such as media. We will examine some of these in later chapters. Before moving on, however, we should translate the research we've considered into more personal terms that illuminate the implications of gender socialization for later life.

▨ The Personal Side of the Gender Drama

Theory and research regarding how we become gendered is only part of the story. Equally important is understanding how gender socialization affects us as we move beyond childhood. To grasp this, we will consider what it means to grow up masculine and feminine in present-day North America.

Growing Up Masculine

What does it mean to be a man in America in the 1990s? Pervasive references to "male privilege" suggest that men, particularly heterosexual white men in the middle and upper classes, have special access to the opportunities and rewards of our society. Further, it is widely understood that our culture reveres masculinity and maleness far more than femininity and womanliness. This is, of course, true as a statement about social values and how they result in privileges for certain groups. It is why American culture is often described as **patriarchal,** which literally means "rule by the fathers." Yet this tells us little about how masculinity constrains and affects individual men who abide by prevailing prescriptions. To understand the drawbacks and advantages of masculinity, let's first consider what several college men say. In the boxes on Randy, Jake, and Charles, we hear of the pressures, expectations, and constraints of manhood as much as the prerogatives and privileges. As Charles tells us, it's a mixed bag. In his book, *The Male Experience,* J. A. Doyle (1989) identifies five themes of masculinity,

JAKE

You asked what it means to be a man today. For me it means that I can expect to get a job and keep it as long as I do decent work. It also means I'll probably have a family to support—or be the major breadwinner for it. It means I don't have to worry about somebody thinking I'm not serious about my work because of my sex. My girlfriend keeps running into this in her job interviews—being treated as if she's not serious about working, when her GPA is higher than mine. I guess going through interviews together has made me aware of how much bias there still is against women. And, yeah, it's made me glad I'm a man.

CHARLES

I don't know what it means to be a man. I do know what it means to be an African-American man. They're not the same thing. Being an African-American man means that people think I'm strong and stupid. They think I can play football but can't be a responsible businessman. It means my woman expects me to provide for her and kids later, but that society thinks I'll run out on them, since everyone thinks black men desert their families. It means when I walk on campus at night, white women cross the street or hook up with some white guy—whether they know him or not—because they think I'm sex crazed and going to rape them. It also means I'm supposed to be aggressive and tough—all the time. It's not okay for me to hurt or need help or be weak—not ever; that's not part of being a man. Jeez, my dad drilled that one into me! It means I can get away with being tough and pushing my weight around, like women can't do that, but I can't get away with being sensitive or giving in to others. It means I get a better job than my wife, but it means I am supposed to, and I can never not think about taking care of my family like she can. It's a mixed bag, which you don't hear a lot about.

R A N D Y

It's funny you asked us to write about what it means to be a man today. I've been trying to figure that out. It's real clear to me that it means I have to make it. Women have a choice about whether to "make their mark" on the world and be successful. I don't. I have to be successful at work, or I am a failure as a man. But I can't figure out exactly what it means to be "successful." I see men who are successful, like my father, and they're slaves to their bosses and their jobs. They don't enjoy life. They're not free to do what they want. They have to always be making it, proving they're successful. Last year my uncle had a heart attack. He was only 51. He was successful, and look what it got him.

ones that weave through the commentaries of these three men. We will consider each of these elements of the male role.

The prime directive is *don't be female*. Doyle (p. 150) calls this the "negative touchstone" of the male role, by which he means that the most fundamental requirement for manhood is not being womanly. Early in life most boys learn they must not think, act, or feel like girls and women. Because this prohibition teaches boys that girls are inferior, it is thought to be one of the bases of the general attitude that females are inferior to males. Any male who shows sensitivity or vulnerability is ridiculed as a sissy, a crybaby, a mama's boy, or a wimp.

The second element of the male role is the command *be successful*, which surfaces when men discuss the concept of masculinity. Men are expected to achieve status in their professions, to be successful, to "make it." They do not have options such as choosing to stay home with children or having a woman provide for family finances. The few men who do this are generally regarded as odd and not manly. Recently, W. Farrell (1991) wrote that men are regarded as "success objects," and their worth as marriage partners, friends, and men is judged by how successful they are at what they do. Training begins early with sports, where winning is stressed. As Alfie Kohn (1986, p. 168) remarks, "The general rule is that American males are simply trained to win. The object, a boy soon gathers, is not to be liked but to be envied, . . . not to be part of a group but to distinguish himself from the others in that group." In childhood and adolescence, being a success means excelling at athletics or academics.

Later in life, this translates into being not just good at what you do but being better than others, more powerful than peers, pulling in a bigger salary than your neighbors, and having a more expensive home, car, and so on, than your friends. Success for men, we might tell Randy, is a comparative issue—it means being better than others. For 20 years in a row, a national survey has reported that the primary requirement for manhood is regarded as being a good provider (Faludi, 1991, p. 65). Salient to most males (Pleck, 1987), the provider role appears to be particularly important to African-American men (Cazenave & Leon, 1987).

A third injunction for the male role is *be aggressive*. Even in childhood, boys are often encouraged to be roughnecks, or at least are seldom scolded for being so. They are expected to fight and not to run from battles or to lose them. Later, sports reinforce early training by emphasizing aggression, violence, and toughness. Coaches psych teams up with demands that they "make the other team hurt, hurt, hurt" or "make them bleed." Perhaps the ultimate training for aggression comes in military service, especially during times of war. "We'll make you into men" promises a recruiting poster. The pledge is really that the military will teach men to fight, to inflict pain on others, to endure it stoically themselves, and to win, win, win.

From childhood on, males learn to be aggressive, to "show what you're made of." In discussing the importance of aggression to masculinity, Doyle (1989, p. 183) calls our attention to the paradox that "aggression is both denounced as a significant social problem and applauded as a masculine attribute." The way aggression is justified for men is that they must protect their rights—they have to retaliate, or seek revenge, when they are violated by another. Not to do so is to be unmanly.

Men's training in aggression seems to be linked to violence (Goldner et al., 1990; Gordon, 1988; Thompson & Walker, 1989), especially violence against women. Because males are taught that women are inferior (remember the prime directive of masculinity: don't be female) and aggressiveness is good, it's not surprising that some men believe they are entitled to dominate women. This belief surfaces in studies of men who rape (Costin & Schwartz, 1987; Scott & Tetreault, 1987). The same belief that "I have a right to do my will on her" is evident in studies of men who abuse their girlfriends and wives (Dobash & Dobash, 1979; Gelles & Straus, 1988). One study (Thompson, 1991) reported that both college women and men who are violent toward their dates have masculine gender orientations, reminding us again that gender and sex are not equivalent terms. Even the judicial system long upheld a man's right to beat his wife within certain limits (a stick no larger than the width of his thumb, which gave rise to the colloquial expression, "the rule of thumb"). Further, some states do not allow a wife to prosecute her husband for rape, since the law holds that carnal relations are a husband's right—regardless of his wife's willingness. Thus, laws condone men's aggression against women.

A fourth element of the male role is captured in the injunction *be sexual*. Men should be interested in sex—all the time, anytime. They are expected to have a number of sexual partners; the more partners a man has, the more of a "stud" he is (Gaylin, 1992). Even in the 1990s, many fraternities still have rituals such as recognizing brothers who "made it" at the last fraternity event. During rush, one fraternity recently issued invitations with the notation B.Y.O.A., which one of my students easily translated for me: Bring your own ass.

A number of writers (Brownmiller, 1993; Faludi, 1991; French, 1992; Russell, 1993) have criticized men's inclination to treat women as sex objects, which clearly demeans women. This tendency is encouraged by socialization that stresses sexual conquests and virility as essential to manhood. Less often noted is that the injunction to be sexual also turns men into sex objects. Sex isn't a free choice when you have to perform to be a man. Some men resent the expectation that they should always be interested in sexual activity.

Finally, Doyle says the male sex role demands that men *be self-reliant*. Men are expected to be confident, independent, autonomous. The Marlboro Man was an extremely effective advertising image because he symbolized the independence and toughness of masculinity. A "real man" doesn't need others, particularly women. He depends on himself, takes care of himself, and relies on nobody. This is central to social views of manliness. As we noted earlier, male self-development typically begins with differentiation from others, and from infancy on most boys are taught to be self-reliant and self-contained (Thompson & Pleck, 1987). Men are expected to be emotionally reserved and controlled: It's not manly to let feelings control oneself or to need others. These five aspects of masculinity clearly reflect gender socialization in early life and lay out a blueprint for what being a man means and calls for in contemporary America. Yet these views are not necessary or healthy. Individual men have options about whether they will embody society's traditional definition of masculinity, and many men are crafting

KEVIN

I'm a man, a normal man, okay? I mean I like girls, and I like to have sex. Sometimes. But that's not all I think about. It's not all I want with women. And frankly sometimes I'm not in the mood. But a man can't say that. If he does, then people think there's something wrong with him. You have to be on — always ready, always drooling for sex to prove you're a man. We don't have any freedom to say "I'm not in the mood" or "I'm not interested." Once I told a girl that when she came on to me, and she asked me if I was gay. I'm not gay. But I'm not a constant sex machine either.

alternative identities for themselves. In later chapters we'll discover examples of ways to revise masculine identity.

Growing Up Feminine

What does it mean to be feminine in the United States in the 1990s? Casual talk and media offer us two quite different versions of modern women. One suggests that women now have it all: They can have careers, marriage, and children. They can get jobs formerly closed and rise to the top levels of their professions; they can have egalitarian marriages with liberated men and raise nonsexist children. At the same time, other communication from the culture intones a quite different message. It tells us women may be able to get jobs, but fewer than 20% will actually be given opportunities to advance. Crime statistics warn us rape is rising, as is battering of women. We discover that married women may have careers, but over 80% of them still do the majority of housework and child care. Medical researchers warn that eating disorders among women are epidemic, and media relentlessly carry the message that youth and beauty are women's ticket to success. Some social analysts claim that our society's attitude toward women is so negative that it is misogynistic, or woman hating. This may be an overstatement, yet within it lies more than a grain of truth. America idolizes women at the same time that it exploits and degrades them. The existence of two such discrepant cultural attitudes gives us a clue that prevailing images of women are conflicting and confusing. The boxes on Jeanne, Jana, Bernadette, and Debbie give us a better understanding of what femininity means, as these women explain how they feel about being a woman. These women recognize cultural expectations

JEANNE

Hungry. That's what being a woman means to me. I am hungry all of the time. Either I'm dieting or I'm throwing up, because I ate too much. I am scared to death of being fat, and I'm just not made to be thin. My genes don't cooperate. I am large boned and everyone in my family tends toward plumpness, but I can't be that way. I gain weight just by smelling food. I think about food all the time — wanting it but being afraid to eat, eating but feeling guilty. It's a no win situation. I'm obsessed, and I know it, but I can't help it. How can I not think about my weight all the time when every magazine, every movie, every television show I see screams at me that I have to be thin to be desirable?

of women that have been noted by researchers and social commentators. We can identify five themes in current views of femininity and womanhood.

The first theme is that *appearance still counts*. Women are still judged by their looks. They must be pretty, slim, and well dressed to be desirable. Inducing girls to focus on appearance begins in the early years of life when girls are given dolls and clothes, both of which invite them to attend to appearance. Gift catalogs for children regularly feature makeup kits, adornments for hair, and even wigs so that girls learn early to spend time and effort on looking good. Dolls, like the ever-popular Barbie, come with accessories such as extensive wardrobes so that girls learn dressing well is important. Teen magazines for girls feature fashion and

J A N A

like being a woman today. It's the best time ever to be female, because we can have it all. When I finish my B.A., I plan to go to law school, and then I want to practice. I also want to have a family with two children. My mother couldn't have had the whole package, but I can. I love the freedom of being a woman in this time — there's nothing I can't do.

B E R N A D E T T E

think expectations of women today are impossible. I read magazines for working women, since I plan to work in business when I graduate. They tell me how to be a good leader, how to make tough decisions and keep others motivated, how to budget my time and advance in an organization. Then in the same magazines there's an article on how to throw a great dinner party with a three-course meal plus appetizers and dessert. Am I supposed to do that after working from 8 to 6 every day to advance in business? Somehow the husband's role in all of this never gets mentioned. It's all supposed to come together, but I don't see how. It seems to me that a career is a full-time responsibility and so is running a home, yet I get the feeling I'm supposed to do both and keep my cool all the time. I just don't see how.

DEBBIE

To me it means I'd better include the expenses of cosmetics, beauty salons, health clubs, and super clothes in my budget from now on. I have to worry about being attractive. I have to look good or I'm a failure as a woman. Guys don't face that. If a guy looks bad it's okay, but not a girl. I've seen this in classes a lot. In one class I had last term, we had a woman professor, who was really fabulous. She really knew her stuff, and she was interesting and funny and smart. But her clothes were out of style and sometimes rumpled like she didn't iron them. I heard a lot of comments about how "sloppy" she was. In another class of mine the man who taught it wore the same jacket almost every day. It was frayed at the sleeves and just kind of ratty, and his shirts were usually wrinkled. So I said something once about his sloppy dress, and my friend just laughed at me and said I ought to appreciate his "eccentric" style. See what I mean? It's a real double standard that you don't hear about much. Whatever else may have changed about views of women, the demand to look good hasn't.

grooming sections and are saturated with ads for makeup, diet aids, and hair products. Like Jeanne said, nearly every magazine, film, and television show spotlights a beautiful woman. The cultural injunction that women must be pretty is unambiguous and unabated (Wolf, 1991).

At the opening of this chapter, I asked you to respond to the question "If you woke up tomorrow and found you had changed into the opposite sex, how would your life be different?" That question comes from a study (Tavris & Baumgartner, 1983) of 2,000 children in grades 3 through 12. One of the clearest findings was that both boys and girls recognized the importance of appearance for girls. Even children as young as 9 understand that girls' success depends on looking good. The boys responded that if they woke up female, they certainly hoped they were gorgeous, because unattractive females are outcasts. When girls considered waking up as boys, they noted it would be a relief not to have to worry about looks all the time. One 10th grader (p. 92) said "I would go back to bed, since it would not take very long to get ready for school."

Cultural expectations for beauty include being slim—or even thin. Jeanne's comments are particularly poignant as she points out that the requirement to be slender can become tyrannical. She's not alone in her obsession with eating or her ways of coping with the societal expectation of thinness in women. In a survey of 33,000 young women, 42% of the respondents said losing weight was more important and would make them happier than success at work (Wooley &

Wooley, 1984). Eating disorders such as anorexia nervosa and bulimia are epidemic and rising as women try to conform to the requirement for thinness. This rigid expectation literally kills thousands of women annually (Wolf, 1991), just to meet the cultural demand for excessively slender bodies (Rodin, Silberstein, & Striegel-Moore, 1985). Women seldom feel they will be loved, respected, or accepted based on their achievements, values, or personality unless they are also attractive.

A second cultural expectation of women is *be sensitive and caring.* Girls and women are supposed to care about and for others and to be nice, responsive, supportive, and friendly. It's part of their role as defined by culture. A number of studies (Aronson, 1992; Hochschild, 1989; Okin, 1989; Wood, 1993c) reveal that women do the majority of caregiving for the whole culture. From assuming primary responsibility for young children to taking care of elderly, often sick or disabled relatives, women are the ones who do the preponderance of hands-on caring. In interviews with adult daughters who care for their aging mothers, Aronson (1992) found that daughters thought this was required to meet society's definition of being "good women." Giving care to others is part of being a woman.

Major responsibilities for children and needy relatives are not the only care burdens expected of women: They are also supposed to be nice, deferential, and helpful in general, whereas men are not held to the same requirements (Hochschild, 1975, 1979, 1983). In their survey of school children, Tavris and Baumgartner (1983) found that both boys and girls recognized there were greater restrictions on girls' activities than on those of boys: They perceived that girls have to do more for others and less for themselves. The girls said that if they were to wake up male, they'd be able to "do anything." They would have more freedom because they wouldn't have to focus on others' needs.

There is one activity that both boys and girls in the study of school children saw as a female advantage. Girls and women are allowed to express feelings more openly than are boys and men. Males are expected to be "calm and cool," as one of the school children remarked; they cannot let on how they really feel, especially if they are afraid of things. Cultural views of femininity include expressiveness, which may explain why women often seem more aware of and comfortable talking about feelings than men are.

A third persistent theme of femininity is *negative treatment by others.* According to substantial research, this still more or less goes with the territory of being female. Supporting this theme are the differential values our culture attaches to masculinity and femininity. Janeway's (1971) early findings that devaluation is built into the feminine role in our culture remains true more than two decades after she first reported it. It's not only built into cultural views, but typically is internalized by individuals, including women. Through communication with parents, teachers, peers, and others and through media and education, girls learn that boys get more respect and more opportunities. It is a lesson retained as girls mature into womanhood. For instance, Hochschild (1983) has shown that female flight attendants are more often abused by passengers than their male peers. Further, Hochschild revealed that both male and female flight attendants understand this pattern and accept it.

The knowledge that American society values males more than females is imparted early as responses from school children make clear. Girls who imagined waking up as boys said (p. 94), "My dad would respect me more if I were a boy" and "My father would be closer because I'd be the son he always wanted." Early awareness of cultural disregard for women, coupled with ongoing elaboration of that theme, erodes the foundations of self-esteem and self-confidence. Given this, it's no wonder that girls and women generally suffer more depression and have lower self-confidence and belief in themselves than males: From birth they've been told that they *are* worth less than their male peers (French, 1992).

Another aspect of negative treatment of women is the violence inflicted on them. They are vulnerable in ways men generally are not to battering, rape, and other forms of abuse (Goldner et al., 1990; Gordon, 1988; Thompson, 1991). Tavris and Baumgartner (1983) found that even 9-year-old boys and girls realize women are subject to violence from others. Contemplating waking up female, the boys said (p. 94), "I'd have to know how to handle drunk guys and rapists" (eighth grader); "I would have to be around other girls for safety" (sixth grader); "I would always carry a gun for protection" (fourth grader). Vulnerability to violence is part of femininity in Western culture.

Be superwoman is a fourth theme emerging in cultural expectations of women, one well expressed by Bernadette. Jana's sense of exhilaration at "being able to have it all" is tempered by the realization that the idea that women *can* have it all appears to be transformed into the command that they *must* have it all. It's not enough to be just a homemaker and mother or just have a career—young women seem to feel they are expected to do it all.

Women students talk with me frequently about the tension they feel in trying to figure out how to have a full family life and a successful career. They tell me that in interviewing for jobs they have to make compromises to locate where their romantic partners have jobs. They ask me how to stay on the "fast track" in business when they foresee taking off at least some time to have one or more children. How, they ask, can I advance in business like a man when I also have to be a mother? The physical and psychological toll of trying to do it all is well documented in women (Faludi, 1991; Friedan, 1981; Hochschild, 1989), and it is growing steadily as women find that changes in the workplace are not paralleled by changes in home responsibilities. Perhaps it would we wise to remember that superwoman, like superman, is a comic character, not a viable model for real life.

In a recent issue of *Newsweek*, Sally Quinn (1993) wrote an article titled "Look Out, It's Superwoman." In it, Quinn detailed the many roles Hillary Rodham Clinton is filling, from being First Lady to being mother and fan at her daughter's soccer matches, to being a policy-maker in charge of health care reform in the United States, to arranging for dinners at the White House, to participating in high-level policy-making meetings of cabinet members. The new "First Lady Plus," wrote Quinn, "is doing it all . . . as Superwoman, the role model for the '90s" (p. 25). Although Hillary Rodham Clinton's abilities and involvements are impressive, not every woman must be as multitalented, energetic, and capable as she is in order to be a successful and valuable individual and member of a family and society. As an individual woman she is admirable; as a single model she may be less constructive for the rising generation of women.

A final theme of femininity in the 1990s is one that reflects all of the others and the contradictions inherent in them. *There is no single meaning of feminine anymore.* Society no longer has a consensual view of who women are or what they are supposed to do, think, and be. A woman who is assertive and ambitious in a career is likely to meet with approval, disapproval, and curiosity from others. A woman who chooses to stay home while her children are young will be criticized by many women and men, envied by others, respected by some, and disregarded by still others. Currently, multiple views of femininity are vying for legitimacy. This makes being a woman very confusing. Yet it also underlines the excitement and possibilities open to women of this era to validate multiple versions of femininity. Perhaps, as Sharon suggests, there are many ways to be feminine, and we can respect all of them.

SHARON

It surely is confusing — I'll say that. My mother and I talk about women, and she tells me that she's glad she didn't have so many options. She says it was easier for her than me because she knew what she was supposed to do — marry and raise a family — and she didn't have to go through all of this identity crisis that I do. I see her point, yet I kind of like having alternatives. I know I wouldn't be happy investing my total self in a home and family. I just have to be out doing things in the world. But my best friend really wants to do that. She's marrying a guy who wants that too, so as soon as they've saved enough to be secure, they plan for her to quit work to raise a family. I know someone else who says she just flat out doesn't want to marry. She wants to be a doctor, and she doesn't think she can do that well plus take care of a home and family, so she wants to stay single. I'm still figuring out how much to try to balance things. I don't really know yet if I will or won't have kids, but it's nice to know I can choose to go either way. My mother couldn't.

Prevailing themes of femininity in North America reveal both constancy and change. Traditional expectations of attractiveness and caregiving to others persist, as does the continuing devaluation of anything considered feminine. Change, however, is signaled by expanding opportunities and less consensus on what a woman must do and be. There are different options, which may allow women with different talents, interests, and gender orientations to define themselves in diverse ways and to chart life courses that suit them as individuals.

*S*ummary

In this chapter, we have considered formative influences on gender identity and how they are reflected later, in adult life. Beginning with Mead's symbolic interactionist theory, we saw that children are literally talked into membership in the human community. Through interaction, we learn how others see us and import their views into our self-conception so that how we view ourselves is inevitably laced with social overtones. We rely on internal dialogues to resist social views of gender or to conform to them by guiding thought, feeling, and action. Interactions with others also affect the structure of the psyche, which is the core of human identity. Because this process occurs in our first stage of life, it profoundly shapes our sense of who we are as gendered individuals. We build on the psychic understanding of gender through interaction with parents, teachers, peers, and others whose communication provides us with both direct instruction and models of femininity and masculinity.

Theory and research about gender identity have practical, personal implications. Communication about being masculine and feminine in childhood affects how we define ourselves as adults, what feelings we allow and suppress, what constraints we experience on our activities, and how we judge our basic self-worth. In offering their ideas about what it means to be a man or a woman in present-day North America, a number of young writers translated theoretical material into accounts of how cultural expectations frame and inform their concrete lives. We learned that many men think society expects them to be successful, aggressive, sexually interested and active, self-reliant, and—above all—not feminine. College women tell us being feminine today means that appearance counts more than intelligence or personality; that there are restrictions on activities ranging from professional opportunities to vulnerability to violence; that others will treat them negatively; and that, increasingly, they experience a pressure to do it all—meet traditional expectations of homemaking and mothering while simultaneously being dynamic, successful, and intensely involved in careers. Most of all, young women say there is no single, clear view of femininity, which is equally a source of confusion, on one hand, and a source of excitement about options, on the other.

Communication plays a primary role in shaping gender identity. It is through interaction with others that we come to understand how society defines masculinity and femininity and what specific individuals such as parents, teachers, and peers expect of us. Communication creates gendered identities by transforming us from biological males and females into gendered individuals.

Before we leave our discussion of influences on gender identity, it's important to reiterate the role of personal choice in defining ourselves. Socialization is not as relentless and deterministic a force as it may sometimes seem. Clearly, we are influenced by the expectations of our culture as those are communicated to us in interaction with individuals and institutions. Yet we also contribute to social understandings of gender. By reflecting on how our society views masculinity and femininity and how those expectations of gender are communicated to us, we enlarge our capacity to think critically about the desirability of cultural views in general and their appropriateness for each of us in particular.

It's also important to remember that social views of gender are not self-sustaining. They endure only to the extent that individuals and institutions persist in reproducing them through their own activities. Through our own communication and the ways that we embody masculinity and femininity, we participate in reinforcing or altering cultural views of masculinity and femininity. Shifts in social expectations of gender that emerged in students' descriptions of the meaning of manliness and womanliness clue us to the important realization that what gender means is not fixed — it changes. How it changes and what sorts of revisions it includes depend on individual and social practices that question existing views of gender and argue for altered conceptions. In the next chapter, we will consider how individuals have participated in various rhetorical movements that challenge and redefine cultural understandings of what it means to be masculine and feminine.

𝒟iscussion Questions

1. How important do you think the early years (birth until 5) are in shaping gender identity? To what extent do you think your sense of being masculine or feminine was established in the first few years of your life? Has it changed since?

2. How does George Herbert Mead's concept of "self-as-object" apply to the processes of creating and refining gender identity? How does being able to see, evaluate, and reflect on yourself and your activities affect how you enact gender? Have you ever resisted cultural prescriptions for your gender? If so, how did the capacity to reflect on yourself influence your ability to depart from widely held views of gender?

3. Would you describe your ego boundaries as relatively permeable or rigid? How did you develop a sense of yourself as more connected to others or independent of them? How do your ego boundaries influence your current relationships with

others? How do permeable ones enrich life and relationships? How might they constrain and limit someone? What are the advantages of rigid ego boundaries? How might they restrict a person?

4. What kinds of toys did you receive as a child? Were you encouraged to like and play with "gender-appropriate" toys? Did you ever ask for a toy that your parents told you was not appropriate for you? Are there differences in how parents responded to men and women students' interest in cross-gender toys?

5. What kinds of chores and responsibilities did you have growing up in your family? Were they consistent with social definitions of your gender? Did you help with outside work or activities inside the home? Did you ever resent what you were told to do and what you were told was not your job?

6. How did your parents model masculinity and femininity? Explain how parents (mother, stepmother, father, stepfather) represented what it means to be feminine and masculine. Does your own embodiment of gender reflect influences from them?

7. Answer the question at the beginning of the chapter for yourself: "If you woke up tomorrow and found you had changed into the opposite sex, how would your life be different?" How consistent are your responses with those from the Tavris and Baumgartner study discussed in this chapter?

8. Do you think the five themes of masculinity discussed in this chapter apply to men today? If you are a man, do you feel you're expected to be successful, aggressive, sexual, self-reliant, and not feminine? How do these social expectations affect your options and your comfort as a person? If you are a woman, are these five themes ones you associate with masculinity and expect in men? How might this be limiting for your relationships?

9. Do you think the five themes of femininity identified in this chapter still apply to women? If you are a woman, do you feel you are supposed to be attractive and sensitive to others? Do you expect to be treated negatively (from being trivialized to being vulnerable to rape) because of your sex? To what extent do you feel pressured to be superwoman — be it all, do it all? If you are a man, are the themes of femininity ones that are part of your thinking and expectations about women? How might endorsing these themes limit your relationships with women?

10. Write a page or so describing what it means to you to be a man or a woman today. Specify what you like and dislike about being a woman or a man. As a class, discuss your views of femininity and masculinity and the ways in which those are comfortable and inhibiting for your lives.

$\mathcal{T}$he Rhetorical Shaping of Gender: Women's, Men's, and Gender Movements in America

We've highlighted cultural influences on gender identity by probing how social views of gender are passed on to individuals through communication by parents, peers, and teachers. Equally important is communication individuals use to influence cultural views of masculinity and femininity. While it's true that gender is socially created, it's also true that individuals make up society and have an impact on its perspectives.

We've also seen that gender varies across cultures and over time within a single culture. For instance, in the early 1800s, masculinity was equated with physical potency, but today masculinity is tied to economic power and success. Views of femininity have also changed so that women are no longer seen as frail and too uninformed to vote. Changes such as these do not just happen. Instead, they grow out of rhetorical movements that alter cultural understandings of gender and, with that, the rights, privileges, and perceptions of women and men. For this reason, any effort to understand relationships among gender, communication, and culture must include an awareness of how rhetorical movements sculpt social meanings of men and women.

Rhetoric is persuasion, and rhetorical movements intend to persuade people to take certain points of view, to change existing attitudes, laws, and policies. In examining American rhetorical movements concerned with gender, we will discover how each movement sought to define gender and whom it sought to persuade. We will first consider a number of women's movements, which have altered the meaning, roles, status, and opportunities of women in America. Second, we'll explore the more recent phenomena of men's movements through which men are attempting to redefine what masculinity means on both personal and social levels. We will then discuss two movements that respond to specific branches of women's and men's movements. As we survey these rhetorical movements, we'll discover that collective efforts to alter views of women and men are anything but uniform. Both women's and men's efforts reflect diverse views of gender and aim for sundry social impacts. Insight into diverse rhetorical movements regarding gender allows us to appreciate the complexity of the ongoing cultural conversation about the meanings of masculinity and femininity. Further, it may allow you to define more clearly where your own values and goals place you within the range of movements about gender.

▇ Women's Movements

Although many women younger than 30 refuse the label "feminist" (Wallis, 1989), every person's life has been deeply affected by feminist movements, beginning with ones that demanded women's right to pursue higher education. A widely held misconception is that feminism began in the 1960s. This, however, disregards over a century's history in which women's movements had significant impacts. It also implies feminism is one thing when really there have been and are many forms of feminism. Beginning in the early 1800s, rhetorical movements to define women's nature and rights occurred in two waves.

During both waves, two distinct ideologies have informed movement goals and efforts at change. One tradition, called liberal, enlightenment, or minimalist (Crawford, 1988; Hare-Mustin & Marecek, 1988; Yellin, 1990), holds that women and men are basically alike and equal in all important respects. Therefore, goes the reasoning, they should have access to the same roles, rights, privileges, and opportunities to participate in various aspects of life. A second, quite different ideology, which is referred to as cultural, structural, or maximalist, holds that women and men are essentially unlike one another. If women differ from men in important ways, then different roles, rights, and activities should be assigned to each. As we survey women's movements, we'll see how these conflicting ideologies lead to diverse rhetorical goals and strategies.

The First Wave of Women's Movements

Roughly spanning the years from 1840 to 1925, the first wave of women's movements included both liberal and cultural branches. As we will see, the contradictory views of women implicit in these two movements ironically worked together to change the status and rights of women in society.

Women's rights movement. Activism aimed at enlarging women's rights grew out of women's efforts in other reform movements (Campbell, 1989a, p. 4). Prior to focusing on **women's rights** themselves, many women in the early 1800s engaged in other reform movements such as abolition and temperance (Yellin, 1990). These early reformists discovered that their efforts to instigate changes were hampered by their lack of a legitimate public voice. Thus, a prerequisite for effective political action about any issue was securing their own rights, most particularly the right to speak and be counted in public and civic arenas.

In 1840, Lucretia Coffin Mott was chosen as one of America's representatives to the World Anti-Slavery Convention in London (Campbell, 1989a, p. 4), but she was barred from participation because of her sex. At the convention, Mott met Elizabeth Cady Stanton, who accompanied her husband who was a delegate, and the two women discussed the indignation and unfairness of Mott's exclusion. Later, Mott, Stanton, and other women in America who believed women were entitled to rights denied by law organized the first women's rights convention. Held in New York in 1848, the Seneca Falls Convention marked the beginning of women's vocal efforts to secure basic rights in America — ones granted to white men by the Constitution. Women, including Elizabeth Cady Stanton, delivered speeches, which was not something considered appropriate for women in that era. The keynote address, titled the "Declaration of Sentiments," was ingeniously modeled after the Declaration of Independence. In paraphrasing that statement of rights, the speech proclaimed (Campbell, 1989b, p. 34):

> We hold these truths to be self-evident: that all men and women are created equal; that they are endowed by their Creator with certain inalienable rights, that among these are life, liberty, and the pursuit of happiness.

Continuing in the language of the Declaration of Independence, Cady Stanton cataloged specific grievances women had suffered under the "unjust government of men," including denial of the right to vote, exclusion from nearly all types of higher education, restriction on employment, and denial of property rights on marriage. Following Cady Stanton's stirring oratory, 100 men and women

(Campbell, 1989b, p. 33) signed a petition supporting specific rights for women except the right to vote. Instrumental to passage of this resolution were the persuasive pleas of former slave Frederick Douglass (Campbell, 1989b, p. 33).

While Douglass's support of women's suffrage was critical for ratification at Seneca Falls, it does not signify widespread participation of black citizens in the women's rights movement. In fact, although there were originally strong links between abolitionist efforts and women's rights, these dissipated. Believing that if slavery could be abolished, so could women's disenfranchisement (O'Kelly & Carney, 1986, p. 140), women's rights activists initially connected their campaign to efforts to enfranchise black men, but many abolitionists and some feminists believed that the movement for black men's voting rights had to precede women's suffrage. During this time, many black women thought their white sisters had defined women's problems in terms of issues that mattered more to whites and had ignored grievous differences caused by race. Forced to choose between allegiance to their race and allegiance to their gender, most black women of the era chose race. Thus, the women's rights movement became almost exclusively white in its membership and interests.

What happened in 1848 did not yield immediate results. Women's efforts to secure the right to vote based on the argument that the Constitution defined suffrage as a right of all individuals fell on deaf ears. Women, it seemed, were still not considered individuals, but rather the property of men. In 1872, two years

A I N ' T   I   A   W O M A N ?

Sojourner Truth, a slave, was a primary spokeswoman for the double oppression suffered by black women in the 1800s. In her most famous speech, "Ain't I a Woman?" she pointed out the ways in which white women enjoy privileges never extended to black women and thus their feminist concerns often overlook the circumstances of minority women's lives. Speaking in 1851 in response to a heckler at a national women's rights convention, her words rang out (Folb, 1985; hooks, 1981):

> That man over there says that woman needs to be helped into carriages, and lifted over ditches, and to have the best place everywhere. Nobody ever helps me into carriages or over mud-puddles, or gives me any best place. And ain't I a woman?
>
> I have ploughed, and I planted, and gathered into barns.... And ain't I a woman?

after black men received the right to vote, Susan B. Anthony and other women registered and attempted to cast votes, but they were turned away at the polls and arrested. Only 48 years later would women win the right to vote, and that occurred, in part, as a result of a second ideology within the first wave of women's movements.

The cult of domesticity. Many actively engaged women of this era did not identify with the women's rights movement. They disagreed with the basic claim that women and men are equal and alike in important respects. Instead, **cultural feminists** argued that women and men differ in fundamental ways. They believed that, compared with men, women were more pure, moral, nurturing, concerned about others, and committed to harmony. Unlike women's rights activists, cultural feminists of this period did not challenge the domestic roles assigned to women; in fact, they celebrated the "cult of domesticity" as the ideal of femininity or "true womanhood" (Welter, 1966). Belief in women's moral virtue led cultural feminists to form various reform organizations such as the Women's Christian Temperance Union and to fight for child labor laws, rights of women prisoners, and policies of peace.

Cultural feminists' belief in women's higher morality reflected prevalent Victorian conceptions of women. Ironically, this ideology led to securing women's right to vote. Cultural feminists gave speeches that argued women should be allowed to vote, because this would curb the corruption of political life. Women's moral virtue, they claimed, would reform the political world that was debased by the control of immoral men. This rhetorical strategy eventually carried women to victory in their struggle to gain political franchise. On August 26, 1920, the amendment granting women the right to vote was passed and ratified.

While the combined force of cultural and liberal women's movements was necessary to win suffrage, the deep ideological chasm between these two groups was not resolved. Nor did securing voting rights immediately fuel further efforts to enlarge women's rights, roles, influence, and opportunities. Few women exercised their hard-won right to vote (Campbell, 1989a, p. 6), and in 1925 an amendment prohibiting child labor was not ratified, which signaled the close of the first wave of women's movements (Campbell, 1989a, p. 6).

After this, women's movements in America were relatively dormant for nearly 35 years. This time of quiescence resulted from several factors. First, America's attention was concentrated on winning two world wars. When those were over, energies focused on creating families and enjoying America's world dominance. In this climate of nationalistic pride, conservative political views prevailed, and these were not conducive to further gains in women's political, social, and professional rights.

Further contributing to the dormancy surrounding women's activism was the fact that women's "place" in the domestic sphere had not been disputed

REPRODUCTIVE RIGHTS

Birth control has been a major issue in both waves of women's movements. In the 19th century, Elizabeth Cady Stanton first raised the idea of "voluntary motherhood" as a prerequisite to women's freedom (Gordon, 1976). Later, Margaret Sanger emerged as the most visible proponent of women's access to birth control, arguing, "No woman can call herself free who does not own and control her body. No woman can call herself free until she can choose consciously whether she will or will not be a mother" (Rossi, 1974, p. 533). Many other first-wave activists either were disinterested in reproductive issues or were critical of any focus on women's sexual emancipation.

Tension over reproductive issues resurfaced in the second wave of women's movements in America. While many feminist groups such as NOW support women's right to choose, other groups such as Feminists for Life (FFL) argue that abortion is wrong and violates basic feminine values, including respect for life itself.

successfully in the first wave of women's movements. Because rhetoric of the women's rights movement focused on the single issue of voting rights, and cultural feminists' voices affirmed women's traditional roles, broader reforms in cultural views of women were impeded. The failure to address a range of inequities women suffered led to further erosions in women's opportunities. For instance, during the Great Depression when jobs were scarce, most employers refused to hire women as long as there were men who needed jobs. Persisting gender inequities festered for a number of years without any rhetorical movements to address them.

The Second Wave of Women's Movements

Between 1960 and today, a second wave of American women's movements has emerged. As increasing numbers of women claim a voice in defining who they are and what rights, roles, and opportunities they should have, new traditions of feminism are born and join in the chorus about women's identity. As in the first wave of women's movements, both liberal and cultural ideologies coexist in the second wave, sometimes in harmony, often in tension. Also consistent with the first era of women's activism, the movements of the second wave spring from different sources, seek diverse goals, and pursue distinct rhetorical strategies.

Radical feminism. Perhaps the first form of feminism to emerge in this century was **radical feminism,** which grew out of another social movement, New Left politics, which focused on protesting the Vietnam War, racial discrimination, and governmental abuses. As women participated side by side with men in objecting to American involvement in Vietnam and egregious racial injustices at home, it became clear that the women were not being treated equally. They did the same work as their male peers and risked the same hazards of arrest, beatings, and expulsion, but women were treated as subordinate. Men dominated and kept a monopoly on New Left leadership, while women activists were expected to make coffee, type news releases and memos, do the scut work of organizing, and be ever-available for the males' sexual recreation. Women were generally not allowed to represent the movement in public—their voices were not recognized or heard.

In 1964, women in the Student Nonviolent Coordinating Committee (SNCC) who argued for female equality within the New Left movement were met with rigid, sexist attitudes. Stokely Carmichael, one of the major leaders for civil rights, responded to women's demands for equality by telling them that "the position of women in SNCC is prone." In 1965, women in the Students for a Democratic Society (SDS) found no receptivity to their demands for equality (O'Kelly & Carney, 1986). Outraged by men's total disregard for their rights and men's refusal to extend the democratic, egalitarian principles they preached to gender equality, women became disillusioned. Many women simply withdrew from the New Left organizations, since male domination seemed unshakable. A second response was distrust of formal organizations and the kind of hierarchy they breed. Building on the belief that formal structures encourage social stratification, many women migrated out of the formal New Left movement to form their own organizations.

In 1968, women organized and held the first national meetings where they began to chart the principles and practices that would define one branch of contemporary feminism and would become the center of its rhetoric. Central to what they created were new forms of communication, which became the heart of radical feminism (Campbell, 1973). A primary radical feminist communication technique was "rap" groups or consciousness-raising groups, where women gathered together to talk informally about personal experiences with sexism. Radical feminists' commitment to equality and their deep suspicion of stratification led them to practice communication that ensured equal participation by all members of rap groups. For instance, some groups used a system of chips in which each woman was given an equal number of chips at the outset of a rap session. Each time she spoke, she tossed one of her chips into the center of the group. When her chips were all "cashed in," she could not contribute further, and other, less outspoken women had an opportunity to speak. This technique was valuable because it recognized the importance of women's voices and encouraged individual women to find and use their voice.

THE FAMOUS BRA BURNING (THAT NEVER HAPPENED!)

One of the most widespread perceptions of feminism is based on the bra burning of 1968, in which media reported that a number of radical feminists burned their bras to protest the Miss America pageant's focus on women as sexual objects.

In planning a response to the pageant, protesters considered a number of guerrilla theater techniques to dramatize their disapproval of what the pageant stood for and how it portrayed women. They decided to protest by throwing false eyelashes, bras, girdles, and so forth into a trash can in front of reporters. They also put a crown on a large pig labeled "Miss America" and led it around the pageant. In early planning for the protest, some members suggested burning bras, but this idea was discarded (Hanisch, 1970). However, a reporter heard of the plan and reported the event on national media. Millions of Americans accepted it as a fact, and even today many people refer to feminists as "those bra-burning women."

It made a great story, it captured public interest, and it supported media caricatures of radical feminists as crazy, extremist, man-hating women. The only problem is, not a single bra was burned at that time!

Consciousness-raising groups as well as working committees in radical feminist organizations were leaderless. Reflecting disillusion with formal organizations like SDS and SNCC in which members vied for power, leaderless discussions allowed each woman to contribute to conversations without having any person in charge of anyone else. A third innovative communication form that radical feminists employed was guerrilla theater, in which they engaged in public communication to dramatize issues and arguments. Although public rhetoric was not a primary focus of radical feminism, it occurred occasionally. Protests against the Miss America pageants in 1968 and 1969, for instance, included throwing cosmetics and constrictive underwear for women into trash containers to demonstrate rejection of a view of women as sex objects.

The radical feminist movement achieved some notable results. Perhaps the most important outcomes of this movement were that it enhanced individual women's self-esteem and voice, built solidarity among women, and empowered grass-roots support for women's issues. Through consciousness-raising and collective efforts, radical feminists organized a women's health movement, which has helped women recognize and resist sexist and dictatorial attitudes of doctors and become knowledgeable about their own bodies (Boston Women's Health Club Book Collective, 1976; the Diagram Group, 1977). Radical feminists' refusal to organize formally, however, precluded them from ever assuming a strong profile in shaping public policies that affect women. Their rhetorical strategies focused on affirming and empowering individual women more than on persuading the general public to change its views of women.

Middle-class, liberal feminism. A second major form of liberal feminism in our era goes by various labels: middle-class feminism, **liberal feminism,** and NOW. This movement was fueled by Betty Friedan's landmark book, *The Feminine Mystique* (1963). Recognized as the major persuasive text launching this movement, Friedan's book highlighted "the problem that has no name," by which she meant the vague, chronic discontent that many middle-class American women felt. Surrounded by their children and hard-working husbands, with matching appliances in their three-bedroom suburban ranch houses and station wagons in the drives, these women were living "the American Dream." They were supposed to be happy and feel gratified. Not only were many middle-class homemakers not happy, but they felt guilty about their malaise. Most women, in fact, felt so guilty at feeling dissatisfied that they kept their feelings to themselves. Because there had been no public rhetoric to make the problem salient to the general population, few women realized that their feelings were widely shared.

Friedan's book named the problem and defined it as a political issue, not a personal one. Friedan told women there was a legitimate reason they felt dissatisfied, since their confinement to homelife kept them from developing personal and professional interests. Of course they loved their families and valued their good fortune in life, yet that wasn't enough for all women. Many also wanted opportunities to participate in public and work life, and they wanted to develop personal interests and ambitions as well as to care for families. Friedan pointed out that the reasons women were not able to pursue personal development were political: American institutions, including laws and prevailing values, kept women confined to domestic roles that squelched fulfillment in arenas outside of homelife. Around the nation, one group of women — middle-class white wives and mothers — resonated to Friedan's message. In it they found validation for their discontent and a hope for change.

Acting from the liberal ideology that women and men are alike in important respects and, therefore, entitled to equal rights and opportunities, the movement spawned by Friedan's book is embodied in NOW, the National Organization for Women, which works to secure political, professional, and educational equity for women. Founded in 1966 with Betty Friedan acting as an organizer, NOW is a public voice for equal rights for women. It has been extremely effective in enacting rhetorical strategies that have brought about concrete changes in laws and policies that enlarge women's opportunities and protect their rights. Consider some of the advances for women that liberal feminism has achieved:

♦ In 1964, the Civil Rights Act was amended to include sex, along with race, religion, and nationality, as an illegal basis for employment discrimination.

♦ Executive Order 11246 was modified to prohibit gender discrimination in employment by holders of federal contracts.

♦ NOW supported federally financed child-care centers, which make it possible for many women to be employed.

♦ NOW documents sexism in children's books and programs and publishes its findings so that parents and teachers may make informed choices about media for their children.

♦ NOW, along with other organizations, has stimulated reforms in credit and banking practices that disadvantage women.

♦ NOW has enlarged equity in sports so that women now have greater, though still inequitable, opportunities in athletics.

♦ In 1971, NOW formed the National Women's Political Caucus, to support women who seek elective and appointive public office.

Liberal feminism, particularly as exemplified by NOW, has led the way in identifying and combating institutional practices and laws that exclude women from positions of influence in public and professional life. The rhetorical strategies of this movement include lobbying, speaking at public forums, drafting legislation, and holding conventions where plans are formed and further strategies are developed. For those women who want equal opportunities to participate in the existing structures of our society, this form of feminism has been liberating.

HELEN

That's me. I'm a liberal feminist. I believe women and men ought to have the same opportunities to get work and to advance. And I think they should get equal pay for equal work. I think more extreme kinds of feminism that try to change the actual structure of the society are just too idealistic to be at all effective. What I want is my place in society. I guess you could say I want a "piece of the action."

Yet liberal feminism has little to offer other women who endorse the belief that women are distinct from men and therefore have different needs and abilities and deserve different opportunities. For those endorsing this ideology, various forms of cultural feminism are more compelling.

Separatism.   Some women believe, as first-wave cultural feminists did, that women are fundamentally different from men in the value they place on life, equality, harmony, nurturance, and peace. Finding that these values gain little hearing in a capitalist society that is wedded to competition and power mongering, some women adopt a revolutionary goal of forming all-women communities where feminine values can flourish without intrusion from men and the aggressive, individualistic, oppressive values of capitalism. They strive for life-styles and communities in which people are interdependent and live in mutual respect and harmony.

Separatists believe it is impossible and/or a poor use of their generative energies to attempt to reform the male-oriented culture of America. Instead, they simply choose to remove themselves from the mainstream and live in tune with communal values and respect for life, including life of people, animals, and the earth. In adopting this course of action, separatists not only remove themselves from mainstream culture but also foreclose opportunities to alter dominant social values. They do not assume a public voice to critique the values they find objectionable, so they have no real impact on social views. In this sense, they exercise

HERLAND

Herland is a feminist utopian novel published in 1915 and reissued in 1979. In it, author Charlotte Perkins Gilman describes a matriarchal society in which feminine traditions infuse personal and social life. *Motherlove* is the religion of Herland, and the *Maternal Pantheism* is the prime goddess.

All women inhabitants of Herland live in a communal fashion in which everyone is committed to helping others and the collective society. They are peace loving, life affirming, and vegetarian, avoiding at all costs activities that harm any life form, including the earth itself.

The drama of the story begins when a small group of men accidentally enter Herland and try to make sense of a culture in which competition gets them nowhere, power is not coveted, and individual self-interest only hampers personal happiness.

little pragmatic or political influence. Yet their very existence defines an alternative vision of how we might live—one that speaks of harmony, cooperation, and peaceful coexistence of all life forms.

Structural feminists.   Structural feminists, or modern-day cultural feminists, are less extreme than separatists but embrace the same basic ideology and goals. Women in this group contend women are different from men, although most are skeptical of claims that the differences are innate or biological (Donovan, 1985, p. 61). Instead, a majority of modern cultural feminists believe that women's traditional position in the domestic sphere of life has led them to develop more nurturing, supportive, cooperative and life-giving values than those men learn through participation in the public sphere. Operating from standpoint theory, which we considered in Chapter 2, Sara Ruddick (1989), for instance, claims that the process of mothering young children cultivates in women "maternal thinking," which is marked by attentiveness to another and personal involvement with another's health, happiness, and development. Unlike separatists, structural feminists see woman's place as in the roles traditionally prescribed by society.

Structural feminists engage in several kinds of communication. While many, perhaps a majority, take no public voice, believing that to be inconsistent with traditional roles for women, others do speak out. Some structural feminists enter into legal debates in an effort to secure unique legal rights for women because of their sex. For instance, some structural feminists argue that laws need to recognize that only women bear children and, thus, they have special needs that must be legally protected. Other structural feminists engage in rhetoric that demeans other forms of feminism, arguing that liberal feminists are not "real women," or at least

---

R E G I N A

If I had to put myself in one or another of the feminist categories, I guess I'd say that I'm more of a cultural feminist. I don't see much to be gained by having equal rights to participate in institutions that are themselves all wrong. I don't believe dog-eat-dog ethics are right. I don't want to be part of a system where I can advance only if I slit somebody else's throat or step on him or her. I don't want to prostitute myself for bits of power and favor in a business. I would rather work for different ways of living, ones that are more cooperative like win-win strategies. Maybe that means I'm a dreamer, but I just can't motivate myself to work at gaining status in a system that I don't respect.

not "good women." Finally, much of the rhetoric of structural feminists seeks to persuade others to incorporate women's values and viewpoints into public structures in order to enhance the quality of politics, professional activity, and cultural life in general.

Lesbian feminists.   Arguing that only women who do not orient their lives around men can be truly free, **lesbian feminists** define themselves as woman-identified. One theorist (cited in Koedt, 1973, p. 246) states, "Feminism is the theory; lesbianism is the practice." Some people argue that homosexuals should keep their sexual lives private just as heterosexuals do. In response, lesbian feminists point out, "That's exactly the point: We don't think employers and others should be able to pry into our private lives and deny us jobs and housing because of the gender of our sweethearts" ("A New Court Decision," 1992). It is others, not lesbians, who seem determined to bring lesbians' sexuality into the spotlight.

Among lesbian feminists there is disagreement about the essence of lesbianism. While some (Rich, 1980) voice the view that lesbianism is a continuum of sharing and support among women, others (Zita, 1981) emphasize sexuality between women as the core of lesbianism. Despite disagreement about the importance of sexuality, lesbian feminists are united in the focus on certain core issues that specifically affect lesbians' lives. High in priority is fighting for basic civil rights through passage of legislation that prohibits job discrimination on the basis of sexual orientation. Lesbians are also concerned with discrimination in insurance coverage, housing, and property rights. Battles over these issues are currently being waged in legislative chambers across the nation. For instance, in *Soroka* v. *Dayton Hudson Corporation* (1991), the California Court of Appeals ruled that questions about sexual orientation may not be included on job applications, since this violates applicants' rights to privacy. For lesbian feminists, the primary goals are to live as women-identified women and to make it possible for women in committed, enduring relationships to enjoy the same property, insurance, and legal rights granted to heterosexual spouses. The rhetoric of lesbian feminists has two characteristic forms. Much communication by lesbian feminists is responsive to criticism from the culture: Lesbians defend their life-style and choice of partners against rhetorical attacks from the media, the public, and sometimes other feminists. More recently, some lesbian feminists have adopted more proactive rhetorical strategies to assert their value, rights, and integrity. In the coming years, we will probably see further evolution in the rhetoric of lesbian feminists.

Revalorists.   Yet another group of modern feminists is committed to valuing traditionally feminine skills, activities, and perspectives that have been marginalized in this society. The members of this group are often called **revalorists** because they seek to revalue women and their contributions to cultural life. In addition, revalorists want to re-cover women whose contributions to public life have been excluded from histories of America. Revalorists often use unusual language to call attention to what they are doing. For instance, they talk about re-covering, not recovering, women's history to indicate they want to go beyond the prevailing male perspectives that have created history and views of women. Instead, their goals are to re-cover the contributions of women and to precipitate cultural acknowledgment of their values and validity.

Examples of revalorists' efforts include Karlyn Campbell's series of books titled *Man Cannot Speak for Her* (1989a, 1989b), in which her goal (1989a, p. 1) is "to restore one segment of the history of women." Another example, from a different field, is physicist Evelyn Fox Keller's efforts (1983, 1985) to make known Barbara McClintock's brilliant work in genetics, which science books have disregarded. In re-covering women's contributions, revalorists contribute to a more complete, more accurate history of North America and the people composing it.

Other revalorists' efforts focus on celebrating women's traditional activities and skills. Carol Gilligan (1982), for instance, highlights women's commitment to caring. Her research led her to theorize that women's morality is grounded in desires to care for others and respond to human needs. Before Gilligan's work, moral maturity had been defined by standards more characteristic of men, which focus on being fair and protecting individual rights. The importance of Gilligan's contribution is twofold: First, it makes us aware of an alternate moral perspective that has its own distinctive structure and coherence. Second, Gilligan refused to define the care perspective as less valuable than the fair perspective. Instead, she argued that women and men have distinct and distinctly valid moral viewpoints, thus affirming the legitimacy of women's ways of seeing and acting on the world. Following up Gilligan's work, Mary Belenky and her colleagues (1986) identified ways of knowing that seem more characteristic of women than of men. All of these revalorist efforts aim to give women and their values and activities "equal time" and equal value in public awareness and recognition. The broad goal of revalorists, then, is to increase the value and salience of skills, activities, and philosophies derived from women's traditional roles (Donovan, 1985, p. 62).

Revalorist rhetoric is consistent with the movement's broad goal of heightening public awareness of and respect for women's ways. Some revalorists seek public forums in which to raise the status of activities and roles traditionally associated with women. Through speeches and other symbolic forms such as art, the beauty and integrity of women's traditional roles are affirmed and promoted. Exhibitions of women's traditional arts such as weaving and quilt-making are examples of rhetorical strategies that rely on symbols other than words to persuade.

Among revalorist and liberal feminists there are fundamental disagreements that often lead to tensions. From a liberal feminist perspective, celebrating women's traditional activities and inclinations appears repressive, since it seems to value what results from oppression. For instance, caring for others may reflect skills women developed to please those who controlled their lives — sometimes literally (Janeway, 1971; Miller, 1986). Revalorists respond to this criticism by arguing that not to celebrate women's traditional activities is to participate in widespread cultural devaluations that have long shaped perceptions of women. This controversy is part of the ongoing cultural conversation about the meaning and value of femininity.

Womanists.   A final group of second-wave activists call themselves **womanists** to differentiate themselves from other feminists. Picking up the first-wave criticism of feminism as being white, middle-class feminism, many African-American women have defined a viewpoint that embodies their racial and gender identities. Their goals are to make others aware of the exclusionary nature of feminism as it has been articulated by middle-class white women and to educate others about the ways in which gender and race oppression intersect in the lives of women of color. Liberal, or middle-class, feminism, say the womanists, speaks only to the experiences, concerns, and situations of members of a privileged race in America. bell hooks (1990), among other womanists, notes that African-American women's oppression is bound up with both race and gender and cannot be addressed by a middle-class feminist agenda that is ignorant of how racism and sexism come together in the lives of minority women.

Women of color have a distinctive cultural history that is seldom recognized, much less addressed, by the white, middle-class women who have dominated women's movements of both waves. In remaining ignorant of experiences of non-white, non-middle-class women, white feminists may inadvertently participate in the very kind of oppression they claim to oppose (Joseph & Lewis, 1981). Key differences between white and African-American women's situations are that a

M E L I T A

Finally, I have a word to describe who I am as an African-American woman. I am a womanist. It's been confusing for me, because I do believe I suffer discrimination because I am a woman. But I know that what happens to me also has to do with my black skin — always my race is part of my oppression in this country. So when some of my white friends would talk to me about feminism and why I should be a feminist, they just didn't understand some of the issues in my life. Their feminism is white as the snow. I'm not. It's like Sojourner said, "Ain't I a woman?" Well I am, and I'm also an African-American. I'm a womanist.

woman of color "remains single more often, bears more children, has less education, earns less, is widowed earlier and carries a heavier economic burden as a family head than her white sister" (Lerner, 1972, p. 597).

Nearly two decades ago, a number of African-American women who were disenchanted with white, middle-class feminism but who were committed to women's equality began organizing their own groups. Feminist organizations such as Black Women Organized for Action and the National Black Feminist Organization sprang up and quickly attracted a number of members. These organizations were more effective than mainstream liberal feminism in cutting across class lines to include working-class women and to address issues of lower-class African-American women in their agenda. Their goals included reforming welfare organizations so that they respond more humanely to poor women and increasing training and job opportunities so that women of color can improve the material conditions of their lives (Hertz, 1977). Primary rhetorical strategies employed by womanists include consciousness-raising and support among women of color, lobbying decision-makers for reforms in laws, and community organizing to build grass-roots leadership of, by, and for women of color.

One of the most pressing challenges before women today is building coalitions among different kinds of women, coalitions that create a truly inclusive movement in which attention to common struggles and oppressions does not obscure awareness of real and important differences among women. If this does not happen, women with diverse experiences, cultural histories, and interests may remain divided against each other, an outcome that will hardly enhance women's solidarity or ability to instigate reform in how women are regarded and treated.

As we have seen, the "women's movement" is really a collage of many movements that span over one and a half centuries and include a range of political and social ideologies as well as diverse understandings of women's identities, needs, and value. The different goals associated with feminism are paralleled by a broad scope of rhetorical strategies, ranging from private empowerment through consciousness-raising and support to public lobbying and stump speaking. The issue of whether a person is a feminist is considerably more complicated than it first appears. Whether you define yourself as a feminist or not, you have some views of women's identities, rights, and nature. It may be that each of us needs to ask not just whether we are feminists, but *which* kind of feminist we are.

Men's Movements

Men's voices have only recently joined the cultural conversation about gender. During the first wave of American feminism, men were largely uninvolved with issues of gender. Most opposed women's efforts to gain rights, although a few like Frederick Douglass actively supported women's struggles for equality and are considered feminists. It is only in the last two decades that men in any number have begun to question the nature and effects of social views of masculinity and to define issues in men's lives.

Like the women's movement, the men's movement is really a collection of different movements with different views of men and diverse, sometimes conflicting, political and personal goals and rhetorical strategies. Also like their feminist parallels, men's movements are evolving, with new ones constantly emerging to spotlight specific issues for men's attention. Diverse views of men and masculinity are considered in umbrella forums such as men's studies courses, increasingly popular on many campuses, and the Men's Studies Association. In addition, in August of 1992, *The Journal of Men's Studies* was launched to report research on men and to explore various approaches to masculinity (Gross, D., 1990). In addition to these broad foci, there are many men's groups that have more specific viewpoints, pursue more limited goals, and adopt particular communication practices. To gain appreciation of the range of issues and ideologies entailed in men's movements, we will discuss three particular branches.

Profeminist Men's Movements

Only one sector of the men's movements shares the liberal or enlightenment ideology of mainstream feminism. Sometimes referred to as "new age men" or "sensitive males," **male feminists**, or profeminist men, emerged from the upheaval in the 1960s. Although many men in student activist organizations like SNCC and SDS ridiculed women who accused them of sexism, not all New Left men responded negatively. A number of them perceived truth in the women's charges, and they were ashamed when confronted with the hypocrisy between their political efforts to end discrimination and their own discrimination against women. These men worked to reform their own attitudes and behavior and bring both in line with the egalitarian ideology they espoused. Male feminists believe that women and men are basically alike in important respects and, therefore, they should enjoy the same privileges, opportunities, rights, and status in society. For the most part, these men have linked themselves and their rhetoric to mainstream, liberal feminism. Out of this perspective, two distinct concerns emerge, one focused on women and the other on men.

Because they believe in the equality of the sexes, male feminists support women's battles for equitable treatment in society. They have participated in efforts to increase women's rights during both the first and second waves of American feminism. During the 1972 campaign to ratify the ERA (Equal Rights Amendment), many men gave time, effort, and resources to the battle to gain legal recognition of women's equality. They joined women in seeking public platforms from which to advocate for women's equality and rights. After the amendment

TEXT OF THE EQUAL RIGHTS AMENDMENT

Equality of the rights under the law shall not be denied or abridged by the United States or by any State on account of sex.

was voted out of Congress in 1972, 28 states quickly ratified it, and its passage seemed assured.

However, a Stop ERA campaign led by Phyllis Schlafly and generously financed by conservative political and business interests stymied progress of the legislation. By 1973, of the needed 38 states, 35 had ratified the amendment, but the remaining ones — conservative southern and western states — refused to support passage, and the ERA was defeated. Throughout struggles to gain ratification, male feminists worked alongside women. They lobbied, canvased neighborhoods, made speeches in public settings, and helped organize and mount the campaign to gain legal recognition of women's equality.

Male feminists also support other issues embraced by women feminists. For instance, men who consider themselves feminists generally endorse efforts to gain equal pay for equal work, to end discrimination against qualified women in academic and professional contexts, and to increase parental leaves and child-care facilities that are necessary for families in which both parents work. Actor Alan Alda is a particularly well-known example of a male feminist, who lent his voice to the fight for ERA and other issues important to liberal feminist women. An equally important kind of communication employed by male feminists is personal persuasion, used to convince particular others to alter discriminatory attitudes and practices. For instance, one of my friends who considers himself a feminist challenged his firm's policy of paying women less salary than it paid to men in equivalent positions. He thought the action was wrong, and he used his voice and his credibility to speak out.

Another interest of male feminists is their personal growth beyond restrictions imposed by society's prescriptions for masculinity. Because they believe that men and women are alike in most ways, male feminists want to develop the emotional capacities that society encourages in women but prohibits in men. Specifically, many male feminists claim that social expectations of masculinity force men to repress their feelings, and this diminishes men's humanity and makes their lives less satisfying than they could be (Hudson & Jacot, 1992).

Agreeing with liberal feminist women, men in this movement regard cultural prescriptions for gender as toxic to both sexes. Whereas for women social

N O C M

The National Organization for Changing Men defines itself as an activist organization that promotes positive changes in men. NOCM is pro-men, pro-women, and pro-gay in its philosophy. Through formal and informal efforts, NOCM attempts to bring about personal, political, and social changes designed to foster equality of men and women and gay and straight people.

Information on the organization's goals, activities, and membership procedures may be obtained by contacting the national organization:

NOCM
P.O. Box 24708
Los Angeles, CA 90024-0099

codes have restricted professional development and rights, for men they have sealed off feelings (Brod, 1987; Hearn, 1987). Male feminists think that in restricting men's ability to understand and experience feelings, society has robbed them of an important aspect of what it means to be human. A major goal of male feminists is changing this. They encourage men to get in touch with their feelings and to be more sensitive, caring, and able to engage in meaningful close relationships.

The male feminist movement includes both informal, interpersonal communication and more organized political efforts. Formal, public action in this movement dates to 1975, when the first Men and Masculinity Conference was held in Tennessee. The conference has met annually since then to discuss the meaning of masculinity, to establish a network of support for men, and to identify and talk about problems and frustrations inherent in how our culture defines masculinity (Doyle, 1989, p. 307). The most prominent male feminist organization is NOCM, the National Organization for Changing Men (originally called NOM, the National Organization for Men), which has nearly 1,000 members. This enterprise sponsors workshops with speakers and group discussions to expand men's awareness of ways in which their emotional development has been hindered by restrictive social views of masculinity. In addition, the workshops attempt to help men change this state of affairs by offering them guidance in how to become more feeling and sensitive. Often these groups serve as safe testing grounds in which men can experiment with expressing their feelings, needs, and problems.

NOCM makes discriminations in its judgment of human qualities. While members argue that some qualities, such as courage and ambition, traditionally associated with masculinity are valuable in all humans (women as well as men), it condemns other conventionally masculine qualities such as aggression, violence, and emotional insensitivity. One of the most important achievements of NOCM is its Fathering Task Group; this group issues a newsletter called *Fatherlove*, which promotes nurturance of children and involvement of fathers (Doyle, 1989, p. 311).

Equally important are informal group discussions where men meet to explore the joys, frustrations, privileges, and problems of being men. Modeled after the consciousness-raising groups popular with radical feminists, these groups encourage men to talk about what our society expects of men and what problems this creates for them. Through discussion, men practice their goal of getting in touch with their emotions. They try to learn how to talk openly with other men about feelings, fears, concerns, and frustrations. Topics like these are ones men are socialized to avoid, since they increase vulnerability and reflect a need for others, both of which violate social expectations for independence. The communication of this men's movement, then, includes both public rhetoric in support of women's rights and men's personal development and more private, small-group communication in which men explore with each other what they feel and how they might change attitudes and behaviors they find unworthy.

Promasculinist Men's Movements

A number of men's groups fit within the second camp of men's movements. This branch, labeled promasculinist (Fiebert, 1987), sees feminism and its ideology as in conflict with men's interests (Freedman, 1985). Many promasculinist men demean their profeminist brothers by calling them male bashers and accusing them of contributing to negative stereotypes of men. A primary rhetorical strategy of this group is debating, or attacking, those men who define themselves as male feminists. Promasculinists and profeminist men also split in their attitudes toward homophobia and gay men. The promasculinist camp does not focus on homophobia, which profeminist men see as underlying all men's — gay and straight alike — inability to form close relationships with other men. The issue of gay rights is not a primary concern for promasculinist men, who tend to either ignore or denigrate gay men. Profeminist men, in contrast, are committed to supporting gay concerns and to eliminating oppression faced by gay men. They regard social prohibitions against affection between men as undesirable.

Free Men.   In sharp distinction to male feminists, one branch of the men's movement calls itself **Free Men** and includes specific organizations such as MR, Inc. (Men's Rights, Incorporated); the National Coalition for Free Men; and

NOM (National Organization of Men). Free Men aim to restore men's pride in being "real men." By "real men," this group means men in the traditional macho image — modern-day John Waynes who are tough, rugged, invulnerable, and self-reliant. Free Men see male feminists as soft and unmanly and defile them with epithets such as "the men's auxiliary to the women's movement" (Gross, D., 1990, p. 12). In fact, Free Men say that profeminist men are not part of the men's movement at all. Interestingly, when men of this movement took the name NOM, the feminist men who had originally called *their* organization NOM changed its name to NOCM to emphasize that they were in favor of *changing* traditional men's roles, not reinforcing them.

Free Men have an interesting attitude toward gender oppression. Although they recognize that women have suffered some discrimination, they think the inequities society heaps on men are far greater and worthy of more attention and correction. According to this group, the primary burden of masculinity is the provider role. Assigning that to men, they argue, makes men little more than meal tickets whose worth is measured by the size of their paychecks and their titles. Warren Farrell (1991, p. 83), for instance, claims that men are relentlessly oppressed by the "24-hour-a-day psychological responsibility for the family's financial well-being." While women perceive working outside the home as one of several courses of action open to them, Farrell notes that "almost all men see bringing home a healthy salary as an obligation, not an option." Many men believe a woman will not love them if they are not successful and good providers.

Another issue important to Free Men and related groups such as NOM is laws that abridge fathers' rights. According to Sidney Miller, a New York attorney

K A T E

It figures. Let women start to get anywhere, just let us make the smallest dent in the oppression we've always fought under, and men will horn in on our turf. So now they're oppressed, are they? I never heard of anything so ridiculous in my life! If they are oppressed — which I don't think they are — then whose fault do they think it is? Let's face it, men set up the system the way that it is and they set it up so they're right in the center and get all the privileges. If they don't like how it has worked out, don't blame women and don't try to take attention off the discrimination they created against women by crying out that men are oppressed. That's really crazy stuff.

who founded NOM, custody laws must be reformed to remedy blatant discrimination against fathers (Gross, D., 1990). Women usually win custody of children, yet fathers are required to pay child support. To be forced to pay for children when you're not allowed to be a full parent is rampant discrimination, say Free Men.

Specific issues like fathers' rights, however, are subordinate to Free Men and NOM members' greater concern that men are being robbed of their masculinity. Targeting feminism as the primary source of men's loss of their masculinity, promasculine men claim that "men have been wimpified. They've been emasculated" (Gross, D., 1990, p. 13). Longing for the return of traditional roles and men's unquestioned supremacy, Free Men want women to return to positions of subordination and attitudes of deference and docility. With this, they believe, men will regain their rightful places as heads of families and unquestioned authorities. To advance this agenda, free men engage in rhetoric ranging from lobbying for reform of laws they claim discriminate against men to condemning feminist men and women in public and private communication. Before dismissing this branch of the men's movement as extremist, notice that NOM has over 8,000 members, and the membership roll for the National Coalition for Free Men now exceeds 5,000.

Mythopoetic men.   The final branch of the men's movement we will discuss has garnered the greatest publicity and so is the best known form of men's movement. Blending aspects of men's studies, feminist men, and Free Men, the **mythopoetic movement** was founded by poet Robert Bly. The goal of the mythopoetic movement is to rediscover the deep, mythic roots of masculine thinking and feeling. Bly and other leaders argue that doing this will restore men to spiritual, emotional, and intellectual wholeness (Keen, 1991).

Mythopoetics agree with feminist women and men that the male role is toxic, yet they argue it was not always so. They claim ideal manhood existed during ancient times and the Middle Ages, when men were self-confident, strong, and emotionally alive and sensitive. As exemplars of ideal manhood, mythopoetics cite King Arthur, Henry David Thoreau, Walt Whitman, and Johnny Appleseed (Gross, D., 1990, p. 14). Mythopoetics think men's former connections to the earth and other men were ripped asunder by modernization, the Industrial Revolution, and feminism. Men were taken away from their land and, with that, from ongoing contact with life itself and their roles as stewards of the land (Kimbrell, 1991). At the same time that men were isolated from their earthy, natural masculinity (Gross, D., 1990, p. 14), industrialization separated men from their families. When men began working outside of the home, young boys lost fathers who could initiate them into manhood and teach them how to relate spiritually and emotionally to other men.

FACTS ABOUT THE MYTHOPOETIC MOVEMENT

- By 1990, over 50,000 men had participated in nature retreats at a cost of $200 + per participant.

- *MAN!,* the national quarterly devoted to the movement, has over 3,500 subscribers.

- *Wingspan,* another national quarterly of the movement, has a (free) circulation of more than 125,000 readers.

- In the Northeast alone, over 163 mythopoetic groups have formed in communities.

- Robert Bly's book *Iron John* enjoyed over 30 weeks on the bestseller list.

Source: Adler, with Duignan-Cabrera, & Gordon, 1991.

While mythopoetics do believe that men have been separated from their feelings, their views depart dramatically from those of profeminist men (Keen, 1991). Rather than encouraging men to become more like women in learning to be sensitive and caring, Bly and his followers think feminism has caused men's emotional deficits. Feminism is seen as making men "soft" and decidedly unmasculine because it robs men of emotional virility. Bly finds male feminists troublesome because he thinks they are moving down a counterproductive path. In "soft males," Bly says, "there's not much energy" (Wagenheim, 1990, p. 42). Stating this view more strongly, some mythopoetics (Allis, 1990, p. 80) charge that "the American man wants his manhood back. Period. . . . [F]eminists have been busy castrating American males. They poured this country's testosterone out the window in the 1960s." So one rhetorical strategy of mythopoetics is to debunk and put down male feminists and to provide a counterstatement to male feminists' public arguments about masculinity.

What do mythopoetics advocate for masculinity? They insist men need to recover the *distinctly male mode of feeling,* one that is fundamentally different from female feelings endorsed by profeminist men. They need to reclaim courage, aggression, and virility as masculine birthrights and as qualities that can be put to the service of bold and worthy goals as they were when knights and soldiers fought for causes. Central to modern man's emotional emptiness, argues Bly, is **father hunger,** a yearning need to be close to another man and to build deep, spiritual bonds with him. To remedy this, Bly and other leaders of the movement speak out in public settings to urge men to get in touch with their grief and, from there, to begin to rediscover their deep masculine feelings and spiritual energies. An especially influential form of persuasion by mythopoetics is Robert Bly's book *Iron John*, which is the major rhetorical text of this movement. This book, which explains mythopoetic views and recounts ancient myths of manhood, was a national best seller for over 30 weeks, making it a rhetorical message that captured a wide audience.

To facilitate this process, there are workshops and retreats that allow men to "come together in nature alone, in the absence of women and civilization" (Gross, D., 1990, p. 14). In the natural world, men can recover their sense of brotherhood and distinctively male feelings, ones repressed by industrialization and feminism. At nature retreats, men gather in the woods to beat drums, chant, and listen to poetry and mythic stories, all designed to help them get in touch with their grief over father hunger and to move beyond that to positive masculine feeling. As this suggests, favored mythopoetic forms of communication are storytelling, chanting, and affirming what it considers the deep roots of distinctively masculine feelings.

Men's movements, like ones focused on women's issues, are diverse and internally contradictory. While some men consider themselves feminists and work

CHUCK

Bly's ideas sound pretty strange to me. I can't identify with chanting in the woods with a bunch of other guys to find my manhood. Heck, I didn't know I'd lost it! But if I were to be serious about this stuff, I guess I'd say there might be something to it. I mean I do like to get together with brothers in my fraternity, and being with a group of just men does have a different kind of feeling than being with women or women and men. Like we're more uninhibited, more rough, and more loud than when girls are around. I guess I do feel more manly or something in those groups.

Another thing that interests me about what Bly says is the stuff about absent fathers. I'm not sure I'd go so far as to say I have the father hunger he talks about or that I have deep grief, but I do feel my father and I should have been closer. I never saw much of him when I was growing up. He worked all day and wanted to relax at night, not spend time with us kids. I wish I'd known him better — in fact, I still do wish it. I think a lot of guys feel that way.

with women for gender equality in society as well as attempt to become more sensitive themselves, other men see feminism as the source of much of modern men's problems, and they feel threatened by women's progress toward more equal status. Men's movements range from efforts to advance women's position to active attacks on women's resistance to traditional, subservient roles. Members of men's movements engage in public and private forms of communication that contribute to the cultural conversation about gender — what it means and how it affects the individual men and women who live under its edicts.

Other Movements Focused on Gender

Before concluding our survey of rhetorical movements about gender, we should consider two that are not branches of women's or men's movements. One of these, the backlash, attempts to discredit and disable feminism. The other, ecofeminism, seeks to integrate a range of positions held by women and men into a single humanistic movement committed to a more just, life-affirming philosophy of living.

The Backlash

Feminist movements have brought about substantial changes in women's lives. Their economic opportunities and rewards are better, although still not equal to men's; laws now prohibit discrimination in educational and work contexts; and many women's self-esteem has grown with the positive image of femininity promoted by women's movements. In fact, the very successes of feminism have led to an intense countermovement, called the **backlash** against feminism.

Unlike other gender movements we have considered, the backlash is not a formal operation nor an organized one. Instead, it consists of assorted, disparate kinds of communication that attempt to undermine women's confidence and obstruct further efforts toward equality. Included within the backlash are media misrepresentations of women's successes and problems, judicial rulings that reduce women's freedoms, business practices that covertly restrict women's opportunities, governmental actions that make it difficult for women to gain economic security without abandoning motherhood responsibilities, and popular book writers who scapegoat feminism as the source of problems ranging from loneliness to delinquent children.

The first clear examples of efforts to squelch feminism emerged in the 1970s when Mirabel Morgan launched the Total Woman movement and Helen Andelin founded the Fascinating Womanhood movement, both of which advocated women's return to traditional attitudes, values, and roles in life. The Total Woman movement (Morgan, 1973) reiterated the conventional social view of women as sexual objects and urged women to devote their energies to making themselves sexually irresistible to men. One example of advice given to women was to surprise their husbands by meeting them at the door dressed only in Saran Wrap. Fascinating Womanhood (Andelin, 1975) was grounded in conservative interpretations of biblical teachings, and it emphasized women's duty to embody moral purity and be submissive to their husbands.

Although feminists found the goals of Fascinating Womanhood and the Total Woman movements laughable and regressive, many women and men found them attractive. Over 400,000 women paid to take courses that taught them to be more sexually attractive and submissive to their husbands (O'Kelly & Carney, 1986). Primary support for these movements came from women who were economically dependent on husbands and who embraced conservative values.

Another instance of backlash occurred at roughly the same time, the mid-1970s, when Phyllis Schlafly led the Stop ERA movement and successfully defeated feminist efforts to gain constitutional recognition of women's equality. Taking to the public platform, Schlafly traveled around the nation to persuade people that feminism was destroying femininity by turning women into men. She told women to return to their roles as helpmates and homemakers and affirmed men's traditional roles as head of families. Ironically, although Schlafly argued that women should be deferential and that their place was in the home, her own activities belied this advice. In speaking forcefully in public, she violated her own advice on feminine style. Further, her speaking schedule kept her on the road or writing much of the time, so she was unable to devote much time to being a homemaker or mother.

Isolated activities such as those of Morgan, Andelin, and Schlafly contributed to antifeminist sentiments. The scope and intensity of this movement are described in depth by Susan Faludi in her 1991 book, *Backlash: The Undeclared War on American Women*. Faludi correctly notes that there are two levels of the broad backlash against feminism, and these levels are internally contradictory. On one hand, substantial contemporary rhetoric defines feminism as the source of women's problems as well as broken homes, tension between spouses, and delinquent children. In encouraging women to become more independent, feminism is portrayed as an evil force that turns women into fast-track achievers who have nothing to come home to but microwave dinners. We saw a good example of backlash rhetoric in the 1992 presidential race. Many conservatives bashed Hillary Rodham Clinton for being an assertive, achieving, intelligent woman, and Bill Clinton was ridiculed as unmanly for letting his wife have so much power and voice. Both Clintons took issue with backlash portrayals of Hillary and their marriage, and they argued — successfully, since Bill Clinton won — that their marriage was a partnership between equals. Backlash rhetors argue that rather than helping women, feminism has created more problems for them and has made their lives miserable. Obviously, they conclude, the answer to the problems is to renounce feminism.

A second backlash theme directly contradicts the first one by arguing that women have never had it so good. The media proclaim that women have won their battles for equality, they have made it, all doors are open to them, and they can have it all. Pointing to the slim gains in status and opportunities won by feminists, the backlash announces that all inequities have disappeared and there is no longer any need for feminism. This line of rhetoric has been persuasive with some people, since many individuals in their 20s say they think gender discrimi-nation is history. Yet, as Faludi insightfully asks (p. x), "How can American women be in so much trouble at the same time that they are supposed to be so blessed? If the status of women has never been higher, why is their emotional state

IS THIS EQUALITY?

If women have won their fight for equality, then why:

♦ Do 80% of women who work outside of their homes earn $20,000 or less annually?

♦ Are collegiate women's sports woefully underfunded in comparison with men's sports?

♦ Do women make up two-thirds of all poor adults?

♦ Do 80% of women working outside of the home remain locked in "women's positions," which do not have potential to advance?

♦ Are only two of the Fortune 500 CEOs women?

♦ Do women who work outside the home do a greater percentage of the child care compared with their husbands than they did in 1984?

♦ Does women's standard of living decrease by 35% following divorce while men's rises?

♦ Do 75% of high schools violate Title IX, which bans sex discrimination in education?

♦ Have sex-related murders of women increased since 1976? And why are 33% of those murders committed by husbands or boyfriends?

♦ Does a woman college graduate today earn less than a man with a high school degree?

so low? If women got what they asked for, what could possibly be the matter now?" Faludi concludes her study by pointing out that the backlash has not convinced women to return to traditional roles. Because of their numeric advantage and what Faludi calls the "justness of their cause," she believes women will continue to fight for equality in personal, professional, legal, and social arenas.

Ecofeminism

An entirely different response to women's movements is **ecofeminism,** which is a very young movement. Although there are historical roots in first-wave American feminism, ecofeminism's official inception is usually dated to 1974, when Françoise d'Eaubonne published *La Feminisme ou la Mort,* which translates to mean *Feminism or Death.* This book, although not widely noted at the time, provided the philosophical foundation for ecofeminism and inspired further work that did achieve some visibility. A key event was the first ecofeminist conference, "Women and Life on Earth: Ecofeminism in the 1980s," which was held in 1980.

Foundations for the emergence of ecofeminism came from both American feminist thinkers such as Rosemary Radford Reuther and influential French feminists, including Françoise d'Eaubonne, Luce Irigaray, and Hélène Cixous. Feminists on both continents highlight the connection between efforts to control and subordinate women and desires to dominate nature, which perhaps not coincidentally is called Mother Earth. Liberal theological scholar Rosemary Radford Reuther (1974, 1983) argues that the lust to dominate has brought the world to the brink of a moral and ecological crisis in which there can be no winners. According to Reuther, the quest to exploit and control is ultimately destructive and must end.

Ecofeminism unites the intellectual and political maturity of feminist thought with larger concerns about oppression and life itself. According to Judith Plant, a fortuitously named early proponent of ecofeminism (Sales, 1987, p. 302), this movement

> gives women and men common ground. . . . The social system isn't good for either—or both—of us. Yet we *are* the social system. We need some common ground . . . to enable us to recognize and affect the deep structure of our relations with each other and with our environment.

Perhaps the idea most central to ecofeminism is that oppression, so valued and encouraged by modern civilization, is wrong and destructive of all forms of life, including the natural world. From ecofeminists have come radical critiques of modern social values and the ends to which they lead us. Reuther (1975, p. 83), for instance, claims that "the project of human life must cease to be seen as one of 'domination of nature,' or exploitation. . . . We have to find a new language of ecological responsiveness, a reciprocity between consciousness and the world system in which we live." For ecofeminists, oppression itself is the primary issue, rather than particular instances of oppression. They believe that as long as oppression is culturally valued, it will be imposed on anyone and anything that cannot or does not resist. Thus, women's oppression is best understood as a specific example of an overarching cultural ideology that idolizes oppression. A number of individuals who stood against specific types of oppression have redefined themselves as ecofeminists (Chase, 1991). For instance, many vegetarians, animal rights activists, and peace activists have joined the ecofeminist movement.

The goals of this movement flow directly from its critique of cultural values. Ecofeminists seek to bring themselves and others to a new consciousness of humans' interdependence with all other life forms. They speak out against values that encourage exploitation, domination, and aggression and seek to show how these oppress women, men, children, animals, plants, and the planet itself. Ecofeminists argue that the values most esteemed by patriarchal culture are ones that will destroy us (Diamond & Orenstein, 1990). The rhetoric of ecofeminism proclaims the need to embrace life-affirming values that can transform societies so

E D

As we talked about all of the different movements, none of them struck me as speaking to where I am. I could see bits and pieces that I liked in several, but I didn't really identify with one. Then we discussed ecofeminism, and that hit the nail on the head. It fits for me. I became a vegetarian 12 years ago, long before it was popular. I did that because I didn't want my life to depend on killing any other kind of life. I worry about energy and hope to make my house fully solar powered when I get out of school and back to work again. I try not to harm or take advantage of anything living—from my wife and kids to my dog to even a grasshopper. For me this attitude has been very helpful in reminding me of human arrogance. I see how self-serving we allow ourselves to be. We just don't think about littering or turning up the heat if we're cold or whatever—we use all of the earth's resources to serve our purposes. We make the natural world our servant, and then we abuse and injure it. This is wrong, and it will lead to the death of all of us. So, you can see why I would call myself an ecofeminist now that I know the term.

that we celebrate the integrity and right to existence of diverse life forms. Ecofeminists speak for values such as harmony, respect for diversity, empowerment, cooperation, and nurturance; these values can re-form us into beings who can endure and prosper in balance with the natural world on which we depend.

Summary

Contributing to the cultural conversation about gender are rhetorical movements, which aim to change social views and policies regarding men and women. Launched in 1840, the first wave of feminism included two movements, one advocating women's equality with men and one proclaiming women's difference from men. Ironically, arguments developed by the two rather contradictory movements combined to secure many basic rights for women, including the right to vote. During the second wave of feminism, which began around 1960, even more voices joined the chorus attempting to define women's nature, rights, and roles. Ranging from liberal feminist organizations such as NOW, which engages in public communication, lobbying, and organizing to fight against political and material discriminations against women, to cultural feminists such as revalorists and womanists, contemporary voices offer alternative visions of women and femininity.

Men's movements too have been diverse. Many men joined with women feminists to speak in favor of fundamental equality for women and to free men from oppressive social expectations. Yet other men regard male feminists as traitors who are undermining masculinity itself. Organizations such as Free Men seek to restore ultra-macho ideals of manhood, while the mythopoetic movement encourages men to discover and cultivate a distinctively male mode of feeling and of relating to other men. Against the backdrop of men's and women's movements are two others, which in opposite ways respond to feminist philosophies and efforts at change. The backlash movement is not a coherent, unified rhetorical movement but rather is a mélange of messages that aim to stop further feminist efforts and to reverse some of the victories won through women's activism.

The counterpoint to backlash tendencies is the ecofeminist movement, which aims to merge ecology's respect for nature and life with feminist critiques of oppression and domination. Many think ecofeminism is the single movement with the greatest promise of unifying interests of diverse women and men while also enlarging all humans' capacities to respect and live in harmony with others and the natural world. Whether or not that prediction is borne out, one thing is certain: The cultural conversation about gender will continue. Communication in private and public settings will delineate multiple versions of femininity and masculinity and will seek to persuade us to adopt certain points of view. As the conversation evolves, new voices will join existing rhetorical efforts to define the meaning of masculinity and femininity and the rights, roles, and opportunities available to women, minorities, men, lesbians, and gay men. It's up to you to define your role in the cultural conversation about gender. Some people will be passive listeners. Others will be critical listeners who reflect carefully on others' communication. And still others will claim a voice in the conversation and will be part of active rhetorical efforts to define gender. What role will you choose for yourself?

$\mathscr{D}$iscussion Questions

1. Before reading this chapter, did you know that there were two waves of the feminist movement in the United States? Did you realize there are so many and such diverse forms of feminism? Many people are not aware that feminism is anything larger than the liberal branch of contemporary United States feminism (e.g., NOW). What does limited knowledge of women's movements imply about biases in education?

2. For suffragists in the 1800s, the big issues were voting, education, and access to employment. What do you see as the most important issues for liberal feminism in the 1990s in the United States? What kinds of discrimination and oppression still limit women economically, personally, educationally, professionally, and politically?

3. With which form or forms of feminism do you most agree? With which are you least comfortable? Do you think it's more the case that women should work to have equal rights and opportunities within existing systems (liberal feminisms) or that they should work to change the systems so that they incorporate traditionally feminine values and concerns (cultural feminisms)?

4. What do you think of efforts to revalorize women by uncovering and valuing traditionally feminine activities, values, and identities? For instance, do you think it's desirable to recognize quilting as a kind of art and caring for others as being as important as making a good salary?

5. One of the most important criticisms of contemporary feminist movements is that they have been insensitive to differences caused by race, affectional preference, and class. Do you think this criticism is well justified? Have the most visible feminist efforts reflected primarily the concerns of middle-class, Western, Caucasian women? Have the gains of feminism tended to benefit middle-class heterosexual women more than women of color and lower socioeconomic class? Do you think this should change?

6. Which of the men's movements do you find most consistent with your own values? Do you think men should work to restore traditional male prerogatives and social power, become more sensitive themselves, or change society?

7. Is the mythopoetic movement incorrect in arguing that most men suffer from father hunger — an unmet need to be deeply connected to fathers and other men? What are the implications of men not having close and enduring ties to other men?

8. Do you think there has been a backlash against feminism in the United States? If so, how do you explain cultural resistance to changes in women's status, rights, and identity? What does the intensity of resistance tell us about the importance of gender ideology to our society?

9. Does ecofeminism appeal to you? Why or why not? Some people think ecofeminism diminishes emphasis on the specific kinds of oppression women suffer and is therefore not the most desirable and effective kind of feminism. Other people argue ecofeminism is ideal because it focuses on oppression as the overarching problem that creates not only gender and gender oppression but also the broader social inclination to create hierarchies of what is more and less valuable. Where do you stand on this?

10. Speculate about gender movements in the next decade. Do you see cultural trends that will influence women's and men's movements as well as broad phenomena like the backlash and ecofeminism? Do you think current social issues such as rising emphasis on cultural diversity will recontour some of the movements that now exist? Do you think new movements will arise?

$\mathcal{G}$endered Verbal Communication

- ◆ "I now pronounce you man and wife."
- ◆ Bob babysat his son while his wife attended a meeting.
- ◆ Looking sharp with an updated wardrobe and a chic hairstyle, Geraldine Ferraro is on the campaign trail again.
- ◆ Freshmen find it difficult to adjust to college life.
- ◆ We reached a gentlemen's agreement on how to proceed.

These five sentences are commonplace ones we might hear or read at any time. Each one reflects cultural assumptions about gender. Did any of the sentences bother you? In the first one, did you notice that "man" is portrayed as an individual, while "wife" is defined only by her relationship to the man? In the second sentence, the use of the word *babysat* implies that the father was performing a special service, one we usually pay for; have you ever heard a mother's time with her children called babysitting? The third sentence defines Ferraro in terms of appearance and deflects attention from her qualifications as a political candidate. Unless the fourth sentence refers to first-year students at an all-male school, the word *freshmen* includes only those students who are male. Finally, the term *gentlemen's agreement* expresses the cultural association between men and professional activities.

Throughout previous chapters, we've discussed relationships among communication, gender, and culture. In this and the following chapter we add depth to those prior discussions by concentrating specifically on how communication reflects and expresses cultural views of gender. This chapter concentrates on how verbal communication interacts with social life and gender, and Chapter 6 traces relationships among nonverbal communication, culture, and gender. It is increasingly clear that language both expresses and sustains gendered relationships. We live in a symbolic environment in which our thoughts and actions are influenced by communication in its many forms. As we will see, language and nonverbal behaviors play critical roles in creating and perpetuating gendered identities and social patterns.

We will probe how verbal and nonverbal communication reflect and shape cultural understandings of masculinity and femininity. In addition, we will consider how individuals embody cultural expectations about communication—that is, how individual women's and men's communication reflects gendered identities. In concert, these two themes underline the cyclical process whereby cultural views of gender are communicated to individuals, who exemplify them personally and thereby perpetuate cultural expectations of masculine and feminine identities and styles of interacting.

▰▰▰ The Nature of Human Communication

Chapter 1 defined communication as "a dynamic, systemic process in which meanings are created and reflected in human interaction with symbols" (Wood, 1992a). Central to this definition is the understanding that communication is symbolic behavior. Unlike other animals, which rely on signal communication, humans interact with symbols. Signal communication is concrete and unambiguous and, therefore, it doesn't require interpretation. For instance, when I point to the floor my dog, Madhi, knows to lie down. The hand signal has a definite, unvarying meaning so she reacts automatically without having to think. Life gets considerably more complex when we enter the realm of symbolic activity. In fact, many philosophers and scientists who have tried to understand how we differ from other animals believe that the ability to think symbolically is the distinguishing quality of humans. It is what allows us to plan, invent, envision new possibilities, and remake ourselves and our world. (Sagan and Druyan, 1992, offer an excellent and readable summary of research on this topic.)

Not all symbols are linguistic or verbal. For instance, art is symbolic (Langer, 1953), as is dance (Langer, 1979). Both represent feelings and sensations, and both require interpretation. In Chapter 6, we will discuss some nonverbal symbols. For now, our focus is language, and all language is symbolic; in fact, language is one of the most complex symbol systems we have. Our nature as symbolic beings transforms us from biological creatures, who respond to the concrete world as it exists, into thinking beings who interpret, interact with, and remake our world through symbols (Langer, 1953, 1979). This implies that the symbols we use shape our understandings of the world and our own places within it.

Verbal Communication Expresses Cultural Views of Gender

In his analysis of humans' use of symbols, philosopher Ernst Cassirer (1978) identified five implications of symbolic ability. He realized that the power of symbols lies in the kinds of thought and action they enable; symbols allow us to define, organize, and evaluate experiences and people, think hypothetically, and reflect on ourselves. Discussing each of these implications of symbolic behavior will illuminate ways in which verbal communication expresses cultural views and expectations of women and men.

Language Defines Gender

The most fundamental implication of symbolic ability is that symbols define phenomena. We use symbols to name objects, people, feelings, experiences, and other phenomena. Because symbols are not concrete or tied naturally to things, the language we use selectively shapes our perceptions. The names we apply emphasize particular aspects of reality and neglect others (Wood, 1992a, p. 65). We cannot describe things in their total complexity, so the labels we choose highlight only certain qualities. What we emphasize is guided in part by cultural values, so that we name those things or aspects of things that are important in society's perspective. For instance, in America, we define dogs as pets, companions, guards, and even members of our family, and we act toward them in loving, protective ways. In cultures where dogs are not pets, but instead are pests, food, or working beasts, they are not given personal names and are not treated with kindness.

Symbols of masculinity and femininity vary across cultures (Philips, Steele, & Tanz, 1987). In Western society, our language negates women's experience by denying and dismissing women's importance and sometimes their very existence. In so doing, it represents men and their experiences as the norm and women and their ways as deviant. This marginalizes women (Bem, 1993; Spender, 1984a,b).

Male generic language excludes women. **Male generic language** is language that purports to include both women and men, yet specifically refers only to men. Examples are nouns such as *businessmen, chairmen, mailmen,* and *mankind,* and pronouns such as *he* to refer to both women and men. Some people think it is understood that women are included in terms such as *mankind* and *chairman.* This viewpoint, however, is not supported by research on how people interpret male generic language.

Research demonstrates conclusively that masculine generics are perceived as referring predominantly or exclusively to men. When people hear them, they think of men, not women. In an early study of the effects of male generics (Schneider & Hacker, 1973), children were asked to select photographs for a textbook with chapter titles of "Urban Man" and "Man in Politics" or "Urban Life" and "Political Behavior." The children nearly always chose pictures of men when the titles included male generics. When the titles did not refer to men only, the children chose more photographs that portrayed both sexes. What they saw as included in the chapters was shaped by the language in titles.

Other researchers (Gastil, 1990; Hamilton, 1991; Switzer, 1990; Todd-Mancillas, 1981) have conducted similar studies and reported that male generics do lead to perceiving males and not females as included. In a particularly interesting study, J. S. Hyde (1984) asked students from first grade through college to make up a story about an average student. When the instructions referred to the average student as "he," only 12% of students composed a story about a female. However, when the instructions defined the average student as "he or she," 42% of the stories were about females. W. Martyna (1978) found that female students took longer to process male generic pronouns (*he, him*) than inclusive pronouns (*they, he* or *she*). In summarizing her investigation, Martyna explained that we have to ponder whether male generics do or do not include females, so it takes longer to comprehend language that explicitly refers only to men.

A N D Y

For a long time I thought all of this stuff about generic *he* was a bunch of junk. I mean it seemed really clear to me that a word like *mankind* obviously includes women or that *chairman* can refer to a girl or a guy who chairs something. I thought it was pretty stupid to hassle about this. Then last semester I had a woman teacher who taught the whole class using *she* or *her* or *woman* whenever she was referring to people as well as when she meant just women. I realized how confusing it is. I had to figure out each time whether she meant women only or women and men. And when she meant women to be general, I guess you'd say generic for all people, it still made me feel left out. A lot of the guys in the class got pretty hostile about what she was doing, but I kind of think it was a good way to make the point.

One of the effects of male generic language is that it makes men seem more prominent and women less prominent than they are in real life. To the extent that our language refers to men and not women, we come to perceive men as more visible than they are, while women become invisible. Speaking to this concern, A. Sheldon (1990) wrote of her experiences as a mother. She had noticed that her 6½-year-old daughter used male generic language to describe her stuffed toys. When she asked her daughter why she called a stuffed animal "he," her daughter responded that "there are more he's than she's" (p. 4). In making us think there are more he's than she's, Sheldon (p. 5) contends, our language "is tricking us all" into perceiving as dominant a group that factually is less than 50% of the population.

According to N. M. Henley (1989), male generic language reduces awareness of women and tends to result in perceiving women as excluded or exceptions to the rule. This affects comprehension of language, views of personal identity, and perceptions of women's presence in various spheres of life. There is also reason to think that exclusionary language in classrooms inhibits women's learning. Researchers have even shown that male generics influence career aspirations by implying that most professions are for men (Bem & Bem, 1973).

Responding to the incontestable evidence that male generics distort perceptions, the newest *Webster's Dictionary* ("No Sexism Please," 1991, p. 59) follows a policy of avoiding male generics and other sexist language. In addition to avoiding man-linked words, the new dictionary cautions against other ways of defining men as the standard and women as the exception. For instance, it discourages **spotlighting**, which is the practice of highlighting a person's sex. Terms such as *lady doctor* and *woman lawyer* define women as the exception in professions and thereby reinforce the idea that men are the standard.

Women are defined by appearance and relationships. A second way that language expresses cultural views of gender is by defining men and women in different ways. Women tend to be defined by appearance and/or relationships with others, while men are more typically defined by activities, accomplishments, and/or positions. Differences in how women and men are defined reflect society's views of women as decorative, emotional, and sexual and men as independent, active, and serious.

Media offer countless examples of defining women by their physical qualities. Headlines announce "Blonde wins election," causing us to focus on the candidate's sex and physical appearance rather than her qualifications and plans for office. Coverage of women's sports, which is disproportionate compared with that for men's sports, frequently focuses on women players' appearance rather than their athletic skills. Stories on female athletes often emphasize wardrobes ("Chris is changing her style with a snappy new outfit"), slimmed-down bodies ("She's gotten back in shape and is looking good on the field"), and changed hairstyles ("When she stepped on the court, fans noticed her lightened hair"), while stories about male athletes focus on their athletic abilities ("He sunk two dream shots").

Similarly, coverage of women in professional and political life regularly directs attention to appearance, which influences readers to notice women's looks more than issues germane to their occupations. News reports far more frequently mention appearance when the story is about a woman than when it concerns a man (Foreit, Agor, Byers, Larue, Lokey, Palazzini, Patterson, & Smith, 1980). The sexist bias in descriptions of women reinforces the cultural view of women as decorative objects whose identity hinges on physical appeal. Much more than men, women's attractiveness is central to how society judges them (Wolf, 1991), and this is reflected in verbal communication.

Our language also reflects society's view of women as defined by their relationships rather than as independent agents. In an extensive survey of news stories, one research team (Foreit et al., 1980) found that a woman's marital status was mentioned 64% of the time, while a man's marital status was noted in only 12% of stories. In prime-time television, even professional women are still depicted primarily in relation to their families (Lott, 1989). For instance, although Claire Huxtable on the popular series "The Cosby Show" was an attorney, viewers saw her almost entirely in her role as wife and mother. Her career was invisible, and her stereotypical feminine roles were accented.

The cultural association of women with relationships is explicitly expressed in the words *Miss* and *Mrs.*, which designate, respectively, unmarried and married women. There are no parallel titles that define men in terms of whether they are married. The alternative term *Ms.* to designate a woman without identifying her

ROBYN

I get so angry reading the stories about women athletes—that is, when I can find them. Half of the time they aren't even reported or are buried in a tiny corner of the sports section, while the big stories are about male athletes. But even when they are reported, women get so trivialized. Reports dwell on how petite, tiny, and cute a woman gymnast is. What does that have to do with her abilities? And I just read one that focused on how a great woman tennis player is aging and doesn't look as good as she had 5 years ago. Give me a break! Then you find stories about how so-and-so has lightened her hair or started wearing softer tennis outfits or whatever. What does any of that have to do with how a woman plays her sport?

by her marital status is a relatively new addition to the language and one not yet fully accepted. It was not until 1987 that *The New York Times* would print "Ms." if a woman preferred that title (Stewart, Stewart, Friedley, & Cooper, 1990). The extent to which our society defines women by marriage and family is further evidenced in the still-prevalent tradition of a wife adopting her husband's name on marrying. Symbolically, she exchanges her individual identity for one based on her relationship to a man: Mrs. John Smith.

There are a number of alternatives to the traditional ways of naming ourselves. Many women revise their first names in order to project a more serious, mature identity. For instance, one of my students, who had been called Kathy for 18 years, began asking people to call her Kate or Katherine, either of which suggests a stronger image than Kathy. When I began graduate studies, I asked family and friends to quit calling me Julie and use Julia instead, because I thought Julia sounded more mature and professional. Last names too reflect identity. Some women choose to retain their own names when they marry. A number of men and women adopt hyphenated names such as Johnson-Smith to symbolize the family heritage of both partners. In some countries, such as Spain, both the mother's and father's family names are used to construct children's family names. Another alternative, less practiced so far, is renaming oneself to reflect matriarchal rather than patriarchal lineage. This involves changing a last name from that of the father's family to that of the mother's. Because that course of action, however, still reflects male lineage—that of the mother's father—some women use their mothers' first names to create a matriarchal last name: for example, Lynn Edwards's daughter, Barbara, might rename herself Barbara Lynnschild. In coming years, we will doubtlessly see other alternatives to traditional naming practices. Their existence reminds us of the importance we attach to naming and of our power to use language creatively.

Language names what exists. Finally, consider the pivotal power of language to name what does and does not exist. We attend to what we name and tend not to recognize or reflect on phenomena we leave unnamed. Spender (1984b) argues that not to name something is to deny it exists or matters, to negate it. The power of naming is clear with sexual harassment and date rape. Only recently has the term *sexual harassment* entered our language (Wise & Stanley, 1987). For most of history, sexual harassment occurred frequently, as later research showed (see Wood, 1992b, 1993f for a summary), but it was unnamed. Because it wasn't named, sexual harassment was not visible or salient, making it difficult to recognize, think about, or stop.

Why was sexual harassment not named for so long? Scholars suggest that the world is named by those who hold power, and what affects those people is what they notice and acknowledge with names (Kramarae, Thorne, & Henley, 1978; Spender, 1984a). Because men held (and still hold) the majority of power in

LISA

When we were talking about how naming makes us aware of things, it rang a bell for me. My first semester here I had a lab instructor who made me really uncomfortable. I was having trouble with some of the material, so I went to see him during office hours. He moved away from his desk and sat beside me. Then he sort of touched my arm and knee while I was trying to show him my work. I felt really bad. I kept trying to edge away, but he just moved too. Then he started cornering me after class and suggesting we get lunch together. I didn't know what to do. I wondered if I was doing something that made him think I was interested or maybe I was overreacting to him, but I just know I felt uncomfortable. Finally, one day he stopped me after class and told me that he might be able to help me with my grade if I would go out with him that weekend. And you know what? I still didn't understand what was happening. I knew I didn't want to date him, and I knew he could hurt my grade, but I didn't know it was sexual harassment. If that happened again today, I'd know what to call it, and I'd also know I could do something about it. So I understood the stuff about names being important.

professional life and because sexual harassment was rarely a problem for them, it was unnamed. If sexual harassment was discussed at all, it was with language that obscured its violation and ugliness (Wood, 1993f, 1994): "Making advances" and "being pushy" fail to convey the abusiveness of sexual harassment. Only when the term *sexual harassment* was coined did we call attention to the wrongness of unwanted behavior that objectifies and humiliates individuals and ties sexuality to security and advancement. And only with this awareness were efforts to redress sexual harassment devised.

Similarly, the term *date rape* did not exist a decade ago. Although a number of men forced their dates to have sex, there was no term to describe what occurred. Victims of date rape had no socially recognized way to name what happened to them. They had to deal with their experience without language that acknowledged a date could commit rape. Consequently, it was not much discussed, and victims were left without ways to define and think about arrant violations that had lifelong repercussions. Bereft of ways to define what happened, victims of date rape were handicapped in efforts to understand, much less resolve, their experiences. These two examples make clear the power of naming—it allows us to see more clearly what exists and to think about it in ways possible only with symbolic designation.

Verbal communication is a primary means by which cultural definitions of gender are expressed and sustained. By excluding women, defining them as exceptions to the male standard, or depicting them in terms of appearance and relationships, language reinforces cultural stereotypes of femininity. In defining men by their activities and achievements and not by their relationships, language fortifies the traditional view of men as independent, assertive agents.

Language Organizes Perceptions of Gender

A second implication of humans' symbolic nature is that we use language to organize experience and perceptions. Because language is abstract, not concrete, we can classify phenomena and think in terms of generalizations. Suzanne Langer (1979), one of the most influential philosophers of language, recognized that humans inevitably construct understandings by abstracting from their experiences and feelings. Calling symbols "vehicles for the conceptions of objects" (p. 60), Langer pointed out that symbols allow us to translate concrete sense data into symbolic forms, so that we may conceive and reflect on them. The organizing function of language expresses cultural views of gender by stereotyping men and women and by encouraging polarized perceptions of gender.

Stereotyping gender.   Because symbols are abstract, they allow us to think in general ways and to understand broad concepts like democracy, freedom, religion, and gender. While our ability to think in broad categories is useful in many ways, it is also the source of **stereotypes**, which sometimes misrepresent individuals. A stereotype is a broad generalization about an entire class of phenomena based on some knowledge of some aspects of some members of the class (Wood, 1992a, p. 70). When we stereotype, we use a general label to define specific members of a class. For example, on learning that a woman is lesbian, some people see her only in terms of her affectional preference—all else about her is unperceived, so her uniqueness is lost, as is an understanding of how she is like some heterosexuals and different from some other lesbians. As this example illustrates, relying on stereotypes may lead us to overlook important particularities of individuals and to perceive them only in terms of what we consider common to a general category.

Verbal communication groups men and women, masculine and feminine into broad stereotypical categories. Women are classified as emotional, while men are classified as rational; men are defined as strong, while women are stereotyped as physically weaker. Because cultural stereotypes promote these views of men and women, they restrict perceptions of others and of ourselves. For instance,

A L I C E

When I was 13 years old, I started having blackouts where I'd just shut down for a few minutes, although I stayed conscious. When I came out of the spells I wouldn't remember what happened, but others would tell me I had been babbling. My mother took me to a doctor, who said not to worry about it. He said it was normal for teenaged girls to be flighty and hysterical. He didn't do any tests or even examine me. He just told mother it would go away when I matured.

My mother was furious and called him an idiot. She then took me to another doctor and another, and they both agreed with the first one. She didn't buy it, and we kept making the rounds until we found one doctor who wanted to run some tests before making any diagnosis. He did a CAT scan, which showed that I had a rare form of epilepsy. It is a condition that develops in early adolescence and causes blackouts, sometimes with odd talking during them. He put me on a medicine that stopped them. But if we had listened to those other doctors, I wouldn't have been treated — except as a *normally* hysterical young girl.

women's arguments are sometimes dismissed as being emotional when, in fact, they entail evidence and reasoning. The stereotype that women are emotional provides a frame that may lead people to judge women's ideas in terms of the stereotype, not the reality. Similarly, a man who accepts the cultural view of masculinity may be unable to recognize, much less act on, strong emotions because they don't fit within his stereotype of what it means to be a man. Thinking of others stereotypically can cause us to misperceive them, which can have severe consequences.

Encouraging polarized thinking.   A second implication of language's organizing function is encouraging polarized thinking. Polarized, or dichotomous, thinking involves conceiving things as opposites. More than many languages, English emphasizes polarities. Something is right or wrong, good or bad, appropriate or inappropriate. Our vocabulary emphasizes all-or-none terms and includes few words that indicate degrees. This makes it difficult for us to think in terms of variation and range (Bem, 1993).

Polarized language and thought are particularly evident in how we think about gender: The world gets divided into two realms — one for males, the other for females. Then we are all expected to conform to the stereotyped molds or suffer the consequences of negative social judgments. Research indicates that women who use assertive speech associated with masculinity are judged as arrogant and uppity, while men who employ emotional language associated with femininity are often perceived to be wimps or gay (Rasmussen & Moley, 1986). Activities and feelings are either feminine or masculine. A man is what a woman is not; a woman is what a man is not. In truth, of course, most of us have a number of qualities, some of which our society designates as feminine and some of which it defines as masculine. Polarized thinking about gender encouraged by our language restricts us from realizing the full range of human possibilities. By being aware of the tendencies to stereotype and think in polar terms, we enhance our capacity to question and resist limiting conceptions of masculinity and femininity (Bem, 1993).

Language Evaluates Gender

Language is not neutral. It reflects cultural values and is a powerful influence on our perceptions. Related to gender, language expresses cultural devaluations of females and femininity. It does this by trivializing, deprecating, and diminishing women and things defined as feminine.

Women are often trivialized by language. They are frequently demeaned by metaphors that equate them with food (dish, feast for the eyes, good enough to eat, cheesecake, cookie, cupcake, hot tomato, honey pie) and animals (chick, pig, dog, cow, bitch). They are described as possessions (his wife, my secretary, or my girl). S. A. Basow (1992, p. 142) notes that accounts of how this country was settled include statements such as "Pioneers moved West, taking their wives and children with them." This description portrays only men as the pioneers and women and children as among the possessions the pioneers took along.

Women are also trivialized by descriptions that belittle their accomplishments or activities. For instance, not long ago on my campus, two administrators, one woman and one man, spoke out sharply against a particular proposal under consideration. The local newspaper reported that the male administrator "expressed deep concern and outrage," while the woman "was piqued." To label her reaction "piqued" is to imply it was frivolous, lightweight, or otherwise not to be taken seriously.

Women are also deprecated by language that devalues them. One researcher (Stanley, 1977) found 220 terms for sexually permissive women but only 22 for sexually promiscuous men. The disproportionate number of sexually insulting words that refer to women reflects society's negative views of women and their sexuality. Women are further deprecated when topics of particular importance to women are marginalized and treated as insignificant. Frequently, women newsmakers and issues that affect women are not covered or are buried in the leisure or life-style sections of newspapers ("Study Reports Sex Bias," 1989).

Third, women and what is feminine are diminished by language. This happens in a number of ways. Quite often, diminutive suffixes are used to designate

R A Y

> I really disagree about language being biased against women. I do think of women as soft and sweet and delicate, and that's how they ought to be. So it makes sense for me to call my girlfriend *muffin* and even things like *powder puff* sometimes. I want her to be that way—feminine. And I think of her as a girl too—she doesn't have to be as grown up as I do after all.

women as deviations from the standard form of the word: *actress, suffragette, majorette.* Calling women *girls* (a term that technically refers to a female who has not gone through puberty) diminishes them by defining them as children, not adults ("No Sexism, Please," 1991). Women's significance is also diminished by linguistic practices such as male generics.

Language Enables Hypothetical Thought

Particularly important to our thinking about gender is the fact that symbols allow hypothetical thought. Hypothetical thought concerns things that do not exist in the moment. Because symbols are abstract, they allow us to think about not just what is, but also what will or might be and what has been. In turn, this enables us to think of past, present, and future and to conceive of alternatives to current states of affairs. To understand the power of hypothetical thought, consider your own commitment to earning a college degree and launching a career. Although these ideas have no material basis in the actual world, they are real enough to you to motivate years of work.

Humans are the only life form that does not accept the world as it is (Cassirer, 1978; Wood, 1992a). We constantly imagine alternatives to what currently exists, which is why humans invent things (electricity, computers, refrigeration), devise systems (transportation, banking), and improve technology and medicine (immunizations, CAT scans). When we see a disease such as AIDS, we don't just accept it; instead, we imagine finding a cure and effective treatments. Our ability to name alternatives to what exists is the source of much progress in human life.

Hypothetical thought has been very influential in defining what gender means. As we saw in Chapter 4, many of the first-wave feminists envisioned the day when women could vote, attend universities, and own property. It was imagining these possibilities that inspired the courage and effort required to instigate changes in social views of women and activities appropriate for them. Years later in the second wave of feminism, many liberal feminists imagined laws that would prohibit sex discrimination on the job, and this idea motivated them to actions that made this a reality. Those involved with the backlash, too, rely on hypothetical thinking in their efforts to define gender. They recall former times when women were subservient, and they try to persuade others to reclaim that vision of womanhood. Whether pushing to move forward or backward in time, people engage in hypothetical thinking to define and work toward alternatives to prevailing views of genders.

Hypothetical thought is important in individuals' gender identity, as well as in rhetorical movements. Each of us has to decide what it means to be a woman or a man. We understand society's views and expectations, yet we are not compelled to accept those as given. Sometimes we challenge cultural definitions of gender and define our personal identities outside of culturally approved prescriptions. Imagine your ideals of women and men. What are they like? How might you realize them? In entertaining these questions, you are engaging in hypothetical thought, which gives you entry into possibilities for defining yourself that transcend those that have been defined within our society.

Language Allows Self-Reflection

This final implication of symbolic ability is especially relevant to thinking about our own gendered identities. Because we are symbol users, we name not only phenomena around us but also ourselves. We are able to self-reflect, a capacity that seems highly developed only in humans (Rosenberg, 1979). George Herbert Mead's insight into how we take the self-as-object, which we discussed in Chapter 3, allows us to stand outside of ourselves to describe, critique, and direct our activities.

If we don't like the self we see, we are able to change it—to alter how we act and how we define our identity (Wood, 1993b). We do this by combining our capacities to think hypothetically and to self-reflect. For instance, one alternative to traditional sex-typing is androgyny. The term **androgyny** comes from the Greek language. The Greek word *androgynos* combines the root word *aner*, which means man, with *gyne*, which means woman. Androgynous people identify with qualities the culture defines as masculine and feminine, instead of identifying with only those assigned to one sex. Androgynous women and men are, for example, both assertive and sensitive, both ambitious and compassionate (Bem & Bem, 1973; Bem, 1993).

Many people reflect on cultural views of gender and decide these don't really fit them well. They feel they are more flexible in attitudes and behaviors than is recognized by social definitions of gender, so they define themselves as androgynous. A number of women choose not to be as passive as the culture prescribes for femininity, and they work to be more assertive. Men also may decide to resist social prescriptions for masculinity by showing sensitivity and vulnerability in appropriate situations as well as strength and toughness in others. Researchers have explored the effects of resisting cultural prescriptions for gender. Findings suggest that androgynous women tend to be more healthy, adjusted, satisfied, and competent than their sex-typed sisters (Heilbrun, 1986; Heilbrun & Han, 1984). Research indicates that girls and women who defy gender prescriptions for passivity and dependence tend to become leaders and to have higher self-esteem than ones who conform to sex-typing (Hemmer & Kleiber, 1981).

It is less clear whether androgyny is as beneficial for men. Some investigations indicate that androgynous members of both sexes score higher on measures of self-esteem (Lamke, 1982), psychological development (Waterman & Whitbourne, 1982), personal adjustment (Jackson, 1983), and flexibility (Wheeless, 1984). All of these studies focus on personal and social effectiveness. When researchers examine behaviors and attitudes germane to professional and civic activities, however, androgynous females again are better off than sex-typed ones, but androgynous males do not appear to have an advantage over sex-typed males. For men, high scores on measures of adjustment and competence seem to result primarily from possession of traits regarded as masculine, rather than from any blend of masculine- and feminine-associated qualities (Hall & Taylor, 1985; Markstrom-Adams, 1989).

The mixed findings on the effects of androgyny make sense when we consider the differential value our culture places on masculinity and femininity. Because masculinity is esteemed by society, men may not benefit from adding qualities associated with femininity. On the other hand, incorporating masculine traits into their personal styles may advance women's effectiveness as well as their adjustment. They are adopting qualities regarded as masculine and, thus, ones more valued by society (Hall & Taylor, 1985; Miller, 1986; Mills & Bohannon, 1983). As you reflect on yourself and what gender means to you, androgyny is one alternative to conventional sex-typing that you might consider.

Language Is a Process

Before leaving our discussion of ways in which language reflects and shapes cultural views of gender, we should remind ourselves that communication and cultural understandings are processes. Both change over time. When existing language is inadequate to describe our experiences, we coin new words. Examples are *sexual harassment, date rape, Ms.,* and even the term *sexist language.* Language is not frozen but rather can be reformed to reflect and to reshape our understandings of gender. We are not prisoners of language—unless we choose to be.

In the first section of this chapter, we saw that language expresses cultural views of gender. It does so through its capacities to define, classify, evaluate, name alternatives to the status quo, and enable self-reflection. Language reflects the gender assumptions and prescriptions of society, yet language is not static. It changes, and we may choose to reform prevailing language if we believe it contributes to distorted perceptions and gender discrimination. We become more effective communicators and more empowered people when we recognize ways in which language influences perceptions of masculinity and femininity. With awareness come choice and the possibility of defining your identity in ways that reflect your own needs and values. Awareness and choice also enable us to participate in social change.

Gendered Interaction: Masculine and Feminine Styles of Verbal Communication

Language not only expresses cultural views of gender but also constitutes individuals' gender identities. The communication practices we use define us as masculine or feminine; in large measure, we create our own gender through talk. Because language constitutes masculinity and femininity, we should find generalizable differences in how women and men communicate. Research bears out this expectation by documenting rather systematic differences in the ways men and women typically use language. You probably don't need a textbook to tell you this, since your own interactions may have given you ample evidence of differences in how women and men talk.

What may not be clear from your own experiences, however, is exactly what those differences are and what they imply. If you are like most people, you've sometimes felt uncomfortable or misunderstood or mystified in communication with members of the other sex, but you've not been able to put your finger on what was causing the difficulty. In the pages that follow, we'll try to gain greater insight into masculine and feminine styles of speech and some of the confusion that results from differences between them. We want to understand how each style evolves, what it involves, and how to interpret verbal communication in ways that honor the motives of those using it.

Gendered Speech Communities

Writing in the 1940s, Suzanne Langer introduced the idea of "discourse communities." Like George Herbert Mead, she asserted that culture, or collective life, is possible only to the extent that a group of people share a symbol system and the meanings encapsulated in it. This theme recurred in Langer's philosophical writings over the course of her life (1953, 1979). Her germinal insights into discourse communities prefigured later interest in the ways in which language creates individual identity and sustains cultural life. Since the early 1970s, scholars have studied **speech communities,** or cultures. William Labov (1972, p. 121) extended Langer's ideas by defining a speech community as existing when a group of people share a set of norms regarding communicative practices. By this he meant that a communication culture exists when people share understandings about goals of communication, strategies for enacting those goals, and ways of interpreting communication.

It's obvious we have entered a different communication culture when we travel to non-English-speaking countries, because the language differs from our own. Distinct speech communities are less apparent when they use the same language that we do, but use it in different ways and to achieve different goals. The communication culture of African-Americans who have not adopted the dominant pattern of North American speech, for instance, relies on English yet departs in interesting and patterned ways from the communication of middle-class white North Americans. The fact that diverse groups of people develop distinctive communication patterns reminds us again of the constant interaction of communication and culture. As we have already seen, the standpoint we occupy in society influences what we know and how we act. We now see that this basic tenet of standpoint theory also implies that communication styles evolve out of different standpoints.

Studies of gender and communication (Campbell, 1973; Coates, 1986; Coates & Cameron, 1989; Hall & Langellier, 1988; Kramarae, 1981; Lakoff, 1975; Tannen, 1990a, 1990b) have convincingly shown that in many ways women and men operate from dissimilar assumptions about the goals and strategies of communication. F. L. Johnson (1989), in fact, asserts that men and women live in two different worlds and that this is evident in the disparate forms of communication they use. Given this, it seems appropriate to consider masculine and feminine styles of communicating as embodying two distinct speech communities. To understand these different communities and the validity of each, we will first consider how we are socialized into feminine and masculine speech communities. After this, we will explore divergencies in how women and men typically communicate. Please note the importance of the word *typically* and others that indicate we are discussing generalizable differences, not absolute ones. Some women are not socialized into feminine speech, or they are and later reject it; likewise, some men do not learn or choose not to adopt a masculine style of communication. What follows describes gendered speech communities into which *most* women and men are socialized.

The Lessons of Childplay

We've seen that socialization is a gendered process in which boys and girls are encouraged to develop masculine and feminine identities. Extending that understanding, we now explore how socialization creates gendered speech communities. One way to gain insight into how boys and girls learn norms of communication is to observe young children at play. In interactions with peers, boys and girls learn how to talk and how to interpret what each other says; they discover how to signal their intentions with words and how to respond appropriately to others' communication; and they learn codes to demonstrate involvement and interest (Tannen, 1990a). In short, interacting with peers teaches children rules of communication.

Initial insight into the importance of children's play in shaping patterns of communication came from a classic study by D. N. Maltz and R. Borker (1982). As they watched young children engaged in recreation, the researchers were struck by two observations: Young children almost always play in sex-segregated groups, and girls and boys tend to play different kinds of games. Maltz and Borker found that boys' games (football, baseball) and girls' games (school, house, jumprope) cultivate distinct understandings of communication and the rules by which it operates.

Boys' games.   Boys' games usually involve fairly large groups — nine individuals for each baseball team, for instance. Most boys' games are competitive, have clear goals, and are organized by rules and roles that specify who does what and how to play. Because these games are structured by goals, rules, and roles, there is little need to discuss how to play, although there may be talk about strategies to reach goals. Maltz and Borker realized that in boys' games, an individual's status depends on standing out, being better, and often dominating other players. From these games, boys learn how to interact in their communities. Specifically, boys' games cultivate three communication rules:

1. Use communication to assert yourself and your ideas; use talk to achieve something.
2. Use communication to attract and maintain an audience.
3. Use communication to compete with others for the "talk stage," so that they don't gain more attention than you; learn to wrest the focus from others and onto yourself.

These communication rules are consistent with other aspects of masculine socialization that we have already discussed. For instance, notice the emphasis on individuality and competition. Also, we see that these rules accent achievement — doing something, accomplishing a goal. Boys learn they must *do things* to be valued members of the team. It's also the case that intensely close, personal relationships are unlikely to be formed in large groups. Finally, we see the undercurrent of masculinity's emphasis on being invulnerable and guarded: If others

ALAN

I got the message about not letting other guys beat me when I was just 10. Every day on my way home from school, this other boy who was 4 or 5 years older would wait for me so that he could beat on me. I got tired of this, so I talked to my dad about it, hoping he'd help me. But he just lit into me some kind of bad. He told me not to ever, ever come to him again saying some other guy was beating up on me. He told me if that guy came after me again, I should fight back and use something to hit him if I had to.

Sure enough, the next day that dude was waiting for me. When he hit me, I picked up the nearest thing—a two-by-four on the ground—and hit him on the head. Well, he had to go to the hospital, but my dad said that was okay because his son had been a man.

are the competition from whom you must seize center stage, then you cannot let them know too much about yourself and your weaknesses.

Girls' games.   Turning now to girls' games, we find that quite different patterns exist, and they lead to distinctive understandings of communication. Girls tend to play in pairs or in very small groups rather than large ones. Also, games like house and school do not have preset, clear-cut goals, rules, and roles. There is no analogy for the touchdown in playing house. Because girls' games are not structured externally, players have to talk among themselves to decide what they're doing and what roles they have. Playing house, for instance, typically begins with a discussion about who is going to be the daddy and who the mommy. This is typical of the patterns girls use to generate rules and roles for their games. The lack of stipulated goals for the games is also important, since it tends to cultivate in girls an interest in the process of interaction more than its products. For their games to work, girls have to cooperate and work out problems by talking: No external rules exist to settle disputes. From these games, Maltz and Borker noted, girls learn normative communication patterns of their speech communities. Specifically, girls' games teach three basic rules for communication:

1. Use collaborative, cooperative talk to create and maintain relationships. The *process* of communication, not its content, is the heart of relationships.

2. Avoid criticizing, outdoing, or putting others down; if criticism is necessary, make it gentle; never exclude others.

3. Pay attention to others and to relationships; interpret and respond to others' feelings sensitively.

These basic understandings of communication echo and reinforce other aspects of feminine socialization. Girls' games stress cooperation, collaboration, and sensitivity to others' feelings. Also notice the focus on process encouraged in girls' games. Rather than interacting to achieve some outcome, girls learn that communication itself is the goal. Whereas boys learn they have to do something to be valuable, the lesson for girls is *to be*. Their worth depends on being good people, which is defined by being cooperative, inclusive, and sensitive. The lessons of child's play are carried forward. In fact, the basic rules of communication that adult women and men employ turn out to be only refined and elaborated versions of the very same ones evident in girls' and boys' childhood games.

Gendered Communication Practices

In her popular book, *You Just Don't Understand: Women and Men in Communication*, linguist Deborah Tannen (1990b, p. 42) declares that "communication between men and women can be like cross cultural communication, prey to a clash of conversational styles." Her study of men's and women's talk led her to identify distinctions between the speech communities typical of women and men. Not surprisingly, Tannen traces gendered communication patterns to differences in boys' and girls' communication with parents and peers. Like other scholars (Bate, 1988; Hall & Langellier, 1988; Kramarae, 1981; Treichler & Kramarae, 1983; Wood, 1993a), Tannen believes that women and men typically engage in distinctive styles of communication with different purposes, rules, and understandings of how to interpret talk. We will consider features of women's and men's speech identified by a number of researchers. As we do, we will discover some of the complications that arise when men and women operate by different rules in conversations with each other.

Women's speech. For most women, communication is a primary way to establish and maintain relationships with others. They engage in conversation to share themselves and to learn about others. This is an important point: For women, talk *is* the essence of relationships. Consistent with this primary goal, women's speech tends to display identifiable features that foster connections, support, closeness, and understanding.

Equality between people is generally important in women's communication (Aries, 1987). To achieve symmetry, women often match experiences to indicate "You're not alone in how you feel." Typical ways to communicate equality would be saying, "I've done the same thing many times," "I've felt the same way," or "Something like that happened to me too and I felt like you do." Growing out of the quest for equality is a participatory mode of interaction in which communicators respond to and build on each other's ideas in the process of conversing (Hall & Langellier, 1988). Rather than a rigid you-tell-your-ideas-then-I'll-tell-mine sequence, women's speech more characteristically follows an interactive pattern in which different voices weave together to create conversations.

Also important in women's speech is showing support for others. To demonstrate support, women often express understanding and sympathy with a friend's situation or feelings. "Oh, you must feel terrible," "I really hear what you are saying," or "I think you did the right thing" are communicative clues that we understand and support how another feels. Related to these first two features is women's typical attention to the relationship level of communication (Wood, 1993a, 1993b; Wood & Inman, 1993). You will recall that the relationship level of talk focuses on feelings and the relationship between communicators rather than on the content of messages. In conversations between women, it is common to hear a number of questions that probe for greater understanding of feelings and perceptions surrounding the subject of talk (Beck, 1988, p. 104; Tannen, 1990b). "Tell me more about what happened," "How did you feel when it occurred?" "Do you think it was deliberate?" "How does this fit into the overall relationship?" are probes that help a listener understand a speaker's perspective. The content of talk is dealt with, but usually not without serious attention to the feelings involved.

A fourth feature of women's speech style is conversational "maintenance work" (Beck, 1988; Fishman, 1978). This involves efforts to sustain conversation by inviting others to speak and by prompting them to elaborate their experiences. Women, for instance, ask a number of questions that initiate topics for others: "How was your day?" "Tell me about your meeting," "Did anything interesting happen on your trip?" "What do you think of the candidates this year?" Communication of this sort opens the conversational door to others and maintains interaction.

Inclusivity also surfaces in a fifth quality of women's talk, which is responsiveness (Beck, 1988; Tannen, 1990a, 1990b; Wood, 1993a). Women usually respond in some fashion to what others say. A woman might say "Tell me more" or "That's interesting"; perhaps she will nod and use eye contact to signal she is engaged; perhaps she will ask a question such as "Can you explain what you mean?" Responsiveness reflects learned tendencies to care about others and to make them feel valued and included (Kemper, 1984; Lakoff, 1975). It affirms another person and encourages elaboration by showing interest in what was said.

A sixth quality of women's talk is personal, concrete style (Campbell, 1973; Hall & Langellier, 1988; Tannen, 1990b). Typical of women's conversation are details, personal disclosures, anecdotes, and concrete reasoning. These features cultivate a personal tone in women's communication, and they facilitate feelings of closeness by connecting communicators' lives. The detailed, concrete emphasis prevalent in women's talk also clarifies issues and feelings so that communicators are able to understand and identify with each other. Thus, the personal character of much of women's interaction sustains interpersonal closeness.

A final feature of women's speech is tentativeness. This may be expressed in a number of forms. Sometimes women use verbal hedges such as "I kind of feel you may be overreacting." In other situations they qualify statements by saying "I'm probably not the best judge of this, but . . ." Another way to keep talk provisional is to tag a question onto a statement in a way that invites another to respond: "That was a pretty good movie, wasn't it?" "We should get out this weekend, don't you think?" Tentative communication leaves open the door for others to respond and express their opinions.

There has been controversy about tentativeness in women's speech. R. Lakoff (1975), who first noted that women use more hedges, qualifiers, and tag questions than men, claimed these represent lack of confidence and uncertainty. Calling women's speech powerless, Lakoff argued that it reflects women's socialization into subordinate roles and low self-esteem. Since Lakoff's work, however, other scholars (Bate, 1988; Wood & Lenze, 1991b) have suggested different explanations of women's tentative style of speaking. Dale Spender (1984a), in particular, points out that Lakoff's judgments of the inferiority of women's speech were based on using male speech as the standard, which does not recognize the distinctive validity of different speech communities. Rather than reflecting powerlessness, the use of hedges, qualifiers, and tag questions may express women's desires to keep conversation open and to include others. It is much easier to jump into a conversation that has not been sealed with absolute, firm statements. A tentative style of speaking supports women's general desire to create equality and include others. It is important to realize, however, that people outside of women's speech community may misinterpret women's intentions in using tentative communication.

Men's speech. Masculine speech communities define the goals of talk as exerting control, preserving independence, and enhancing status. Conversation is an arena for proving oneself and negotiating prestige. This leads to two general tendencies in men's communication. First, men often use talk to establish and defend their personal status and their ideas, by asserting themselves and/or by challenging others. Second, when they wish to comfort or support another, they typically do so by respecting the other's independence and avoiding communication they regard as condescending (Tannen, 1990b). These tendencies will be more clear as we review specific features of masculine talk.

To establish their own status and value, men often speak to exhibit knowledge, skill, or ability. Equally typical is the tendency to avoid disclosing personal information that might make a man appear weak or vulnerable (Derlega & Chaiken, 1976; Lewis & McCarthy, 1988; Saurer & Eisler, 1990). For instance, if someone expresses concern about a relationship with a boyfriend, a man might say "The way you should handle that is . . . ," "Don't let him get to you," or "You ought to just tell him . . ." This illustrates the tendency to give advice that Tannen reports is common in men's speech. On the relationship level of communication, giving advice does two things. First, it focuses on instrumental activity—what another should do or be—and does not acknowledge feelings. Second, it expresses superiority and maintains control. It says "I know what you should do" or "I would know how to handle that." The message may be perceived as implying the speaker is superior to the other person. Between men, advice giving seems understood as a give-and-take, but it may be interpreted as unfeeling and condescending by women whose rules for communicating differ.

A second prominent feature of men's talk is instrumentality—the use of speech to accomplish instrumental objectives. As we have seen, men are socialized to do things, achieve goals (Bellinger & Gleason, 1982). In conversation, this is often expressed through problem-solving efforts that focus on getting information, discovering facts, and suggesting solutions. Again, between men this is usually a comfortable orientation, since both speakers have typically been socialized to value instrumentality. However, conversations between women and men are often derailed by the lack of agreement on what this informational, instrumental focus means. To many women it feels as if men don't care about their feelings. When a man focuses on the content level of meaning after a woman has disclosed a problem, she may feel he is disregarding her emotions and concerns. He, on the other hand, may well be trying to support her in the way that he has learned to show support—suggesting ways to solve the problem.

A third feature of men's communication is conversational dominance. Despite jokes about women's talkativeness, research indicates that in most contexts, men not only hold their own but dominate the conversation. This tendency, although not present in infancy, is evident in preschoolers (Austin, Salehi, & Leffler, 1987). Compared with girls and women, boys and men talk more frequently (Eakins & Eakins, 1976; Thorne & Henley, 1975) and for longer periods of time (Aries, 1987; Eakins & Eakins, 1976; Kramarae, 1981; Thorne & Henley, 1975). Further, men engage in other verbal behaviors that sustain conversational dominance. They may reroute conversations by using what another said as a jump-off point for their own topic, or they may interrupt. While both sexes engage in interruptions, most research suggests that men do it more frequently (Beck, 1988; Mulac, Wiemann, Widenmann, & Gibson, 1988; West & Zimmerman, 1983). Not only do men seem to interrupt more than women, but they do so for different reasons. L. P. Stewart and her colleagues (1990, p. 51) suggest that men use interruptions to control conversation by challenging other speakers or wresting the talk stage from them, while women interrupt to indicate interest and to respond. This interpretation is shared by a number of scholars who note that women use interruptions to show support, encourage elaboration, and affirm others (Aleguire, 1978; Aries, 1987; Mulac et al., 1988).

Fourth, men tend to express themselves in fairly absolute, assertive ways. Compared with women, their language is typically more forceful, direct, and authoritative (Beck, 1988; Eakins & Eakins, 1978; Stewart et al., 1990; Tannen, 1990a, 1990b). Tentative speech such as hedges and disclaimers is used less frequently by men than by women. This is consistent with gender socialization in which men learn to use talk to assert themselves and to take and hold positions. However, when another person does not share that understanding of communication, speech that is absolute and directive may seem to close off conversation and leave no room for others to speak.

Fifth, compared with women, men communicate more abstractly. They frequently speak in general terms that are removed from concrete experiences and distanced from personal feelings (Schaef, 1981; Treichler & Kramarae, 1983). The abstract style typical of men's speech reflects the public and impersonal contexts in which they often operate and the less personal emphasis in their speech communities. Within public environments, norms for speaking call for theoretical, conceptual, and general thought and communication. Yet, within more personal relationships, abstract talk sometimes creates barriers to knowing another intimately.

Finally, men's speech tends not to be highly responsive, especially not on the relationship level of communication (Beck, 1988; Wood, 1993a). Men, more than women, give what are called "minimal response cues" (Parlee, 1979), which are verbalizations such as "yeah" or "umhmm." In interaction with women, who have learned to demonstrate interest more vigorously, minimal response cues generally inhibit conversation because they are perceived as indicating lack of involvement (Fishman, 1978; Stewart et al., 1990). Another way in which men's conversation is generally less relationally responsive than women's is lack of expressed sympathy and understanding and lack of self-disclosures (Saurer & Eisler, 1990). Within the rules of men's speech communities, sympathy is a sign of condescension, and revealing personal problems is seen as making one vulnerable. Yet women's speech rules count sympathy and disclosure as demonstrations of equality and support. This creates potential for misunderstanding between women and men.

Misinterpretations Between Women and Men

In this final section, we explore what happens when men and women talk, each operating out of a distinctive speech community. In describing features typical of each gender's talk, we already have noted differences that provide fertile ground for misunderstandings. We now consider several examples of recurrent misreadings between women and men.

Showing support.   The scene is a private conversation between Martha and George. She tells him she is worried about her friend. George gives a minimum response cue, saying only "Oh." To Martha this suggests he isn't interested, since women make and expect more of what D. Tannen (1986) calls "listening noises" to signal interest. Yet, as Tannen (1986, 1990b) and A. Beck (1988) note, George is probably thinking if she wants to tell him something she will, since his rules of speech emphasize using talk to assert oneself (Bellinger & Gleason, 1982). Even without much encouragement, Martha continues by describing the tension in her friend's marriage and her own concern about how she can help. She says, "I feel so bad for Barbara, and I want to help her, but I don't know what to do." George then says, "It's their problem, not yours. Just butt out and let them settle their own relationship." At this, Martha explodes: "Who asked for your advice?" George is now completely frustrated and confused. He thought Martha wanted advice, so he gave it. She is hurt that George didn't tune into her feelings and comfort her about her worries. Each is annoyed and unhappy.

The problem here is not so much what George and Martha say and don't say. Rather, it's how they interpret each other's communication—actually, how they *misinterpret* it, because each relies on rules that are not familiar to the other. They fail to understand that each is operating by different rules of talk. George is respecting Martha's independence by not pushing her to talk. When he thinks she directly requests advice, he offers it in an effort to help. Martha, on the other hand, wants comfort and a connection with George—that is her purpose in talking with him. She finds his advice unwelcome and dismissive of her feelings. He doesn't offer sympathy, because his rules for communication define this as condescending. Yet within Martha's speech community, not to show sympathy is to be unfeeling and unresponsive.

"Troubles talk."   Tannen (1990b) identifies talk about troubles, or personal problems, as a kind of interaction in which hurt feelings may result from the contrast between most men's and women's rules of communication. A woman might tell her partner that she is feeling down because she did not get a job she wanted. In an effort to be supportive, he might respond by saying, "You shouldn't feel bad. Lots of people don't get jobs they want." To her this seems to dismiss her feelings—to belittle them by saying lots of people experience her situation. Yet within masculine speech communities, this is a way of showing respect for another by not assuming that she or he needs sympathy.

Now let's turn the tables and see what happens when a man feels troubled. When he meets Nancy, Craig is unusually quiet because he feels down about not getting a job offer. Sensing that something is wrong, Nancy tries to show interest

J A Y

Finally I understand this thing that keeps happening between my girlfriend and me. She is always worrying about something or feeling bad about what's happening with one of her friends. I've been trying to be supportive by telling her things like she shouldn't worry, or not to let it get her down, or not to obsess about other people's problems. I was trying to help her feel better. That's what guys do for each other — kind of distract our attention from problems. But Teresa just gets all huffy and angry when I do that. She tells me to stuff my advice and says if I cared about her I would show more concern. Finally, it makes sense. Well, sort of, but I still think the rules she uses are strange.

by asking, "Are you okay? What's bothering you?" Craig feels she is imposing and trying to get him to show a vulnerability he prefers to keep to himself. Nancy probes further to show she cares. As a result, he feels intruded on and withdraws further. Then Nancy feels shut out.

But perhaps Craig does decide to tell Nancy why he feels down. After hearing about his rejection letter, Nancy says, "I know how you feel. I felt so low when I didn't get that position at Datanet." She is matching experiences to show Craig that she understands his feelings and that he's not alone. Within his communication rules, however, this is demeaning his situation by focusing on her, not him. When Nancy mentions her own experience, Craig thinks she is trying to steal the center stage for herself. Within his speech community, that is one way men vie for dominance and attention. Yet Nancy has learned to share similar experiences as a way to build connections with others.

The point of the story.   Another instance in which feminine and masculine communication rules often clash and cause problems is in relating experiences. Typically, men have learned to speak in a linear manner in which they move sequentially through major points in a story to get to the climax. Their talk tends to be straightforward without a great many details. The rules of feminine speech, however, call for more detailed and less linear storytelling. Whereas a man is likely to provide rather bare information about what happened, a woman is more likely to embed the information within a larger context of the people involved and other things going on. Women include details not because all of the specifics are important in themselves but because recounting them shows involvement and allows a conversational partner to be more fully part of the situation being described.

Because feminine and masculine rules about details differ, men often find women's way of telling stories wandering and unfocused. Conversely, men's style of storytelling may strike women as leaving out all of the interesting details. Many a discussion between women and men has ended either with his exasperated demand, "Can't you get to the point?" or with her frustrated question, "Why don't you tell me how you were feeling and what else was going on?" She wants more details than his rules call for; he is interested in fewer details than she has learned to supply.

Relationship talk.   "Can we talk about us?" is the opening of innumerable conversations that end in misunderstanding and hurt. As Tannen (1986) noted in an earlier book, *That's Not What I Meant*, men and women tend to have very different ideas about what it means to talk about relationships. In general, men are inclined to think a relationship is going fine as long as there is no need to talk about it. They are interested in discussing the relationship only if there are particular problems to be addressed. In contrast, women generally think a relationship is working well as long as they can talk about it with partners. The difference here grows out of the fact that men tend to use communication to do things and solve problems, while women generally regard the *process* of communicating as a primary way to create and sustain relationships with others. For many women, conversation is a way to be with another person — to affirm and enhance closeness. Men's different rules stipulate that communication is to achieve some goal or fix some problem. No wonder men often duck when their partners want to "discuss the relationship," and women often feel a relationship is in trouble when their partners are unwilling to talk about it.

These are only four of many situations in which feminine and masculine rules of communication may collide and cause problems. Women learn to use talk to build and sustain connections with others. Men learn that talk is to convey information and establish status. Given these distinct starting points, it's not surprising that women and men often find themselves locked into misunderstandings.

Interestingly, research (Sollie & Fischer, 1985) suggests that women and men who are androgynous are more flexible communicators, who are able to engage comfortably in both masculine and feminine styles of speech. The breadth of their communicative competence enhances the range of situations in which they can be effective in achieving various goals. On learning about different speech rules, many couples find they can improve their communication. Each partner has become bilingual, and so communication between them is smoother and more satisfying. When partners understand how to interpret each other's rules, they are less likely to misread motives. In addition, they learn how to speak the other's language, which means women and men become more gratifying conversational partners for each other, and they can enhance the quality of their relationships.

Summary

In this chapter, we have explored a range of ways in which verbal communication intersects with gender and culture. The first focus we pursued highlighted how language reflects and sustains cultural views of masculinity and femininity. By defining, classifying, and evaluating gender, language reinforces social views of men as the standard and women as marginal and men and masculinity as more valuable than women and femininity. From generic male terms to language that demeans and diminishes women, verbal communication is a powerful agent of cultural expression. We also saw, however, that symbolic abilities allow us to think hypothetically and, therefore, to imagine alternatives to existing patterns of meaning. In addition, the self-reflexivity promoted by our symbolic capacity invites us to examine critically how we have defined masculinity and femininity in general and our own gender identities in particular. We have the capacity to revise cultural perspectives through the language we use and the identities we express in our own communication.

The second theme of this chapter was that women and men constitute their gender identities through their styles of communication. Because males and females tend to be socialized into distinct speech communities, they learn different rules about the purposes of communication and ways to indicate support, interest, and involvement. Because women and men have some dissimilar rules for talk, they often misread each other's meanings and misunderstand each other's motives. This frequently leads to frustration, hurt, and tension between people who care about each other. Appreciating and respecting the distinctive validity of each style of communication is a foundation for better understanding between people. Further, learning to use different styles of communication allows women and men to be more flexible and effective in their interactions with each other.

Discussion Questions

1. How important is language in influencing how we think about gender in general and our own gender identity in particular? For instance, do you think inclusive language (*he or she, mail carrier*) is important and should be used? Why?

2. Read several newspapers and gather examples of differences in how language describes women and men. Do you find examples of women being described by appearance, marital status, and family life? Are such descriptions pertinent to why they are featured in news stories?

3. Think about naming, specifically about naming yourself. If you are a woman, do you plan to keep your name if you marry? If you are a man, do you expect (or want) your partner to change hers? Would you consider adopting her name instead? What do conventions governing women's names tell us about cultural views of gender?

4. The chapter discusses the importance of naming in making us aware of phenomena. For instance, *date rape* and *sexual harassment* are relatively new terms that call to our attention activities that historically were not noticed or regarded as noteworthy. Are there other phenomena today that need naming? For what gender issues do we not have terms? For instance, does existing language provide us with a way to describe women who have been independently successful and acted autonomously and then enter roles that link them to men? Hillary Rodham Clinton is a good example of this. Do we need a term for this? What other gender issues are not yet named?

5. What do you think of the concept of androgyny? Do you think it is desirable for women, for men, for both? Why or why not? With which aspects of your gender identity are you satisfied and dissatisfied? What are you doing to alter aspects of your gender identity that you find confining or inappropriate for you personally?

6. Think back to your childhood games. Which games did you play? What rules for using talk were implicitly promoted in the games you tended to play? Do you see how engaging in childhood activities may have affected your style of verbal communication?

7. Did reading this chapter give you any insights into difficulties and misunderstandings you may have experienced when talking with the other gender? Are you able to identify ways in which your assumptions about how to talk with others reflect the gender culture into which you were socialized?

8. Now that you have a clearer understanding of general differences in the genders' verbal styles, what are you going to do about it? How will what you've learned affect how you communicate and how you interpret others' communication?

9. Try to follow the rules of talk generally *not* typical for your gender. Can you develop proficiency in another style of talking? How might enlarging your communication repertoire affect your relationships?

10. The next time you have a conversation in which you feel that gendered rules of talk are creating misunderstandings, try to translate your expectations to the person with whom you are talking. For instance, if you are a woman talking with a man about a problem, he might try to help by offering advice. Instead of being frustrated by his lack of attention to your feelings, try saying to him, "I appreciate your suggestions of what I might do, but I'm not ready to think about how to fix things yet. It would be more helpful to me if you'd help me work through my feelings about this issue." Discuss what happens when you explain what you need or want from others.

$\mathcal{G}$endered Nonverbal Communication

In this chapter, we continue to explore relationships among communication, gender, and culture. Whereas in Chapter 5 we focused on verbal communication, we now turn our attention to nonverbal behavior. The nonverbal dimension of communication is extensive and important. Some scholars, in fact, consider it more significant than verbal language, since our nonverbal behaviors are estimated to carry from 65% (Birdwhistell, 1970) to 93% (Mehrabian, 1981) of the total meaning of communication. Like language, nonverbal communication is related to gender and culture in two ways: It expresses cultural meanings of gender, and men and women construct their gender identities through differences in their nonverbal communication. In this chapter, we will consider some of the ways in which nonverbal behaviors express and sustain meanings of gender in our society.

Nonverbal communication consists of all elements of communication other than words themselves. It includes not only visual cues (gestures, appearances) but also vocal features (inflection, volume, pitch) and environmental factors (use of space, position) that affect meanings. Like language, nonverbal communication is learned through interaction with others. Also like verbal communication, nonverbal behaviors reflect and reinforce social views of gender and encourage individuals to embody them in distinctive feminine and masculine styles. As we will see, nonverbal communication frequently reinforces cultural views of women as passive, affiliative, decorative, and responsive and of men as active, aggressive, dominant, and independent. We will identify functions and types of nonverbal communication and then concentrate on gender-differentiated patterns of nonverbal communication to understand how cultural views of masculinity and femininity are embodied in the nonverbal styles of men and women.

▄▄ Functions of Nonverbal Communication

Researchers who have studied nonverbal communication identify a number of functions it serves. It supplements verbal communication, regulates interaction, and conveys the bulk of the relationship level of meaning in interaction. In each of these areas there are some consistent gender differences.

Nonverbal Communication Supplements Verbal Communication

Two communication scholars (Malandro & Barker, 1983) identified five ways in which nonverbal behaviors interact with verbal messages to influence meanings. First, nonverbal communication may *repeat* words, as when you say "right" while pointing to the right. Second, we may nonverbally *contradict* a verbal message. For example, the statement "I'm fine" would be contradicted if a speaker were trembling and on the verge of tears. Nonverbal behavior may also *complement* or augment verbal communication by underlining a verbal message. The statement "I never want to see you again" is more forceful if accompanied by a frown and a threatening glare. Fourth, sometimes we use nonverbal behaviors to *replace* verbal ones. Rather than saying "I don't know," you could shrug your shoulders. Finally, nonverbal communication may *highlight* or accent verbal messages, telling us which parts are important. "I love *you*" means something different than "*I* love you" or "I *love* you," because different words are emphasized with cues of volume and inflection.

Because masculine socialization emphasizes self-assertion and dominance, we would expect men to use more nonverbal behaviors than women to complement, repeat, and highlight their verbal messages. This increases the visibility and force of what they say. Instruction in femininity highlights relationships, deference, and expressiveness, so women specialize in nonverbal functions such as complementing and highlighting that add personal emphasis and feeling to their communication. Each of these functions adds meaning to the verbal messages.

Nonverbal Communication Regulates Interaction

Malandro and Barker (1983) also pointed out that nonverbal communication regulates verbal interaction. We use body posture and especially eye contact to signal others that we wish to speak or that we are through speaking (Eckman, Friesen, & Ellsworth, 1971). Whereas women frequently use nonverbal signals to invite others into conversation, men more frequently use them to discourage others from speaking. For instance, if a man does not maintain eye contact with a woman who is talking, she is likely to perceive him as uninterested, and she may cease talking. Similarly, we signal others that we want to hear from them by looking their way. In classrooms, raised hands announce a desire to talk, and averted gazes are often silent requests that teachers not call on people.

Nonverbal Communication Establishes the Relationship Level of Meaning

A final and particularly important function of nonverbal communication is to convey relationship levels of meaning that define identities and relationships between communicators. While words may disguise feelings, we tend to believe that nonverbal behaviors reveal inner feelings, attitudes, and emotions. As Aino Sallinen-Kuparinen (1992, p. 163) noted in a recent review, "Nonverbal communication is a relationship language." In most cases, the overall feeling or style of relationships is expressed nonverbally (Burgoon, Buller, Hale, & deTurck, 1989; Sallinen-Kuparinen, 1992). The relationship function of nonverbal behavior is particularly germane to gender, since women and men in general differ in the relationship messages they communicate. Three primary dimensions of relationship level communication are responsiveness, liking, and power (Mehrabian, 1981), each of which is linked to gender.

Responsiveness. The first dimension of the relationship level meaning in communication refers to how aware of and responsive to others we seem. Nonverbal cues of responsiveness include lively gestures, inflection, eye contact, and attentive body posture (Mehrabian, 1981). Responsiveness conveys interest and involvement, so it's not surprising that it is part of the relationship level of communication. You are probably familiar with the importance of responsiveness in your role as a student. Jon Nussbaum (1992, p. 175) reports that students learn more when they have teachers who use nonverbal responsiveness behaviors such as vocal expressiveness, relaxed body posture, eye contact, and smiling.

Both women and men display responsiveness, yet they do so in rather distinctive ways. Socialized to be affiliative, women tend to engage in responsive nonverbal communication that indicates engagement with others, emotional involvement, and empathy. Men, on the other hand, are socialized to focus on status and power, and this is mirrored in their nonverbal responsiveness. More than women, men use gestures and space to command attention and vocal inflection and volume to increase the strength of their ideas and positions (Frieze & Ramsey, 1976; Hall, 1987; Major, Schmidlin, & Williams, 1990).

There are also general differences in how expressively men and women respond to others. Women tend to be more expressive of emotions than men, a finding that reflects socialization that promotes this in women and curbs it in men. Men are encouraged to assert themselves, while women are taught to react, listen, and respond (LaFrance & Mayo, 1979; Markel, Long, & Saine, 1976). Brenda Ueland (1992, pp. 106–107) observes that women have developed skill at listening, while men "lose it because of their long habit of striving in business, of self-assertion. And the more forceful men are, the less they can listen."

By extension, women are expected to respond expressively to others. Smiling sends the message "I am approachable, interested, friendly," which conforms to cultural ideals of femininity. This is less evident in African-American women, who generally don't smile as much as Caucasian women. Similarly, attentive eye contact is practiced less by many African-American women than by Caucasian women (Halberstadt & Saitta, 1987), reminding us that the meaning of femininity is constructed and varies among diverse groups. In general, if a white woman does not smile and maintain eye contact, others are likely to think something is wrong with her; conversely, a man who *does* smile a lot and look steadily at others may be suspect (Chesler, 1972; Henley, 1977). So ingrained is gender socialization that women find it difficult not to smile, even when they deliberately try to refrain.

Women not only tend to display feelings more clearly but also seem to be more skilled than men at interpreting others' emotions. Consistently, researchers (Hall, 1978; Rosenthal, Archer, DiMatteo, Koivumaki, & Rogers, 1974) report that females exceed males in the capacity to decode nonverbal behaviors and more accurately discern others' emotions.

Perhaps you are wondering why this is so. The same question occurred to a number of scholars, whose investigations yield two explanations. One hypothesis is that women are socialized to be more attentive to feelings. Beginning with birth, most females are encouraged to be sensitive to others and to relationships. In addition, there may be some physiological influence, since the right hemisphere of the brain in which women specialize is used to interpret emotions (Saxby & Bryden, 1985). It makes sense that this focus of feminine socialization would teach women how to read others' emotions (Noller, 1986; Rosenthal & DePaulo, 1979). Further, as R. Buck (1976) pointed out, the contexts of women's socialization—

ELAINE

I never thought it would be so hard not to smile. When you challenged us in class to go one day without smiling except when we really felt happy, I thought that would be easy. I couldn't do it. I smile when I meet people, I smile when I purchase things, I even smile when someone bumps into me. I never realized how much I smile — all the time.

What was most interesting about the experiment was how my boyfriend reacted. We got together last night and I was still working on not smiling. He asked me what was wrong. I told him "nothing." Now I was being perfectly nice and talkative and everything, but I wasn't smiling all the time like I usually do. He kept asking what was wrong, was I unhappy, had something happened — even was I mad. I pointed out that I was being as friendly as usual. Then he said yeah, but I wasn't smiling. I told him that I just didn't see anything particular to smile about, and he said it wasn't like me. I talked with several other women in our class, and they had the same experience. I just never realized how automatic smiling is for me.

relationships — provide them with more opportunities to refine their skills in reading nonverbal cues. Related to this is women's standpoint as caregivers who have consistently tended to children, the elderly, and sick people (Hewlett, 1986, 1991; Okin, 1989; Ruddick, 1989). Women also far outnumber men in caring professions such as social work, counseling, nursing, and human resources. Women's involvement in caring provides them with a standpoint different from those whose lives do not routinely center on nurturing. This standpoint cultivates skill in recognizing human needs and feelings (Wood, 1993c).

A second explanation that many scholars (Deaux, 1976; Janeway, 1971; Leathers, 1986; Major, 1980; Willis, 1966) find credible is that women's decoding skill results from their standpoint as subordinate members of society. The idea that women's nonverbal skills are linked to gender-differentiated power within our society was first suggested in 1951 by H. M. Hacker. Since then, a number of scholars (Hall, 1979; Janeway, 1971; Miller, 1986; Tavris, 1992) have amassed considerable evidence in support of the idea that those who are oppressed learn to interpret others in order to survive. N. M. Henley (1977) analyzed the nonverbal behaviors of people in subordinate positions and found consistent patterns for minorities, women, and individuals in subservient roles. This suggests that a standpoint associated with more or less power may explain gender differences in decoding emotions and attitudes.

KRISTA

I buy the power explanation for women's decoding skill. I know that I learned to do this from my mother. My father is very moody, and you have to know how to read him or there's trouble ahead. I remember when I was a little girl, my mother would tell me not to ask daddy for something or not to tell him about things at certain times because he was in a bad mood. I asked her how she knew, and she gave me a blueprint for reading him. She told me when he was mad he fidgeted and mumbled more and that he got real quiet when he was upset. Later she taught me other things like how to tell when he's getting angry about something — his eyebrows twitch. She made it seem like a science, and I guess it was in a way. But she sure knew how to read his moods, and that's how we stayed out of his way when he was on the warpath.

The argument that people in subordinate positions learn to interpret others' moods and feelings is supported by substantial research. B. Bettelheim (1943) showed that prisoners in concentration camps learned to interpret their captors' feelings and moods. Similarly, B. Puka (1990) demonstrated consistency between the emotional sensitivity typical of women and that found in prisoners, slaves, and other oppressed groups. For women, minorities, and others who are oppressed, decoding is a survival skill. Women's decoding skills probably result from a combination of socialization and how power is distributed in society. In emphasizing nurturing and pleasing, female socialization motivates women to care and provides them with opportunities to refine their skills in interpreting and responding to others' feelings. In addition, their historically subordinate position renders emotional perceptiveness useful in ensuring their acceptance, as well as their comfort and safety.

Liking.   A second aspect of responsiveness is liking. We use nonverbal behaviors to signal that we like or dislike others. Albert Mehrabian (1971) identifies important nonverbal cues of liking as vocal warmth, standing close to others, touching, and holding eye contact in face-to-face positions. Because females are socialized to be nice to others and to form relationships, they tend to employ more nonverbal communication that signals liking than do men (LaFrance & Mayo, 1979; Stewart et al., 1990). For instance, women stand and sit more closely in conversation than do men (Rosengrant & McCroskey, 1975), and women, particularly Caucasian ones, engage in more eye contact with others than do men (Ellsworth & Ludwig, 1972; Ellsworth & Ross, 1975; Henley, 1977).

Feminine socialization emphasizes building connections with others, while masculine socialization stresses independence. These learned orientations account for general differences in women's and men's tendencies to express affiliation nonverbally.

Power, or control. The third aspect of the relationship level of meaning in communication is power, or control, which involves dominance and power relationships between communicators that are defined through interaction. Control issues in conversations include who defines topics, directs conversation, interrupts, and defers. While many nonverbal behaviors convey control messages, three are especially important: vocal qualities, touch, and use of space. In all three categories, men generally engage in more nonverbal efforts to exert control than do women (Henley, 1977; Tannen, 1990b). For instance, compared with women, men tend to use greater volume and stronger inflection to highlight their ideas and add to the force of their positions (Eakins & Eakins, 1978). Men also tend to touch women more in nonaffiliative or aggressive ways that indicate and reinforce status differences (Deaux, 1976; Henley, 1977; LaFrance & Mayo, 1979; Leathers, 1986; Major, 1980). For instance, bosses often touch secretaries, but the reverse is rare (Spain, 1992). In addition, men command and use more personal space than women; they take up more space in sitting and standing, a difference not attributable to body size alone (Henley, 1977; LaFrance & Mayo, 1979; Mehrabian, 1972). Even at very young ages, boys are taught to seek and command more space than girls (Harper & Sanders, 1975), a finding that reflects the emphasis on independence in male socialization. In terms of nonverbal cues of power, then, men generally exceed women in behaviors that communicate dominance and control in relationships. When nonverbal efforts to dominate are combined with men's generally greater verbal dominance, we see a pattern whereby men tend to control mixed-sex conversations and, consequently, they often hold more power in relationships with women.

Now that we have seen how nonverbal communication functions to supplement verbal communication, regulate interaction, and define relationships, we are ready to explore how it reflects and sustains cultural definitions of gender. We will discover that nonverbal messages reiterate society's views of masculinity and femininity, reminding us constantly of gendered expectations for women and men.

Patterns of Nonverbal Communication

Throughout this book we have noted that our society defines masculinity and femininity in particular ways and then communicates its meanings through cultural institutions and practices. In our society, women are defined as and expected to be decorative, passive, affiliative, and responsive to others. Society expects men to be achieving, independent, and dominant. These basic cultural views of gender are evident in nonverbal communication about males and females as well as in nonverbal messages directed toward them. In addition, the nonverbal styles of interaction that men and women typically learn are distinctive in many respects and function to constitute gendered identities for individuals. Examining these topics will illuminate further means by which culture constructs gender.

Artifacts

Artifacts are personal objects that influence how we see ourselves and express the identity we create for ourselves. Beginning with pink and blue blankets used by many hospitals, personal objects for children define them as masculine or feminine. Parents send artifactual messages through the toys they give to sons and daughters. Typically, boys are given toys that invite more active and rough play, while girls are given playthings that emphasize nurturing, domestic activities, and appearances (Caldera, Huston, & O'Brien, 1989; Lawson, 1989; Pomerleau, Bolduc, Malcuit, & Cossette, 1990). One implication of sex-differentiated toys, as Miller (1987) pointed out, is that they cultivate different cognitive and social skills. Despite evidence that sex-typing restricts development, many parents continue to favor sex-differentiated toys. As we saw in Chapter 3, parents, especially fathers, tend to discourage children's interest in toys and activities that are judged not to be sex appropriate (Antill, 1987; Fagot, 1978; Lytton & Romney, 1991). These artifacts are powerful communicators of what males and females are supposed to be and do.

One clear indicator of cultural views of gender is toy catalogs. Even 1992 catalogs for children's gifts featured pages titled "For Girls," with play kitchen appliances, makeup and hair accessories, and pink tutu outfits! The pages labeled "For Boys" show soldiers and science equipment, swords and shields, and building

D A N

I don't care what the experts say about bringing kids up, no son of mine will get any dolls. I think that's just stupid. Boys aren't supposed to play with dolls and stuff like that. I didn't, and I turned out okay. I played with normal guy toys like model planes and cars and erector sets and computers. I did have a G.I. Joe, though. I guess it would be okay with me if my son played with one of them, but no Barbies.

sets. Most of the girls' pages were predominantly pink with other pastel colors, while the pages displaying items for boys used bolder colors. Carrying cultural views of gender, these catalogs and those who purchase from them tell girls they are supposed to be pretty, soft, and nurturing, whereas they instruct boys to be active, adventurous, and aggressive.

Movement away from sex-stereotyped toys is slow. For instance, the 1993 American International Toy Fair featured for the first time ever "genderbenders," which are toys designed to bend conventional views of gender (Lawson, C., 1993). This sounds like progress until we consider more carefully specific toys introduced as genderbenders. The big one for girls is an action figure—only the second one ever for girls (She-Ra was the first, and she hasn't been made since 1988). The Wonder Woman action doll has fluffy long hair and a stereotypical and unrealistic female figure, and her weapon for fighting evil is a magic wand that disperses bubbles! For boys, trolls are being promoted to encourage them to play with dolls, but these trolls are stereotypically male action figures and have names such as "Troll Warriors" and "Battle Trolls." So the big change in toys isn't much of a change at all.

Beyond childhood, artifactual communication continues to manifest and promote cultural definitions of masculinity and femininity. Although clothing has become less sex distinctive than in former eras, there are still differences in fashions for women and men. Men's clothes generally are not as colorful or bright as women's clothing (although this has attenuated in recent years), and they are designed to be functional. Pockets in jackets and trousers allow men to carry wallets, change, keys, and miscellany. The relatively loose fit of men's clothes and the design of men's shoes allow them to move quickly and surely. Thus, men's clothing deemphasizes physical appearance and enables activity.

Women's clothing is quite different. Consistent with a view of women as decorative objects whose value depends on appearance, clothing is designed to call attention to women's bodies and to make them attractive to viewers. Form-fitting skirts, materials that cling to the body, and details in design contribute to making women look decorative. Many women's clothes have no pockets or ones not large enough to hold wallets and keys without distorting the line of the garment. Further, most shoes for women are designed to call attention to their legs at the cost of comfort and safety—how quickly can you run in 2-inch heels?

Other artifactual communication reinforces cultural views of women and men. Advertisements for food, homemaking, and childrearing feature women, reiterating the view of women as mothers and the view of men as uninvolved in parenting. Products associated with heavy work, cars, and outdoor sports feature men. Also, consider the artifacts that women are encouraged to buy to meet the cultural command to be attractive: The cosmetics industry alone is a multi-million-dollar business in the United States; products to condition, straighten, curl, color, and style hair are similarly thriving. Women are taught to like and

BETH

Women's clothes—that's my pet peeve. I mean, why is it I have to choose between being comfortable and looking nice? Guys don't have to. I'm interviewing for jobs this semester, so I have to wear suits a lot of days, and they make me miserable. The jackets are cut close and don't let me move freely, and the skirts are made to ride up when I sit down. And shoes! They're the pits. To wear nice-looking shoes—ones that look professional—I have to be masochistic. Even in the good lines of shoes, the toes on pumps cramp my toes. There's no way I can walk fast when I need to get somewhere when my body is strapped in a suit and my feet are bound.

want jewelry, which reflects and reinforces images of women as decorative objects. Later, in the chapter on media, we will pursue in greater detail how advertising reinforces social views of gender.

Proximity and Personal Space

In 1968, E. T. Hall coined the word **proxemics** to refer to space and our use of it. As researchers began studying space, they realized it is a primary means through which cultures express values and shape patterns of interaction (Hall, 1959, 1966; Sommer, 1959, 1969). Early work revealed that different cultures have different norms for how much space people need and how closely they interact. For instance, in Latin American countries, people interact at closer distances than in reserved societies like the United States (Hall, 1959, 1966). Different cultures also have distinct understandings of personal space. In some countries, houses for big families are no larger than small apartments in America, and the idea of private rooms for individual members of families is unheard of. As these examples indicate, cultural views are evident in proxemic behavior.

Proxemics offers keen insight into the relative power and status accorded to various groups in society. Space is a primary means by which a culture designates who is important, who has privilege. Consider who gets space in our society. You'll notice that executives have large offices, although there is little functional need for so much room. Secretaries, however, are crowded into cubbyholes that overflow with file cabinets and computers. Generally there is a close correlation between status and the size of a person's home, car, office, and so forth. Who gets space and how much space they get indicate power. In fact, both Daphne Spain

(1992) and Leslie Weisman (1992) have shown in detail how the use of space in the United States designates lesser status for women and minorities. Now think about the amount of space women and men typically have in our society. As we have seen, early socialization encourages boys to go out on their own and girls to stay closer to adults and home. From these patterns, boys come to expect space for themselves, while girls learn to share space with others (Evans & Howard, 1973; Harper & Sanders, 1975; Lewis, 1972).

Gender-differentiated use of space continues in adult life. Think about your family. Did your father have his own room, space, or chair? Did your mother? One researcher (Frieze & Ramsey, 1976) reported that many men have private studies, workshops, or other spaces that others do not enter freely, but few women with families have such spaces. My students initially disagreed with Frieze's report and informed me their mothers had spaces. When we discussed this, however, it turned out mothers' spaces were kitchens and sewing rooms—places they do things for other people! Years ago, Virginia Woolf gave a famous lecture titled "A Room of One's Own," in which she argued that women's ability to develop and engage in creative, independent work is hampered by not having an inviolate space for themselves. A century later, most women still do not have a room of their own.

Proxemics also concerns how space is used. Again, think of your family. Who sat at the head of the table—the place reserved for a leader? In most two-parent families, that position belongs to the man and symbolizes his leadership of the family. Now consider the extent to which men's and women's spaces are invaded by others. We have already seen that men are more likely than women to have spaces that are "off limits" to others. Yet this is not the only way in which men's territory is more respected than that of women.

Early research (Henley, 1977; Sommer, 1965) identified **territoriality** as an aspect of proxemics. Territoriality refers to our sense of personal space or our private area that we don't want others to invade. Yet not everyone's territory is equally respected. People with power tend to invade the spaces of those with less power (Henley, 1977). Paralleling this is the finding that men invade women's spaces more than women invade men's spaces and more than men invade other men's spaces (Evans & Howard, 1973; Willis, 1966). Invasions of space are sometimes interpreted as sexual harassment, because too much closeness communicates a level of intimacy that may be perceived as inappropriate in work and education situations (Poire, Burgoon, & Parrott, 1992).

What happens when a person's private territory is invaded? This question has intrigued many researchers including, most recently, Judee Burgoon and her colleagues (Burgoon, Buller, Hale, & deTurck, 1988; Burgoon & Hale, 1988; Poire, Burgoon, & Parrott, 1992). One way people respond is to engage in behaviors themselves that attempt to restore their privacy zone (Burgoon & Hale, 1988; Poire, Burgoon, & Parrott, 1992). For instance, if someone moves too close for comfort, you might step back to create distance. Similarly, there is the well-known "elevator phenomenon" in which people are often crowded more closely than they like, so everyone looks up or down as if to say "I'm really not this close to you, and I am not trying to intrude." Further, we know that when personal territory is invaded, men tend to respond negatively and sometimes aggressively to defend their territory (Fisher & Byrne, 1975), while women tend to yield space or flee their territory rather than challenge the intruder (Polit & LaFrance, 1977). These patterns reflect cultural teachings that tell men to be aggressive in protecting their rights and instruct women to defer. Proxemics reflects cultural understandings that men are entitled to more space and that they are less subject to invasion than women.

Tactile Communication, or Touch

The first of our senses to develop, touch is an important form of nonverbal behavior. **Tactile communication,** or touch, from parents and other adults communicates different messages to boys and girls. Studies of parent-child interaction reveal that parents tend to touch sons less often and more roughly than they touch daughters (Condry, Condry, & Pogatshnik, 1983; Frank, 1957; Frisch, 1977). Daughters are handled more gently and protectively. Early tactile messages teach boys not to perceive touching as affiliative, while girls learn to expect touching from others and to use touch affiliatively (Goldberg & Lewis, 1969).

While women are more likely than men to initiate hugs and touches that express support, affection, and comfort, men more often use touch to direct others, assert power, and express sexual interest (Deaux, 1976; Leathers, 1986). These gendered patterns of proxemic and touching behavior are linked to the problem of sexual harassment (Wood, 1993b, 1993f, 1994). The meaning of touching, of course, depends on more than touch per se. As Judee Burgoon and her colleagues have shown (Burgoon, Buller, & Woodall, 1989), how we interpret touch depends on factors such as its duration, intensity, frequency, and the body parts touching and being touched. Because masculine socialization encourages men to enter the private spaces of others, particularly women, and to use touch to establish power, they may engage in touching that women co-workers will perceive as harassing (Poire, Burgoon, & Parrott, 1992). Men are more likely to invade others' spaces and to use touch to assert power, even when their interest is unwelcome. Women's training to be nice to others may make them reluctant to speak forcefully to a boss or co-worker whose touches are unwanted. Socialization practices and the gendered identities they foster shed light on sexual harassment in workplaces and educational institutions. For this reason, women and men need to be aware of gendered patterns and resist those that contribute to sexual harassment.

Finally, in discussing tactile communication, we must recognize the different degrees of sheer strength men and women in general can exert. Because men are

ROSEANN

I'm not paranoid or anything, but men really do have more physical strength, and they can use it against me. A few months ago, I was out with this guy I'd been seeing for a while. We weren't serious or anything, but we had gone out a few times. Well, we were at his place listening to music when he started coming on to me. After a while, I told him to stop because I didn't want to go any further. He grinned and pinned my arms back and asked what I was going to do to stop him. Well, I didn't have to, thank goodness, because he didn't really push, but just the same I had to think there really wasn't anything I could have done if he had. That's always there when I'm with a guy—that he could overpower me if he wanted to.

generally larger and stronger than women, they tend to have more physical confidence and to be more willing to use physical force than women. In an extensive analysis of the psychology of power, H. M. Lips (1981, p. 188) pointed out that "men can physically dominate women by beating their wives, girlfriends, daughters, and sisters. Rape and the threat of rape are also used as a coercive form of male social control over women." When men's physical confidence and sense of entitlement are carried to an extreme, they become violence against women. This tendency is encouraged by media representations of women as passive and powerless (Franzwa, 1975) and of men as sexually aggressive (Marks, 1979). We are bombarded with cultural messages telling us men can and should use power and women should not. If we incorporate these beliefs into our own identities, we perpetuate the cultural script handed down to us. By reflecting on these messages about gender, we empower ourselves to resist them in our own actions. Physical coercion is seldom the only or most appropriate means of achieving goals.

Facial and Body Motion

This area of nonverbal communication reflects a number of gendered patterns. We have already noted some of these: For instance, in general women reflect feminine socialization by smiling even when they are not genuinely happy, a pattern more true of Caucasian than African-American women (Halberstadt & Saitta, 1987). In addition, women tend to tilt their heads in deferential positions, condense their size, and allow others to invade their spaces. Men too tend to enact patterns they were taught by displaying less emotion through smiles or other facial expressions, using larger gestures, taking more space, and being more likely

R A N D A L L

It sounds kind of stupid when we talk about it, but it's true that a guy has to return another guy's stare if he wants to hold his own. It's like a staring contest. Sometimes on a street, another guy will meet my eyes. When I notice, then he's locked into holding the stare, and that means that I have to too. It's like that old joke about the first one to blink loses. It's kind of dumb, but I'd feel strange not returning another guy's gaze. Like a wimp or something.

to encroach on others' territories. In combination, these gender-differentiated patterns suggest that women's facial and body motions generally signal they are approachable, friendly, and unassuming. Men's facial and body communications, in contrast, tend to indicate they are reserved and in control.

A particularly interesting area of facial behavior is communication with the eyes. Called by poets "the mirrors of the soul," eye expressions indicate love, anger, fear, interest, challenge, and a range of other emotions. Men and women tend to differ in how they use their eyes to communicate. Women signal interest and involvement with others by sustaining eye contact, while men generally do not hold eye contact. These patterns reflect lessons from childhood in which girls learned to maintain relationships and boys learned to vie for status—to show interest in others may jeopardize your own position. Consistent with the image of women as interactive, researchers have shown that women not only give but also receive more facial expressions of interest and friendliness (Feldman & White, 1980). There is one exception to males' generally low eye contact. Among primates, the eyes are used to challenge and threaten (Pearson, 1985). Particularly challenging is a prolonged stare. While women seldom engage in staring, men use it to challenge others, particularly other men, and to assert their status (Pearson, 1985, p. 245). Men in my classes tell me that they cannot refuse to return a stare without losing face and appearing cowardly.

Paralanguage

Vocal cues that go along with verbal communication are called **paralanguage**. While there are some physiological differences in male and female vocal organs (the larynx and pharynx), these do not account fully for differences in women's and men's paralanguage. For instance, the larger, thicker vocal folds of male larynxes do result in lower pitch, but the difference between the average

WENDY

All my life I've had to live with the "dumb blonde" label. I am blonde. I am also pretty and petite, and it's true that this makes others perceive me as dumb and immature. That's what people always think before they get to know me. And they act toward me as if I were dumb, and they don't expect me to be mature and stuff. What really gets me is that sometimes I get hooked into their impression of me, and I start *acting* the part of the dumb blonde. Why can't a girl be feminine and smart both?

pitch of male speakers and the pitch of female speakers exceeds that explained by physiology. To understand why women and men tend to have divergent paralanguage, we must once again consider socialization processes. What vocal cues would you expect of someone taught to be deferential, polite, and caring? What would you expect of someone encouraged to be assertive, emotionally reserved, and independent? Your expectations probably match pretty closely with differences in male and female paralanguage that have been identified. In general, women use soft pitch, low volume, and a lot of inflection. Men tend to use their voices to assert themselves and command the conversation, which means they use low pitch, strong volume, and limited inflection. Further, men discourage others from talking by interrupting and responding with minimum and delayed "umms" (Tannen, 1990b; Zimmerman & West, 1975).

One interesting study sheds light on cultural stereotypes of men and women. D. W. Addington (1968) asked participants to judge the personalities of people on the basis of vocal qualities, which he experimentally manipulated. Women with breathy, tense voices were judged to be pretty, feminine, petite, shallow, immature, and unintelligent. Men with throaty, tense voices were judged to be mature, masculine, intelligent, and sophisticated. Addington concluded that when women are perceived as feminine, other aspects of the feminine gender stereotype—such as being flighty, immature, and unintelligent—are attributed to them. Perceptions of men as masculine are accompanied by the assumption that they are intelligent and mature.

Physical Characteristics

American society is preoccupied with physical appearance. More than many cultures, ours places a premium on personal attractiveness and makes it salient to us. It is unsurprising, then, that attractiveness is closely related to self-esteem and ability to form social and personal relationships (Byrne, London, & Reeves, 1968). While both sexes are judged by attractiveness, there are some important differences in the kind of judgments made and the implications of these judgments. Overall, the physical ideals our culture defines for males are less oppressive and less tied to individual worth than those defined for females. We will explore this issue in some detail, since mounting evidence demonstrates that physical and psychological problems result from trying to fit cultural images of femininity and masculinity.

Both men and women are affected by cultural standards of attractiveness. Research indicates that members of both sexes tend to be dissatisfied with their bodies (Chaiken & Pliner, 1987; Mintz & Betz, 1986; Mishkind, Rodin, Silberstein, & Striegel-Moore, 1987; Tucker, 1983). The nature and scope of dissatisfaction, however, differ between the sexes. Men who are dissatisfied with their weight or muscularity—primary requirements for masculine attractiveness—tend to confine their concerns to their bodies. They may dislike physical features, but that seldom affects how they feel about their competence, worth, and abilities (Mintz & Betz, 1986). For women, dislike of their bodies—particularly weight—often affects overall self-esteem. In other words, women generalize from the specific idea that their bodies don't meet the cultural standard to the broad evaluation that they are unworthy and unattractive (AAUW, 1991; Mintz & Betz, 1986).

The difference between women's and men's feelings about their bodies makes sense when we consider cultural definitions of the two sexes. Women's greater concern about physical appearance reflects our culture's emphasis on physical attractiveness in women (Silverstein, Perdue, Peterson, & Kelly, 1986; Spitzack, 1993; Wolf, 1991). Unfortunately, women who fall short of cultural ideals are judged more harshly and negatively than men who do not meet the cultural benchmark (Basow & Kobrynowicz, 1990; Feingold, 1990; Tiggemann & Rothblum, 1988). Inherent in social views of femininity is attractiveness, so not to be attractive by arbitrary standards is to be unfeminine.

What is designated as the ideal female form, however, is not constant. Like other aspects of gender, attractiveness varies across cultures and over time within any single society. The intense emphasis on thinness is a relatively new standard of feminine beauty. Some of the most famous art (for instance, Peter Paul Rubens's paintings of women) features women with more voluptuous, more fleshy bodies than would be favorably regarded today. Interested in changes in views of feminine beauty, N. Wolf (1991) investigated when and why standards for women's weight have changed in America. Her analysis yielded the interesting insight that there is a strong correlation between cultural pressures for women to be body conscious and women's gains in social, professional, and political equality. She notes that "dieting and thinness began to be female preoccupations when Western women received the vote" (p. 184). The preoccupation was precipitated by media's use of thinner models than had been featured previously.

THE SOCIAL CONSTRUCTION OF FEMININE FORM

In the late 1960s and through the 1970s, women began entering the work force in large numbers, and, more than in previous eras, women sought professional positions—ones on a level with those of many men. Interesting changes in the media's persuasions toward women accompanied this change in women's role:

♦ The number of articles on dieting rose 70% between 1968 and 1972.

♦ In the entire year of 1979, there were 60 articles in the popular press about dieting; in just the month of January 1980, there were 66 articles on dieting.

♦ By 1984, over 300 recently published diet books filled the shelves of bookstores and libraries.

♦ Whereas a generation ago, female models weighed only about 8% less than the average American woman, today they weigh 23% less.

♦ The average model, dancer, or actress today weighs less and looks more thin than 95% of the female population in the United States.

Source: Wolf, N. (1991). *The beauty myth.* New York: William Morrow.

During the second wave of feminism in America, as women became more visible in professional spheres and a portion assumed prominent positions, women's magazines suddenly were crowded with articles on how to lose weight and look slimmer. The natural weight of healthy, normal women was recast as "*the existential female dilemma*" (Wolf, 1991, p. 67). Many women responded to cultural demands to lose weight in order to meet the newly fashioned ideal of womanhood.

How serious is the problem? Recent investigations reveal that the cultural message to women that they must be thin to be successful has precipitated severe problems. Many women think constantly about appearance, particularly weight. In one survey (Wooley & Wooley, 1984), a majority of adult women rated losing 10 to 15 pounds more important than success in work or love. In her book *The Beauty Myth*, Wolf (1991, p. 186) reports that on any given day, 25% of the women in America are dieting, and an additional 50% are just finishing or just starting diets. And dieting starts early: It is rampant among girls in the fourth and fifth grades (Seligman et al., 1987). Even in high school, up to 75% of women report being preoccupied with losing weight ("Nearly Half," 1991). This is not the way it has always been. Wolf (1991, p. 186) points out that the number of high school girls who think they are overweight rose from 50% to 80% between 1966 and 1969. This number has increased exponentially in recent years, especially for young girls.

The cultural mandate to be thin has a number of serious effects on women who internalize that value. Women who have negative body images are more likely to be depressed (Mintz & Betz, 1986). Further, the pressure to be thin has ushered in an epidemic of eating disorders, of which women are the primary sufferers. J. J. Brumberg (1988) estimates that as many as one in five women students in the United States has or has had an eating disorder. The effects can be deadly: According to the American Anorexia and Bulimia Association, thousands

THE TOLL OF BEING THIN

♦ Eighty percent of American females have dieted by the age of 18.

♦ Eleven percent of high school seniors have an eating disorder.

♦ Nine of 10 bulimics (those who binge food and then purge it) are female.

♦ Nine of 10 sufferers of anorexia nervosa (self-starvation) are female.

♦ Bulimics are usually within 10 pounds of normal weight.

Source: An "All-Consuming Passion." (1991, May 13). *Newsweek*, p. 58.

JILL

Eating disorders are epidemic all right. What's more, they aren't even hidden. A lot of us just accept it as a way to keep from gaining weight. In my sorority it's almost a joke by now that most of us will be in the bathroom right after dinner throwing up. Nobody thinks anything about it anymore. Sometimes I worry when I hear about people who die from it, but I think that's pretty rare, isn't it?

of American women die each year of anorexia alone (Wolf, 1991, p. 182). And the latest models introduced in 1993 magazines are reviving the excessively thin look (LeLand & Leonard, 1993).

Perhaps you are wondering if there is some kind of profile for those likely to become obsessed with weight and/or to develop eating disorders. Very recent research provides some answers to this question. First, we know that women are far more likely than men to be preoccupied with weight and physical attractiveness ("An All-Consuming Passion," 1991). Second, women who are highly sextyped (they have internalized the culture's views of femininity) are more susceptible to cultural ideals for women's weight than are androgynous women (Franzoi, 1991). Women who resist contemporary standards of excessive thinness are more able to accept themselves regardless of how much they weigh. Third, a number of studies (Levinson, Powell, & Steelman, 1986; Thomas, 1989; Thomas & James, 1988) indicate that African-American women generally are better at resisting the cultural messages than Caucasian women. Although many African-American women do perceive themselves as weighing more than they would like, they tend to be less dissatisfied and less extreme in punishing themselves for a few extra pounds. Also, African-American women less often develop eating disorders than Caucasian women, perhaps because weight is judged less negatively by African-American men than by Caucasian ones (Root, 1990).

Because our culture is increasingly emphasizing men's bodies, more and more men are exercising and/or working out with weights to develop the muscularity promoted as ideal (Mishkind et al., 1987; Tucker, 1983). A few men do develop eating disorders, although the incidence is rare compared with that for women. The greater risk for men is compulsive exercising and/or use of potentially lethal steroids to attain the cultural ideal of strength. One group of men, however, is particularly likely to be concerned about appearance and to develop eating disorders: gay men. M. D. Siever (1988) argues that physical appearance is more tied to self-worth for gay than straight men, because gay men, like straight women, must attract other men. Thus, the same reasons may explain straight women's and gay men's preoccupation with thinness and their heightened vulnerability to eating disorders: Both groups want to attract men.

In concert, identified gender differences in nonverbal behavior reflect rather distinctive masculine and feminine styles. In general, women are more sensitive to nonverbal communication; display more interest, attention, and affiliation; constrict themselves physically; are given and use less space; use touch for affiliative purposes but are touched more; and restrict body gestures more than men. Reflecting cultural messages to them about how to enact masculinity, men's nonverbal communication tends to signal power and status, to assert themselves and their agenda, to command territories, and to shroud their emotions from public display.

▬ Implications of Gendered Nonverbal Communication

What is the meaning of general differences in women's and men's nonverbal communication? The concept of speech communities helps us understand gendered nonverbal codes. Just as male and female speech communities have alternative rules of talk, so do they include divergent rules for nonverbal communication. You will recall that Maltz and Borker (1982) found that through peer interaction boys learn to use talk to assert themselves, to compete for attention and status, and to control conversations. Girls, on the other hand, learn to use communication to create relationships, include and support others, and notice and respond to others' feelings. These principles also show up in the nonverbal styles of girls and boys, women and men.

It is probably not wise to try to establish which style is "better" or "more effective" in an absolute sense, since that depends on situations and purposes of communication. Instead, let's think about how each mode fits within the context of cultural values and what that implies for perceptions, opportunities, and self-concepts of men and women. Identifying cultural views doesn't necessarily mean we will accept them. If we find that social views restrict individuals, we may resist them and appreciate different nonverbal styles on their own terms. This allows us to act as agents of change who reform cultural understandings that evaluate one style as standard and all others as inferior.

The Cultural Context of Nonverbal Communication

The meaning of behaviors reflects social agreements that are created and sustained through communication. As a number of theorists (Harding, 1991; Tavris, 1992; Weedon, 1987) point out, meanings of femininity and masculinity are sculpted through interactions and perpetuated through ongoing cultural activities. Not only is gender socially constructed, but also the meanings attached to nonverbal behaviors are constructed through cultural communication. Given this, it's worthwhile to consider how feminine and masculine nonverbal communication styles fit within and reflect larger cultural patterns. We begin by noting that Western society values communality and agency differently. Agency, which involves power, activity, and achievement, is held to be more important, more significant than communality, which focuses on relationships and community. Thus, our culture accords unequal worth to feminine and masculine nonverbal styles. The values it confers on each reflect larger cultural patterns — in fact, the overall ethos of the culture.

The differential values assigned to agency and communality have long been noted by scholars and social critics. Further, attention has been paid to the paradox in socializing roughly half of the population to do and be something that is devalued by the culture. This was dramatically illustrated in a classic study conducted more than two decades ago. A research team (Broverman, Broverman, Clarkson, Rosenkrantz, & Vogel, 1970) prepared a list of traits that reflected a broad range of human qualities. They then asked 79 male and female clinicians (psychiatrists, psychologists, and social workers) to check the attributes they thought described "normal, healthy women." Next, the clinicians checked traits they associated with "normal, healthy men." Finally, clinicians selected characteristics of "normal, healthy adults." The findings were clear and startling: Normal women were described as dependent, deferential, unassertive, concerned with appearance, submissive, emotional, and uncompetitive. In contrast, clinicians described normal men as independent, aggressive, competitive, not submissive, more rational than emotional, and ambitious. Associated with normal adults were the qualities used to describe normal men. From these clinical judgments, two conclusions follow. First, the clinicians perceived stereotypically masculine characteristics as the standard, or norm, for healthy adults. Second, being a normal, healthy woman was seen as incompatible with being a normal, healthy adult.

Unfortunately, the bias favoring masculine qualities, as described in the study by Inge Broverman and her colleagues, continues to linger in society. Writing in 1973, Karlyn Campbell pointed out that Western culture values agency, action, doing, achievement, and ambition — in short, the qualities encouraged in men and discouraged in women. She noted that the conflict between femininity and adulthood, between being a woman and being successful, creates a constant paradox for women. As Campbell concluded, too often a woman has to choose between being perceived as feminine and being perceived as effective — she cannot simultaneously meet both sets of standards because they are mutually exclusive.

Although the bias favoring qualities associated with men has reduced somewhat since the study by Broverman et al., it is still the case that stereotypically masculine traits are viewed more positively than are stereotypically feminine qualities (Basow, 1992; Williams & Best, 1990). Accordingly, men who demonstrate power, independence, control, and achievement are highly regarded. Men who do not are disdained. Women who embody the qualities esteemed in our society are usually judged as unfeminine, while women who do not enact these qualities are judged as feminine but ineffective (Wood & Conrad, 1983). Thus, the styles women are taught by their speech communities are devalued by the culture at large, and the communicative practices emphasized in masculine speech communities gain respect and status in Western culture. Yet we need to remember that cultural beliefs are not sacred dogma etched in stone. Instead, they are constructed, sustained, and sometimes altered as members of a society interact in ways that constantly remake social values. We may either accept or challenge existing views of masculinity and femininity, as well as the values currently attached to communality and agency.

Respecting Differences in Nonverbal Communication

The ways we learn to communicate nonverbally reflect the circumstances of our socialization and present lives, as well as the qualities and goals we have learned to value. Gender, race, class, communicative experiences, and personal contexts combine to influence individuals' nonverbal communication styles. This implies we should recognize different nonverbal styles as simply different—not better and worse, just different. Because our culture emphasizes hierarchy and our language encourages polar thinking, it's hard to realize that different ways can be equally valid. If we cannot do this, however, we wind up operating from very egocentric perspectives, which fail to respect others on their own terms.

Misinterpretation of nonverbal styles is frequent. Men may perceive a woman who defers as less confident of her own point of view than a man who advances his position assertively. Similarly, a woman could easily judge a man to be insensitive and domineering if he keeps an impassive face, offers little response to her talk, and promotes his agenda. Yet such judgments reflect the communication rules we have learned, ones that may not apply to others' ways of expressing themselves. If we impose our values on behaviors that emanate from an alternative standpoint that is not guided by the rules we take for granted, then we distort others' communication by viewing it within a perspective alien to it. Greater accuracy in interpreting others' nonverbal communication results from understanding and respecting differences in how people use nonverbal behaviors and the alternative goals promoted by different communicative modes.

Respecting differences calls on us to suspend judgment based on our own perspectives and to consider more thoughtfully what others mean *in their own terms*, not ours. This might lead you to ask for clarification of intent from conversational partners whose nonverbal communication patterns diverge from your own. For example, it might be constructive to say to someone less facially expressive than you, "I don't know how you're feeling about what I just said, because your face doesn't show any reaction. Could you tell me what you feel?" Conversely, understanding may be enhanced when someone with a masculine, assertive nonverbal style says to his or her more deferential partner, "I'm not sure where you stand, because you seem to be responding more to my ideas than expressing your own. I'm interested in your opinion." Communicative techniques such as these enable us to show respect for nonverbal differences and, at the same time, to transcend their potential to create misunderstandings.

Understanding and respecting different forms of nonverbal communication does not imply that you have to give up your own style. That would be as counterproductive as discounting a style different from yours. All that under-standing and respect require is an honest effort to appreciate what another says on his or her own terms. At first this is difficult, because we have to get past our own egocentric ways of perceiving the world in order to interpret other people from their standpoints. People who commit to doing this say that it becomes easier with practice.

There's another benefit to learning to understand and respect alternative styles of nonverbal communication. It enhances your personal effectiveness by increasing the range of options you have for communicating with different people in diverse contexts and for varied reasons. Now that you are aware of gendered patterns in nonverbal communication, you may reflect on your own behaviors. Do you fit the patterns associated with your gender? Are you comfortable with your style and the effects it has, or would you like to alter your nonverbal behavior in some respects? By reflecting on your own nonverbal communication, you em-power yourself to create consciously a style that reflects the identity you assign to yourself.

$\mathcal{S}$ummary

In this chapter, we have seen that nonverbal communication expresses cul-tural views of gender, and men and women learn different styles of nonverbal interaction. Social definitions of women as deferential, decorative, and relation-ship-centered are reinforced through nonverbal communication that emphasizes their appearance, limits their space, and defines them as touchable. Views of men as independent, powerful, and in control are reflected in nonverbal behaviors that accord them larger territories and greater normative rights to invade others by entering their space and touching them. Consistent with how nonverbal commu-nication defines men and women are differences in how they use it. While women tend to embody femininity by being soft-spoken, condensing space and yielding territory, and being facially responsive, men are likely to command space and volume, defend their turf, and adopt impassive facial expressions to keep feelings camouflaged. These differences grow out of socialization in distinctive speech communities.

Recognizing the value of alternative styles of communication, both verbal and nonverbal, allows you to appreciate the richly diverse ways humans express themselves. It also enables you to reflect with increased insight on the patterns esteemed in our society and the extent to which different ones are assigned to women and men. In turn, this enables you to resist those social meanings you find unconstructive, to revise your own nonverbal communication to reflect the iden-tity you want, and to work toward changing the values our society assigns to masculine and feminine modes of expression. In doing this, you speak back to society and claim your right to participate in the processes of constructing the meanings of masculinity and femininity and the values assigned to different forms of communication.

*D*iscussion Questions

1. Observe people in your classes, in restaurants and stores, walking around campus, and in the media. Do you see gendered patterns of nonverbal communication that were identified in this chapter? Do women smile, hold eye contact, and use condensed space more than men? Do men use larger motions and more relaxed posture and command more space than women? What is the cumulative impact of gender-linked nonverbal styles in influencing perceptions of women and men?

2. Think back to the years when you were growing up. What artifacts were part of your environment? What kinds of toys did you have? What color was your room, bedspread, and so on? What sort of clothes did you have? How did these artifacts reflect and reinforce social views of your gender?

3. In recent years, there have been changes in clothing styles, particularly ones for women. Compared with a decade ago, there are many more women's fashions that are loose-fitting, comfortable, and unisex in style. What do such changes indicate about changes in social views of women? Is nonverbal communication — in this case artifacts — causing or reflecting changes in cultural definitions of femininity, or is it doing both?

4. Think about how space was organized in your family's home or homes. Did your parents have their own special territories — ones others were not supposed to use or interrupt? Did your father and mother or stepparents have equal amounts of space? Was there a head seat at your dining table? If so, who generally occupied it?

5. As a class, try an experiment and discuss your findings. Violate one of the nonverbal expectations for nonverbal communication for your gender. If you are a woman, you might try to go a day without smiling or refuse to make eye contact when others are talking to you. If you are a man, you might try to smile constantly or hold very steady eye contact with others in conversation. Notice how people respond, both in things they say to you and in their nonverbal reactions to your behavior. As a class, discuss what this experiment tells you about social expectations of gender and communication.

6. Are gender prescriptions for appearance strong in our society? How powerful is the cultural pressure to be thin? Does it affect men as much as women? How intense is the social expectation that men should be muscular and strong? Why might there be differences in social expectations for strength and thinness? How do cultural

views of nonverbal communication reproduce gender? How can you and society as a whole resist unhealthy expectations regarding appearance?

7. Enlarge your communication repertoire by developing some of the nonverbal interaction skills more typical of the other gender. If you are a man, try using more expressive facial gestures and eye contact when you talk with others, especially women. Do they respond differently to you when you seem more attentive? If you are a woman, experiment with using space differently — take a central seat in a discussion group instead of a side one, for instance. Do you see differences in how others respond to you?

PART III

Gendered Communication in Practice

CHAPTER SEVEN

Gendered Close Relationships

PAIGE

Honestly, I almost left my boyfriend when we had our first fight after moving in together. It was really a big one about how to be committed to our relationship and also do all the other stuff that we have to do. It was major. And after we'd yelled and all for a while, there seemed to be nothing else to do—we were just at a stalemate in terms of conflict between what each of us wanted. So Ed walked away, and I sat fuming in the living room. When I finally moved out, I found him working away on a paper for one of his courses, and I was furious. I couldn't understand how he could concentrate on work when we were so messed up. How in the world could he just put us aside and get on with his work? I felt like it was a really clear message that he wasn't very committed.

M A R K

Sometimes I just don't know what goes on in Ellen's head. We can have a minor problem — like an issue between us, and it's really not serious stuff. But can we let it go? No way with Ellen. She wants "to talk about it." And I mean talk and talk and talk and talk. There's no end to how long she can talk about stuff that really doesn't matter. I tell her that she's analyzing the relationship to death and I don't want to do that. She insists that we need "to talk things through." That may work for her, but, honestly, it makes no sense to me. Why can't we just have a relationship, instead of always having to talk about it?

Perhaps you have found yourself in situations such as those Mark and Paige describe. If you are a man, Mark's predicament may remind you of ones in your own life. If you are a woman, Paige's frustration may be more familiar to you. What they describe reflects gendered orientations toward close relationships. For Mark, as for most people socialized into masculinity, the purpose of talking is to accomplish some goal or solve some problem; for his partner, talking about the relationship is a primary means to intimacy. Paige cannot understand how Ed could concentrate on his paper when there is a problem between them; for Ed, the paper is a way to distract himself from something that matters very much. If Paige and Ed and Mark and Ellen do not figure out that their gendered viewpoints are creating misunderstandings, they will continue to find themselves at cross-purposes.

In this chapter, we will focus on dynamics in women's and men's close relationships. As we have seen already, a range of communicative processes teach us cultural definitions of masculinity and femininity. To the extent that these views are internalized, women and men tend to develop gendered ways of experiencing and expressing closeness. Incongruencies between feminine and masculine meanings of closeness and ways of communicating affection are sources of much misunderstanding and hurt.

To begin our discussion, we will consider alternative meanings closeness may have for masculine and feminine individuals. Next we'll explore two kinds of close, personal relationships. First, we will examine friendships to understand the ways affection is communicated and experienced between same-sex and different-sex friends. A second type of close relationship is romantic bonds between heterosexuals, gays, and lesbians. Here, too, we will discover that gender-differentiated patterns of communication permeate interpersonal attachments. As we explore dimensions of human relationships, we want not only to understand masculine and feminine inclinations but also to appreciate each on its own terms. Equally important, we want to consider alternatives to cultural prescriptions for how men and women should interact in their significant relationships.

The Meaning of Close, Personal Relationships

Defining Close, Personal Relationships

Of the many relationships we form, only a few become close and personal. These are the ones that occupy a special place in our lives and affect us more than other, less important associations we have. Close relationships are ones that endure over time and in which participants depend on one another for various things from support to material assistance. Yet not all relationships marked by continuing interdependence are personal. For instance, two colleagues might work together for many years and help each other in varied ways without ever becoming personally involved. In close, personal relationships, the essence is particular individuals who have strong feelings for each other (Blumstein & Kollock, 1988; Brehm, 1992). If a social partner leaves or dies, a replacement may be found and the functional relationship continues; when a personal partner leaves or dies, the relationship ends.

Gender and Closeness

There are notable differences in the ways women and men generally approach close relationships. Distinctive expectations, interaction patterns, and ways of interpreting others reflect gendered identities and communication styles. While the next section in this chapter discusses these in detail, what you have already read in prior chapters suggests basic gender differences that could affect personal relationships. We know that masculine socialization emphasizes independence, instrumental activity, aggression and emotional reserve, and use of talk to gain status and control. In contrast, feminine socialization fosters interconnections with others, emotional disclosiveness, responsiveness and support of others, and use of communication to build and sustain relationships. What do these differences mean? Among researchers there has been disagreement about how to interpret differences between men's and women's ways of relating to others. While some scholars argue that men's interpersonal styles are inferior to women's, others think the two styles are distinct yet equally valid. So that you may evaluate these two viewpoints, we will consider each.

"Male deficit model."   Based on a long-standing cultural definition of women as "relationship experts," our society tends to regard women as more interpersonally sensitive and competent than men. Because women are perceived as relationship experts, their ways of forming relationships and interacting with others are presumed to be "the right ways." Operating from this premise, a number of researchers consider men's ways of relating to be inadequate. This view, the **male deficit model,** maintains that men are not adept at intimacy because they are less interested and/or able than women to disclose emotions, reveal personal information, and engage in communication about intimate topics.

The central assumption of the male deficit model is that personal, emotional talk is the hallmark of intimacy. With this assumption in mind, researchers began to study how women and men interacted in close relationships. In a classic investigation M. A. Caldwell and L. A. Peplau (1982) measured the intimacy of men's and women's friendships by how much intimate information they confided in friends — a mode of communication generally more used by women than by men. Given this measure of intimacy, it is not surprising that women were found to be more intimate than men in this and similar studies. Findings such as this led to judgments that men's ways of relating are inadequate. J. O. Balswick and C. W. Peek (1976) argued that men's inexpressiveness is a tragedy of our society. The solution recommended is for men to overcome masculine socialization by getting in touch with their feelings and learning to communicate openly and expressively (Pleck & Sawyer, 1974; Tognoli, 1980).

The trend to privilege women's ways of relating and disparage men's was heightened in the 1960s by the rhetorical movements we considered earlier. A point of view that gained salience during this era was that men are emotionally repressed and would be enriched by becoming more aware and expressive of their feelings. Both women and men who were feminists found merit in this idea, and many men committed to developing their emotional sides and to expressing those more openly in their relationships. In the 1980s, the male deficit model continued to prevail. Researchers claimed that men "feel threatened by intimacy" (Mazur & Olver, 1987, p. 533); men are "lacking in mutual self disclosure, shared feelings and other demonstrations of emotional closeness" (Williams, 1985, p. 588); men suffer from "stunted emotional development" (Balswick, 1988); men do not know how to experience or communicate feelings (Aukett, Ritchie, & Mill, 1988); and men should learn to talk openly about their emotions (Tognoli, 1980).

Even now, much academic and popular sentiment holds that men do not have deep feelings and/or are unskilled in expressing emotions and caring. A number of books written in the last few years state that personal disclosures are the crux of intimacy, women have more intimate relationships than men, boys' friendships lack the emotional depth of girls' friendships, and males focus on activities to avoid intimacy (see Wood & Inman, 1993). What needs to be asked is whether we should assume that activities cannot lead to intimacy and whether emotional and personal disclosures are the only way to create closeness. Questions like these led to a second interpretation of differences between how men and women, in general, create and experience closeness.

Alternate paths model.   The **alternate paths** explanation agrees with the male deficit model that gendered socialization is the root of differences in women's and men's typical styles of interacting. It departs from the deficit model, however, in important ways. First, the alternate paths viewpoint does not presume that men lack feelings and emotional depth, nor that relationships and feelings are unimportant in men's lives. Rather, this explanation suggests that masculine socialization constrains men's comfort in verbally expressing feelings and, further, that it limits men's opportunities to practice emotional talk. A second important distinction is that the alternate paths model argues that men *do* express closeness in ways that they value and understand—ways that may differ from those of feminine individuals but that are nonetheless valid.

F. Cancian (1987, 1989) calls attention to the "feminization of love," meaning that the ways we have learned to think about close, personal relationships are heavily gendered. As a culture, she suggests, we use a "feminine ruler" to define and measure closeness. She also argues that using a specifically feminine standard (emotional talk) automatically misrepresents and devalues masculine modes of caring in the same way that using male standards to measure women's speech distorts the unique qualities of women's communication. Cancian argues that men's and women's ways of demonstrating affection, however different, are equally valid when judged on their own terms. She states (1987, p. 78), "There is a distinctive masculine style of love, . . . but it is usually ignored by scholars and the general public."

Influenced by this viewpoint, S. Swain (1989) studied men's perceptions of their close friendships. He discovered that men develop a closeness "in the doing"—a kind of connection that grows out of engaging in activities. His research suggests men engage in activities not as a substitute for intimacy, but, in fact, as an alternate path to closeness. Other scholars (Paul & White, 1990; Tavris, 1992; Wright, 1988) agreed and began to study how men express closeness and what they appreciate from others as demonstrations of caring. D. Sherrod's (1989, p. 168) research led him to conclude that men's friendships are no less intimate than women's, but "men generally do not express intimacy through self-disclosure." There is also increasing evidence that talking about problems may be less effective than diversionary activities in relieving men's stress and enhancing feelings of closeness between men (Riessman, 1990; Swain, 1989; Tavris, 1992).

The safest conclusion may be that males generally do not express their feelings in feminine ways, just as women tend not to express theirs in masculine ways. This suggests some men may find that intimate talk doesn't make them feel close, just as some women feel that instrumental demonstrations of commitment are disappointing. This may be a case in which the genders really do have different languages. If so, then becoming bilingual is a necessity for healthy relationships. Understanding alternative ways of creating and sustaining intimacy empowers us to create and participate in a range of connections with others who matter to us.

▩ Gendered Friendships

As we explore women's and men's communication in friendships and romantic commitments, keep in mind the possibility that we may be seeing only different, not differently valuable, orientations toward closeness. The goal is not to judge which is better but to understand and learn from each orientation.

Commonalities in Men's and Women's Friendships

Before we consider differences between the genders, we should note that there are some important commonalities in masculine and feminine views of friendship. According to Sherrod (1989), both women and men value intimate same-sex friends, and both agree on basic qualities of close friendships: intimacy, acceptance, trust, and help. Other researchers (Berscheid, Snyder, & Omoto, 1989; Jones, 1991) concur that in many respects there are no substantial differences between the sexes' friendships. Recently, M. Monsour (1992, p. 289) concluded, "There are more similarities than differences in the meanings given to intimacy by participants in cross-sex and same-sex friendships." In summary, men and women generally share similar views of the importance of close friendship and some of its key qualities.

Differences Between Women's and Men's Friendships

Against the backdrop of commonalities in the genders' understandings of friendships, we now explore general differences in how women and men typically create friendships and how they communicate feelings of closeness. As we consider this topic, we want to be careful not to misinterpret distinct styles by assuming that one is the absolute standard.

As early as 1982, Paul Wright pointed to interaction style as a key difference between women's and men's friendships. He noted that women tend to engage each other face to face, while men usually interact side by side. By this, Wright meant that women communicate directly and verbally with each other to share themselves and their feelings. Men more typically share activities and interests with friends. Wright suggested that what is central to friendship differs between the sexes: For men, it tends to be doing things together; for women, being and talking together is the essence of close, personal relationships. Among researchers (Becker, 1987; Buhrke & Fuqua, 1987; Paul & White, 1990; Reisman, 1990; Riessman, 1990), there is consensus on the distinction between talking face to face and doing side by side that Wright found differentiated men's and women's friendship styles.

The fact that women use talk as a primary way to develop relationships and men generally do not underlies four gender-linked patterns in friendship. First, communication is central to women friends, while activities are the primary focus of men's friendships. Second, talk between women friends tends to be expressive and disclosive, focusing on details of personal lives, people, relationships, and feelings; talk in men's friendships generally revolves around less personal topics such as sports, events, money, music, and politics. Third, in general, men assume a friendship's value and seldom discuss it, while women are likely to talk about the dynamics of their relationship. Finally, women's friendships generally appear to be broader in scope than those of men. Let's now see how these differences lead to unique kinds of friendship between women, between men, and between men and women.

Women's Friendships: Closeness in Dialogue

In an early study, E. J. Aries and F. L. Johnson (1983) reported that women use talk to build connections with friends. They share their personal feelings, experiences, fears, and problems in order to know and be known by each other. In addition, Aries and Johnson noted, women exchange information about their daily lives and activities. By sharing details of lives, women feel intimately and continuously connected to one another (Rubin, 1985; Schaef, 1981; Wood, 1992d). To capture the special quality of friendship that women create through talking, C. S. Becker (1987) described women's friendships as "an evolving dialogue" through which initially separate worlds are woven together into a common one. Becker wrote (p. 65), "As time spent together continues and each woman brings important parts of her life into the friendship, a world of shared meanings and understanding is created." The common world of women friends grows directly out of ongoing communication that is the crux of closeness between women.

Talk between women friends tends to be personal and disclosive (Aries & Johnson, 1983; Buhrke & Fuqua, 1987; Reisman, 1990; Wood & Inman, 1993). In general, for women feeling close is facilitated by knowing each other in depth. To achieve this, women tend to talk about personal feelings and disclose intimate information. They act as confidantes for one another, respecting the courage required to expose personal vulnerabilities and inner feelings. Consistent with gender socialization, women's communication also tends to be expressive and supportive (Aukett, Ritchie, & Mill, 1988; Rubin, 1983; Schaef, 1981; Wright & Scanlon, 1991). Typically, there is a high level of responsiveness and caring in women's talk, which lends a therapeutic quality to women's friendships (Aries & Johnson, 1983). The more permeable ego boundaries encouraged by feminine socialization cultivate women's ability to empathize and to feel a part of each other's life.

Because women are socialized to be attentive, supportive, and caring, certain problems may arise in their relationships. Clinicians have pointed out that feminine norms of communication make it difficult for women to deal with feelings of envy and competition (Eichenbaum & Orbach, 1987; Rubin, 1985). It is not that women do not experience envy and competitiveness, but rather that they think it's wrong to have such feelings. Being jealous of a friend lies outside of cultural prescriptions for femininity, so women may repress or avoid talking with each other about these "taboo" feelings. Avoidance, however, may harm friendships by creating barriers and distance. For this reason, clinicians like Luise Eichenbaum and Suzie Orbach advise women to recognize and learn to deal openly with envy and competition. It's also the case that women may find it difficult to override socialization's message that they are supposed to be constantly available and caring. Thus, when women lack the time or energy required to nurture others, they may feel guilty and self-critical (Eichenbaum & Orbach, 1983; Miller, 1986). The responsiveness and caring typical of women's friendships both enriches and constrains people socialized into feminine rules of relating.

JANICE

One of the worst things about being female is not having permission to be selfish or jealous or *not* to care about a friend. Usually, I'm pretty nice and I feel good for my friends when good things happen to them, and I want to support them when things aren't going well. But sometimes I don't feel that way. Like right now, all my friends and I are interviewing for jobs, and my best friend just got a great offer. I've had 23 interviews and nothing so far. I felt good for Sally, but I also felt jealous. I couldn't talk about this with her, because I'm not supposed to feel jealous or to be selfish like this. It's just not allowed, so my friends and I have to hide those feelings.

Another quality of communication between women friends is an explicit focus on their relationship. The friendship itself and the dynamics between women are matters of interest and discussion (Winstead, 1986). Because women are socialized to attend to interpersonal processes and relationships, they tend to be sensitive to what happens between friends. It is not unusual for women to state affection explicitly or to discuss tensions within a friendship. The ability to recognize and deal with interpersonal difficulties allows women to monitor their friendships and improve them in ways that enhance satisfaction.

A final quality typical of women's friendships is breadth (Caldwell & Peplau, 1982; Weiss & Lowenthal, 1975; Wright, 1982; Wright & Scanlon, 1991). With close friends, women tend not to restrict their disclosures to specific areas, but to invite each other into many aspects of their lives. Because women talk in detail about varied aspects of their lives, they know each other in complex and layered ways (Aries & Johnson, 1983; Eichenbaum & Orbach, 1983, 1987; Rubin, 1983, 1985). Typically, this renders close friendships between women broad in scope (Buhrke & Fuqua, 1987). In summary, women's friendships tend to develop out of the central role accorded to communication, which allows disclosures, expressiveness, depth and breadth of knowledge, and attentiveness to the evolving nature of the relationships. Because they know the basic rhythms of each other's life, women friends often feel interconnected even when not physically together.

Men's Friendships: Closeness in Doing

Like women, men value friendships and count on friends to be there for them (Mazur, 1989; Monsour, 1992; Sherrod, 1989). However, the ways men create and express closeness differ from those of women. Activities, rather than talk, are generally the center of most men's friendships (Aries & Johnson, 1983; Duck, 1988; Mazur & Olver, 1987; Paul & White, 1990; Reisman, 1990; Riessman, 1990; Wood & Inman, 1993). Beginning with childhood, interaction between males revolves around shared activities, particularly sports (Maltz & Borker, 1982; Monsour, 1992; Swain, 1989). Scott Swain's (1989) phrase "closeness in the doing" captures the way most men create and experience friendships. Over two-thirds of men in Swain's study described activities other than talking as the most meaningful times with friends. Engaging in sports, watching games, and doing other things together cultivate a sense of camaraderie and closeness between men (Sherrod, 1989; Williams, 1985). Whereas women tend to look for confidantes in friends, men more typically seek companions. And much of the research on men's friendships suggests they perceive talking as a limited way to be close (Cancian, 1987; Monsour, 1992; Swain, 1989).

JOEL

The best thing about guys' friendships is that you can just relax and hang out together. With women you have to be on — intense, talking all the time — but with guys you can just be comfortable. It's not like we're not close, but we don't have to talk about it or about our lives all the time like girls do. It's more laid back and easygoing. I don't know about other guys, but I feel a lot closer to guys than to girls.

Growing out of the emphasis on activities is a second feature of men's friendships: an instrumental focus. Men tend to do things for people they care about (Cancian, 1987; Sherrod, 1989). Swain (1989) describes men's friendships as involving a give and take of favors, skills, and assistance. Because masculine socialization discourages verbal expressions of affection and stresses concrete action, men generally regard doing things as a primary way to demonstrate affection. Instead of being the focus of interaction, for men talk tends to accompany activities and be about impersonal topics, especially sports (Aries & Johnson, 1983; Sherman & Haas, 1984). Between men, there is often a sense of reciprocity, where one offers expertise in repairing cars and the other provides computer skills — an exchange of favors that allows each man to hold his own while showing he cares about the other. The masculine inclination toward instrumentality also surfaces in how men help each other through rough times. Rather than engaging in explicit, expressive conversation about problems as women often do, men are more likely to help a friend out by distracting him from troubles with diversionary activities (Cancian, 1987; Riessman, 1990; Tavris, 1992).

Third, men's relationships are distinguished by what Swain (1989) labeled "covert intimacy." In contrast to the overt expressions of caring between women, men tend to signal affection through indirect, nonverbal means. These include joking, engaging in friendly competition, razzing, and being together in comfortable companionship. Perhaps because men are socialized not to express personal feelings, most find it awkward to say "I care about you" or "Our relationship really matters to me," or to hug, all of which are comfortable for women. Instead, men tease, interact without explicitly discussing their friendship, and touch each other in sports or engage in affectionate punches and back slapping (Mazur & Olver, 1987; Swain, 1989). An exception to this is androgynous men, who, more than their sex-typed brothers, engage in expressive, emotional communication (Williams, 1985).

L E E

I don't know what girls get out of sitting around talking about problems all the time. What a downer. When something bad happens to me, like I blow a test or break up with a girl, the last thing I want is to talk about it. I already feel bad enough. What I want is something to distract me from how lousy I feel. That's where having buddies really matters. They know you feel bad and help you out by taking you out drinking or starting a pickup game or something that gets your mind off the problems. They give you breathing room and some escape from troubles; girls just wallow in troubles.

Finally, men's friendships are often, although not always, more restricted in scope than are women's. A number of researchers (Bell, 1981; Burhke & Fuqua, 1987; Davidson & Duberman, 1982; Weiss & Lowenthal, 1975) report that men tend to have different friends for various spheres of interest rather than doing everything with any single friend. From their study, P. H. Wright and M. B. Scanlon (1991) reported that men's relationships tend to center around specific, structured activities. Thus, Jim might meet Ed for racquetball matches, get together with Bob for poker, and have Randy as a drinking buddy. Because they tend to limit friendship to particular areas, men may not share as many dimensions of their lives as is typical of women friends. Overall, then, men's friendships involve shared activities, instrumental demonstrations of commitment, covert intimacy, and limited spheres of interaction.

In summary, distinctive patterns of communication define unique qualities of men's and women's friendships. Women tend to see closeness as sharing themselves and their lives through personal communication. Men more typically create closeness by sharing particular activities and interests and by doing things with and for others. Describing these gender differences, L. Rubin (1985) wrote that men bond nonverbally through sharing experiences, while women become intimate through communicating.

Friendships Between Women and Men

Differences typical of how women and men experience and express closeness make friendships between the sexes particularly interesting. They pose unique challenges and offer special opportunities for growth. Because our culture so heavily emphasizes gender, it is difficult for women and men not to see each other in sexual terms (Johnson, Stockdale, & Saal, 1991; O'Meara, 1989). Even when cross-sex friends are not sexually involved, an undertone of sexuality often punctuates cross-sex friendships.

Another impediment to friendship between women and men is sex segregation in our society. Beginning with childhood, males and females are often separated, as are their activities. We have Boy Scouts and Girl Scouts, rather than Scouts, and most athletic teams are gender segregated. As boys and girls interact with same-sex peers and enter into separate speech communities, differences are compounded by learning different styles of interaction. Because males and females generally learn alternative rules for communicating, there is greater potential for misunderstanding as well as awkwardness in mixed-sex friendships. This seems especially true for African-Americans whose culture is more rigidly sex segregated than that of Caucasians (Gary, 1987).

Despite these difficulties, many women and men do form friendships with each other and find them rewarding. In mixed-sex friendships, each partner has something unique to offer as the "expert" in particular areas. Women may lead the way in providing personal support, while men tend to have more skill in using activities to increase closeness. Years ago, an insightful psychiatrist (Sullivan, 1953) claimed that intimacy and companionship are basic needs of all humans, ones that men and women are differentially encouraged to cultivate in themselves. For women, a primary benefit of friendships with men is fun — companionship that is less emotionally intense than that with women friends (Basow, 1992). For men, an especially valued benefit of closeness with women is access to emotional and expressive support, which tend to be infrequent in friendships between men. Men say they receive more emotional support and therapeutic release with women than with men friends. The greater supportiveness of women also is reported by women, who say they receive less of it from men than from women friends (Aries & Johnson, 1983; Aukett, Ritchie, & Mill, 1988; Reisman, 1990). This may explain why both sexes seek a women friend in times of stress, and both women and men are generally more comfortable self-disclosing to women than to men (Buhrke & Fuqua, 1987; Eichenbaum & Orbach, 1983; Rubin, 1985). These patterns reflect cultural views that it is women who nurture, support, and care for others.

Differences in men's and women's communication styles show up in friendships between them. In general, men talk more and demand more attention, response, and support than they offer to women with whom they are friends. Women often find there is less symmetry in their friendships with men than with other women, a pattern that echoes the male-dominant model in society at large. Thus, both women and men perceive women as more attentive, caring, and responsive, and both sexes report that friendships with women are more close and

CHRISTY

Sometimes I feel like this one guy is really using me. He calls and wants to come over whenever he's feeling bad, and then he dumps on me. He wants me to help him—to listen to his problems and provide some comfort, I guess. But he only talks about himself and his problems. He has no interest in my life. He never asks how things are with me. It's a one-way street. Maybe it's true that men don't know how to express support for others, but I really don't care. It's just no good being in a relationship that meets only one person's needs.

satisfying than those with men (Aries & Johnson, 1983; Buhrke & Fuqua, 1987; Weiss & Lowenthal, 1975).

Differences in men's and women's ways of creating and sustaining friendships also surface in other kinds of close relationships. As we will see, the basic gendered patterns discussed here are prominent in dating and romantic commitments.

◼ Gender and Intimacy

Nowhere else are cultural expectations of masculinity and femininity so salient as in romantic relationships. The cultural script for romance stipulates a number of "rules" that are well known to us: First, the romantic ideal promoted by our culture is decidedly heterosexual, which excludes gay and lesbian couples, although they make up at least 10% of the population. The cultural script also specifies other things: Women should be attracted to men, and men should be attracted to women; more feminine women and more masculine men are desirable; men should initiate, plan, and direct activities and have greater power within the relationship; women should facilitate conversation, generally defer to men, but control sexual behavior (Brehm, 1992); men should excel in status and earning money, and women should assume primary responsibility for the relationship, the home, and the children; men should be autonomous, and women should depend on men. This heavily gendered cultural script is well understood by most people. In fact, in a recent study (Rose & Frieze, 1989), college students were asked to define the content of men's and women's roles on a first date, and there was virtually unanimous agreement on who did various things and when they were appropriate. The elements of this script are evident in both dating relationships and enduring commitments.

Developing Romantic Intimacy

Insight into what heterosexual men and women seek in romantic partners may be gleaned from reading personal advertisements. Ads written by men emphasize the importance of stereotypically feminine physical qualities using words such as *attractive, slender, petite,* and *sexy.* Women's ads for male partners emphasize status and success and include words such as *secure, ambitious, professional,* and *successful* (Davis, S., 1990; Smith, Waldorf, & Trembath, 1990). Both women's and men's views of desirable partners, then, reflect cultural gender expectations, emphasizing success in males and beauty in females.

The conventional heterosexual dating script calls for women to be passive and men to take initiative. Although many people, especially women, claim not to believe in these gender stereotypes, research suggests that most heterosexuals conform to them (Cochran & Peplau, 1985; Riessman, 1990; Rubin, 1983). Conformity seems to reflect both our internalized sense of how we are supposed to be and the belief that the other sex expects us to meet cultural gender ideals. Thus, women tend to play feminine and men tend to play masculine, each reflecting and perpetuating established social views of gender.

There are exceptions to compliance with cultural scripts. Androgynous individuals, who break from rigid cultural definitions of masculinity and femininity, behave in more flexible, less stereotypical ways (DeLucia, 1987). There is also less role playing between gay men and even less between lesbian women (Kurdek & Schmitt, 1986b, 1986c, 1987). Because gays and lesbians are of the same gender, male-female differences are less salient than in heterosexual romances. The tendency for greater role playing between gay men than between lesbian women, however, may reflect masculine socialization, which fosters manipulation to gain power (Blumstein & Schwartz, 1983; Kurdek & Schmitt, 1986c; Wood, 1993e).

Is one gender more romantic than the other? Contrary to folklore, research (Brehm, 1992) indicates men tend to fall in love sooner and harder than women do. The cultural gender script that calls for men to initiate may explain why they take the lead in declaring love. There are also differences in what love generally means to women and men. For men, it tends to be more active, impulsive, sexualized, and game playing than for women, whose styles of loving are more pragmatic and friendship focused (Cancian, 1987; Hendrick & Hendrick, 1986; Riessman, 1990). For instance, men may see love as taking trips to romantic places, spontaneously making love, and engaging in ploys to surprise a partner. Women might more typically think of quiet, extended conversation in front of a fire or a general comfort and security in each other's presence.

Within love involvements, women are generally expected to assume the role of "relationship expert." This has long been recognized in heterosexual relationships (Cancian, 1987; Tavris, 1992; Wood, 1993a), and most researchers attribute women's association with taking care of the relationship with socialization that encourages women to be more relationship-oriented than men. Further evidence of the belief that women take care of relationships comes from studies of homosexual commitments. In lesbian couples, partners tend to take mutual responsibility for nurturing the dyad and for providing emotional direction and support (Eldridge & Gilbert, 1990; Kurdek & Schmitt, 1986c; Wood, 1993e). Because both women are likely to have internalized feminine identities, both are attentive to intimate dynamics. Gay couples, on the other hand, are least likely to have a partner who nurtures the dyad and provides emotional leadership (Kurdek & Schmitt, 1986b; Wood, 1993e).

Relationships that continue and deepen typically progress through stages of initiating, intensifying (falling in love), working out problems, and making a commitment. Development of lesbian and gay romantic attachment parallels that of heterosexuals with stages of initiation, intense infatuation, and maturing commitment (Kurdek & Schmitt, 1986a). Over time, couples work out norms for interacting, and they create private cultures (Wood, 1982). While each couple forms a unique private culture, generalizable gendered patterns are evident. Despite efforts to increase equality between the sexes, enduring heterosexual love relationships, in general, continue to reflect traditional gender roles endorsed by

SABRINA

To tell you the truth, even if my sexual preference were for men, I think I'd live with a woman. I've tried both sides of the track, and there's no comparison in the two kinds of relationship. When I used to date men and have relationships with them, I was always the one who had to do the caring. I had to prop them up emotionally and take care of them. They never did that for me. I had to point out when there was an issue in the relationship we needed to work out, and they still dragged their feet. By now I've had several serious relationships with women, and it's a different world. My partner right now is just as caring as I am. I don't get drained by doing it all, and neither does she. And relationship problems don't fester either, because both of us see them and want to do something about them.

the culture (Riessman, 1990; Wood, 1993a). Men tend to be perceived as the "head of the family" and the major breadwinner; women tend to assume primary responsibility for domestic labor and child care; and men tend to have greater power (Wood, 1993a, 1993c).

Because gender distinctions are not as salient, gay and lesbian relationships depart from the roles characteristic of heterosexual couples. Research (Brehm, 1992) suggests that both gay and lesbian commitments resemble best-friend relationships with the added dimensions of sexuality and romance. Following the best-friends model, lesbian relationships tend to be monogamous and high in emotionality, disclosure, and support, and partners have the most equality of all types of relationships (Blumstein & Schwartz, 1983; Eldridge & Gilbert, 1990; Kurdek & Schmitt, 1986c). Gay couples are less monogamous (and more tolerant of extrarelationship sexual involvements), keenly sensitive to power issues, and lowest of all relationships in expressiveness and nurturance (Blumstein & Schwartz, 1983; Kurdek & Schmitt, 1986b; Wood, 1993e).

Committed Relationships

Once two people commit to a future of intimacy, partners develop patterns of interaction that reflect their desires for a loving relationship. Complicating their efforts are gendered identities, which incline women and men toward distinct understandings of how to create and communicate closeness. Gendered orientations influence four primary dimensions of couple involvement: modes of expressing care, satisfying needs for autonomy and connection, responsibility for relational maintenance, and power balance. As we will discover, these dynamics are influenced by distinctive assumptions, styles, and preferences emphasized by masculine and feminine socialization.

Gendered modes of expressing care.   As we have seen, women generally create and express closeness through personal talk, while men rely more on instrumental activities. This difference complicates heterosexual partners' efforts to achieve intimacy. A. W. Schaef (1981, p. 150) has noted that "women are often hurt in relationships with men because they totally expose their beings and do not receive respect and exposure in return." Conversely, men may be threatened or resentful when women want them to be more emotionally expressive than they find comfortable. To many men, intensely personal talk feels more intrusive than loving.

For women, ongoing conversation about feelings and daily activities is a primary way to express and enrich connections between people (Tannen, 1990b; Wood, 1993a, 1993b). Communication processes are the core of the relationship. The masculine speech communities in which most men are socialized, however,

PHIL

What does my girlfriend want? That's all I want to know. She says if I really loved her, I'd want to be together and talk all the time. I tell her all I do for her. I fix her car when it's broken; I give her rides to places; I helped her move last semester. We've talked about marriage, and I plan to take care of her then too. I will work all day and overtime to give her a good home and to provide for our family. But she says, "Don't tell me what you *do* for me," like *do* is a bad word. Now, why would I do all this stuff if I didn't love her? Just tell me that.

regard the function of talk as solving problems and achieving goals. Thus, unless there is some problem, men often find talking about a relationship pointless, while women are more likely to feel that continuing conversation is the best way to keep problems from developing (Riessman, 1990; Schaef, 1981; Tannen, 1990b; Wood, 1986). These mismatched views of talking pave the way for misunderstandings, hurt, and dissatisfaction.

Modes of expressing closeness further reflect and reproduce gender by the different ways men and women tend to demonstrate they care. C. K. Riessman (1990) maintains that women and men differ in what intimacy means. For women, she says (p. 24), closeness is identified with "communicating deeply and closely," while for men "talk is not the centerpiece." The instrumental focus encouraged in men motivates them to show affection by doing things with or for others. By extension, heterosexual partners have distinctive ways of showing they care and count different things as evidence that a partner cares. This creates a likelihood that women and men may not recognize each other's styles of communicating care.

Not only are modes of expressing caring generally different for women and men, but there is a cultural bias favoring the feminine style. This goes back to the Industrial Revolution, which took men away from homes and bifurcated life into public and private spheres. According to F. Cancian (1989, p. 18), "With the split between home and work and the polarization of gender roles, love became a feminine quality." Since that time, love has been measured by a "feminine ruler," which assumes that women's ways of loving are *the right ways*.

The feminine bias in views of love is illustrated by a classic study (Wills, Weiss, & Patterson, 1974) on the effects of increased demonstrations of affection between spouses. Husbands were instructed to engage in affectional behaviors toward their wives, and then the wives' responses were measured. When one wife

SHARON

Whoops! I thought I had my act together on this gender stuff, and most of this course has been a review of stuff I already knew, but the unit on how men and women show they love each other was news to me. It made a lot of sense when I thought about it, and it really turned my head around about my boyfriend. I'm always fussing at him for not showing me he cares. I tell him he takes me for granted and if he really loved me he'd want to talk more about personal, deep stuff inside him. But he bought me a book I'd been wanting, and a couple of weeks ago he spent a whole day fixing my car because he was worried about whether it was safe for me—I thought of that when we talked about the guy in the experiment who washed his wife's car. I guess he *has* been showing he cares for me, but I haven't been seeing it.

showed no indication of receiving more affection, the researchers called the husband to see if he had followed instructions. Somewhat irately, the husband said he certainly had—that he had thoroughly washed his wife's car. Not only did his wife not experience this as affection, but the researchers themselves claimed he had "confused" instrumental with affectional behaviors. Doing something for someone was entirely disregarded as a valid way to express affection! This exemplifies the cultural bias toward feminine views of loving. It also illustrates a misunderstanding that plagues many heterosexual love relationships.

Gay and lesbian couples tend to have less discrepant understandings of the purpose of communication. Gay men, like their heterosexual counterparts, tend to engage in little emotional and intimate dialogue and do not process their relationship constantly (Wood, 1993e). Lesbians, on the other hand, generally create the most expressive and nurturant communication climates of any type of couple, since both partners typically are socialized into feminine forms of interaction and, thus, value talk as a means of expressing feelings and creating closeness (Blumstein & Schwartz, 1983; Wood, 1993e). Lesbian partners' mutual attentiveness to nurturing and emotional openness may explain why, as a group, lesbian relationships are more satisfying than gay or heterosexual ones (Eldridge & Gilbert, 1990; Kurdek & Schmitt, 1986c).

Gendered needs for autonomy and connection. Researchers and clinicians (Baxter, 1990; Bergner & Bergner, 1990; Goldner, Penn, Sheinberg, & Walker,

1990; Scarf, 1987; Thompson & Walker, 1989) state that autonomy and connection are two basic needs of all humans. We all need to feel we have both personal freedom and meaningful interrelatedness with others. What may differ is how much of each of these we want and how partners coordinate preferences. Masculine individuals tend to want greater autonomy and less connection than feminine persons, whose relative priorities are generally reversed. It is not that men want *only* autonomy and women want *only* connection. Both genders tend to want both, yet the proportionate weights women and men assign to autonomy and connection generally differ.

Desires for different degrees of autonomy and connection frequently generate friction in close relationships, particularly heterosexual ones. Many couples are familiar with a pattern called "demand-withdraw" (Christensen & Heavey, 1990) or "pursuer-distancer" (James, 1989). The dynamic of this pattern is that one partner (usually the woman) seeks emotional closeness through disclosive, intimate communication, and the other partner (usually a man) withdraws from a degree of closeness that stifles his need for autonomy. The more one pursues, the more the other distances; the more one withdraws from interaction, the more the other demands talk and time together. Socialized toward independence, masculine individuals need some distance to feel comfortable, while feminine persons feel closeness is jeopardized and they are rejected when a partner retreats from intimate talk (Wood, 1993a). The irony is that the very thing that creates closeness for one partner impedes it for the other. As you might suspect, this pattern is less prominent in gay and lesbian relationships in which both partners tend to have congruent desires for autonomy and connection.

More hurtful than the pattern itself, however, are partners' tendencies to interpret each other using rules that distort the other's behavior. For instance, to think that a man who wants time alone doesn't care for his partner or value a relationship is to interpret his actions through the rules of femininity. Similarly, to perceive a woman who wants intimate conversation as intrusive is to misjudge her by applying masculine standards. While the pursuer-distancer pattern may persist in relationships, we may eliminate the poison of misinterpretation by respecting different needs for autonomy and connection (Bergner & Bergner, 1990).

Responsibility for relational health.   Lesbian partners generally share responsibility for keeping their relationship healthy. Because most lesbians, like the majority of heterosexual women, learn feminine ways of thinking and acting, both partners tend to be sensitive to interpersonal dynamics and willing to work out conflicts to enrich their bond (Blumstein & Schwartz, 1983; Wood, 1993e). Sharing responsibility for safeguarding a relationship lessens the pressure on each partner and also reduces the potential for conflict over investing in the relationship.

Against the standard set by lesbians, heterosexual couples do not fare so well in distributing responsibility for relational health. Women are widely expected to be "relationship specialists," and both men and women tend to assume that women are more responsible for relationships and better at keeping them on track (Janeway, 1971; Miller, 1986; Okin, 1989; Rubin, 1985; Tannen, 1990). Because relationships and interpersonal sensitivity are not promoted in masculine socialization, men often are less aware of (Wamboldt & Reiss, 1989; Wood & Lenze, 1991b) and less skilled in reading the nuances of personal interaction (Christensen & Heavey, 1990; Rubin, 1985; Wood, 1993a; Wood & Inman, 1993). Summarizing much research in this area, L. Thompson and A. J. Walker (1989, p. 849) concluded that wives "have more responsibility than their husbands for monitoring the relationship, confronting disagreeable issues, setting the tone of conversation, and moving toward resolution when conflict is high."

The expectation that one person should take care of relationships often cultivates problems. It inequitably burdens one partner, while exempting the other person from responsibility (Cancian, 1987; Miller, 1986; Schaef, 1981; Thompson & Walker, 1989). In addition, it is difficult for one person to meet relationship responsibilities if a partner does not acknowledge and work on matters that jeopardize relational health. What can happen is that the partner expected to safeguard the relationship is perceived as a nag by someone who fails to recognize problems until they become very serious (Tavris, 1992). This can separate intimates into what J. Bernard (1972) years ago called "his marriage" and "her marriage," a situation in which spouses have different, often conflicting, views of their relationship. Separation and the tension it generates are less likely when both partners take responsibility for the health of their commitment. Not surprisingly, research shows that the highest levels of couple satisfaction result when both partners follow the lesbian pattern of sharing responsibility (Gunter & Gunter, 1990; Peterson, Baucom, Elliott, & Farr, 1989; Steil & Turetsky, 1987).

Gendered power dynamics.   All relationships involve power issues, and these particularly reflect gender patterns. The social view of women as less powerful than men carries over into intimacy. Even in the 1990s, traditional views of male dominance remain relatively intact in the perceptions of intimate partners (Riessman, 1990). Both women and men believe that men should be more powerful, and this varies only slightly when a female partner's job equals a male's in prestige and salary (Anderson & Leslie, 1991; Hochschild, 1989; Steil & Weltman, 1991).

Consistent with social prescriptions for masculinity, men are expected to have higher job status and earn greater salaries than women (Farrell, 1991). When this expectation is not met, many heterosexual couples either experience dissatisfaction or engage in a variety of rationalizations to convince themselves the husbands are of greater status and value (Anderson & Leslie, 1991; Hochschild, 1989;

Steil & Weltman, 1991). The pressure for men to be primary breadwinners is especially arduous for African-Americans, since job discrimination makes it difficult for many African-American men to earn enough to support families (Doyle, 1989; Wilkie, 1991).

As you might predict, problems fostered by believing that men should be more powerful are absent in lesbian relationships, which tend to be highly egalitarian. On the other hand, power issues are accentuated in gay relationships, where partners may engage in constant competition for dominance (Blumstein & Schwartz, 1983; Kurdek & Schmitt, 1986a, 1986b). The expectation of male dominance in heterosexual relationships is reflected in three important ways: division of labor, patterns of influence and decision making, and violence between partners.

One of the clearest indicators of power is how equitably labor is divided between partners. On this matter, deeply gendered patterns continue to prevail in heterosexual relationships. Writing in 1991, J. R. Wilkie reported that only 17% of marriages today have a single male wage earner, while nearly two-thirds of couples are dual workers. This pattern deviates from that of former eras when males were more frequently the only or primary providers of income.

What has not changed with the times, however, is the distribution of responsibility for domestic chores and care of children and other relatives (Ferree, 1988; Nussbaum, 1992; Okin, 1989; Thompson & Walker, 1989). By and large, these responsibilities are still carried entirely or predominantly by women, regardless of whether they work outside of the home. Dubbing this the "second shift," sociologist Arlie Hochschild (1989) found that the majority of wives employed outside of their homes have a second-shift job when they get home. In only 20% of dual-worker families do husbands contribute equally to homemaking and child care. Further, it is almost always women who assume responsibility for parents and in-laws who need assistance (Wood, 1993c). According to *Newsweek* ("The Daughter Track," 1990), the average woman in the United States will spend 17 years raising children and 18 years caring for elderly parents and in-laws. From all reports, she will also do the bulk of cleaning, cooking, and shopping, regardless of her job responsibilities outside of the home. In stark contrast to the rise in the number of women working outside of their homes, the amount of housework and child care that husbands do has risen only 10% (from 20% to 30%) in nearly three decades (Pleck, 1987).

Not only do women work more than men at home, but the work they do is generally more taxing and less gratifying. For instance, while men's contributions tend to be sporadic, variable, and adjustable in timing (repairing an appliance, mowing the lawn), the work women typically do is repetitive, routine, and constrained by deadlines. Further, more than men, women engage simultaneously in multiple tasks. For example, many women help a child with homework while preparing dinner. These features render women's work in the home less gratifying

(Hochschild, 1989). This is also true of child care. While mothers tend to be constantly on duty, performing repetitive caretaking such as fixing meals, giving baths, and supervising activities, fathers more typically volunteer for irregular and fun child-care activities such as a trip to the zoo. Sporadic excursions for recreation and adventure are more fun for both parents and children than the constant, necessary activities of caretaking.

Another way in which women's contributions to homelife are greater is in terms of what Hochschild (1989) termed **psychological responsibility**, which is the responsibility to remember, plan, and make sure things get done. For instance, it may be that spouses agree to share responsibility for taking a child to medical and dental visits, but it is typically the wife who is expected to remember when various inoculations are due, schedule appointments, notice when the child needs attention, and keep track of whose turn it is to take the child. Similarly, partners may share responsibility for preparing meals, but who takes charge of planning menus, keeping inventory on what's in the home, making shopping lists, and getting to the grocery store to buy what's needed? All of this planning and organization is a psychological responsibility that is often not counted in couples' agreements for sharing the work of a family. Psychological responsibility is an ongoing burden that transcends the actual time and energy needed to do a job and requires constant awareness.

The consequences of women's "second shift" are substantial. Hochschild (1989) reported that among the couples she studied, women were extremely stressed, fatigued, and susceptible to illness, because they were constantly trying to meet the double responsibilities of their jobs inside and outside of the home. In addition, the inequity of the arrangement is a primary source of resentment and dissatisfaction, especially for women, and of marital instability. Marital stability is more closely tied to equitable divisions of housework and child care than to a couple's income (Fowers, 1991; Hochschild, 1989; Suitor, 1991).

Another clue to power dynamics is whose preferences prevail when partners differ. Research repeatedly finds that in both spouses' minds, husbands' preferences usually count more than those of wives on everything from how often to engage in sexual activity to who does the housework (Schneider & Gould, 1987; Paul & White, 1990; Thompson & Walker, 1989). Further, we know that masculine individuals (whether female or male) tend to use more unilateral strategies to engage in and to avoid conflicts (Snell, Hawkins, & Belk, 1988). Feminine individuals more typically try to please, defer, submit, or compromise to reduce tension, and they employ indirect strategies when they do engage in conflict (Howard, Blumstein, & Schwartz, 1986; Miller, 1986; White, 1989).

More than feminine or androgynous persons, individuals with masculine identities tend to deny problems or to exit situations of conflict, thus enacting the masculine tendency to maintain independence and protect the self. Feminine persons, in contrast, tend to initiate discussion of problems and stand by in times of trouble (Rusbult, 1987). As you might suspect, the tension between masculine and feminine ways of exerting influence is less pronounced in lesbian relationships, where equality is particularly high. For gay partners, power struggles are especially common, sometimes being a constant backdrop in the relationship (Blumstein & Schwartz, 1983; Kurdek & Schmitt, 1986b).

Finally, gendered power dynamics underlie violence and abuse, which are means of exercising dominance over others. Mounting evidence demonstrates that violence and abuse are not rare but are fairly common in relationships. Not confined to any single group, violence cuts across race, ethnic, and class lines. Researchers estimate that at least 28% and possibly as many as 50% of women suffer physical abuse from partners, and even more suffer psychological abuse (Brock-Utne, 1989; French, 1992; Roberts, 1983). Verbal violence has recently been identified as a major problem ("The Wounds of Words," 1992). Further, violence seems to be rising in dating relationships (Mahlsted, 1992).

Violence is strongly linked to gender in two ways. First, it is inflicted primarily by those most frequently socialized into masculine identities: Less than 5% of violence against a partner is committed by women (Kurtz, 1989). In the United States, a woman is beaten every 12 seconds by a man, and four women are beaten to death daily (Brock-Utne, 1989). Further, women are 600% more likely to be brutalized by an intimate than are men (French, 1992, p. 190). Violence is also linked to masculine identity and cultural ideologies of male dominance. Cross-cultural research indicates that partner abuse, like rape, is lowest in societies that have ideologies of sexual equality and harmony among people and with nature; it is most frequent in cultures that are stratified by sex and that believe in male dominance of women (Levinson, 1989). Clinical studies of men who batter women have convinced researchers (Goldner et al., 1990, p. 344) that abusive relationships "are not unique but, rather, exemplify in extremis the stereotypical gender arrangements that structure intimacy between women and men generally." Like rape, battering and abuse seem to be promoted by cultural ideals linking masculinity with aggression, strength, control, and domination.

Particularly convincing evidence that violence is more connected to gender than sex comes from a recent study by Thompson (1991). Based on reports from 336 undergraduates, Thompson found a high degree of violence in dating relationships. Sex alone, however, did not explain the violence. What Thompson discovered is that violence is linked to gender, with abusers—both male and female—being more masculine and less feminine in their gender orientation. This led Thompson to conclude that physical aggression is associated with traditional views of masculinity and a self-definition based on control, domination, and power.

It also seems that violent relationships endure because of gendered identities of partners. For the relationship to continue once abuse has begun, partners must agree (however unconsciously) that one partner, usually the man, has more power

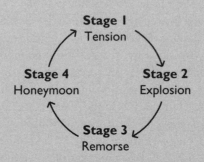

Stage One: Tension builds and the abusive partner blames the other for problems or for not being supportive. Typically, the abuser begins psychological battering with insults, threats, taunts, and intimidation. Victims, especially ones in chronically abusive relationships, learn to spot cues and to be extremely compliant and not to do anything to annoy the partner. This seldom helps, since the abuser is looking for an excuse to relieve frustration by exerting power over another.

Stage Two: An explosion occurs. Tension erupts into physical violence, and one or more battering incidents occur. The abuser may wait until the victim is relaxing quietly or even asleep and then attack. Often victims require hospital care. Sometimes they are pregnant and miscarry.

Stage Three: The abuser appears contrite and remorseful. The abuser may apologize to the victim and typically promises it will never happen again. The victim sees the "good person" inside and remembers what led to commitment or marriage.

Stage Four: This is the "honeymoon phase." The abuser acts courtly and lovingly. The victim becomes convinced the abuse was an aberration that will not recur—even if it has repeatedly.

And then the whole cycle begins anew.

and has the right to exert it, even brutally, against the other. The dynamic is supported when the abused partner, usually a woman, has a feminized identity that leads her (or him) to be unassertive, loyal, and deferential (Goldner et al., 1990). Because feminine socialization emphasizes compliance and passivity, and because women are often economically dependent on men, many women stay in abusive situations to fulfill the feminine ideals of caring for others and keeping their families together.

Close relationships reflect the distinctive expectations and interpersonal orientations encouraged by feminine and masculine socialization. In turn, these are evident in four processes central to intimacy: how partners express and experience caring, preferences for balances of autonomy and connection, responsibility for maintaining relationships, and power dynamics. Each of these dimensions of close relationships is deeply influenced by the gendered identities of participants in friendships and romantic commitments.

*S*ummary

So what are close relationships? What is "caring"? Is it one kind of activity and orientation that women are better at than men? Or, like so many human experiences, are there multiple forms of caring, and does it mean different things to different people? We have seen that widely held social views of friendships and love relationships reflect primarily feminine values and marginalize or dismiss masculine styles of enacting closeness. Whether we wish to accept these cultural views is up to us.

We have the capacity to transcend conventional viewpoints and enlarge our own understandings to reflect the diverse and intriguing ways that men and women create and express intimacy. Throughout this book, we have seen that cultural institutions and practices shape our understandings of ourselves, others, and social life. At the same time, to the extent that we understand some of the influences on us, we are empowered to question them and to resist those that we find undesirable. Further, because we interact with our culture, we may influence the understandings that compose its ideology. This pertains to how we understand and engage in closeness just as it applies to how we define our personal identities.

Social definitions of friendship and intimacy reflect traditional stereotypes of men's and women's roles so that men are expected to have more power and status, require more autonomy, and assume less responsibility for domestic and caretaking duties than women. While these gendered patterns may work for some, they are not satisfying to growing numbers of people. As friends and committed partners discover the limits and disadvantages of traditional gender roles, they are experimenting with new ways to form and sustain relationships.

Many who resist prevailing cultural gender scripts discover new and exciting dimensions of their personal potential, ones not cultivated by rigid roles. For instance, men who are single fathers or who devote themselves to caring for their parents heighten their abilities to empathize and provide comfort, and they create rich, intimate relationships with others that traditional prescriptions for masculinity precluded (Kaye & Applegate, 1990; Risman, 1989). Women who pursue substantial careers develop senses of increased personal agency and confidence in their judgment and value (Hochschild, 1975; McGowen & Hart, 1990; Wood, 1983b). Illustrations such as these remind us that we can venture beyond conventional definitions of identity and relationships if we choose to. In so doing, we edit cultural scripts, using our own lives as examples of alternative visions of women, men, and the kinds of relationships they may form with each other. By contributing these to the cultural collage, we enrich our individual and interpersonal lives and the social fabric as a whole.

𝒟iscussion Questions

1. The author discussed different perspectives on how men express and experience closeness. Do you think that men really are less able to engage in closeness than women, as the male deficit model claims, or that men and women simply have different ways of experiencing and communicating closeness? How does the theory you accept affect your behaviors and interpretations of others?

2. Think about your friendships with women and men. How are they different from one another? In what ways are they similar? Are your experiences with friends consistent with general patterns identified in the chapter? What are the values and limitations of same- and cross-sex friendships in your life?

3. Keep experimenting with expanding your personal repertoire. This time, try to enlarge the ways in which you create and build friendships by engaging in some modes that you have not typically used. If you have relied primarily on talk to build closeness, see what happens when you do things with friends. Do you experience a "closeness in the doing"? If your friendships have tended to grow out of shared activities, check out what happens if you talk with friends without some activity to structure time. As a class, discuss what you learn.

4. Do you see gendered patterns of interaction in your romantic relationships? Think about gender-linked differences in how partners express care, power, interest in the relationship, and needs for autonomy and connection. Are these points of difference and perhaps tension in your romantic relationships? Does knowing about gender-linked patterns regarding these issues affect how you interpret what happens in your own relationships?

5. If members of your class are willing, discuss differences in gay, lesbian, and heterosexual romantic relationships. Are gay and lesbian relationships "easier" in the

sense that partners are more likely to share gender-linked attitudes about what closeness is and how to build it? How is relational maintenance handled in gay men's relationships? Is there ever too much focus on the relationship in lesbian couples? What might heterosexuals learn from gay and lesbian relationships?

6. Have you ever experienced the pursuer-distancer pattern in your own relationships? Explain how it occurs and how it feels to you. Does what you learned in this chapter affect how you feel about this pattern? Do you think you will behave differently or interpret interaction differently in the future?

7. Think about how power was distributed in the family or families in which you grew up. If both parents or stepparents worked, did they share equitably in childcare and household responsibilities?

8. Now think about your own relationships. How is power distributed within them? Who decides what you'll do, where you'll go, how you'll spend money, when you'll get together, and how you'll spend time? Do you see connections between power and gender in your relationships?

9. Within your own relationships, who assumes responsibility for taking care of the relationships' health? Do you and your partner invest equal effort in thinking about yourselves as a couple? Do you work equally to identify and resolve tensions in your relationship? Are you satisfied with how relationship responsibility is distributed? If not, what might you do to work out a more gratifying system for your relationship?

10. How pervasive is violence in romantic relationships of your generation? Have you ever used or been abused by physical power? What about abuses of verbal power? Do you agree with the text's argument that gender and violence are linked? How might we challenge and change cultural structures and practices that build connections between masculinity and violence?

$\mathcal{G}$endered Education: Communication in School Settings

♦ The longer males attend school, the higher their self-esteem, achievement, and ambition; the longer females attend school, the lower their self-esteem and aspirations.

W hat is wrong with this picture? "Equality of educational opportunity" is one of our country's pledges to citizens. Yet if education is equal for all, how is it that men and women do not reap equivalent benefits from schooling? How can a process alleged to enhance our personal and professional lives fail to do that for slightly more than half of those who participate in it? That is the question we will try to answer in this chapter as we consider schools as institutions that communicate cultural values regarding gender.

Schools are powerful agents of socialization. They are the one specific institution specifically charged by society with responsibility for teaching us about our culture: its history, traditions, practices, beliefs, and values. In addition, schools teach us who is important and who is not; who influenced the directions of history, science, literature, and social organization; and what possibilities and responsibilities exist for various individuals in the society. By implication, schools join with other socializing agents to communicate what identities we are expected to assume and what personal, civic, and vocational opportunities are open to us.

Finally, schools teach by example. The organization of education and the roles of males and females in schools implicitly communicate a model of "normal" life and the status of various people.

As we continue to unravel the sources of gender ideology, we will discover that schools contribute in major ways to the process of gendering individuals. From preschool through graduate programs, communication within educational institutions reproduces cultural views of women as subordinate, passive, deferential, and unachieving and of males as dominant, independent, and achieving. This is not the intended purpose of education, and it is a process that many educators themselves do not consciously realize is occurring. Nonetheless, as we will see, schools provide powerful lessons in gender.

In addition to the explicit agenda of education, there is a **hidden curriculum** (Lee & Gropper, 1974), which reinforces sexist conceptions of women and men. This hidden curriculum consists of institutional organization, content, and teaching styles that reflect gender stereotypes and have the effect of sustaining gender inequities by privileging white males and marginalizing and devaluing female and minority students. After we have explored these three dimensions of the hidden curriculum, we will identify their implications for women's and men's personal and professional lives. Finally, we will consider alternative efforts to reform educational institutions so that a hidden curriculum no longer disadvantages some students. Examining these issues may give us insight into the reasons that males' self-esteem and aspirations rise and females' decline in proportion to the extent of their participation in education.

■ The Organization of Schools

Both symbolic interactionism and standpoint theory highlight the ways in which social institutions and practices organize cultural life and normalize values. As we have seen in prior chapters, social order may be thought of as a primary means by which a culture's values are communicated to individuals so that they come to see a particular organization as natural, normal, and the "way we do things." A pivotal way that an arbitrary social order is represented as normal is by having institutions embody it. As we participate in these institutions, we come to see the prevailing order as natural, and we then reproduce it in our own identities and actions (West & Zimmerman, 1987). Thus, institutions normalize cultural values and instill them in individuals by modeling them as standard and correct.

Schools Perpetuate Gender Inequities

Educational institutions reflect the gender stratification of the culture at large and encourage us to see the unequal status and value assigned to women

GENDER STRATIFICATION IN EDUCATION

Percentages of positions held by women in educational institutions:

Level	Teachers	Principals/ Presidents
Elementary	86.2	18
Junior high	61.4	3
Senior high	47.0	2
College	7.4	10

Source: *Academe*. (1990, March/April). Some dynamic aspects of academic careers: The urgent need to match aspirations with compensation. Pp. 3–20.

and men as normal. The actual organization of schools communicates strong messages about relationships among gender, identity, value, and opportunities. Think about your elementary and high schools. Who were the teachers? Who were the principals? Which of the two had more authority? Who were the aides, cafeteria workers, and secretaries? From our earliest experiences in schools, we learn that males have authority—the principal is the primary authority figure in elementary and secondary schools, and the chancellor or provost is in charge at colleges and universities. The head person is usually male, while most women are in subordinate positions—teachers and support staff. Further, at higher levels of education where the position of teacher has more status, the number of women decreases (*Academe*, 1990).

Schools Limit Career Aspirations

Although most students are not consciously aware of the trends shown in the box on "Gender Stratification in Education," they nonetheless pick up the gender message that men are authorities and women are subordinates. In an interesting study (Paradise & Wall, 1986), researchers compared the perceptions of first graders in schools with male and female principals. They found that students were much more likely to think that both women and men could be principals when they had a woman principal than when they had a man principal. In mirroring gender stereotypes of our society, the organization of schools instills in students the belief that men belong in positions of authority and power and women do not.

At higher levels, gendered school organization continues to affect perceptions of career opportunities and appropriate roles for women and men. At colleges and universities, faculty are predominantly male, especially at senior levels. At the entry level of assistant professor, approximately 40% of faculty nationwide are female. The percentage decreases to 26% at the level of associate professor, and it plummets to a mere 13% at the highest faculty level of full professor (*Academe*, 1990). The figures are even more unsatisfactory for African-Americans, who represent only about 4% of faculty, roughly equally divided between women and men (Snyder, 1987).

Schools Lack Female and Minority Role Models

A primary consequence of the prominence of male and white faculty is a lack of role models for women and people of color. Further, the few women and minority faculty members are overburdened with disproportionate requests for committee service and advising (Phillips, Gouran, Kuehn, & Wood, 1993; Welch, 1992). Consequently, they are less likely to see positions in higher education as viable career options for themselves. Several studies have confirmed the relationship between the presence of women and minorities in schools and minority and women students' career aspirations. L. A. Gilbert and S. L. Evans (1985) found that female faculty are important role models for women students, providing concrete examples of the fact that women can hold positions of authority. Not surprisingly, women students' level of ambition and self-confidence are highest in women's high schools (Lee & Marks, 1990) and colleges (Rice & Hemmings, 1988; Tidball, 1989), where women hold nearly all positions of status and authority. Similarly, African-American faculty serve as role models, who influence the likelihood that African-American students will pursue further education and ambitious professions (Fleming, 1984; Freiberg, 1991; Lee & Marks, 1990). This research makes it clear that while we all benefit from interacting with people like us, white male students are given an advantage in that they are provided with more role models who underline their value and encourage them to establish high personal, social, and professional goals. This leads many educators to argue that separate schools for women and minorities provide them with better educations and greater self-esteem (Kelly, 1989; Rice & Hemmings, 1988).

CAROL

I remember when I had my first woman professor at the university. At first I was surprised to see she was our teacher, and I wasn't sure how I felt about that. But she really knew her stuff, and she was really good at getting us involved, so the classes were interesting. Then I went to talk to her about my paper, and she asked me about my plans after college and whether I'd thought about graduate school. I hadn't, but she told me she thought I was capable, and she encouraged me. That was in my first semester junior year, and now that I'm in my final semester, I have been accepted in graduate school. I would never have thought of myself as able to do graduate work, and none of my male professors had suggested it. But she really believed in me and helped me believe in myself.

▪ Curricular Content

The hidden curriculum is further implemented through the actual content of education. As we will see in this section of the chapter, a number of studies have shown that academic curricula at all educational levels are permeated by materials that communicate gender stereotypes. Beginning in the 1970s, researchers examined educational content to determine what it communicates about women and men. For over 20 years, reports have documented pervasive and persistent sexism in instructional materials and particularly in the language used in teaching and learning settings.

Misrepresentation of White Men as Standard

Readers in elementary school perpetuate gender stereotypes in several ways. First, they represent males as standard by overrepresenting men and underrepresenting women. Misrepresentation of the sexes was first discovered in a classic investigation conducted in 1972 (Women on Words and Images, 1972). Titling their study "Dick and Jane as Victims," the researchers reported that in the 2,760 stories examined, there were approximately three males for every one female. In biographies, males outnumbered females by an even higher percentage—approximately six to one. When males are the focus of the majority of stories, students are led to believe males are the norm, the standard, in society.

Perhaps you are thinking that "Dick and Jane as Victims" is interesting but that it is irrelevant to education today, two decades later. The same idea occurred to P. Purcell and L. Stewart (1990), so they replicated the study recently. They found that although the numbers of male and female characters are more nearly equal now, other sex stereotypes persist. Males are still featured in two-thirds of the pictures and photographs in books, so they still appear to be more standard than females. Perhaps more important, Purcell and Stewart found that both sexes were portrayed in sex-stereotyped ways: Females were shown depending on males to help and rescue them; males were portrayed as engaging in more adventurous activities than females, and males continue to be depicted in a wider range of careers. A related study (Tetenbaum & Pearson, 1989) of elementary readers found that male characters are more visible, more active, and involved in areas of life considered important in our society.

The male-standard bias in our society is further reflected in theories taught in schools. For instance, prominent theories of human moral and cognitive development have for years been based on studies that relied exclusively on male subjects. Thus, the ways in which males develop morally were universalized to members of both sexes (Gilligan, 1982; Wood & Lenze, 1991b). As we saw in earlier chapters, however, males and females are socialized in different contexts and ways that lead to distinct moral orientations. In general, feminine socialization prioritizes caring for others and responding to their needs, while masculine socialization emphasizes being fair to others and respecting their rights. Not surprisingly, when women were measured by a theory that excluded their experiences, they were judged to be less mature than men on whom the theory is based. By representing male moral development as standard, instruction has distorted understanding of the range and forms of human morality.

The Invisibility of Women

Sex-stereotypical portrayals of men as standard, active, and successful and women as invisible or marginal, passive, and dependent continue in books used at secondary and college levels. Consider how history is presented and who figures prominently in making it. Accounts of wars, for instance, focus on battles and military leaders. Seldom noted are the contributions of women both on the battlefields and at home. Who kept families intact and food on the table while men fought? Who manufactured supplies for men on the front? Chronicles of important events, such as the civil rights movement, focus on male leaders' speeches and press conferences and obscure the ways in which women made the movements possible. We know of the contributions of Stokley Carmichael and the Reverend Martin Luther King but remain uninformed of Ella Baker's pivotal efforts in organizing neighborhoods in support of civil rights. The few women who are presented tend to be exceptional cases who distinguished themselves on men's terms and in men's contexts, while women who had an impact in settings less privileged in our culture remain hidden (Spitzack & Carter, 1987). Women virtually disappear in historical accounts of our country and the world (Kramarae, Schultz, & O'Barr, 1984).

Women's experiences and perspectives have been similarly excluded from other academic subjects. For instance, women's experiences are seldom represented in theories of interpersonal relationships, small-group communication, public speaking, and other areas (Bowen & Wyatt, 1993). A. Oakley (1974) has shown that sociology defines political institutions, areas of work, and civic leadership in ways that reflect males' experiences and push those of women to the periphery. Theories of family life, Oakley notes, fail to include housework and cooking, which are clearly issues of real importance to *some* members of families.

M. M. Ferree and E. J. Hall (1990) discovered that women are conspicuously absent even in current college textbooks. Speech communication has also presented males as standard in some of its curricular content. For instance, Karlyn Campbell (1991, p. 33) has documented that "in recently published public address anthologies and public speaking textbooks, women are grossly underrepresented." She argues that in omitting women's speeches and women speakers, the field has undermined the goal of public speaking courses, which is to empower students to speak. Women, she observes, are not empowered when their courses teach them that only men and men's speaking merit study. Whether the field is literature, in which male authors predominate, or science, in which males are portrayed as virtually the only people to make discoveries, the trend is the same: Women's contributions are minimized or altogether neglected (Spender, 1989). One text even describes Madame Curie, two-time winner of the Nobel Prize, as her husband's "helpmate" (Basow, 1992, p. 150).

Misrepresentation of Human Experiences

When education makes women invisible and distorts their experiences by using male standards, social life as a whole is distorted. It is (mis)represented from the perspective of one group: white heterosexual males who had and have status and position. While a six-shooter receives six pages of discussion in one history book, the role and experiences of frontier women merit a mere six lines (Bate, 1988). Another widely used history text devotes a scant two sentences to the movement for women's right to vote. The male bias in curricular materials is further detected in the practice of defining historical epochs by their effects on men while totally neglecting their impact on the lives of women. It is ironic that the Renaissance is known as the period of rebirth and progress in human life when, in fact, it reduced the status and opportunities of most women (Kelly-Gadol, 1977).

As in other areas we have discussed, sexism in education intersects with other forms of discrimination: racism, classism, and heterosexism. Not just any males are presented as the standard; it is white, heterosexual, middle- and upper-class men who are depicted as the norm. How often have you studied important people who were lesbian or gay? How much of your education has focused on describing and explaining the lives and contributions of economically disadvantaged people? Have your courses taught you about black women and men in journalism, music, science, literature, and other fields? Criticizing the white bias in education, Linda Carty (1992) notes that blacks are invisible in college education, where the reference point has been and remains white males.

THE INVISIBILITY OF WOMEN'S ACHIEVEMENTS

Do you know how these women influenced our culture?

Maria Goeppert-Mayer   Ellen Goodman
Mary Wollstonecraft   Aphra Behn
Mary Manley   Barbara McClintock

Maria Goeppert-Mayer won the Nobel Prize in physics in 1963 but was not offered a full-time faculty position in an American university until the probability of her receipt of the award was made known.

Mary Wollstonecraft authored *The Vindication of Women's Rights*, a key text in the first wave of American feminism.

Mary Manley, who lived from 1663 to 1724, was a political journalist of considerable influence.

Ellen Goodman is a Pulitzer Prize–winning contemporary journalist.

Aphra Behn (1640–1689) was an abolitionist, writer, spy, and social activist. Her book *Oroonoko* provided one of the first popular accounts of the horrors of slavery. During her life, she traveled to the West Indies, where she supported a slave rebellion, was a spy for Charles II, published 13 novels along with collections of poetry, and produced 17 of her plays in London.

Barbara McClintock showed that the structure of DNA is subject to rearrangement and, thus, reprogramming, which is the basis of much current genetic work (Keller, 1985).

What are the consequences of biases in curricular materials? First, they reflect and perpetuate the general social practice of making women invisible. When we do not learn of women's contributions, the ways they shaped history, science, and literature, their activities, and the impact of events on women, then we misunderstand our collective life. We are given a partial and, therefore, false understanding of the subjects we study. This has three important implications. First, we may come to assume that males and male experiences are the standard for society and that men have made the only significant contributions (Gastil, 1990; Hamilton, 1991; Sheldon, 1990; Switzer, 1990).

K E V I N

I don't buy the stuff about history being distorted, and I don't think we should rewrite all of our books to make it look like women have done more just because that's politically correct. I'm fed up with all of this stuff in my classes that tries to convince us women and minorities did things. History is history, science is science, and saying women did things doesn't make it so.

T E R E S A

When I went home over break, I was telling my daddy about this class, and he got all upset when I started explaining the distortions in education. He started ranting that education was being ruined by a bunch of misguided liberals who are putting political correctness before truth. So I asked him why women who did things weren't in the textbooks and why the ways that women affected history aren't discussed. If education is supposed to present the "truth," I told him, then why hasn't it? He said I was getting my head filled with junk, and I would not have a good understanding of history and science and stuff because it would be guided by political correctness, not accuracy. So I said to him that it's just a matter of *whose* politics are in control. It seems to me that it was pretty political to write books in the first place that ignored what a lot of women and minorities did, but that kind of political correctness is consistent with my father's values.

A second implication of curricular bias is that it restricts everyone's knowledge. Commenting on the tendency to marginalize women's experience and define subject areas by male standards, D. Smith (1987) cautions that this deprives men, as well as women, of knowledge both about women's contributions to culture and about areas of life in which, historically, women have predominated. By marginalizing women's activities and contributions, education defines cultural life as the life of men. Third, on a more personal level, distortions and stereotypes in instructional content encourage men to see themselves as able to fulfill high ambitions and to affect the course of events, whereas these stereotypes discourage women from those self-perceptions. By implication, both women and men are taught to see women as less able to lead, have impact, and exert influence (American Association of University Women, 1991; Henley, 1989).

▰ Educational Processes

A third dimension of the hidden curriculum consists of communication processes in educational settings that devalue women and their ways of learning and expressing knowledge. Through inequitable expectations of and responses to male and female students, and through privileging masculine forms of communication, educators often unintentionally communicate that women students are inferior to male students.

Unequal Attention to Males and Females

The most obvious way in which teachers' communication expresses the view that males are more important than females is in the sheer amount of attention given to students. From preschool through graduate education, teachers pay more attention to male students. Further, research (Epperson, 1988; Hall & Sandler, 1982, 1984) indicates that teachers actually give male students more individualized instruction and time than they devote to female students.

Another way in which educational processes foster intellectual development in boys and men more than in girls and women is by reinforcing different qualities in male and female students. While teachers praise males for academic interest and achievement, they offer more support to female students for being quiet and compliant (Fagot, 1984; Gold, Crombie, & Noble, 1987; Sadker & Sadker, 1986). This pattern was first noticed in elementary classrooms, but later research has shown that it continues throughout all levels of education (Hall & Sandler, 1982; Sandler & Hall, 1986; Wood & Lenze, 1991a).

Doonesbury

BY GARRY TRUDEAU

DOONESBURY copyright 1992 G. B. Trudeau. Reprinted with permission of UNIVERSAL PRESS SYNDICATE. All rights reserved.

Not Taking Women Students Seriously

In an essay titled "Taking Women Students Seriously," Adrienne Rich (1979) calls attention to the fact that men routinely are treated as serious students, whereas women often are not. Women students are frequently praised for their appearance, personalities, and nurturing inclinations, while their academic abilities and achievements receive no comment (Hall & Sandler, 1982, 1984). When professors show an interest in men's ideas and encourage them to work further, but do not extend this attention to women students, the clear message is that males are more academically serious—and worthwhile.

Compounding this are differences in how academic advisers and faculty mentors often counsel male and female students. Consistently, more generous time, effort, and encouragement are given to males than to females (Hall & Sandler, 1984; Sandler & Hall, 1986). Women are often discouraged from pursuing challenging careers and encouraged instead to focus on family life and/or undemanding careers (Lacher, 1978). Further, as we noted earlier, the limited number of women in positions of authority in education reduces the likelihood that female students will find role models who could support their aspirations ("Where Have All the Smart Girls Gone?" 1989).

Sexual harassment is a particularly appalling instance of the devaluation of women. Indicative of the overall lack of regard for women as students and persons, sexual harassment is widespread on college campuses (Hughes & Sandler, 1986; Wood, 1992b). Women faculty and staff report they are sexually harassed by colleagues and administrators (Kreps, 1992; Wood, 1992b). Male students routinely harass women with cheers, jeers, lewd suggestions, and uninvited physical touches, and this is apparently considered normal by many students (Malovich & Stake, 1990; Paludi, 1990). In 1992 ("Fraternities Raise Consciousness, Not Hell," 1992), students at a southern university protested the fraternity

JEANNE

It's just ceaseless, the way men harass women on this campus. If it's not construction workers making dirty remarks as you walk by, it's guys lined up in front of the cafeteria rating us as we walk by. If it's not that, it's professors who give you the once over or let their eyes wander during a conference. It's just nonstop. Sometimes I feel like screaming, "Quit treating me like a pinup and notice I am a student who just wants to learn without hassle."

practice of using a "pig book," which contained photos of first-year students. Fraternity brothers select the most attractive entering women students and invite them to fraternity parties called "cattle drives," at which the brothers and pledges encourage them to drink and then take sexual liberties.

Sexual harassment is not confined to peer interactions. Some faculty treat women in classes as sex objects rather than as serious students. Ranging from provocative remarks to offers of higher grades for sexual favors, instances of sexual harassment by faculty are substantial (Hughes & Sandler, 1988). These create a climate of intimidation in which many women students' sexuality is made more salient to them than their intellectual activities and interests. Sexual harassment defines women in sexual terms and subjects them to intrusion and abuse by more powerful males. In treating women as sexual objects, harassment ignores and undermines their status as students and tells them they are not taken seriously as members of an intellectual community.

Classroom Communication

Education further devalues women students through communication practices that favor and reward male students more than female ones. We will consider two of these practices: different ways teachers communicate to male and female students and instructional styles that benefit males more than females.

Gender biases in communication with students. In 1982, a pioneering study by R. M. Hall and B. R. Sandler called attention to a variety of verbal and nonverbal communication practices that convey the hidden curriculum by providing less recognition and encouragement for female students than for male students. That investigation and other similar ones (Krupnick, 1985; Sadker &

Sadker, 1986; Spender, 1989) identified the following communication behaviors of teachers as ones that devalue women students:

♦ Professors are more likely to know the names of male students than female ones.

♦ Professors maintain more eye contact and more attentive postures when talking to male students than when addressing female students.

♦ Professors ask more challenging questions of male students.

♦ Professors give longer and more significant verbal and nonverbal responses to males' comments than to those of females. When male students cannot respond to a question, they tend to be given additional time along with encouragement and coaching until they come up with a good answer; when female students do not answer correctly, instructors frequently move on.

♦ Faculty call on male students more often.

♦ Faculty are more willing to make time and to devote longer periods of time to confer with male students than with female students.

♦ Female students' contributions are interrupted, ignored, or dismissed more often than those of males.

♦ Faculty extend and pursue comments by male students more than those of female students.

You may be wondering why we would bring up an 11-year-old study in a discussion of communication in education. Regrettably, the most recent investigations confirm the persistence of a range of behaviors that suggest male students are taken more seriously and regarded more favorably than female students. In 1990, C. G. Krupnick ("Researcher," p. 10A) reported that men get more than do women for the dollars they spend on education. She reported that the biases found in 1972 persevere and continue to create inequities in men's and women's educations. In 1992, the American Association of University Women Educational Foundation commissioned a comprehensive review of 1,331 studies of gender and educational practices. The result was a report titled "How Schools Shortchange Girls" ("Sexism in the Schoolhouse," 1992), in which evidence was amassed to show that female students continue to receive less attention, less encouragement, and less serious regard than their male peers. Other evidence of current sexism included issues we have discussed in previous sections of this chapter: stereotypical images in textbooks, disproportionate inclusion of male authors and historical figures and neglect of women, lack of recognition and encouragement of women students who have high career ambitions, and an increasing tolerance for sexist remarks and sexual harassment.

Doonesbury

BY GARRY TRUDEAU

Not coincidentally, this recent report also found that "girls enter first grade with the same or better skills and ambitions as boys. But, all too often, by the time they finish high school, 'their doubts have crowded out their dreams'" ("Sexism in the Schoolhouse," 1992, p. 62). The evidence from this study led to the conclusion that the hidden curriculum creates a downward intellectual mobility cycle in which "girls are less likely to reach their potential than boys" (p. 62). The reasons for this pattern seem to lie in the cumulative effects of communication that devalues women students and that presents white heterosexual males as normal and important, and females, gays, lesbians, and people of color as marginal.

Instructional style. Teaching processes also disadvantage women students by favoring a classroom climate more conducive to male modes of learning and achievement. In Chapter 5, we discussed the speech communities in which men and women are socialized, and we discovered that these communities encourage distinctive understandings of how to communicate. In general, males learn to use talk to assert themselves and compete, while females see talk as a way to build cooperative relationships with others. Relatedly, recent research (Belenky, Clinchy, Goldberger, & Tarule, 1986) suggests that women may also learn in more interactive, collaborative ways than most men prefer. With these differences in mind, consider what kind of classroom climate would foster learning and involvement for each gender.

The expected and rewarded patterns of classroom participation are consistent with masculine rules of communication and inconsistent with feminine forms (Hall & Sandler, 1982, 1984; "Sexism in the Schoolhouse," 1992; Wood & Lenze, 1991a). Given this, it is not surprising that males are more comfortable and find learning easier than females, since classroom climates so often employ masculine communication styles (Gabriel & Smithson, 1990; Tannen, 1991). From grade school to graduate school, classroom climates typically emphasize assertion, competition, and individual initiative. Students are encouraged to compete with each other in class discussions, performances, and tests. Further, assignments emphasize individual efforts and seldom allow for collaborative work. Assertion and self-confidence are more rewarded than are questioning and tentative statements. In all of these respects, the traditional educational climate reflects and enables men's participation and achievement more than that of women. Many classrooms are actually masculine speech communities, which renders them ineffective in empowering individuals who employ feminine styles of communication. People who have learned to use communication to build relationships and collaborate with others find it uncomfortable to compete, to assert themselves over others, and to speak in absolute terms that don't invite others to participate. This may explain why many women students in coeducational institutions speak up less often in classrooms.

The effects of instruction favoring one gender's speech style are linked to the sex of students and teachers. In 1983, Paula Treichler and Cheris Kramarae reported on an experimental class that primarily used styles of interaction and learning reflective of women's speech communities: discussion, group projects, interactive teaching and learning, cooperative review sessions, and interaction in which students collaborate rather than compete with each other. Women students particularly responded to this learning environment, and men in the class at first found it uncomfortable but came to realize it had distinctive values and enlarged their learning. Recent research (Crawford & MacLeod, 1990; Statham, Richardson, & Cook, 1991) indicates that women college faculty tend to encourage more participatory classroom climates than do male instructors. Not surprisingly, in classroom environments that are inclusive and invite collaboration, women students take more active roles, participating in relative equity with their male peers. These findings suggest that women, like men, excel in settings that favor and affirm their ways of thinking and communicating. By implication, the ideal instructional style might blend masculine and feminine modes of communicating, which would enable all students to participate comfortably some of the time and stretch all students to supplement their styles of interacting by learning additional ones.

In summary, the hidden curriculum consists of three interrelated factors. First, the organization of educational institutions reiterates the gender stratification of Western society in which males are defined as authorities and women as subordinates. Second, curricular content marginalizes women's contributions in areas ranging from genetics to literature, suggesting that males are both the standard and more valuable, influential, and active than females. Third, educational processes, including teachers' communication and classroom climate, send the message that males are taken more seriously as students and are given greater opportunity to participate fully in education than are women.

This hidden curriculum creates educational settings that are dramatically inequitable: They are hospitable to men but are chilly climates for women (Hall & Sandler, 1982, 1984; Sandler & Hall, 1986). The specific behaviors we have discussed, coupled with other practices such as use of male-generic language, work together to impede the efforts and confidence of women students. Simultaneously, they reinforce a gendered social order (Hamilton, 1988). While some of the issues we have noted here appear small, in tandem they work to disempower women students. Although each specific form of gender inequity in education might seem minor, the *cumulative* impact can be overwhelming in communicating constantly that women are less valued, less respected, and less able than their male peers.

Certainly not all women students are derailed by gender biases that permeate education. Probably you know some women students who are very successful academically; perhaps you are one yourself. The gender inequities in education we have discussed, like other forms of gender discrimination, have predictable *general* consequences on women as a group. This doesn't mean some individual women aren't exceptions. Clearly, some are, either because they have not adopted social views of femininity and therefore they employ more masculine styles of learning and communicating, and/or because they are able to overcome the biases in education. The point is that no student—woman or man—should have to work against the odds to gain an education. Learning should be equally accessible to all.

The information presented so far in this chapter provides insight into why females' self-esteem, as well as that of minorities, erodes and white males' esteem rises in proportion to the amount of time spent in education. The organization, curricular content, and pedagogical processes standard in most educational environments undermine the confidence, career ambitions, and overall sense of esteem of women and people of color. Because this opposes our culture's commitment to equal opportunity education for all, a number of efforts have been devised to remedy the inequities that punctuate American education. In the final section of this chapter, we consider four of those efforts and the ways in which each attempts to create educational environments that value and empower women and men equally.

▪ Efforts to Redress Inequities in Educational Systems

A desire to correct gender and sex discrimination (as well as other types of discrimination) has led to a variety of solutions. Four particular means to ending discrimination are equal opportunity, affirmative action, quotas and goals, and increasing sensitivity to gender issues in educational content and processes. These methods are related in that each is a response to existing inequities, and each proposes a specific way of correcting those. Because these remedies are related, we sometimes don't recognize distinctions among them, and we may confuse different efforts at reform. Yet affirmative action is not the same thing as quotas, and it's certainly not reverse discrimination. Understanding the methods of redressing inequities and how they differ is important so that we may evaluate arguments for and against them and decide our own positions. Although this chapter focuses specifically on education, keep in mind that efforts to redress discrimination transcend the specific context of schooling. The remedies we will discuss apply to gender inequities in general — in educational settings as well as in other areas of life.

Equal Opportunity Laws

Laws prohibiting discrimination began with the landmark *Brown* v. *Board of Education* case in 1954. In deciding the case for Brown, the United States Supreme Court overturned the "separate but equal" doctrine that had allowed separate educational systems for white and African-American citizens. While this was the start of laws to guarantee civil liberties, equal opportunity legislation is not confined to racial discrimination. Following *Brown* v. *Board of Education*, a number of laws were passed in the 1950s and 1960s to prohibit discrimination against individual members of minority groups, including racial minorities and women. Two primary examples of **equal opportunity laws** are Title VII of the Civil Rights Act of 1964, which prohibits discrimination in employment on the basis of race, color, religion, sex, or national origin, and Title IX, which forbids discrimination in educational programs receiving federal aid.

Passed in 1972, Title IX states that "no person in the United States shall, on the basis of sex, be excluded from participation in, be denied benefit of, or be subjected to discrimination under any program or activity receiving Federal financial assistance." Covered by this law are standards of admission, courses and academic majors, counseling, financial aid, and athletic programs. Some institutions also ban discrimination on the basis of other factors such as sexual preference, disability, and age. While Title IX is considered the primary federal law regarding discrimination on the basis of sex, it is not the only one. Others are Title IV of the 1964 Civil Rights Act, the Women's Educational Equity Act of 1974 and 1978, an amendment to the 1976 Vocational Education Act, and laws pertaining to specific institutes and foundations (Klein, 1985; Salomone, 1986).

Equal opportunity laws focus on discrimination against *individual* members of classes. For instance, complaints filed with the Equal Employment Opportunity Commission must claim that a particular person suffered discrimination because of sex, race, or other criteria named in laws (Public Agenda Foundation, 1990). Equal opportunity does not ask whether a group (women, Hispanics) is underrepresented or has been treated inequitably; instead, it focuses specifically on discrimination against individuals. Further, the equal opportunity strategy focuses on *present* practices, so historical patterns of discrimination are irrelevant. For example, a university with a record of not admitting women into a particular program is not subject to suit unless a particular individual can prove she personally and currently suffered discrimination on the basis of her sex. Governmental obligation extends only to present, individual equality of opportunity. Equal opportunity is assessed on a case-by-case basis.

Although Title IX prohibits sex discrimination, for years it lacked regulations to ensure its implementation (Mickelson & Smith, 1992). Further, the scope of this law was weakened in 1984 when the Supreme Court narrowed its application from whole institutions to only specific programs and activities that receive federal money. Despite laws, sexism and discrimination against women persist in educational settings. In this chapter, we have seen how curricular materials, school organization, and educational processes unequally benefit women and men. Equal opportunity legislation fails to address the impact of historical patterns of discrimination and covert biases, so these continue to riddle educational practice and to falsify the pledge of equal opportunity for all.

Affirmative Action Policies

President Lyndon Johnson used his 1965 commencement address at Howard University to inaugurate a new strategy for combating discrimination. Saying that recent passage of civil rights legislation was important but insufficient to end discrimination, Johnson called for policies that address the weight of historical prejudice. He said, "You do not take a person who for years has been hobbled by chains and liberate him, bring him to the starting line of a race and then say, 'you are free to compete with all the others.'" Johnson went on to argue that equality of opportunity, which is the guarantee of civil rights legislation, must be matched with equality in results. To do this, he claimed, there must be measures to compensate for historical patterns of discrimination against groups as well as subtle forms of discrimination such as institutional racism and sexism.

Affirmative action hinges on three key ideas (Public Agenda Foundation, 1990, p. 23). First, because discrimination has systematically restricted the opportunities of *groups* of people, remedies must apply to entire groups, not just to individuals. Second, there must be *preferential treatment* for members of groups that have suffered discrimination in order to compensate for the legacy of discrimination. Third, the effectiveness of remedies is judged by *results*, not intent. If a law does not result in greater presence of women and minorities, then it is ineffective in producing the result of equality.

The goal of affirmative action is to increase the representation in education and in the workplace of available and qualified women, minorities, and other

JERRY

I understand about historical discrimination, but I still don't think affirmative action is right. I am a white male, and I know that means that I have less of a chance of getting a job today than a black person or a female. Even if I am more qualified, they can get it. That isn't right. It's just another kind of discrimination. I didn't do anything to women or blacks. I didn't discriminate against them, so why should I have to pay for what others did?

historically marginalized groups. This focus causes some to question the fairness of affirmative action policies (summarized in Witt, 1990). They argue that insisting on greater numbers of women in athletic or academic programs results in excluding more qualified white males. What many people do not realize is that affirmative action includes two important limitations. First, the goal is to increase the number of *qualified* members of historically marginalized groups, so there is no pressure to admit, hire, or promote women and minorities who lack necessary qualifications. Affirmative action policies also recognize the *limited availability* of historically underrepresented groups. Because of long-standing discriminatory practices, there may be fewer women and minorities who are qualified to participate in certain programs and activities. Affirmative action only attempts to increase the number of qualified members of minority groups, commensurate with their availability.

To understand how affirmative action policies work, it's important to distinguish between *qualified* and *most qualified*. Consider an example: Jane Evans and John Powell are the final two candidates for the single remaining opening in a medical school that requires a 3.2 undergraduate grade point average and a 1200 on the medical aptitude exam. Jane's undergraduate average is a 3.4, while John's is a 3.6. On the entrance exam she scores 1290, and he scores 1300. Although his qualifications are slightly better than hers, both individuals clearly meet the school's requirements; both are adequately qualified. In such a case, affirmative action would require admitting Jane instead of John, because she meets the qualifications and does so despite historical patterns that discourage women from studying sciences and math, which are primary in premed schooling. The fact that she overcame disadvantages to become qualified suggests that Jane will succeed in medical studies if she is given the opportunity.

As columnist William Raspberry (1990) points out, affirmative action is necessary to translate goals of equality from empty theory into concrete realities.

N I C O L A

Quotas are the only thing that can work. The laws aren't enforced, so they don't help, and affirmative action is just a bunch of talk. I've watched both my parents discriminated against all of their lives just because of their skin color. All the laws and pledges of affirmative action haven't done a damned thing to change that. Quotas cut through all of the crap of intentions and pledges and say point blank there will be so many African-Americans in this company or this school or whatever. That's the only way change is ever going to happen. And when I hear white dudes whining about how quotas are unfair to them, I want to throw up. They know *nothing* about unfair.

Unlike equal opportunity legislation, affirmative action recognizes the impact of historical patterns of discrimination and the ways in which they disadvantage whole groups of people. Thus, this remedy aims to make up for the effects of a long heritage of bias by giving slight preference to individuals whose qualification was achieved in spite of obstacles and discrimination.

Quotas and Goals

Quotas. Perhaps the most controversial effort to redress discrimination is the **quota system**. Building on affirmative action's focus on end results, quotas specify that a number or percentage of women and/or minorities must be admitted to schools, hired in certain positions, or promoted to defined levels in institutions. For instance, a university might stipulate that it has a quota of 50% women in athletic programs or 30% women at the faculty level of full professor. A binding quota requires a specified number or percentage of women regardless of circumstances such as merit. If a medical school has an unmet quota of women to be admitted, it must admit women applicants even if they lack the required academic average and entrance exam score.

A famous case relevant to quotas was brought in 1978 when Allan Bakke sued a school, claiming that the school's quota of minority admissions had resulted in rejecting him, a white male, in favor of less qualified minority applicants. Bakke won his case on the grounds that he had been a victim of "reverse discrimination." In her 1990 race for the California governorship, Dianne Feinstein pledged that if she won, she would appoint women to half of the offices in her administration. She reasoned that women are more than half of the voters in

California, so a representative number—half—of state administrators should be women. This stand cost Feinstein votes because many people viewed her quotas as reverse discrimination. As J. Beck (1990) noted, "Laws and policies that discriminate in favor of one race or sex or ethnic group discriminate against other people."

Goals. Goals are different than quotas, although the two are frequently confused. A goal states an institution's intention to achieve representation of minorities or women. For instance, a university could establish the goal of having women make up 30% of faculty at the full professor rank by the year 2000. Goals call for no flexibility on qualifications and they do not require results. If the university in our example had only 13% women full professors (the current nationwide percentage) by 2000, there would be no penalty nor even any need to develop new strategies. The university could simply announce that its new goal is to have 30% women full professors by the year 2010. Goals are more flexible than quotas, which many consider an advantage. However, goals also lack enforcement provisions, which means their effectiveness depends entirely on the commitment of those charged to pursue them. For this reason, groups that have been victims of discrimination are often skeptical of goals as a serious effort to increase equity (Witt, 1990).

Ironically, both quotas and goals can work *against* women and minorities. D. Maraniss (1991) points out that just as they function to let in minorities, so too can they exclude people. The numbers specified by quotas and goals can be interpreted and used as a maximum number of women and minorities, rather than a minimum. In our example, the 30% number established for women full professors could be used to keep more than 30% of the professoriate from being female, even if 40% of those qualified for promotion were women. Departments may hire an African-American or woman scholar and then cease to consider other female and minority applicants for future openings—they've met their quota by employing one. Because both quotas and goals establish limits, they can be used to exclude as well as include.

Goals and quotas can work against women and minorities in a second way. When goals or quotas are in effect, members of institutions may assume women and minorities got in only because of their sex or race. When this happens, individual women and people of color are not regarded as capable members of the school, business, or trade. Others may overlook their qualifications and accomplishments and simply discount them as "quota fillers." One implication of this is that women and minorities—regardless of their qualifications—may be resented by peers who think they didn't earn membership in the institution. In addition, if others discount the abilities of minorities and women, they are unlikely to take them seriously and give them important responsibilities that allow achievement and opportunities that lead to advancement.

Increasing Sensitivity to Gender Issues

A final remedy for persistent discrimination is enhancing sensitivity to gender discrimination through training and through creating curricular materials that do not foster inequity. This strategy assumes that many people are unaware of the range of ways in which educational institutions devalue and disadvantage women. If lack of awareness is the problem, then a promising solution is to make people conscious of practices that inadvertently devalue and marginalize women and to provide materials that incorporate women and their experiences. This strategy focuses attention on creating nonbiased curricular materials and developing teacher training programs that heighten educators' sensitivity to gender biases they may not have recognized.

Implementing this solution requires developing programs that inform educators and students of subtle biases and introducing them to alternative instructional materials and styles of teaching. For instance, a program of nonsexist education for 3- to 5-year-olds was developed (Koblinsky & Sugawara, 1984) and implemented. Both girls and boys who participated in the special program had substantially less sex-stereotypical views than they had before the program and than their peers in regular programs manifested. At some universities, faculty and staff have developed workshops on sexual harassment and gender discrimination in classrooms. Students, staff, and faculty who attend these learn how some of their communication and course content may exclude women and people of color. In addition, participants in these workshops are introduced to methods to make their classrooms more inclusive and more equitable for people of color and women. Of course, not everyone cares about inequities, and many people are not

GEORGE

I like the idea of training in gender sensitivity. Part of the orientation program when I came here was a program in sexism and racism. Until I attended that, it never occurred to me that words like *girl* could offend, and I had never realized Confederate flags would seem like bigotry to blacks. Maybe I was naive, but I really didn't understand those things, and now that I do, I don't do them anymore. And then courses like this one make me aware of other things, like how I interrupt women and that keeps men dominant. I think a lot of the discrimination is really insensitivity and is really not deliberate. Once people understand that certain words and actions hurt, they'll stop.

willing to make changes, especially ones that may limit some of their own privileges. Thus, an important drawback of gender-sensitivity programs is that they require personal commitment and interest from educators.

A complementary way to decrease gender bias in education is to provide teachers with materials that allow them to teach more inclusively. For instance, Karlyn Campbell (1989a, 1989b, 1993) followed her call for including women speakers in public address courses by producing three volumes of material on the lives and speeches of important women orators. H. Tierney has published a series of books that document women's contributions in the sciences (1989); literature, arts, and education (1990); and history, philosophy, and religion (1991). A colleague and I (Wood & Lenze, 1991b) published an article in which we explained how to incorporate both women's and men's developmental paths into instruction on communication and self-development. Similarly, another colleague and I (Wood & Inman, 1993) published an essay that showed ways to include masculine modes of creating and expressing closeness in curricular units on communication within friendships.

While education has historically not been an equally empowering environment for women and men, this appears to be changing. Noteworthy trends, such as those we have discussed, indicate that many educators are becoming more aware of the hidden curriculum and the covert, subtle ways in which it creates inequitable learning climates for men and women. Further, increasing numbers of teachers are reading articles on gender sensitivity and attending workshops that help them discover subtle biases in their own instruction. It is also encouraging to see the wealth of materials being written by scholars so that there are resources for those who wish to include women's contributions and perspectives along with those of men in order to make educational content representative of the range and diversity of people who compose and participate in cultural life.

Finally, we should realize that a number of students are taking active roles to challenge and change sexism, racism, and heterosexism in education. Many students, including a number of men, are taking courses in women's studies and African-American studies to enrich the breadth of their education. Further, they often use what they learn in those classes to call attention to white male standards in other courses they take. More than once my students have helped me see where my teaching inadvertently excluded minorities, and they've frequently provided me with resources so that I could learn about people and issues I should include. After taking my course in gender and communication, students sometimes report back to me that they have used what they learned in our course to challenge sexism in other classes. For instance, one man told me he had asked a professor to stop using male-generic language, and the professor had stopped. Another student said she had used her knowledge to intervene in a class where males interrupted females and where the professor paid more attention to male students' comments. Whenever a woman was interrupted, she would say "I'd like to hear what Jane was saying"; whenever a woman student's ideas were dismissed, she would find a way to credit the woman in her own comments: "I think Mary had a good point when she said, . . . and I'd like to extend it." As powerful agents of change, students are a major force in charting the future of education.

*S*ummary

In this chapter, we have gone beneath the surface of education to examine the hidden curriculum, which creates unequal educational opportunities for women and men. The hidden curriculum consists of three elements. First, in mirroring the gender stratification of society in which men are defined as superior and women subordinate, educational institutions model these as normal to students, a process that re-creates inequity. Second, curricular content devalues women by excluding them and their experiences, perspectives, and contexts from instruction. In so doing, it represents men and male experiences as the norm, or standard, and women and their experiences as marginal, unimportant, or deviant. Third, teachers' communication contributes to gendered education by giving men students greater attention, respect, and recognition than women students. In a number of ways, teachers and staff of educational institutions communicate to women that they are less valued and less able than their male peers. Historically, the combination of these elements reproduces gender inequities within school settings, making education a process that generally enables men more than women.

Because serious and damaging inequities diminish education, there are major efforts to reduce discrimination and to increase the equality of educational opportunities and results. Existing remedies of equal opportunity, affirmative action, quotas and goals, and increasing sensitivity to gender issues will probably be augmented by other strategies in future years. Students, too, are working to remake education by claiming their voices and exerting their influence to correct practices that disadvantage, devalue, or dismiss women and minorities. As we learn more about the ways education is gendered, additional means of diminishing inequities will be devised in an effort to realize the American pledge of truly equal education for all citizens.

*D*iscussion Questions

1. How many role models have you found in the schools you've attended? Which of your teachers have given you ideas about who you might become and what you might do in life? As a class, discuss this and notice whether women, men, and minority students report finding equal numbers of role models in educational settings.

2. Examine one or more of the textbooks used in other courses you are taking this term. Do you see examples of the hidden curriculum in these books? Are men

represented as standard by male-generic language, disproportionate references to men and their activities, and theories that reflect masculine more than feminine interests and orientations?

3. What are the consequences for knowledge of overrepresenting men and underrepresenting women and their experiences? Using standpoint logic, ask how our understandings are affected when issues, disciplines, and content of knowledge are defined from the standpoint of only some members of a culture.

4. As you attend classes this term, notice patterns of communication in them. Do teachers call on male and female students equally? Do they respond with equivalent interest and encouragement to students of both sexes?

5. If you have both women and men as professors, do you see differences in their styles of teaching? Do they rely equally on lecture and participative discussion? Do they engage students in similar ways, or are there differences in the formality, friendliness, and so forth of their interactions with students?

6. Think about your experiences as a student. In elementary and secondary school, what did your teachers praise about your work? What did they criticize? Are your experiences consistent with patterns identified in the chapter?

7. How prevalent is sexual harassment on your campus? Are women students forced to endure jeers, suggestive comments, and so forth? How does this affect women's comfort and confidence as students? Does your school have a sexual harassment officer or an office where you can report harassment? Is there an official policy against it?

8. As a class, discuss different instructional styles. Do you prefer structured classes in which professors lecture and students talk little? Or do you prefer more interactive classes in which you participate? How do these different styles of instruction affect your learning? What kinds of learning and personal development does each style promote?

9. As a class, discuss various efforts to redress discrimination in education. Now that you understand distinctions among equal opportunity, affirmative action, quotas, and goals, discuss advantages and problems of each. Do you think policies should focus on an individual or on group discrimination? Should they compensate for historical patterns of discrimination?

10. Are goals or quotas more desirable? Can goals really work when there is no provision to make sure they are enforced? Are quotas too binding to be acceptable? If goals don't result in less discrimination, then what might? As a class, design a policy that you think would best eliminate discrimination while not severely penalizing individuals and groups who have not suffered discrimination.

$\mathcal{G}$endered Media: The Influence of Media on Views of Gender

In this chapter, we examine another important form of communication about gender: From newspapers to MTV, media interact with cultural images of gender and with individual identities in three ways. First, media reflect cultural values and ideals about gender. They portray women, men, and relationships between the sexes in ways that mirror widely shared understandings and ideals. Second, media reproduce cultural views of gender in individuals. By defining "normal" women, men, and relationships, media suggest how we should be as women and men. Third, media are gatekeepers of information and images. To a significant extent, they control what we see and know by deciding what programs to air, what news stories to feature, how to represent issues and events, and how to depict women and men. By selectively regulating what we see, media influence how we perceive gender issues, ourselves, and men and women in general.

To launch our exploration of how media reflect and shape understandings of gender, we will first establish the significance of media in cultural life. Next,

MEDIA'S MISREPRESENTATION OF AMERICAN LIFE

The media present a distorted version of cultural life in our country. According to media portrayals:

> White males make up two-thirds of the population. The women are less in number, perhaps because fewer than 10% live beyond 35. Those who do, like their younger and male counterparts, are nearly all white and heterosexual. In addition to being young, the majority of women are beautiful, very thin, passive, and primarily concerned with relationships and getting rings out of collars and commodes. There are a few bad, bitchy women, and they are not so pretty, not so subordinate, and not so caring as the good women. Most of the bad ones work outside of the home, which is probably why they are hardened and undesirable. The more powerful, ambitious men occupy themselves with important business deals, exciting adventures, and rescuing dependent females, whom they often then assault sexually.

we will identify basic themes and trends in media's images of women, men, and relationships between the sexes. Third, we will examine media's role in shaping our understanding of issues related to gender. Finally, we will ask how media's portrayals of gender issues and of men and women contribute to misconceptions of issues, violence against women, psychological and physical problems of men and women, and limited views of our human possibilities.

The Prevalence of Media in Cultural Life

How important are media in shaping our views of our world, ourselves, and gender? Consider what we know about the extent to which media are part of our lives. In a relatively short span of years, television has saturated American life. While only 9% of households owned televisions in 1950, by 1991 nearly all American households (98.3%) own a television, and two-thirds of households own more than one set (Television Bureau of Advertising, 1991, p. 2). Well over half of all households now own videocassette recorders (Edmondson, 1987), which suggests home film viewing is substantial. Cable penetration is now 60.2% (Television Bureau of Advertising, 1991, p. 2). The average household receives more than 28 stations (*American Demographics*, February 1990, p. 4), and at least one television is on more than 7 hours a day. Television reaches more people than any other medium, with 89% (18- to 54-year-olds) to 94% (those over 55 years old) watching television in a given day (Television Bureau of Advertising, 1990, p. 4). Children and adolescents are heavy viewers, averaging 2 to 3½ hours daily (Television Bureau of Advertising, 1991, p. 7), and some watch as many as 7 hours in a single day (Gerbner & Gross, 1976; Nielsen Media Research, 1989). By age 16, many adolescents have spent more time in front of a television than in school, and the amount of viewing is even higher for most African-Americans (Brown, Childers, Bauman, & Koch, 1990; Tangney & Feshbach, 1988).

Beyond television, media continue to pervade our lives. While walking or riding through any area, we take in a nearly endless procession of billboards that advertise various products, services, people, and companies. Magazines abound, and each one is full of stories that represent men and women and their relationships, thereby suggesting what is "normal." The hundreds of magazines available make it possible for just about anyone to select the kind of coverage she or he wants. In 1991, *Playboy* had 3,488,006 subscribers, while *Newsweek* had 3,211,958 and *Family Circle* had 5,431,779 ("Mediaworks," 1991, p. 37). Advertisements, which make up nearly half of some magazines, tell us what we need and where to buy it if we are to meet cultural standards for women and men. Radios, Walkmans, and stereo systems allow us to hear music as much of the time as we wish, while home videos are doing a record business as Americans see more films than ever. In 1991, 72.5% of homes had at least one VCR (Television Bureau of Advertising, 1991, p. 2). Newspapers, which circulate to over 62 million homes (Newsprint Information Committee, 1992, p. 18), news programming, and talk shows provide us with a horizon on our world, contemporary issues, and the roles of various people in shaping cultural life. Popular advice books and gothic novels are top sellers, and pornographic print and visual media are readily available to anyone who is interested.

▇ Themes in Media

Of the many influences on how we view men and women, media are the most pervasive and one of the most powerful. Woven throughout our daily lives, media insinuate their messages into our consciousness at every turn. All forms of media communicate images of the sexes, many of which perpetuate unrealistic, stereotypical, and limiting perceptions. Three themes describe how media represent gender. First, women are underrepresented, which falsely implies that men are the cultural standard and women are unimportant or invisible. Second, men and women are portrayed in stereotypical ways that reflect and sustain socially endorsed views of gender. Third, depictions of relationships between men and women emphasize traditional roles and normalize violence against women. We will consider each of these themes in this section.

Underrepresentation of Women

A primary way in which media distort reality is in underrepresenting women. Whether it is prime-time television, in which there are three times as many white men as women (Basow, 1992, p. 159), or children's programming, in which males outnumber females by two to one, or newscasts, in which women make up 16% of newscasters and in which stories about men are included 10 times more often than ones about women ("Study Reports Sex Bias," 1989), media misrepresent actual proportions of men and women in the population. This constant distortion tempts us to believe that there really are more men than women and, further, that men are the cultural standard.

Other myths about what is standard are similarly fortified by communication in media. Minorities are even less visible than women, with African-Americans appearing only rarely (Gray, 1986; Stroman, 1989) and other ethnic minorities being virtually nonexistent. In children's programming when African-Americans do appear, almost invariably they appear in supporting roles rather than as main characters (O'Connor, 1989). While more African-Americans are appearing in prime-time television, they are too often cast in stereotypical roles. In the 1992 season, for instance, 12 of the 74 series on commercial networks included large African-American casts, yet most featured them in stereotypical roles. Black men are presented as lazy and unable to handle authority, as lecherous, and/or as unlawful, while females are portrayed as domineering or as sex objects ("Sights, Sounds, and Stereotypes," 1992). Writing in 1993, David Evans (1993, p. 10) criticized television for stereotyping black males as athletes and entertainers. These roles, wrote Evans, mislead young black male viewers into thinking success "is only a dribble or dance step away," and blind them to other, more realistic ambitions. Hispanics and Asians are nearly absent, and when they are presented it is usually as villains or criminals (Lichter, Lichter, Rothman, & Amundson, 1987).

Also underrepresented is the single fastest growing group of Americans — older people. As a country, we are aging so that people over 60 make up a major part of our population; within this group, women significantly outnumber men (Wood, 1993c). Older people not only are underrepresented in media but also are represented inaccurately. In contrast to demographic realities, media consistently show fewer older women than men, presumably because our culture worships youth and beauty in women. Further, elderly individuals are frequently portrayed as sick, dependent, fumbling, and passive, images not borne out in real life. Distorted depictions of older people and especially older women in media, however, can delude us into thinking they are a small, sickly, and unimportant part of our population.

The lack of women in the media is paralleled by the scarcity of women in charge of media. Only about 5% of television writers, executives, and producers are women (Lichter, Lichter, & Rothman, 1986). Ironically, while two-thirds of journalism graduates are women, they make up less than 2% of those in corporate management of newspapers and only about 5% of newspaper publishers ("Women in Media," 1988). Female film directors are even more scarce, as are executives in charge of MTV. It is probably not coincidental that so few women are behind the scenes of an industry that so consistently portrays women negatively. Some media analysts (Mills, 1988) believe that if more women had positions of authority at executive levels, media would offer more positive portrayals of women.

Stereotypical Portrayals of Women and Men

In general, media continue to present both women and men in stereotyped ways that limit our perceptions of human possibilities. Typically men are portrayed as active, adventurous, powerful, sexually aggressive, and largely uninvolved in human relationships. Just as consistent with cultural views of gender are depictions of women as sex objects who are usually young, thin, beautiful, passive, dependent, and often incompetent and dumb. Female characters devote their primary energies to improving their appearances and taking care of homes and people. Because media pervade our lives, the ways they misrepresent genders may distort how we see ourselves and what we perceive as normal and desirable for men and women.

Stereotypical portrayals of men. According to J. A. Doyle (1989, p. 111), whose research focuses on masculinity, children's television typically shows males as "aggressive, dominant, and engaged in exciting activities from which they receive rewards from others for their 'masculine' accomplishments." Relatedly, recent studies reveal that the majority of men on prime-time television are independent, aggressive, and in charge (McCauley, Thangavelu, & Rozin, 1988). Television programming for all ages disproportionately depicts men as serious, confident, competent, powerful, and in high-status positions. Gentleness in men, which was briefly evident in the 1970s, has receded as established male characters are redrawn to be more tough and distanced from others (Boyer, 1986). Highly popular films such as *Lethal Weapon, Predator, Days of Thunder, Total Recall,*

Robocop, Die Hard, and *Die Harder* star men who embody the stereotype of extreme masculinity. Media, then, reinforce long-standing cultural ideals of masculinity: Men are presented as hard, tough, independent, sexually aggressive, unafraid, violent, totally in control of all emotions, and—above all—in no way feminine.

Equally interesting is how males are *not* presented. J. D. Brown and K. Campbell (1986) report that men are seldom shown doing housework. Doyle (1989) notes that boys and men are rarely presented caring for others. B. Horovitz (1989) points out they are typically represented as uninterested in and incompetent at homemaking, cooking, and child care. Each season's new ads for cooking and cleaning supplies include several that caricature men as incompetent buffoons, who are klutzes in the kitchen and no better at taking care of children. While children's books have made a limited attempt to depict women engaged in activities outside of the home, there has been little parallel effort to show men involved in family and home life. When someone is shown taking care of a child, it is usually the mother, not the father. This perpetuates a negative stereotype of men as uncaring and uninvolved in family life.

Stereotypical portrayals of women. Media's images of women also reflect cultural stereotypes that depart markedly from reality. As we have already seen, girls and women are dramatically underrepresented. In prime-time television in 1987, fully two-thirds of the speaking parts were for men. Women are portrayed as significantly younger and thinner than women in the population as a whole, and most are depicted as passive, dependent on men, and enmeshed in relationships or housework (Davis, 1990). The requirements of youth and beauty in women even influence news shows, where female newscasters are expected to be younger, more physically attractive, and less outspoken than males (Craft, 1988; Sanders & Rock, 1988). Despite educators' criticism of self-fulfilling prophesies that discourage girls from success in math and science, that stereotype was dramatically reiterated in 1992 when Mattel offered a new talking Barbie doll. What did she say? "Math class is tough," a message that reinforces the stereotype that women cannot do math ("Mattel Offers Trade-In," 1992). From children's programming, in which the few existing female characters typically spend their time watching males do things (Feldman & Brown, 1984; Woodman, 1991), to MTV, which routinely pictures women satisfying men's sexual fantasies (Pareles, 1990; Texier, 1990), media reiterate the cultural image of women as dependent, ornamental objects whose primary functions are to look good, please men, and stay quietly on the periphery of life.

Media have created two images of women: good women and bad ones. These polar opposites are often juxtaposed against each other to dramatize differences in the consequences that befall good and bad women. Good women are

JILL

I remember when I was little I used to read books from the boys' section of the library because they were more interesting. Boys did the fun stuff and the exciting things. My mother kept trying to get me to read girls' books, but I just couldn't get into them. Why can't stories about girls be full of adventure and bravery? I know when I'm a mother, I want any daughters of mine to understand that excitement isn't just for boys.

pretty, deferential, and focused on home, family, and caring for others. Subordinate to men, they are usually cast as victims, angels, martyrs, and loyal wives and helpmates. Occasionally, women who depart from traditional roles are portrayed positively, but this is done either by making their career lives invisible, as with Claire Huxtable, or by softening and feminizing working women to make them more consistent with traditional views of femininity. For instance, in the original script, Cagney and Lacey were conceived as strong, mature, independent women who took their work seriously and did it well. It took 6 years for writers Barbara Corday and Barbara Avedon to sell the script to CBS, and even then they had to agree to subdue Cagney's and Lacey's abilities to placate producer Barney Rosenzweig, who complained, "These women aren't soft enough. These women aren't feminine enough" (Faludi, 1991, p. 150). While female viewers wrote thousands of letters praising the show, male executives at CBS continued to force writers to make the characters softer, more tender, and less sure of themselves (Faludi, 1991, p. 152). The remaking of Cagney and Lacey illustrates the media's bias in favor of women who are traditionally feminine and who are not too able, too powerful, or too confident. The rule seems to be that a woman may be strong and successful if and only if she also exemplifies traditional stereotypes of femininity—subservience, passivity, beauty, and an identity linked to one or more men.

The other image of women the media offer us is the evil sister of the good homebody. Versions of this image are the witch, bitch, whore, or nonwoman, who is represented as hard, cold, aggressive—all of the things a good woman is not supposed to be. Exemplifying the evil woman is Alex in *Fatal Attraction*, which grossed more than $100 million in its first four months (Faludi, 1991, p. 113). Yet Alex was only an extreme version of how bad women are generally portrayed. In children's literature, we encounter witches and mean stepmothers as villains, with beautiful and passive females like Snow White and Sleeping Beauty as their good counterparts.

Prime-time television favorably portrays pretty, nurturing, other-focused women, such as Claire Huxtable on "The Cosby Show," whose career as an attorney never entered storylines as much as her engagement in family matters. Hope in "Thirtysomething" is an angel, committed to husband Michael and daughter Janey. In the biographies written for each of the characters when the show was in development, all male characters were defined in terms of their career goals, beliefs, and activities. Hope's biography consisted of one line: "Hope is married to Michael" (Faludi, 1991, p. 162). Hope epitomizes the traditional woman, so much so in fact that in one episode she refers to herself as June Cleaver and calls Michael "Ward," thus reprising the traditional family of the 1950s as personified in "Leave It to Beaver" (Faludi, 1991, p. 161). Meanwhile, prime-time typically represents ambitious, independent women as lonely, embittered spinsters who are counterpoints to "good" women.

Stereotypical Images of Relationships Between Men and Women

Given media's stereotypical portrayals of women and men, we shouldn't be surprised to find that relationships between women and men are similarly depicted in ways that reinforce stereotypes. Four themes demonstrate how media reflect and promote traditional arrangements between the sexes.

Women's dependence/men's independence. Walt Disney's award-winning animated film *The Little Mermaid* vividly embodies females' dependence on males for identity. In this feature film, the mermaid quite literally gives up her identity as a mermaid in order to become acceptable to her human lover. In this children's story, we see a particularly obvious illustration of the asymmetrical relationship between women and men that is more subtly conveyed in other media productions. Even the Smurfs, formless little beings who have no obvious sex, reflect the male-female, dominant-submissive roles. The female smurf, unlike her male companions, who have names, is called only Smurfette, making her sole identity a diminutive relation to male smurfs. The male dominance/female subservience pattern that permeates mediated representations of relationships is no accident. Beginning in 1991, television executives deliberately and consciously adopted a policy of having dominant male characters in all Saturday morning children's programming (Carter, 1991).

Women, as well as minorities, are cast in support roles rather than leading ones in both children's shows and the commercials interspersed within them (O'Connor, 1989). Analyses of MTV revealed that it portrays females as passive and waiting for men's attention, while males are shown ignoring, exploiting, or directing women (Brown, Campbell, & Fisher, 1986). In rap music videos, where African-American men and women star, men dominate women, whose primary role is as objects of male desires (Pareles, 1990; Texier, 1990). News programs that have male and female hosts routinely cast the female as deferential to her male colleague (Craft, 1988; Sanders & Rock, 1988). Commercials, too, manifest power cues that echo the male dominance/female subservience pattern. For instance, men are usually shown positioned above women, and women are more frequently pictured in varying degrees of undress (Masse & Rosenblum, 1988; Nigro, Hill, Gelbein, & Clark, 1988). Such nonverbal cues represent women as vulnerable and more submissive while men stay in control.

In a brief departure from this pattern, films and television beginning in the 1970s responded to the second wave of feminism by showing women who were independent without being hard, embittered, or without close relationships. Films such as *Alice Doesn't Live Here Anymore, Up the Sandbox, The Turning Point, Diary of a Mad Housewife,* and *An Unmarried Woman* offered realistic portraits of women who sought and found their own voices independent of men. Judy Davis's film, *My Brilliant Career,* particularly embodied this focus by telling the story of a woman who chooses work over marriage. During this period, television followed suit, offering viewers prime-time fare such as "Maude" and "The Mary Tyler Moore Show," which starred women who were able and achieving in their own rights. "One Day at a Time," which premiered in 1974, was the first prime-time program about a divorced woman.

By the 1980s, however, traditionally gendered arrangements resurged as the backlash movement against feminism was embraced by media (Haskell, 1988; Maslin, 1990). Thus, film fare in the 1980s included *Pretty Woman,* the story of a prostitute who becomes a good woman when she is saved from her evil ways by a rigidly stereotypical man, complete with millions to prove his success. Meanwhile, *Tie Me Up, Tie Me Down* trivialized abuse of women and underlined women's dependence on men with a story of a woman who is bound by a man and colludes in sustaining her bondage. *Crossing Delancey* showed successful careerist Amy Irving talked into believing she needs a man to be complete, a theme reprised by Cher in *Moonstruck.*

Television, too, cooperated in returning women to their traditional roles with characters like Hope in "Thirtysomething," who minded house and baby as an ultratraditional wife, and even Murphy Brown found her career wasn't enough and had a baby. Against her protests, Cybill Shepherd, who played Maddie in "Moonlighting," was forced to marry briefly on screen, which Susan Faludi (1991, p. 157) refers to as part of a "campaign to cow this independent female figure." Popular music added its voice with hit songs like "Having My Baby," which glorified a woman who defined herself by motherhood and her relationship to a man. The point is not that having babies or committing to relationships is wrong;

rather, it is that media virtually require this of women in order to present them positively. Media define a very narrow range for womanhood.

Joining the campaign to restore traditional dominant-subordinate patterns of male-female relationships were magazines, which reinvigorated their focus on women's role as the helpmate and supporter of husbands and families (Peirce, 1990). In 1988, that staple of Americana, *Good Housekeeping*, did its part to revive women's traditional roles with a full-page ad ("The Best in the House," 1988) for its new demographic edition marketed to "the new traditionalist woman." A month later, the magazine followed this up with a second full-page ad in national newspapers that saluted the "new traditionalist woman," with this copy ("The New Traditionalist," 1988): "She has made her commitment. Her mission: create a more meaningful life for herself and her family. She is the New Traditionalist—a contemporary woman who finds her fulfillment in traditional values." The long-standing dominant-submissive model for male-female relationships was largely restored in the 1980s. With only rare exceptions, women are still portrayed as dependent on men and subservient to them. As B. Lott (1989, p. 64) points out, it is women who "do the laundry and are secretaries to men who own companies."

Men's authority/women's incompetence.   A second recurrent theme in media representations of relationships is that men are the competent authorities who save women from their incompetence. Children's literature vividly implements this motif by casting females as helpless and males as coming to their rescue. Sleeping Beauty's resurrection depends on Prince Charming's kiss, a theme that appears in the increasingly popular gothic romance novels for adults (Modleski, 1982).

One of the most pervasive ways in which media define males as authorities is in commercials. Women are routinely shown anguishing over dirty floors and bathroom fixtures only to be relieved of their distress when Mr. Clean shows up to tell them how to keep their homes spotless. Even when commercials are aimed at women, selling products intended for them, up to 90% of the time a man's voice is used to explain the value of what is being sold (Basow, 1992, p. 161; Bretl & Cantor, 1988). Using male voice-overs reinforces the cultural view that men are authorities and women depend on men to tell them what to do.

Television further communicates the message that men are authorities and women are not. One means of doing this is sheer numbers. As we have seen, men vastly outnumber women in television programming. In addition, the dominance of men as news anchors who inform us of happenings in the world underlines their authority ("Study Reports Sex Bias," 1989). Prime-time television contributes to this image by showing women who need to be rescued by men and by presenting women as incompetent more than twice as often as men (Boyer, 1986; Lichter et al., 1986).

PAUL

I wouldn't say this around anyone, but personally I'd be glad if the media let up a little on us guys. I watch those guys in films and on TV, and I just feel inadequate. I mean, I'm healthy and I look okay, and I'll probably make a decent salary when I graduate. But I am no stud; I can't beat up three guys at once, women don't fall dead at my feet; I doubt I'll make a million bucks; and I don't have muscles that ripple. Every time I go to a film, I leave feeling like a wimp. How can any of us guys measure up to what's on the screen?

Consider the characters in "The Jetsons," an animated television series set in the future. Daughter Judy Jetson is constantly complaining and waiting for others to help her, using ploys of helplessness and flattery to win men's attention. *The Rescuers*, a popular animated video of the 1990s, features Miss Bianca (whose voice is that of Zsa Zsa Gabor, fittingly enough), who splits her time evenly between being in trouble and being grateful to male characters for rescuing her. These stereotypical representations of males and females reinforce a number of harmful beliefs. They suggest, first, that men are more competent than women. Compounding this is the message that a woman's power lies in her looks and conventional femininity, since that is how females from Sleeping Beauty to Judy Jetson get males to assist them with their dilemmas (McCauley, Thangavelu, & Rozin, 1988). Third, these stereotypes underline the requirement that men must perform, succeed, and conquer in order to be worthy.

Women as primary caregivers/men as breadwinners. A third perennial theme in media is that women are caregivers and men are providers. Since the backlash of the 1980s, in fact, this gendered arrangement has been promulgated with renewed vigor. Once again, as in the 1950s, we see women devoting themselves to getting rings off of collars, gray out of their hair, and meals on the table. Corresponding to this is the restatement of men's inability in domestic and nurturing roles. Horovitz (1989), for instance, reports that in commercials men are regularly the butt of jokes for their ignorance about nutrition, child care, and housework.

When media portray women who work outside of the home, their career lives typically receive little or no attention. Although these characters have titles such as lawyer or doctor, they are shown predominantly in their roles as homemakers, mothers, and wives. We see them involved in caring conversations with

KALEB

What burns me up is those programs and commercials that show men as absolute idiots. One of the worst is that one where the mother gets sick and the kids and husband just fall apart without her to fix meals and do laundry. Give me a break. Most guys can do the basic stuff just as well as women, and I'm tired of seeing them made into jokes anytime they enter a nursery or kitchen.

JOANNE

I'd like to know who dreams up those commercials that show men as unable to boil water or run a vacuum. I'd like to tell them they're creating monsters. My boyfriend and I agreed to split all chores equally when we moved in together. Ha! Fat chance of that. He does zilch. When I get on his case, he reminds me of what happened when the father on some show had to take over housework and practically demolished the kitchen. Then he grins and says, "Now, you wouldn't want that, would you?" Or worse yet, he throws up Hope or one of the other women on TV, and asks me why I can't be as sweet and supportive as she is. It's like the junk on television gives him blanket license for doing nothing.

family and friends and doing things for others, all of which never seem to conflict with their professional responsibilities. This has the potential to cultivate unrealistic expectations of being "superwoman," who does it all without ever getting a hair out of place or being late to a conference.

Magazines play a key role in promoting pleasing others as a primary focus of women's lives. K. Peirce's (1990) study found that magazines aimed at women stress looking good and doing things to please others. Thus, advertising tells women how to be "me, only better" by dyeing their hair to look younger; how to lose weight so "you'll still be attractive to him"; and how to prepare gourmet meals so "he's always glad to come home." Constantly, these advertisements emphasize pleasing others, especially men, as central to being a woman, and the message is fortified with the thinly veiled warning that if a woman fails to look good and please, her man might leave (Rakow, 1992).

There is a second, less known way in which advertisements contribute to stereotypes of women as focused on others and men as focused on work. Writing in 1990, Gloria Steinem, editor of *Ms.*, revealed that advertisers control some to most of the *content* in magazines. In exchange for placing an ad, a company receives "complimentary copy," which is one or more articles that increase the market appeal of its product. So a soup company that takes out an ad might be given a three-page story on how to prepare meals using that brand of soup; likewise, an ad for hair coloring products might be accompanied by interviews with famous women who choose to dye their hair. Thus, the message of advertisers is multiplied by magazine content, which readers often mistakenly assume is independent of advertising.

Advertisers support media, and they exert a powerful influence on what is presented. To understand the prevalence of traditional gender roles in programming, magazine copy, and other media, we need only ask what is in the best interests of advertisers. They want to sponsor shows that create or expand markets for their products. Media images of women as sex objects, devoted homemakers, and mothers buttress the very roles in which the majority of consuming takes place. To live up to these images, women have to buy cosmetics and other personal care products, diet aids, food, household cleaners, utensils and appliances, clothes and toys for children, and so on. In short, it is in advertisers' interests to support programming and copy that feature women in traditional roles. In a recent analysis, Lana Rakow (1992) demonstrated that much advertising is oppressive to women and is very difficult to resist, even when one is a committed feminist.

Women's role in the home and men's role outside of it are reinforced by newspapers and news programming. Both emphasize men's independent activities and, in fact, define news almost entirely as stories about and by men ("Study Reports Sex Bias," 1989). Stories about men focus on work and/or their achievements (Luebke, 1989), reiterating the cultural message that men are supposed to do, perform. Meanwhile the few stories about women almost invariably focus on their roles as wives, mothers, and homemakers ("Study Reports Sex Bias," 1989). Even stories about women who are in the news because of achievements and professional activities typically dwell on marriage, family life, and other aspects of women's traditional role (Foreit et al., 1980).

Women as victims and sex objects/men as aggressors. A final theme in mediated representations of relationships between women and men is representation of women as subject to men's sexual desires. The irony of this representation is that the very qualities women are encouraged to develop (beauty, sexiness, passivity, and powerlessness) in order to meet cultural ideals of femininity contribute to their victimization. Also, the qualities that men are urged to exemplify (aggressiveness, dominance, sexuality, and strength) are identical to those linked to abuse of women. It is no coincidence that all but one of the women nominated for Best Actress in the 1988 Academy Awards played a victim (Faludi, 1991, p. 138). Women are portrayed alternatively either as decorative objects, who must attract a man to be valuable, or as victims of men's sexual impulses. Either way, women are defined by their bodies and how men treat them. Their independent identities and endeavors are irrelevant to how they are represented in media, and their abilities to resist exploitation by others are obscured.

This theme, which was somewhat toned down during the 1970s, returned with vigor in the 1980s as the backlash permeated media. According to S. A. Basow (1992, p. 160), since 1987 there has been a "resurgence of male prominence, pretty female sidekicks, female homemakers." Advertising in magazines also communicates the message that women are sexual objects. While men are seldom pictured nude or even partially unclothed, women habitually are. Advertisements for makeup, colognes, hair products, and clothes often show women attracting men because they got the right products and made themselves irresistible. Stars on prime-time and films, who are beautiful and dangerously thin, perpetuate the idea that women must literally starve themselves to death to win men's interest (Silverstein et al., 1986).

Perhaps the most glaring examples of portrayals of women as sex objects and men as sexual aggressors occur in music videos as shown on MTV and many other stations. Typically, females are shown dancing provocatively in scant and/or revealing clothing as they try to gain men's attention (Texier, 1990). Frequently, men are seen coercing women into sexual activities and/or physically abusing them. Violence against women is also condoned in many recent films. R. Warshaw (1991) reported that cinematic presentations of rapes, especially acquaintance rapes, are not presented as power-motivated violations of women but rather as strictly sexual encounters. Similarly, others (Cowan, Lee, Levy, & Snyder, 1988; Cowan & O'Brien, 1990) have found that male dominance and sexual exploitation of women are themes in virtually all R- and X-rated films, which almost anyone may now rent for home viewing. These media images carry to extremes long-standing cultural views of masculinity as aggressive and femininity as passive. They also make violence seem sexy (D. Russell, 1993). In so doing, they re-create these limited and limiting perceptions in the thinking of another generation of women and men.

In sum, we have identified basic stereotypes and themes in media's representations of women, men, and relationships between the two. Individually and in combination these images sustain and reinforce socially constructed views of the genders, views that have restricted both men and women and that appear to legitimize destructive behaviors ranging from anorexia to battering. Later in this chapter, we will probe more closely how media versions of gender are linked to problems such as these.

▪ Bias in News Coverage

Television is the primary source of news for at least two-thirds of Americans (Basow, 1992, p. 160), with newspapers ranking second. This suggests that our understanding of issues, events, and people is shaped substantially by what television and newspapers define as news and the manner in which they present it. As gatekeepers of information, news reporting selectively shapes our perceptions of issues related to gender.

Beginning with the second wave of American feminism in the 1960s, media have consistently misrepresented the goals, activities, and members of women's movements. Because most editors and media executives are men, they have not experienced the daily frustrations women face in a society where they lack rights, opportunities, and status equal to those of men. Some men may feel threatened by women's demands for more prerogatives and for equal treatment. Their lack of personal acquaintance with inequities and their apprehension about women who step out of familiar roles probably account for much of the distortion in coverage of feminism and women.

In the early days of radical feminism, media portrayed feminists as man-hating, bra-burning extremists. The famous bra-burning, in fact, never happened, but was erroneously reported by a journalist who misunderstood the facts (Faludi, 1991, p. 75). This was no isolated effort to discredit the women's movement, since many stories caricatured feminists and undermined women's efforts to gain rights. In the early 1970s, an editor at *Newsday* gave these instructions to a reporter he assigned to research and write a story on the women's movement (Faludi, 1991, pp. 75–76): "Get out there and find an authority who'll say it's all a crock of

---

LOUISE

Talk about biased coverage. Last year a group of us went to Washington, DC, for the big prochoice march. The turnout was fabulous and showed that a lot of women support freedom to choose what happens to their bodies. But was it given coverage? It got less than 1 minute on the nightly news that night, but a big business deal got over 2 minutes, and an athlete's decision to switch teams was the newsmaker interview that night. It was covered in the next day's papers, but not well. It didn't even make the first section in some papers. If you just tuned in the news you could think the whole march never happened. In fact, my mother and father told me they'd heard virtually nothing about it when I got home.

shit." Little wonder that the story that later appeared reported that the women's movement was a minor ripple without much validity or support.

One of the most famous—or infamous—media stunts of the 1980s was another manifestation of the backlash movement against feminism, which consistently received more favorable press than the women's movement itself. The cover story for the June 21, 1986, issue of *Newsweek* was about the so-called man shortage. With dramatic charts showing that chances for marrying plunge precipitously as a working woman ages, *Newsweek* proclaimed that after age 40, a woman was more likely to be killed by a terrorist than to marry, a comment that led one wit to declare that was the best rationale she'd ever heard for terrorism! Behind the headlines, the facts were shaky. The predictions of women's opportunities to marry were based on a study by researchers at Harvard and Yale, but the data of the study were discredited and the study was withdrawn from publication. Did the flaws in the study and its withdrawal get headlines? No way. When the accurate U.S. Census Bureau's figures were released some months later and disproved the bogus study, *Newsweek* relegated that information to a mere two paragraphs in a minor column (Faludi, 1991, pp. 98–100).

Another incident illustrative of media's distortion of feminism came in 1989, when Felice Schwartz, a management consultant, published an article in the prestigious *Harvard Business Review*, in which she argued that women who want to have children cost businesses too much money and should be placed on a separate track in which they do not get the opportunities for advancement that go to men and women who are career oriented. Dubbing this "the mommy track," newspapers and magazines took Schwartz's article as occasion to reassert the viewpoint that women's place really is in the home and that they are lesser players in professional life. Once again, though, facts to support the claim were scant. Schwartz's article was speculative, as was her opinion that most women would willingly trade promotions and opportunities for more time with their families. When the annual Virginia Slims Poll (1990) directly asked women working outside of the home whether they favored mommy tracks, nearly three-fourths thought such a policy was regressive and discriminatory. Schwartz later retracted her suggestions, saying she had erred in claiming women were more expensive as employees than men. Her retraction, however, got little coverage, since Schwartz's revised point of view did not support the media's bias regarding women's roles. Because there was virtually no coverage of Schwartz's change of opinion (Faludi, 1991, p. 92), many people read only the first article and continue to believe it is credible.

Other gender issues have been similarly transformed to fit media's biases. Two instances of bending events to fit stereotypes of gender occurred in the 1990 Gulf War. As substantial numbers of women joined men in fighting, traditional values were shaken. Throughout the war, newspapers and magazines featured melodramatic pictures of children watching mothers go to war, while talk shows asked the question "Should a woman leave her baby to go to war?" (Flanders, 1990). Surely, this is a reasonable question to ask about any parent, but it was rarely applied to fathers. In focusing on women's roles as mothers, the media communicated two gender messages. First, they implied that women — real women — don't leave their children. The second gender message was that fathers are not primary parents. In dismissing fathers' abilities to take care of children while mothers were overseas, media reinforced men's marginality in family life.

The second gender issue out of the Gulf War came when an American woman in the military, along with several men, was taken as a prisoner of war. Rather than presenting this as straightforward news, however, media focused on her femininity rather than on her military role. Newspapers showing photographs of all P.O.W.s featured the male ones in military uniform and the female in a glamour shot from her school yearbook. In highlighting her femininity, media ignited powerful public sentiment about women's fragility, vulnerability, and, therefore, inappropriateness in positions of danger. All attention focused, as the media directed it to, on possibilities of sexual assault of women P.O.W.s, thereby reinforcing images of women as sex objects. Only a year later, we learned of the Tailhook scandal in which numerous male naval personnel sexually harassed female personnel. This made it clear that women are at least as likely to suffer sexual assault from male peers in the service as from enemies who capture them.

When Geraldine Ferraro ran for vice president and Pat Schroeder ran for president in the late 1980s, morning talk shows focused on whether women's hormonal swings disqualified them for leadership. A thorough review of all research on the effects of hormonal cycles on women's abilities (Golub, 1988) somehow never made the airwaves, perhaps because it demonstrated conclusively that women's cycles do not consistently impair their performance. This issue resurfaces virtually every time a woman runs for high office, yet media have yet to cover James Dabbs and Robin Morris's (1990) finding that *male* hormonal cycles *do* affect behavior. A few years later when it was revealed that President Bush was taking Halcion, a drug demonstrated to affect judgment and sometimes to cause hallucinations, scant attention was paid. Facts and fairness were sacrificed in the media's quest to reinforce views of women as irrational, emotional, and frail and men as in control, competent, and able.

Do media representations of events shape our perceptions? To find out, I asked students to answer five questions. First, I asked whether feminists had burned bras to protest inequities; second, whether women who have children cost more to employ than men; third, whether men have hormonal cycles that affect their behavior; fourth, whether women's hormonal swings affect their behavior; and fifth, whether there is a shortage of men for women who want to marry. In every case, the majority of students believed the myths created by media, with nearly all students thinking that women are more expensive to employ and are subject to severe hormonal swings but that men either do not have hormonal cycles or are not affected by them. Too often the messages media create misinform us about issues that affect our lives and perceptions.

Implications of Media Representations of Gender

We have seen that media passes along gendered themes and skews coverage of gender issues. Acting as the announcer of cultural values, media reinforce traditional stereotypes of men and women and of relationships between them. Media encourage us to perceive women as dependent, decorative, passive, and subservient and men as independent, powerful, active, and superior. Besieging us from childhood through adult life, media messages reinforce and reproduce gendered identities.

In this final section of the chapter, we want to probe the consequences of media communication about gender. As we will see, media potentially hamper our understandings of ourselves as women and men in three ways. First, media perpetuate unrealistic ideals of what each gender should be, implying that normal people are inadequate by comparison. Simultaneously, because cultural ideals promoted by media are rigid, they limit views of each gender's abilities and opportunities, which may discourage us from venturing into areas outside of those that media defines for our sex. Second, media pathologize the bodies of men and especially of women, prompting us to consider normal physical qualities and functions as abnormal and requiring corrective measures. Third, media contribute significantly to normalizing violence against women, making it possible for men to believe they are entitled to abuse or force women to engage in sex and for women to consider such violations acceptable.

Fostering Unrealistic and Limited Gender Ideals

Many of the images dispensed by media are unrealistic. Most men are not as strong, bold, and successful as males on the screen. Few women are as slender, gorgeous, and well dressed as stars and models, whose photographs are airbrushed and retouched to create their artificial beauty. Most people will not reach executive positions by the age of 35, and those who do are unlikely to be as glamorous, stress-free, and joyous as the atypical few featured in magazines like *Savvy, Business Week, Fortune,* and *Working Woman.* Further, no woman who is healthy can avoid crossing 40, which is the age at which women virtually disappear from media ("Women on TV," 1990). The relationships depicted in media also defy realistic possibilities, since most of us will encounter problems that cannot be solved in 30 minutes (minus 4½ minutes for commercial interruptions), and most of us will not be able to pursue a demanding career and still be as relaxed and available to family and friends as media characters.

Do idealized images in media really affect us? You might reasonably assume that we all know the difference between fantasy and reality, so we don't accept media images as models for our own lives and identities. Research, however, suggests that the unrealistic ideals in popular media do influence how we feel about ourselves and our relationships. Mediated images seem to function at a less than conscious level as implicit models for our own lives. In Chapter 2, we noted that modeling contributes to development of gender identity. We look to others—including mediated others—to define how we are supposed to be. Especially during the early years when children often do not clearly distinguish reality from fantasy, they seem susceptible to confusing media characters with real people (Woodman, 1991). In one interesting study, M. M. Kimball (1986) compared the sex-stereotypical attitudes of children who lived in areas without television and those in similar areas who watched television. He found that children who watched television had more stereotyped views of the sexes; further, when television was introduced into communities that had not had it, the children's beliefs became more sex typed. Other research confirms the finding that television is linked to sex-typed attitudes in children and adolescents (Morgan, 1987), especially ones in working-class families (Nikken & Peeters, 1988). One exception is programming that presents nonstereotypical portrayals of males and females, which tends to decrease, not fortify, sex stereotypes (Eisenstock, 1984; Rosenwasser, Lingenfelter, & Harrington, 1989).

The effects of media are not limited to childhood. For adolescents, radio is a major influence, with the average listening time being 5 hours a day—slightly less for Caucasians and slightly more for African-Americans, especially African-American females (Brown et al., 1990). While most popular music reflects sex stereotypes (Lont, 1990), this is less true of work composed and/or sung by women (Groce & Cooper, 1990). However, because most songs are written and sung by males, rock and rap music generally reflects a male point of view (Brown & Campbell, 1986) in which women are depicted sexually and negatively (St. Lawrence & Joynder, 1991). Other media stereotypes have similar distorting effects on our identities. For instance, popularized images of men as independent and women as nurturing and as relationship experts encourage women to feel responsible for others and men to regard caring as peripheral in their lives.

A study by J. Shapiro and L. Kroeger (1991) suggests that mediated myths of relationships contribute to socializing people into unrealistic views of what a normal relationship is. In particular, they found that MTV's and rock music's emphasis on eroticism and sublime sex is linked to an expectation of sexual perfectionism in real relationships. Further, Shapiro and Kroeger reported that readers of self-help books tended to have more unrealistic ideals for relationships than did nonreaders. Consequently, those who read self-help books experienced more than typical amounts of frustration and disappointment when their relationships failed to meet the ideals promoted by media.

Of the many influences on how we feel about ourselves and what we expect in our relationships, media are substantial. Clinicians such as A. T. Beck (1988) as well as researchers (Adelmann, 1989; McCormick & Jordan, 1988; Wadsworth, 1989) maintain that unrealistic images of what we and our relationships should be contribute significantly to dissatisfaction and its consequences, including feelings of inadequacy, anorexia, cosmetic surgery, and emotional difficulties. Media's images of women, men, and relationships are ideals—they are not real, and few of us can even approximate the standards they establish. Yet when we are constantly besieged with ideals of how we should look, feel, act, and be, it's difficult not to feel inadequate. As Paul's earlier journal entry indicated, men as well as women may feel woefully deficient if they rely on media characters as models. If we use media as a reference point for what is normal and desirable, we may find ourselves constantly feeling that we and our relationships are inferior by comparison. To the extent that we let ourselves be influenced by the unreal and unreasonable images presented by media, we may be hindered in our ability to enjoy real people and real relationships.

Pathologizing the Human Body

One of the most damaging consequences of media's images of women and men is that these images encourage us to perceive normal bodies and normal physical functions as problems. It's understandable to wish we weighed a little more or less, had better developed muscles, and never had pimples or cramps. What is neither reasonable nor healthy, however, is to regard healthy, functional bodies as abnormal and unacceptable. Yet this is precisely the negative self-image cultivated by media portrayals of women and men. Because sex sells products (Muro, 1989), sexual and erotic images are the single most prominent characteristic of advertising (Courtney & Whipple, 1983). Further, advertising is increasingly objectifying men, which probably accounts for the rise in men's weight training and cosmetic surgery. Media, and especially advertising, are equal opportunity dehumanizers of both sexes.

Not only do media induce us to think we should measure up to artificial standards, but they encourage us to see normal bodies and bodily functions as pathologies. A good example is the media's construction of premenstrual syndrome (PMS). Historically, PMS has not been a problem, but recently it has been declared a disease (Richmond-Abbott, 1992). In fact, a good deal of research (Parlee, 1973, 1987) indicates that PMS affected very few women in earlier eras. After the war, when women were no longer needed in the work force, opinion changed and the term *premenstrual tension* was coined (Greene & Dalton, 1953) and used to define women as inferior employees. In 1964, only one article on PMS appeared; in 1988–1989, a total of 425 were published (Tavris, 1992, p. 140). Drug companies funded research and publicity, since selling PMS meant selling their remedies for the newly created problem. Behind the hoopla, however, there was and is little evidence to support the currently widespread belief that PMS is a serious problem for a significant portion of the female population. Facts aside, the myth has caught on, carrying in its wake many women and men who now perceive normal monthly changes as abnormal and as making women unfit for positions of leadership and authority. Another consequence of defining PMS as a serious problem most women suffer is that it leads to labeling women in general as deviant and unreliable (Unger & Crawford, 1992), an image that fortifies long-held biases against women.

Menopause is similarly pathologized. Carol Tavris (1992, p. 159) notes that books describe menopause "in terms of deprivation, deficiency, loss, shedding, and sloughing," language that defines a normal process as negative. Like menstruation, menopause is represented as abnormalcy and disease, an image that probably contributes to the negative attitudes toward it in America. The cover of the May 25, 1992, *Newsweek* featured an abstract drawing of a tree in the shape of a woman's head. The tree was stripped of all leaves, making it drab and barren. Across the picture was the cover-story headline "Menopause." From first glance, menopause was represented negatively — as desolate and unfruitful. The article focused primarily on the problems and losses of menopause. Only toward the end did readers find reports from anthropologists, whose cross-cultural research revealed that in many cultures menopause is not an issue or is viewed positively. Women in Mayan villages and the Greek island of Evia do not understand questions about hot flashes and depression, which are symptoms often associated with menopause in Western societies ("Menopause," 1992, p. 77). These are not part of their experience in cultures that do not define a normal change in women as a pathology. Because Western countries, especially America, stigmatize menopause and define it as "the end of womanhood," Western women are likely to feel distressed and unproductive about the cessation of menstruation (Greer, 1992).

Advertising is very effective in convincing us that we need products to solve problems we are unaware of until some clever public relations campaign persuades us that something natural about us is really unnatural and unacceptable. Media have convinced millions of American women that what every medical source considers "normal body weight" is really abnormal and cause for severe dieting (Wolf, 1991). Similarly, gray hair, which naturally develops with age, is now something all of us, especially women, are supposed to cover up. Facial lines, which indicate a person has lived a life and accumulated experiences, can be removed so that we look younger — a prime goal in a culture that glorifies youth (Greer, 1992).

Body hair is another interesting case of media's convincing us that something normal is really abnormal. Beginning in 1915, a sustained marketing campaign informed women that underarm hair was unsightly and socially incorrect. (The campaign against leg hair came later.) *Harper's Bazaar*, an upscale magazine, launched the crusade against underarm hair with a photograph of a woman whose raised arms revealed clean-shaven armpits. Underneath the photograph was this caption: "Summer dress and modern dancing combine to make necessary the removal of objectionable hair" (Adams, 1991). Within a few years, ads promoting removal of underarm hair appeared in most women's magazines, and by 1922, razors and depilatories were firmly ensconced in middle America as evidenced by their inclusion in the women's section of the Sears Roebuck catalog.

Media efforts to pathologize natural physiology can be very serious. As we have seen in prior chapters, the emphasis on excessive thinness contributes to severe and potentially lethal dieting, especially in Caucasian women (Spitzack, 1993). Nonetheless, the top female models in 1993 are skeletal, more so than in recent years (Leland & Leonard, 1993). Many women's natural breast size exceeded the cultural ideal in the 1960s when thin, angular bodies were represented as ideal. Thus, breast reduction surgeries rose. By the 1980s, cultural standards changed to define large breasts as the feminine ideal. Consequently, breast augmentation surgeries accelerated, and fully 80% of implants were for cosmetic reasons ("The Implant Circus," 1992). In an effort to meet the cultural standards of beautiful bodies, many women suffered unnecessary surgery, which led to disfigurement, loss of feeling, and sometimes death for women when silicone implants were later linked to fatal conditions. Implicitly, media argue that our natural state is abnormal and objectionable, a premise that is essential to sell products and advice for improving ourselves. Accepting media messages about our bodies and ourselves, however, is not inevitable: We can reflect on the messages and resist those that are inappropriate and/or harmful. We would probably all be considerably happier and healthier if we became more critical in analyzing media's communication about how we should look, be, and act.

Normalizing Violence Against Women

Since we have seen that media positively portray aggression in males and passivity in females, it's important to ask whether media messages contribute to abuse of and violence against women. There is by now fairly convincing evidence (Hansen & Hansen, 1988) that exposure to sexual violence through media is linked to greater tolerance, or even approval, of violence. For instance, P. Dieter (1989) found a strong relationship between females' viewing of sexually violent MTV and their acceptance of sexual violence as part of "normal" relationships. He reasoned that the more they observe positive portrayals of sexual violence, the more likely women are to perceive this as natural in relationships with men and the less likely they are to object to violence or to defend themselves from it. In short, Dieter suggests that heavy exposure to media violence within relationships tends to normalize it, so that abuse and violence are considered natural parts of love and sex.

Dieter's study demonstrates a direct link between sexual aggression and one popular form of media, MTV. Research on pornography further corroborates connections between exposure to portrayals of violence against women and willingness to engage in or accept it in one's own relationships (Russell, 1993). Before we discuss this research, however, we need to clarify what we will mean by the term **pornography**, since defining it is a matter of some controversy. Pornography is not simply sexually explicit material. To distinguish pornography from erotica, we might focus on mutual agreement and mutual benefit. If we use these criteria, pornography may be defined as materials that favorably show subordination and degradation of a person such as presenting sadistic behaviors as pleasurable, brutalizing and pain as enjoyable, and forced sex or abuse as positive. **Erotica,** on the other hand, depicts consensual sexual activities that are sought by and pleasurable to all parties involved (MacKinnon, 1987). These distinctions are important, since it has been well established that graphic sexual material itself is not harmful, while sexually violent materials appear to be (Donnerstein, Linz, & Penrod, 1987).

Pornographic films are a big business, outnumbering other films by 3 to 1 and grossing over $365 million a year in the United States alone (Wolf, 1991). The primary themes characteristic of pornography as a genre are extremes of those in media generally: sex, violence, and domination of one person by another, usually women by men (Basow, 1992, p. 317). More than 80% of X-rated films in one study included scenes in which one or more men dominate and exploit one or more women; within these films, three-fourths portray physical aggression against women, and fully half explicitly depict rape (Cowan et al., 1988). That these are linked to viewers' own tendencies to engage in sexual violence is no longer disputable. According to recent research (Demare, Briere, & Lips, 1988; Donnerstein et al., 1987; Malamuth & Briere, 1986), viewing sexually violent material tends to increase men's beliefs in rape myths, raises the likelihood that men will admit they might themselves commit rape, and desensitizes men to rape, thereby making forced sex more acceptable to them. This research suggests that repeated exposure to pornography influences how men think about rape by transforming it from an unacceptable behavior with which they do not identify into one they find acceptable and enticing. Not surprisingly, the single best predictor of rape is the circulation of pornographic materials that glorify sexual force and exploitation (Baron & Straus, 1989). This is alarming when we realize that 18 million men buy a total of 165 different pornographic magazines every month in the United States (Wolf, 1991, p. 79).

It is well documented that the incidence of reported rape is rising and that an increasing number of men regard forced sex as acceptable (Brownmiller, 1993; Soeken & Damrosch, 1986). Studies of men (Allgeier, 1987; Koss & Dinero, 1988; Koss, Dinero, Seibel, & Cox, 1988; Koss, Gidycz, & Wisniewski, 1987; Lisak & Roth, 1988) have produced shocking findings: While the majority of college men report not having raped anyone, a stunning 50% admit they have coerced, manipulated, or pressured a woman to have sex or have had sex with her after getting her drunk; 1 in 12 men at some colleges has engaged in behaviors meeting the legal definition of rape or attempted rape; over 80% of men who admitted to acts that meet the definition of rape did not believe they had committed rape; and fully one-third of college men said they would commit rape if they believed nobody would find out.

Contrary to popular belief, we also know that men who do commit rape are not psychologically abnormal. They are indistinguishable from other men in terms of psychological adjustment and health, emotional well-being, heterosexual relationships, and frequency of sexual experiences (Segel-Evans, 1987). The only established difference between men who are sexually violent and men who are not is that the former have "hypermasculine" attitudes and self-concepts—their approval of male dominance and sexual rights is even stronger than that of nonrapists (Allgeier, 1987; Koss & Dinero, 1988; Lisak & Roth, 1988; Wood, 1993a). The difference between sexually violent men and others appears to be only a matter of degree.

We also know something about women who are victims of rape and other forms of sexual violence. Between 33% and 66% of all women have been sexually abused before reaching age 18 (Clutter, 1990; Koss, 1990). The majority of college women—up to 75%—say they have been coerced into some type of unwanted sex at least once (Koss, Gidycz, & Wisniewski, 1987; Poppen & Segal, 1988; Warshaw, 1988). A third of women who survive rape contemplate suicide (Koss et al., 1988). It is also clear that the trauma of rape is not confined to the time of its actual occurrence. The feelings that accompany rape and sexual assault—fear, a sense of degradation and shame, anger, powerlessness, and depression—endure far beyond the act itself (Brownmiller, 1975; Wood, 1992b, 1993f). Most victims of rape continue to deal with the emotional aftermath of rape for the rest of their lives (Marhoefer-Dvorak, Resick, Hutter, & Girelli, 1988).

What causes rape, now the fastest growing violent crime in the United States (Doyle, 1989; Soeken & Damrosch, 1986)? According to experts (Costin & Schwartz, 1987; Koss & Dinero, 1988; Koss, Gidycz, & Wisniewski, 1987; Scott & Tetreault, 1987; Scully, 1990), rape is not the result of psychological deviance or uncontrollable lust. Although rape involves sex, it is not motivated by sexual desire. Authorities agree that rape is an aggressive act used to dominate and show power over another person, be it a man over a woman or one man over another,

MYTHS AND FACTS ABOUT RAPE

Myth	Fact
Rape is a sexual act that results from sexual urges.	Rape is an aggressive act used to dominate another.
Rapists are abnormal.	Rapists have not been shown to differ from nonrapists in personality, psychology, adjustment, or involvement in interpersonal relationships.
Most rapes occur between strangers.	Eighty percent to 90% of rapes are committed by a person known to the victim (Allgeier, 1987).
Most rapists are African-American men, and most victims are Caucasian women.	More than three-fourths of all rapes occur within races, not between races. This myth reflects racism.
The way a woman dresses affects the likelihood she will be raped.	The majority — up to 90% — of rapes are planned in advance and without knowledge of how the victim will dress (Scully, 1990).
False reports of rapes are frequent.	The majority of rapes are never reported (Koss, Gidycz, & Wisniewski, 1987). Less than 10% of rape reports are judged false, the same as for other violent crimes.
Rape is a universal problem.	The incidence of rape varies across cultures. It is highest in societies with ideologies of male dominance and a disregard for nature; it is lowest in cultures that respect women and feminine values (Griffin, 1981).

as in prison settings where rape is one way inmates brutalize one another and establish a power hierarchy (Rideau & Sinclair, 1982). Instead, mounting evidence suggests that rape is a predictable outcome of views of men, women, and relationships between the sexes that our society inculcates in members (Brownmiller, 1975; Costin & Schwartz, 1987; Scott & Tetreault, 1987; South & Felson, 1990).

Particularly compelling support for the cultural basis of rape comes from cross-cultural studies (Griffin, 1981; Sanday, 1986), which reveal that rape is extremely rare in cultures that value women and feminine qualities and that have ideologies that promote harmonious interdependence among humans and between them and the natural world. Rape is most common in countries, like the United States, that have ideologies of male supremacy and dominance and a disrespect of women and nature. Cultural values communicated to us by family, schools, media, and other sources constantly encourage us to believe men are superior, men should dominate women, male aggression is acceptable as a means of attaining what is wanted, women are passive and should defer to men, and women are sex objects. In concert, these beliefs legitimize violence and aggression against women.

While the majority of media communication may not be pornographic, it does echo in somewhat muted forms the predominant themes of pornography: sex, violence, and male domination of women. As we have seen, these same motifs permeate media that are part of our daily lives, which generally portray males as dominating in number, status, authority, and will. Substantial violence toward women punctuates movies, television — including children's programming — rock music, and music videos, desensitizing men and women alike to the *un*naturalness and unacceptability of force and brutality between human beings. Thus, the research that demonstrates connections between sex-stereotypical media and acceptance of sexual violence is consistent with that showing relationships between more extreme, pornographic media and acceptance of and use of violence.

Summary

In this chapter, we have seen that media send powerful messages about gender — about who we are as men and women, about the nature of normal relationships between the sexes, and about gender issues. In concert with other cultural institutions and practices, media contribute to gendering our identities and influence how we think about issues, people, and events related to gender.

Ranging from children's cartoons to pornography, media influence how we perceive events in our world, ourselves, each other, and the nature of normal relationships between women and men. Three implications of media representations that stereotype gender and condone male aggression and domination are promoting unrealistic gender ideals in men and women, pathologizing the human

MEDIA ORGANIZATIONS FOR CONSUMER ACTION

To request government investigation or intervention into media operations:

Federal Communications Commission (FCC)
Consumer Assistance Office
1919 M. Street, NW
Washington, DC 20554
Phone: 202-632-7000

The following public organizations are receptive to complaints about sexism and/or violence in programming:

Action for Children's Television (ACT)
46 Austin Street
Newtonville, MA 02160
Phone: 617-527-7870

Goal: To encourage and support quality programming for children.

American Council for Better Broadcasts (ACBB)
120 E. Wilson
Madison, WI 53707
Phone: 608-257-7712

Goal: To support development of critical-viewing skills and broadcasting of good radio and television programs. AABB sponsors education to improve children's critical skills.

Foundation to Improve TV (FIT)
50 Congress Street, Suite 925
Boston, MA 02109
Phone: 617-523-5520

Goal: To support and represent individuals who are attempting to promote healthy uses of television, particularly for children.

body, and naturalizing violence against women. These potential consequences are facilitated by media communication that defines masculinity and femininity in ways that limit us and our possibilities as human beings. Understanding the overt and subtle gender messages in media empowers us to be more critical about what we hear and see and to raise our voices in resistance to media messages we find harmful. As individuals, parents, and citizens we have opportunities and responsibilities to criticize media representations that demean men and women and that contribute to attitudes that harm all of us and our relationships with each other.

$\mathscr{D}$iscussion Questions

1. The author points out that media are pervasive in our society. How much are media part of your life? How many hours a week do you spend watching television and movies, listening to radio and stereo, and reading popular magazines?

2. Watch children's programming on Saturday morning and report back to the class on gender themes you identify. Are men or male characters more prominent than women and female characters? Are there differences in the activities, integrity, intelligence, and so forth of male and female characters? How do you think commercial children's programming influences children's ideas about gender?

3. As a class, select three prime-time weekly television shows that all of you will watch. When you've viewed the programs, discuss the gender roles in them. How are women and men represented? Are there inequalities in the power, stature, and ability of women and men in these shows? To what extent are women portrayed in autonomous and powerful roles? To what extent are men portrayed within relationships and involved in caring for others?

4. Focus on relationships between women and men in television programming. How many relationships seem relatively egalitarian? Are male and female partners shown equally involved in work outside the home and inside of it? Do they participate equally in making decisions that affect them both, or does one partner exercise more influence than the other?

5. As a class, discuss media representations that challenge and change traditional prescriptions for gender and backlash media that reinscribe conventionally gendered roles. Find examples of each. Which is more prevalent? What does the simultaneous existence of both traditional and nontraditional gender images tell us about current social attitudes toward gender?

6. Do you agree with the chapter's criticism of violence and sexual aggression against women in the media? Do you think what happens in the media affects how average women and men define themselves and what is normal in relationships? Why or why not?

7. As a class, watch some MTV programs. Discuss the ways women and men are represented in these. Are women sexually exploited? Are they presented as subject to men's power? What does this imply about men's identity?

8. Watch morning and evening news programming. What kinds of stories do male and female reporters and newscasters present? Are there differences in story content? Are there differences in the communication styles of male and female newscasters?

9. The author suggests that media present unrealistic and unhealthy images of women and men and that this can be harmful. Do you agree? Bring advertisements from magazines to class and discuss the images of women, men, and relationships in them. Are these healthy? What are your options as a reader and consumer?

10. Watch for new products introduced into the market and notice how they are advertised. Are there any examples today like the marketing campaign beginning in 1915 to convince women that underarm hair is undesirable? What relational meanings exist in advertising messages—what do they tell us we should be, do, and think as women and men?

11. Listen to music on popular stations. With others in your class, discuss differences and similarities in music by women and men artists. Do you find there are different themes or alternative emphases in lyrics and music? Are these differences consistent with what you've learned about gendered identities?

CHAPTER TEN

Gendered Organizational Communication

♦ "Would you want a woman with PMS to be able to take the country to war?"

♦ "If he really cared about his family, he'd be putting in extra time to make money, not asking for time off to be home."

♦ "She may get results from her sales team, but she's one hard woman."

♦ "He must feel awful having a wife who makes so much more money than he does."

These four comments illustrate some of the ways in which gender stereotypes surface in organizational settings. The first question, made during a discussion of political candidates, reflects the widespread myth that women's hormonal fluctuations disqualify them for positions of leadership and authority. The second comment, uttered when a new father took advantage of his firm's paternity leave policy, discloses the still prevalent view that men's primary role is as provider and parenting is less important. The third statement reveals a paradox experienced by many women who pursue careers in which men have historically dominated: They may meet the requirements of their jobs or those of femininity, but both cannot be achieved simultaneously. In this example, the qualities that made the woman an effective manager are at odds with those prescribed for femininity. The final remark illustrates a tension for partners in some dual-career relationships whose roles conflict with the traditional view of men as the breadwinners.

All four of the comments underscore powerful ways in which cultural views of gender permeate interaction in organizations. As primary structures of cultural life, institutions reflect and re-create cultural beliefs about gender. Social meanings of masculinity and femininity riddle the structures and routines of schools, workplaces, the legal system, religions, medicine, and commercial and service organizations. In addition, institutions have formal and informal practices that express and reinforce traditional views of women and men by defining and treating members of the two sexes in gender stereotypical ways.

In this chapter, we will explore how cultural views of gender are communicated in institutional settings. We begin by examining stereotypes of women, men, and professional communication that are communicated through concrete practices, such as hiring, placement, promotion, and interaction patterns. We will also evaluate the evidence supporting these stereotypes. Next, we consider organizational communication systems that reflect and perpetuate limiting views of women and men. As we discuss gender stereotypes, we will try to understand how they affect the personal and professional lives of working people.

▆ Institutional Stereotypes of Women and Men

Institutions, like individuals, operate according to beliefs, values, and goals. Collectively, these form a framework that organizes interaction among people who participate in organizations — employees as well as those who use institutions (for example, students in schools, plaintiffs and defendants in courts, customers in business). Institutional beliefs are communicated through structures, policies, and practices. When these beliefs are broad generalizations about women and men as groups, they are gender stereotypes. In this section, we analyze how stereotypes reflect and perpetuate gendered attitudes and identities.

Stereotypes of Women

Writing in 1977, Rosabeth Kanter, who specializes in organizational dynamics, observed that four basic stereotypes of women in our society also operate in organizations. Since Kanter first made this claim, other researchers (Garlick, Dixon, & Allen, 1992; Wood & Conrad, 1983) have corroborated it. According to Kanter, organizations tend to classify women into one of four roles, none of which acknowledges professional competence. The four roles are sex object, mother, child, and iron maiden.

Sex object. This stereotype defines women in terms of their sex and/or sexuality. Frequently, it is expressed in expectations that a woman's appearance and actions should conform to cultural views of femininity. A pleasing appearance is an informal requirement for flight attendants, hostesses, receptionists, and other jobs in which women predominate. The view that women must be conventionally pretty was highlighted in the summer of 1990, when one airline fired a woman from her job as ticketing agent for not wearing makeup. The ticketing agent brought and won a suit on the grounds of sex discrimination, claiming that makeup was not required of male employees and was irrelevant to her job performance. Even though she won the case, the incident dramatically illustrates the institutional expectation that women should be attractive.

The stereotype of women as sex objects is also evident in how co-workers and supervisors interact with women employees. Conversations with women often highlight appearance and obscure performance, reflecting the cultural tendency to judge women by appearance more than competence. Regarding women as sex objects contributes to sexual harassment, which at least 50%, and possibly as much as 90%, of the female work force has experienced in some form ("Ninety Percent," 1988; U.S. Merit Systems Protection Board, 1988; Wood, 1992b). If someone defines a woman by her sex, then flirting, lewd remarks, and inappropriate communication may follow. Sexual harassment reflects perceptions of women as sex objects, not professionals (Strine, 1992).

The sex-object stereotype is also used to define and devalue gay men and lesbians. Like women, gays and lesbians are often perceived almost exclusively in terms of their sexuality, which is hardly the sum of their identities any more than of heterosexuals' identities. Stereotyping homosexuals as sex objects leads to gay bashing, in which lesbians and gays are devalued because of their sexual orientation, while their job performance goes unnoticed. Stereotyping gays and lesbians is particularly prevalent in the military (Gross, J., 1990), which historically barred

---

K E E N A

The sex-object one is the one that really gets to me. I work as a waitress to get through school, okay? So my manager has really been on my case lately about how I should fix my hair nicer and wear more makeup in order to please the customers. Is my job to serve them or to provide them with artistic material? I do my job, and I do it well. I am polite, I check on customers during their meals—nobody's complained about my service. But my super keeps telling me that I'm such a nice-looking girl and that I really should fix myself up more.

known homosexuals from the services. As this book goes to press, military exclusion of gays and lesbians is being challenged by President Clinton's proposal to end discrimination against gays in the services. Sexual harassment also appears particularly rampant in the military, as exemplified recently in the Tailhook scandal, in which male military personnel mauled, violated, and verbally harassed female personnel. Incidents like Tailhook and charges against men of high status and power (Senator Packwood in 1992 and 1993, for example) illustrate long-standing norms that allow or encourage treating women as sex objects (Katzenstein, 1990; Taylor & Conrad, 1992; Wood, 1992b).

Mother. Kanter explains the role of mother as one in which a person is expected to support, nurture, defer, and generally take care of others. In institutional life, the stereotype of women as mothers has both indirect and literal forms. The indirect version of this stereotype involves expectations that women employees will listen to, support, and help others. Regarding women as motherly sources of comfort may explain the tendency to communicate with women co-workers more than with men when support and sympathy are wanted. The mother stereotype also underlies the expectation that women will fix coffee, take notes, and arrange social activities.

Stereotyping women into the role of mother is a source of job segregation by gender, a subtle and pervasive form of discrimination. The growing number of women employed outside of the home suggests greater gender equality in the work force than really exists. By and large, women and men are not competing equally in a single job market but are segregated into two distinct arenas of employment—his and hers (Jacobs, 1989). Approximately three-fourths of women working outside the home fall into one of three types of jobs: clerical/administrative support (28%), service (18%), and administrative/managerial (27%; for example, teaching, human resources) (U.S. Department of Labor, 1991). As these figures suggest, most women's jobs function to support and/or to provide care to others. Thus, we see a pattern in which gender stereotypes about women's roles spill over into the workplace, limiting the positions for which they are considered qualified. Over 90% of employed women work in jobs where the majority of employees are female (Woody, 1989). The jobs into which women are segregated generally have the least prestige and the lowest salaries. Gender and race intersect to influence job segregation, with African-American women even more narrowly stereotyped into mothering jobs than Caucasian women (Morton, 1991; Segal & Zellner, 1992; Woody, 1989, 1992).

The woman-as-mother stereotype also has a literal manifestation. Women employees who have children are often classified as "not serious professionals." Because mothering is consistent with established images of women, this role overshadows perceptions of women's professional skills. Thus, working women who are also mothers may be stereotyped as less committed to work, which justifies excluding them from opportunities for training and advancement. You might think that one way a woman could resist this stereotype is to downplay her role as mother, but that strategy often backfires. If a woman who is a mother does not seem highly committed to her family, then she may be perceived as unwomanly, which will lead to lack of acceptance. During the 1992 presidential campaign, Hillary Rodham Clinton was characterized as hard, manly, and aggressive because she remained active and vocal in her career and politics after having a child (Tannen, 1992).

The mother stereotype can become a self-fulfilling prophecy. In Chapter 5, we discussed stereotyping as one implication of human symbolic capacity. You might recall that when we stereotype by gender, we often act toward others on the basis of a stereotype we designate rather than on the basis of how others actually are and behave. Thus, the language we use in defining others may function to blind us to seeing them outside of categories to which we assign them. For instance, if a manager decides not to offer Maria Constanza a new assignment because he assumes she is preoccupied with her children, then Ms. Constanza is deprived of professional experience. She will not have opportunities to learn what she needs to advance in her job. Later, when the manager is looking for someone who has background and experience in a certain area, he notes that Ms. Constanza is not qualified and attributes this to her being a mother.

Child.   This stereotype reflects the social view of women as less mature, competent, and/or capable of making decisions than men. An early instance of this stereotype was denial of voting rights to women, which was justified with arguments that women, like children, are unable to make important decisions. Stereotyping women as children often transpires under the guise of "protecting women." For example, women once had to have parents' or husbands' permission to get abortions. The issue here is not whether you are for or against abortion, but simply that this policy patronizes women by treating them as children who must have some adult's permission to make a choice. Similarly, not long ago, some states required a woman to get her husband's permission if she wished to be sterilized. Only 2 years ago, a company tried to bar women of childbearing age from working in positions that exposed them to lead, since lead may affect fetuses (it may also affect males' reproductive capacities, but men were not restricted from these jobs). Regardless of whether women employees planned to have children, the company insisted on "protecting women" from the dangers of these jobs (which, incidentally, were higher paying ones in the company). The policy was struck down when a court ruled that a company could not act as the parent of women employees, since women are adults, capable of assessing risks and making their own choices. In essence, the court ruled that organizations have no right to speak for employees, who may assume responsibility for themselves.

The medical profession has been criticized strongly for its patronizing style of communicating with women. Women's complaints about physiological problems and symptoms are too often dismissed by doctors as "female hysteria," with sometimes serious, even deadly consequences (Calderone, 1990). Women report being told "Don't worry" or "You're imagining things" when they discuss symptoms with doctors. Far more often than men, women are given sedatives and relaxants, which reduce anxiety but do nothing to correct physiological conditions that may be cause for legitimate worry (Calderone, 1990; Gomberg, 1986). Stereotyping women as children encourages treating them as such.

In job-related situations, stereotypes of women as children may restrict women's opportunities, so they are less able to demonstrate abilities and to grow professionally. When supervisors, for instance, decide that a project is too demanding for a woman or that it would burden her, they make the decision not to allow her to stretch professionally. Within the military, one argument against allowing women in combat is that they should be protected from the gruesome realities of war. This is somewhat ironic, since women have been involved and killed in every war fought by our nation. In "protecting" women from challenging work, employers often exclude them from experiences that lead to promotion and salary raises, as well as from personal development that comes with rising to meet new challenges. Within the military, for instance, combat duty is essential to advancement.

The stereotypes of women as sex objects, mothers, or children contribute to gender and racial inequities in pay. When employers label women as mothers, sex objects, or children, they tend not to perceive them primarily as employees. And they tend not to pay them as they do males, particularly white males, who are defined as serious workers and as family breadwinners. On average, white women and black men are paid 25% less than their white male peers, and black women make 36% less. The disparity is even greater for Hispanic men, who make 32% less, and Hispanic women, who make 43% less (Hymowitz, 1992, p. 116).

For some jobs, gender and race discrimination are even greater than the averages reveal. For instance, women doctors earn only about 63 cents for every dollar their male peers earn; female managers earn roughly 65 cents for every dollar that male managers earn; and saleswomen make approximately 58% of the salary earned by salesmen (Hilts, 1991; National Commission on Working Women, 1990; U.S. Department of Labor, 1991). This pattern of discrimination continues to hold true even when a man and a woman perform the exact same job. There is a substantial disparity in salary when experience and other qualifications are equivalent for women and men. Level of education does not explain the disparity, since female college graduates earn about what male high school graduates do (Bovee, 1991). Gender and race discrimination persist beyond inequities in starting salaries. As Carol Hymowitz (1992, p. 116) pointed out, for each year on a job, women's hourly salary increases by 7 cents, while men's increases by 24 cents.

Iron maiden. A final stereotype defines a woman as not womanly. She is unfeminine, manly, or, as the opening example stated, "one hard woman." This stereotype reflects the idea that it is unfeminine to be independent, ambitious, directive, competitive, and tough at times. A woman who engages in these behaviors may be labeled an "iron maiden" (Garlick, Dixon, & Allen, 1992).

An example of this occurred in 1990, when Ann Hopkins sued the accounting firm of Price Waterhouse for sex discrimination (Fiske, Bersoff, Borgida, Deaux, & Heilman, 1991). Ms. Hopkins brought in more money in new accounts than any of her 87 male peers, yet 47 of the men were made partner while Ms. Hopkins was not. Executives refused to promote Ms. Hopkins because they perceived her as unfeminine. Describing her as authoritative and too tough, they suggested she could improve her chances for promotion if she wore more jewelry and dressed and behaved more femininely. Ms. Hopkins was promoted after a federal district court ruled that gender stereotyping is a form of sex discrimination and, therefore, illegal. Yet there are many women like Ms. Hopkins who are underpaid and not promoted and who lack the funds and/or confidence to go to court to fight for their rights.

As you can see, all four of these stereotypes define women as undesirable employees. Either women are incompetent (sex object, child), or they are only able to support others in positions of leadership (mother), or they are too unfeminine to be accepted (iron maiden). Each stereotype entails some reason for discounting women as workers; each defines women by sex and gender rather than by job qualifications and performance.

Stereotypes of Men

Within institutional settings, men are also stereotyped. As was true of stereotypes of women, those applied to men reflect entrenched cultural views of masculinity and men's roles. We will discuss three stereotypes of men that limit them in institutional settings: men as sturdy oaks, fighters, and breadwinners.

Sturdy oaks. In Chapter 3, we discussed J. A. Doyle's (1989) view of the male role. Prominent in that is the notion that men are supposed to be tough, unshakable, in control of feelings, and unaffected by pain and problems. R. Brannon and S. Juni (1984) call this the "sturdy oak" image of men as self-contained, self-sufficient pillars of strength. This stereotype of men is reflected in institutional patterns that assume men should not appear weak or reliant on others. In politics, we see dramatic examples of the extent to which men are still expected to be sturdy oaks. In the 1960s, Edmund Muskie lost voters' confidence

DOUG

I almost died during my first year at school. I woke up one night really hurting. My stomach was killing me. I woke my roommate and told him something was wrong, and he told me to quit complaining and go back to sleep. I couldn't, but I lay there all night just hurting. The next morning he asked me if I was okay and I said no, that I hurt too much to even get up. He asked if I wanted him to call "your mama so she can make it all better." What could I say? I said I didn't need her; I'd get by. I got up and struggled to get dressed and go to class, so he wouldn't think I was a sissy. I could barely stand up. On the way to class I fainted and an ambulance came and took me to the hospital. It turned out my appendix had ruptured and I was letting peritonitis set in by toughing it out. I just felt I couldn't complain or seek help when my roommate acted that way—it was like I had to prove myself.

---

in his bid for the presidency because he cried in public, something no "real man" would do. Ronald Reagan ran and ruled as "a man's man," catapulting his role in B-grade western movies into political life. One of George Bush's greatest handicaps as both a candidate and a president was the perception that he was a "wimp." He was perceived as whining, leaning on others, and failing to appear to be "his own man."

How does this apply to men not running for political office? It is directly relevant, since the same sturdy oak stereotype guides perceptions of men in most contexts. Because men are expected to be strong and uncomplaining, they may conceal problems so that others won't perceive them as weak or whining. The cultural mandate that men be self-sufficient probably contributes to the fact that men suffer from stress-related conditions and generally die younger than women. Men who have internalized the sturdy oak ideal may not even acknowledge medical problems and needs to themselves. Obviously, this can have fairly severe consequences, as Doug's story (see the box) illustrates.

The stereotype of sturdy oaks can also affect men's professional performance. If it is not manly to admit doubts or fears, then men take risks that are unwise at times. Similarly, if asking for help is prohibited, then consulting with others for advice or assistance may be ruled out, and decision making may be impeded by lack of important input. If a man does make a mistake, he may feel compelled to hide it. We've seen this with Watergate, Irangate, savings and loan scandals, P.O.W.s left in Vietnam, and other flawed national courses of action and the cover-ups that followed them. In each case, the problem and the later effort to conceal it may have been influenced by efforts to live up to the image of men as self-sufficient sturdy oaks, who need no help and make no errors.

Fighters.   Cultural stereotypes also cast men as fighters—brave warriors who go to battle, whether literally in war or metaphorically in fighting the competition in business. Childhood training to be aggressive, "to give 'em hell," and to win at all costs translates into professional expectations that men should go out there and beat the other guys on Wall Street or in the courtroom. There is no room for being less than fully committed to the cause (your country or your company), less than aggressive, less than eager for combat, or less than ruthless in defeating the competition.

The stereotype of men as fighters echoes other themes of masculinity: dominance, force, and violence. Some interesting research suggests that this cultural definition of manhood may have influenced recent military engagements. M. F. Fasteau (1974), for instance, argues that Vietnam was a way Presidents Kennedy, Johnson, and Nixon demonstrated their toughness—they showed they were "real

FORREST

Last summer I had a supervisor who wrote the book on men as fighters. I took a job selling encyclopedias to make money for the fall. So every morning I set out on my territory, knocked on doors, and tried to sell people these encyclopedias. I did all right I guess. I made the suggested quota most weeks, but I just didn't have the heart to push the books on people who were obviously real poor. The head honcho asked me why I hadn't sold more in one neighborhood, and I told him the people there were really pressed to make ends meet, and they needed food more than encyclopedias. So he read me the riot act—told me those were the very folks who could be talked into buying encyclopedias because they wanted to help their kids get ahead. He told me to pressure them with a line of talk about what they owed their kids and how these books were the whole foundations of their children's lives and success. I told him I couldn't do that, that it was just too pushy. He told me that was what I was supposed to do—push, strong-arm people if I have to, but sell the books. When I checked around with some of the other reps, I found out they do that and they have contests to see who can push the most people into buying books. Maybe I'm not cut out to be a salesman.

men" by waging war. Fasteau's analysis of records on foreign policy reveals that the single greatest goal of U.S. involvement in Vietnam was to avoid a humiliating defeat that would make our country (and the commander in chief) appear weak. A mere 30% of our official reasons for being at war involved commitments to helping the Vietnamese people or saving their country from Chinese rule. President Reagan's invasion of Grenada and President Bush's invasions of Panama and the Persian Gulf have also been questioned by scholars, who think these were premature acts of aggression. Masculine culture seems to encourage such aggressiveness as a way to prove manliness, willingness to fight.

The fighter stereotype is also evident in business and professional life, where being strong, tough, aggressive, and ready to do battle are constant expectations. In their work lives, men may be oppressed by this stereotype, which communicates to them that they are to put the cause, company, or country first and to fight for it with everything they have. One implication of this is that men are often not able to take time from work for family matters without risking disapproval from colleagues and supervisors. While recent surveys (Gibbs, 1990; Saltzman, 1991) indicate that over half of men working outside the home would like to reduce their hours in order to spend more time with families, very few companies and firms in America allow any time off for fathers. Men who do take time are often looked down upon by colleagues and superiors (Pleck, 1986, 1987; Saltzman, 1991). Caring about families and spending time with them is at odds with the fighter stereotype that requires men to make the cause (work) their first priority.

Breadwinners. Perhaps no other stereotype so strongly defines men in our society as does that of breadwinner. Men are expected to be the primary or exclusive wage earners for their families, and achieving this is central to how our society views men's success. Years ago, J. Bernard (1981) noted that maleness is equated with being a good provider so that to be a man is to earn a good income. Recently reprising this theme, W. Farrell (1991) warns that men have become "success objects," defined by others and themselves in terms of their ability to earn good incomes. The breadwinner stereotype is both particularly strong and dangerous for men. Because earning an income is the crux of how our culture defines masculinity, many men feel enormous pressure to meet the ideal. Yet when any single thing so completely defines us, we are imperiled. If a man's ability to earn a good salary ends, then he may be emotionally at risk. This was dramatically illustrated when the Great Depression befell America in 1929. Men who lost their jobs often also forfeited respect for themselves as men, as breadwinners. Feeling psychologically emasculated (Komarovsky, 1940), many men became clinically depressed, and a number committed suicide. They could not live up to the stereotype imposed by the culture.

In our own era, there are risks for men who link their identity and worth to earning a big income. First, there is an uncertain economy in which job security is not assured. To reduce expenses, companies increasingly are cutting employees. Further, many jobs are being replaced by machines, which may render today's qualifications irrelevant 5 or 10 years down the road. This is especially a problem for African-American men and men over 50, who have particularly high levels of unemployment (Wilkie, 1991). Further, few families are able to live on a single income, so both partners work, an arrangement that lessens men's roles as providers for their families. Finally, in some couples, women's salaries exceed men's, which may create tension between gendered expectations and daily life. Similarly, men who define themselves as earners may feel threatened by women colleagues who advance ahead of them. Psychiatrist Willard Gaylin (1992, p. 37) reports that "men commit suicide at a rate of seven to eight times as frequently as women in our culture, and they do it invariably because of perceived social humiliation that is almost exclusively tied to business failures." Noting that working and making a salary define manhood in our culture, Gaylin warns that this is a dangerous foundation for identity and self-esteem, and he encourages men to resist cultural pressures to define their worth by this yardstick.

Yet it is difficult for men to find social legitimation for alternative self-definitions. A second problem with stereotyping men as breadwinners is that it undercuts institutional willingness to allow, much less support, men's involvement with families. Because defining men as sturdy oaks, fighters, and breadwinners ignores men's family commitments, these stereotypes do not facilitate policies that allow men to reduce time at work. This has severe costs both to individual men and families and to our society as a whole. The "father hunger" about which the mythopoetic men's movement speaks is sustained by institutional structures that do not allow men to form close, active relationships with their daughters and sons.

Evaluation of the Facts

Before we leave our discussion of stereotypes, we should evaluate their validity. Convincing evidence suggests that institutional stereotypes of women and men bear little resemblance to reality. Are women less able, less ambitious, and/or less committed to work than men? Based on two decades of intensive study of achievement motivation, A. S. Kahn and J. D. Yoder (1989) concluded there are no significant gender differences in this area. Although women and men may channel motivations to achieve into different areas and activities, they have equivalent desires to accomplish things with their lives. Further, as we will see later, both sexes tend to revise professional goals and communication styles when their career situations call for this.

The stereotypes of men seem equally unwarranted by research. For instance, defining men by their ability to earn big salaries (the breadwinner) is inconsistent with men's own reports that they value family life and want more time for it in their lives. The tendency to minimize men's role in parenting also reflects social belief in a maternal instinct, which turns out to be more myth than fact (Eyer, 1992). Nurturance, like other behaviors, is largely learned. From childhood, girls are encouraged to play with toys that cultivate caregiving (dolls, stuffed toys), to perceive and respond to others' feelings, and to regard relationships as central. These socialized values translate into competent mothering, but they do not make up a maternal instinct. While nurturance generally is not emphasized in boys' socialization, males can learn to nurture, just as many women have learned to assert themselves in ways not encouraged by feminine socialization. As we have seen, considerable research shows men can be just as caring as women, and many find this very gratifying when circumstances allow them to do it. The idea that men cannot nurture or do not wish to seems to have little basis in fact. Therefore, stereotypes of women as sex objects, mothers, children, and iron maidens and of men as sturdy oaks, fighters, and breadwinners have little basis in the abilities that women and men actually have. Nonetheless, because these stereotypes guide how women and men are perceived in institutional contexts, they exert a powerful influence on the professional placement, salaries, and advancement of workers.

■ Stereotypes of Professional Communication

Because men have historically dominated institutional life, masculine forms of communication are the standard in most work environments. Defining men and masculine patterns as normative leads to perceptions that women and feminine styles are not just different, but inferior. In this section, we will examine three stereotypes of communication in the workplace: Masculine communication is equivalent to professional communication; communication styles are stable; and men and women cannot work together effectively. Before doing that, however, let's briefly consider the male norms that define institutional life in general, since these establish the foundation of stereotypes of professional communication.

Male Standards in Institutions

Throughout this book, we have seen that communication, gender, and culture interact to affect one another. A primary way that societies sustain their values is through institutions that reflect and reproduce those values through their structures and practices. The cultural view of men as standard, or normative, is reflected throughout institutional life in the United States. Male standards are evident in our judicial system. Designed to provide "equal justice for all," our legal system's assumption that masculinity is normative leads to inequitable treatment of women. From local levels to the Supreme Court, most judges are men, who typically lack experiences that provide insight into some of the issues and conditions in women's lives (Wood, 1992b). This was particularly evident during the Hill-Thomas hearings in 1991. During these proceedings, a roomful of male congressmen interrogated Anita Hill about her charge that Supreme Court nominee Clarence Thomas had sexually harassed her when she worked for him years earlier. The questioners could not understand (and thus did not believe) why if this happened, Hill had not objected at the time. Out of these hearings came the phrase "They just don't get it," meaning that men may be unable to understand sexual harassment and ways women react to it. If you have never been sexually harassed, and if you have not been taught to be passive, deferential, and friendly, then it may be impossible to understand why many victims of sexual harassment do not firmly, forcefully, and immediately protest harassment.

Other issues that affect women exclusively or primarily may also be ones that men cannot understand and ones to which they would respond differently. For instance, there are cases in which women who have been chronically brutalized by their partners finally defend themselves by killing the men while they sleep. Because the murder takes place when the man is not actually attacking the woman, it fails to fit the legal definition of self-defense. But, argue a number of attorneys, a person who is physically weaker and who has been repeatedly overcome by her partner may not be able to defend herself during an episode of violence. Her homicide may be the only reasonable self-defense, given the circumstances and relative strengths of the two partners. Cases of this sort, along with sexual harassment trials, are forcing the legal system to consider whether its standard, which is literally that of "a reasonable man" (What would a reasonable man do if . . . ?), is fair to women. The "reasonable woman" standard defines different courses of action as reasonable for women, based on their distinctive physical and socialized natures.

The male standard is also evident in religious systems. Not only has God historically been defined as male, but until very recently, only men have been allowed to occupy the highest offices—minister, priest, rabbi. In 1968, feminist theologian Mary Daly critiqued sexism in the church in her book, *The Church and the Second Sex*, and she pursued this theme further in later books titled *Gyn/ecology* (1978), *Beyond God the Father* (1973), and *Outercourse* (1992). While many churches and synagogues continue to discriminate against women, these sexist practices are being challenged. Many denominations now ordain women into the ministry, although even in 1992 the Catholic church reiterated its belief that women should not be priests. Some religions have begun to speak of God as "motherlove and fatherlove" and to revise interpretations of the Bible so that women's presence, contributions, and value are more fully recognized.

With this broad understanding of the male standard that infuses institutional life in our culture, we may now consider three specific implications of assuming men—white heterosexual men—are the model for professional communication.

The Stereotype That Masculine Communication Equals Professional Communication

The male-as-standard norm defines expected communication in professional settings. Leadership, a primary quality associated with professionals, is typically linked with masculine modes of communication—assertion, independence, competitiveness, and confidence, all of which are emphasized in masculine speech communities. Deference, inclusivity, collaboration, and cooperation, which are prioritized in women's speech communities, are linked with subordinate roles rather than with leadership. To the extent that women engage in traditionally feminine communication, then, they may not be recognized as leaders or marked for advancement in settings where masculine standards prevail. The validity of equating leadership with masculinity is open to question, as we will see.

Bias against feminine forms of communication assumes that these are not effective in leading others. This dismisses out of hand communication skills such as supportiveness, attentiveness, and collaboration, all of which appear to enhance morale and productivity in work settings (Helgesen, 1990). Institutional biases against feminine forms of communication also reflect the mistaken belief that style is static and human beings cannot learn new ways to communicate. As we will see, both of these views are open to serious question.

A number of researchers have investigated women's and men's communication in professional situations. Their findings indicate that women and men leaders act similarly in many respects: Both are able to direct and organize collective efforts, and many subordinates judge male and female leaders to be equally effective (Eagly & Johnson, 1990; O'Leary, 1988). Yet, there are differences. Consistently, studies reveal that women, more than men, are motivated to help others. This explains, at least in part, why women with high achievement goals tend to select professions such as teaching, social work, medicine, and human services, while men with strong motivation to achieve are more likely to choose high-status occupations (Bridges, 1989). The inclination to care that is cultivated in women also shows up in *how* women and men do their work. Comparisons of women and men in the same professional roles reveal that women employ more caring, personal styles (Lunneborg, 1990). For instance, female doctors tend to be more compassionate and patient centered than their male counterparts, and female attorneys tend to be more concerned with clients' needs and feelings (Gilligan & Pollack, 1988; Rosener, 1990). The desire to help others is a major factor in both African-American and Caucasian women's choices of jobs and styles of communication in their work (Murrell, Frieze, & Frost, 1991; Woody, 1992).

Similar differences between the managerial styles of women and those of men have been found (Helgesen, 1990). It appears that both women and men enjoy being leaders and being in positions of influence, although there are general differences in how the two sexes enact leadership. Women leaders are more likely to use collaborative, participative communication that enables others, reflecting how their speech communities taught them to interact (Aries, 1987; Helgesen, 1990; Lunneborg, 1990; Rosener, 1990). Men, in general, engage in more directive, unilateral communication to exercise leadership, which is consistent with their learned view of talk as a way to assert self and achieve status (Eagly & Karau, 1991). This suggests that there may be different "tones" to women's and men's leadership.

Does this mean that women are less professional and less able to lead than men? We could draw that conclusion only if research indicated that the style more characteristic of male leaders is also more effective in motivating followers and accomplishing results. Research, however, does not support the belief that masculine qualities are the only ones that yield good leadership. While instrumentality and assertiveness are valued in leaders, so are supportiveness and collaboration, which are communication skills at which women tend to excel. Further, studies indicate that the most effective leadership style employs androgynous communication, which incorporates both relationship-building and instrumental qualities (Cann & Siegfried, 1990). Finally, we should note that the Japanese management style, which is highly cooperative and participative, is increasingly being adopted by American businesses (Kanter, 1983; Helgesen, 1990). Interestingly, it is usually male managers who have to attend workshops to learn this style, since a majority

R O B I N

I always thought it would be weird sort of to have a woman as my boss. I have always had men supervisors, and I guess I kind of thought that men should be in charge. But where I work part-time now, I have a woman as my boss. At first, I was put off by this, and I kind of resented it when she would tell me what needed doing or when she would make suggestions for how I could do the work better. But after a while I began to see that she was really interested in helping me do well, not in throwing her weight around. She was willing to take time to work with me and explain stuff without acting like I should know or like she was superior or anything. And she's also really nice, not just to me but to all the people who work in her office. She remembers what's important in our lives. Like the other day, she asked me how I did on my Chemistry exam, because last week I'd been talking about how worried I am about that course. I don't know what it is exactly, but in that office there is a warmer kind of feeling — more personal or something. I guess I wouldn't worry if I had another female boss.

of women already employ it. While business and industry are increasingly endorsing feminine ways of leading, they have not labeled them "feminine" but "participative" or "transformational." Some people consider the refusal to credit women by naming the style "feminine" to be further evidence that women are dismissed and devalued.

There's one further insight to add to this picture. Men and women may be judged differently for enacting the *same* communication. This highlights the importance of distinguishing between how women and men actually behave and how others perceive them. If communication is perceived through gender stereotypes, then women and men may need to communicate differently to be equally effective. Because cultural views hold that women should be supportive and friendly, not being so may be regarded as a violation of gender role and may result in negative evaluations of women. Relatedly, because highly assertive and instrumental communication is socially defined as masculine, women who engage in it may be branded "iron maidens," a perception that jeopardizes their acceptance and effectiveness (Butler & Geis, 1990; Carli, 1989). Research confirms that others may negatively evaluate women—but not men—whose communication is directive and unresponsive to feelings (Basow, 1990; Bradley, 1981; Gervasio & Crawford, 1989). Because emphatic, directive communication by women is viewed negatively, a more participative, supportive leadership style is likely to be most effective for women leaders (Statham, 1987). Thus, it may well be that the ways in which men and women enact leadership are different, yet equally appropriate and effective in light of gendered expectations that others bring to professional settings.

The Stereotype That Communication Styles Are Stable

The second assumption behind the idea that masculine communication is the essence of professionalism maintains that the communication styles of men and women are permanently set. Earlier chapters in this book demonstrated that our communication styles are learned. We are taught to communicate in particular ways, with females being encouraged to create and sustain interpersonal connections and respond to others, and males being encouraged to emphasize independence and status. Are we bound forever by what we learned in childhood? Are the communication styles we have at the moment set in stone?

To answer this question, we return to standpoint theory, introduced in Chapter 2. According to this perspective, our ways of knowing and acting are influenced by the circumstances of our lives. Thus, the different standpoints of women's and men's lives lead them to distinctive ways of exercising influence and interacting with others, ways that are reflected in how they communicate in their jobs. Yet standpoint theory also suggests that as our standpoints change, so will our ways of thinking and communicating. If this is true, then as women enter into positions requiring forms of communication not fostered in feminine socialization, they should become proficient in new skills. Similarly, as institutions discover that cooperative, supportive communication is important in leadership, men should develop skills in these areas.

It appears that the requirements of jobs influence styles of communication — more so, in fact, than personal styles affect the structure of jobs. Pioneering work in this area (Miller, Schooler, Kohn, & Miller, 1979) found that the structural requirements of women's jobs predicted their self-esteem and communication style more than the converse. A series of studies by C. F. Epstein (1968, 1981, 1982) corroborated these findings by showing that women attorneys who were not assertive, self-confident, or ambitious at the start of their careers became more so as a result of engaging in work that required those qualities. Other investigations (Hochschild, 1975; McGowen & Hart, 1990) demonstrate that women develop communication skills that respond to the conditions of their employment. Some research indicates that women managers may develop even more autonomous and instrumental communication styles than their male peers (Gordon, 1991; Hatcher, 1991).

This suggests that as men and women enter into new settings and take on new roles, they reform their identities and communication patterns to reflect and respond to the norms and requirements of their contexts. Thus, we should realize that communication styles are not fixed entities but rather are processes

NATE

I think it's true that women can learn to communicate in the same ways that men do. I saw that in my mom. Dad died when I was just 11, and up until then mom had been your average mother. She took care of us, and she was real gentle and not at all pushy or demanding. But then she had to go to work to support us. She took a job in a factory in our town, and she was so good at her work she got promoted to supervisor in a couple of years. I watched her become more independent, more sure of herself, and more willing to lay down the law to me and my sisters. Before, she would let us get away with just about anything, but she became more strict and more willing to enforce her rules. I also saw changes in how she dealt with others, like salesmen. She used to let them push her around, but that was old history after she went to work. She just became a stronger person in a lot of ways.

that continually evolve in relation to situations and others with whom we interact. Both sexes can develop communication skills that advance leadership as they find themselves in positions requiring abilities not emphasized in their earlier socialization.

The Stereotype That Men and Women Cannot Work Together Effectively

This stereotype reflects several social beliefs about gender. First, it echoes the idea that women belong in the private sphere of home and family, while men should operate in the public sphere of institutional life. Women who enter the "male domain" of work may be perceived as violating their gender role. Relatedly, because our culture defines women and men as "opposites," it may be thought that their different priorities and ways of communicating would conflict and lead to inefficient business operations. This stereotype boils down to a preference for working with "our own kind," which has been used to justify excluding minorities and lesbians and gay men from many environments. Extending these two ideas, we run into the stereotype of women and men as sexual or romantic partners. Because the sexes historically have related personally and socially, a legacy of romantic/sexual overtones haunts the interaction between women and men (Wood, 1992b). This leads some people to think men and women are so focused on each other as romantic or sexual beings that they cannot work together as colleagues.

Studies of mixed-sex task groups shed light on the validity of these beliefs. While women and men often feel awkward initially when they work together (Aries, 1977; Kanter, 1977), this is usually overcome in a short time, and mixed-sex groups develop comfortable routines for interacting. Second, not only are mixed-sex groups not disruptive to productivity, they actually may enhance the quality of much decision making. Some researchers (W. Wood, 1987) report that groups of men and women are more effective than groups of either just women or just men. Why might this be so? Researchers suspect that when men and women are together, each contributes in important ways to high-quality decision making. Women may specialize in communication that supports and builds team cohesion, and men may initiate more communication focused on logistics of the task. Effective groups need both kinds of communication. While androgynous individuals might well supply both kinds of communication, more sex-typed people specialize. Thus, mixing women and men often improves the quality of decision making and heightens members' satisfaction.

The research relevant to institutional stereotypes of men, women, and professional communication shows that for the most part the stereotypes are not well founded. Both sexes seem motivated to work and to achieve in their jobs, and both seem able to develop communication skills required in their roles. Further, it appears that not only are women and men able to work together effectively, but they may actually complement and enhance each other's competence in professional settings. This suggests that institutional life would benefit in many ways by recognizing the value of traditionally masculine and feminine communication styles and by realizing that individuals, male and female, develop new skills when given opportunities to do so. Relatedly, it appears that individual women and men might enhance their personal effectiveness by cultivating androgynous communication skills so that they are competent in a wide range of behaviors germane to professional life.

In addition to stereotypes, organizational life is gendered by communication systems. We turn now to the final section of this chapter, in which we explore how gender interacts with formal and informal communication systems in organizations.

▇ Gendered Communication Systems in Organizations

All institutions are communication systems, which implies that communication within them reflects and perpetuates values and understandings of "how we do things around here." Within the military, for instance, communication practices rigidly follow a hierarchy, indicating the importance of chain of command in that organization. Soldiers are housed, fed, trained, and drilled together, a practice that encourages cohesion among troops, which is essential to team efforts in battle.

Communication occurs in formal and informal structures and practices of institutions. Formal structures include communication designated by policies and accountability among members of an organization: leave policies, work schedules, performance reviews, who reports to whom, who has authority to authorize and evaluate whom, and so on. Informal structures, which are at least as important as formal ones, concern interactions and norms beyond or in addition to those that are explicitly defined: becoming part of networks, caucusing with colleagues about issues, learning what is required to be on "the fast track," trading favors, gossiping and exchanging information (sometimes hard to distinguish!), advising, mentoring, and so forth. Taken together, formal and informal structures define the culture, or values and understandings, of an organization. As we will see, most organizations have gendered cultures (Nicotera & Cushman, 1992) that affect the professional and personal lives of employees. We will focus on leave policies and schedules, communication climates in organizations, and glass ceilings.

Leave Policies and Work Schedules

Leave policies.   Organizations have policies that stipulate how much time employees are entitled to for disability, illness, and personal reasons; in addition, leave policies specify whether absences are paid or unpaid. Leave policies reflect cultural views of gender roles by clinging to an outdated model of workers and their lives. When America first industrialized, men were considered the primary breadwinners, and most professions were designed to conform to the lives of men who were white, heterosexual, middle class, and married to women who stayed home. Thus, in hiring a man, an organization actually got two workers — a man on the job and a woman who took care of family responsibilities so that the man could focus on his work. Leave policies did not need to take family responsibilities into account, since those were managed by homemaker-wives of employees.

This model no longer fits the majority of workers, half of whom are female, many of whom are single parents, and few of whom have a domestic partner whose full-time responsibility is home and family. Fully 50% of mothers with preschool children work outside of the home today (Moen, 1991; Shelton, 1992; "Study Finds Family Changed Forever," 1992). Changes in the work force, however, have not been paralleled by institutional policies that reflect the needs and situations of most contemporary workers.

The one accommodation that has been made, although only by some companies, is to include pregnancy within legitimate reasons for taking a leave. While a number of organizations include pregnancy and childbirth in the category of "disability," some grant no leave, and some provide no guarantee that a job will be held for a woman who is absent to have a child. In 1989, less than half of women working outside of the home had the option of maternity leaves that provided even partial salary (National Commission on Working Women, 1989). For many women, this forces a choice between having families and having jobs — not a very humane set of options.

Even organizations that do allow leaves for childbirth assume that women are entitled to time away from work, but men are not. This reflects the deeply held social belief that mothers are the primary caretakers and fathers are peripheral to the process of raising children. Leave policies that exclude fathers perpetuate this pattern by making it nearly impossible for men to assume full roles in family life. They also disadvantage mothers by reinforcing the view that women should assume the primary responsibility for caring for children. Relatedly, women who choose to mother and to work outside the home often are treated as second-class employees who receive less salary, status, benefits, social security, and professional opportunities (McHenry & Small, 1989; Shelton, 1992; Warme, Lundy, & Lundy, 1992).

Men too suffer from gender-discriminatory leave policies. Increasingly men, particularly younger ones, see families as an important priority in their lives. A

MATERNITY LEAVES IN VARIOUS COUNTRIES

	Minimum Weeks Allowed	Percent Salary
Sweden*	51	90
France	16–38	84
Italy	20	80
Britain	18	90
Canada	15	60
Germany	14	100
Japan	14	60
Netherlands	7	100
United States	**None****	**None**

Source: Child care. (1992, August 10). *Fortune*, pp. 50–54.

*For both parents combined.
**The 1993 Family and Medical Leave Act does not require all organizations to provide leaves, and it does not apply to all workers.

recent survey ("Working Dads," 1991) revealed that fully 75% of men would accept reductions in career advancement in exchange for more time to spend with families. For many working men, however, this is not a choice, since their companies do not allow paternity leave. Even when it is formally allowed, there is often informal disapproval of men who take it. Basow (1992, p. 176) reports that only 1% of men take formally allowed paternity leave, because they know that others would perceive them as less committed to their jobs. One new father reported that when his daughter was born, he turned down a paternity leave because of "subtle, unspoken, never in print" assumptions that define being on the job as what it takes "to be a player." Another new father said, "It's socially unacceptable. The stigma is still there. . . . Society says a man shouldn't do it" ("Fears for Careers," 1990).

Companies that establish maternity leaves, but not paternity or family leaves, engage in a symbolic process by which women are defined as those who do and should care for children. Fathers and fathering remain unnamed and, therefore, unrecognized as integral to family life (Cornell, 1991; Mann, 1989). The view of women as mothers combines with the stereotype of men as breadwinners to create a situation in which it is exceedingly difficult for men to become actively involved in raising children. As long as men remain unrepresented in the language of caregiving, their roles in the process will be seen as marginal (Weedon, 1987).

The language of leave policies also poses another dilemma. When companies name only maternity, paternity, or parental leaves, they include newborn and newly adopted children within the compass of those for whom it is legitimate to care, but they exclude all others who might need care. Few American organizations have policies that allow workers time to care for disabled or dying parents. As medical technology expands the human life span, there will be a growing number of older citizens, many of whom will need various degrees of assistance. Who will care for these people? How can children take in parents and provide care when they have their own children to care for and when employers make no provisions for family responsibilities? Will we be forced to choose among our children, our parents, and our own livelihoods (Wood, 1993c)? The evidence that generous parental and family leave policies are working in other countries — every industrialized nation except America has a national policy — provides reason to think they could work here also (Hewlett, 1986, 1991; Okin, 1989).

Work schedules. Another way in which formal organizational rules affect men and women employees stems from rigid working schedules generally mandated. The 9-to-5 model of the work day is increasingly giving way to the expectation that 7 or 8 A.M. until 7 or 8 P.M. is normal for "really committed professionals." Obviously, this model — or even the 9-to-5 one — does not accommodate family needs and schedules. Day care is expensive, prohibitively so for many single parents. And day care is not a complete solution, since children are sometimes too sick to attend and arrangements fall through periodically, making it necessary for a parent to take responsibility for child care. Women bear the majority of these responsibilities, taking time off when children are sick or day care is unavailable (Hewlett, 1986, 1991; Hochschild, 1989; Wood, 1993c). Often this forces them into part-time positions, which have many risks for career growth (Warme, Lundy, & Lundy, 1992). This pattern (and its costs to women's careers) reflects the gender stereotype that women are the primary caregivers of children and men who are serious about their careers do not interrupt their work for family matters.

Historically, American businesses and government have not supported family life. In 1985, Representative Pat Schroeder introduced the Family and Medical Leave Act into Congress, but for 8 years it was defeated by backlash politics and conservative administrations. During his single term as president, George Bush vetoed two versions of the family leave bill. President Clinton, however, made instating a family leave bill a top priority. Within a month of his inauguration,

President Clinton signed into law a bill that mandates 12 weeks of unpaid leave for workers to care for family members under certain conditions. Specifically, the bill applies only to employers with 50 or more workers, only to employees who have worked at least 1 year and a minimum of 1,250 hours a year, and only if the workers are not in the top 10% of the company's pay scale. Also, the bill is helpful only to people who can forego a paycheck for 12 weeks. In spite of these rather severe limits on family leaves, the new policy does represent progress. It may signal a new attitude that is more supportive and respectful of family life.

The irony of tightly restricting family leave is that every study of the costs of providing more leave and flexible working hours shows that these not only do not cost businesses, but they frequently save money! In states where employers are required to provide leave time (unpaid) for family care, there has been virtually no hardship for businesses (Ball, 1991). A recent study authorized by the U.S. Small Business Administration ("Hope for Working Families," 1991) surveyed over 3,000 firms about the costs of giving unpaid leaves for family care. The major finding was that for companies with 16 to 99 employees, allowing leaves is $30 a week cheaper than replacing a manager and only 97 cents a week more expensive than replacing a nonmanagerial employee. Costs vary for firms with more than 100 or fewer than 16 employees, but the trend is clear: Providing leave for family responsibilities is not prohibitively expensive for most organizations. Companies such as Aetna, Corning, IBM, and Johnson & Johnson that have pioneered in "family-friendly" policies report that their employee turnover has dropped dramatically and morale has risen comparably ("Mommy Tracks," 1991). Unfortunately, policies that support family involvement, including the 1993 act, are usually available only to highly paid professionals, leaving the majority of workers without any safety net ("Child Care," 1992; Cowell, 1992; Okin, 1989). Here again we see the intersection of race, class, and gender oppression, since workers who are women and minorities in blue-collar jobs are least likely to have family leave policies.

Communication Climates in Organizations

An organization's communication climate includes interaction patterns and communication style. Communication climates are gendered to the extent that they emphasize gender differences, regard one gender as standard, and/or provide differential opportunities to women and men. Mentor relationships and collegial networks, a major aspect of communication climates, are seldom formally defined, yet these can make or break careers.

Hostile environments for women. In our earlier discussion of gender inequities in educational settings, we identified a range of ways in which schools marginalize, devalue, and discriminate against women students. A similar pattern occurs in many organizations, making them hostile environments for women. Because workplaces have historically been designed by and for men, they include language and behavior that men find familiar and comfortable, but women may not.

A key contributor to organizational climates that are hostile to women is language that emphasizes men's experiences and interests. Pervading most workplaces are terms taken from sports (hit a home run, huddle on strategy, ballpark figures, second-string player, come up with a game plan, be a team player, line up, score a touchdown), sexuality (hit on a person, he has balls, he is a real prick, stick it to them; such language also includes calling women employees "hon" or referring to women generally in sexual ways), and the military (battle plan, mount a campaign, strategy, plan of attack, under fire, get the big guns). Whether intentional or not, language related to sports, military, and sexuality functions to bind men together into a community from which many women feel excluded (Hamilton, 1988). The sense of the "old boys' club" is established.

Even in the 1990s, there is often substantial resistance and hostility to women who enter jobs where men predominate (Palmer & Lee, 1990; Schroedel, 1990; Strine, 1992). Women may be given unrewarding assignments, isolated from key networks of people and information, and treated stereotypically as sex objects, mothers, or children. Each of these techniques contributes to a masculinized communication climate and defines women as not "real" members of the team. Sexual harassment further devalues women's professional abilities and highlights their sex, which complicates women's work lives in ways men seldom experience (Strine, 1992; Taylor & Conrad, 1992; Wood, 1993d, 1993f).

The informal network.   Relationships among colleagues are important in creating a sense of fit and providing access to essential information that may not come through formal channels. Because men have predominated in the workplace, most informal networks are largely or exclusively male, giving rise to the term *the old boy network.* Hiring and promotion decisions are often made through informal communication within these networks. For example, Bob knows of a good job prospect and tells Nathan about it while they are golfing; over drinks, Ed comments to Joel about an impressive trainee, so that trainee stands out later when Ed selects people for an important assignment; Mike talks with Ben, John, and Frank about his new marketing plan, so when Mike introduces it formally in a meeting, he has support lined up. Informal communication networks are vital to professional success.

Women tend to be less involved than men in informal networks. They often feel unwelcome, and feminine socialization does not encourage them to assert themselves and claim a position in a group. Further, women may feel out of place because of their minority status. When only one or two women are in a company or at a particular level, they stand out and are aware of their token status (Kanter,

1977; O'Leary & Ickovics, 1991). A sense of difference also is experienced by people of color who confront a sea of white when they enter most professions. Co-workers' behaviors often compound women's and minority people's feeling of being different. R. M. Kanter (1977), for instance, reports that when a woman enters an all-male group, the men tend to intensify masculine behaviors, talking more loudly, crudely, and perhaps profanely in what is probably an unconscious male-bonding process. Similarly, Mary Strine (1992) has shown how sexual harassment in the workplace, in addition to violating women, communicates the message that "you are not wanted here." In the face of communication that defines them as "outsiders," women may avoid informal networks, thus losing out on a key source of information and support.

Mentor relationships. A mentor is a senior colleague who advises and assists a junior employee in building a career. Often faculty do this with graduate students and sometimes with undergraduates. Coaches sometimes do it with players. In the past, fathers frequently tutored sons in running the family business. Having a mentor is at least helpful and sometimes indispensable to career advancement. Both women and minorities are less likely to have mentors than are men of the majority race. Can you guess why?

Several factors account for the low number of women and minority people who have the benefit of mentoring relationships. First, the numbers game works against them. Most of us prefer to interact with people with whom we identify rather than ones who seem different from us. The paucity of women and minorities in senior positions means there are few who identify with new employees who are female and/or minorities. Research indicates that African-American women are least likely of all groups to be mentored (Morrison & Von Glinow, 1990). Men are sometimes reluctant to mentor young women for a variety of reasons: fear of gossip about sexual relations, their assumption that women are less serious than men about careers, and/or feeling less comfortable with women than with men as colleagues. This pattern perpetuates the status quo in which white men gain assistance in climbing the corporate ladder, while women and minorities receive little help.

In an effort to compensate for the lack of networks and mentors available to women, several innovations have arisen. Professional women's networks allow women to share ideas, contacts, strategies for advancement, and information. In addition to furnishing information, these networks provide women with support and a sense of fit with other professionals like them. A number of established professional women also mentor younger women in their fields, even though doing so requires heavy investments of time and energy. Because even women who have earned professional status report that they must continue to work harder than their male colleagues to prove themselves, finding time to mentor is difficult. As men and women become accustomed to interacting as colleagues, they may become more comfortable mentoring each other and forming sex-integrated communication networks.

Glass Ceilings — and Walls?

Finally, we consider what has been called **the glass ceiling**, which is an invisible barrier that limits advancement of women and minorities. In 1991, *U.S. News and World Report*'s lead business story concerned the glass ceiling that blocks women's progress in professions ("Trouble at the Top," 1991). Labeling her report the "glass ceiling initiative," Labor Secretary Lynn Martin revealed that gender discrimination pervades the workplace, particularly at the upper levels. What impedes women's progress, according to this study, is subtle discrimination that limits women's opportunities (p. 41). It might be the stereotype of women as mothers that leads an executive to assume that a working mother would not be interested in a major new assignment, one that could advance her career. It might be seeing a woman in sexual terms so that her competence is overlooked. It might be misinterpreting an inclusive, collaborative style of communication as indicating lack of initiative. All of these stereotypes and misperceptions pose subtle barriers — a glass ceiling that keeps women out of the executive suite.

But glass ceilings may be only part of the problem. A recent report ("Study Says Women Face Glass Walls," 1992, p. B2) suggests that "if the ceiling doesn't stop today's working woman, the walls will." *Glass walls* is a metaphor to describe sex segregation on the job, in which stereotypes lead to placing women in positions that require traditionally feminine skills (assistant to . . . , clerical roles, counseling, human relations). Typically, areas such as human resources do not include a career ladder in which doing well at one level allows advancement to the next. In essence, many positions into which women are placed are dead ends for careers.

Recognizing that subtle, unintentional discrimination is no more acceptable than overt prejudice, some companies are taking steps to break through glass ceilings and walls that unfairly hinder women's career advancement. Arthur Andersen and Company, for example, sponsors gender-awareness training that helps men and women learn to understand and respect each other as colleagues. DuPont has initiated a rotation policy that moves women and men employees through different jobs so that all employees have opportunities to learn about the company and qualify for advancement ("Study Says Women Face Glass Walls," 1992, p. B2). These examples are good models of institutional efforts to accommodate diverse workers and, in the process, enlarge the talent available to organizations.

Formal and informal communication systems establish the climate of a workplace and relationships among employees. While many factors make up the communication systems of an organization, three particularly related to gender are leave policies and schedules, communication climates, and glass ceilings. In each of these areas, gendered beliefs lead to gendered practices, which reflect and perpetuate restrictive views of women and men and, therefore, limit their professional and personal lives. Yet, increasingly, organizational structures and practices are changing to respond to the distinctive skills, experiences, needs, and styles of men and women workers (Reskin & Roos, 1990).

*S*ummary

In this chapter, we have considered a variety of ways in which institutional life intersects with cultural understandings of gender and communication. Views of masculinity and femininity endorsed by society seep into the workplace in the form of stereotypes of women, men, and professional communication and in communication systems that reflect and perpetuate gendered attitudes. While overt and subtle gender bias persists in institutional life, we should remember that only recently have substantial numbers of women sought extended professional careers. As women and men gain experience in communicating with each other as colleagues, and as organizations recognize the distinctive contributions each gender makes to productivity and climate, we should see erosion in some of the barriers that exist today.

Clearly, organizations need to adapt to the nature of the contemporary work force. This will involve recognizing family responsibilities as part of most employees' lives and increasing efforts to accommodate family commitments. In addition, institutions should identify and alter communication practices and climates that create inequitable working environments for diverse employees. Both organizations and individuals will benefit by climates that are equally hospitable to women, men, minority races, and gays and lesbians.

Reforming institutional structures and practices is a priority for young people who are now entering the work force. You and your peers will make up and define the workplace of the future. Through attention to legislation that affects the workplace and through your own participation in it, you may take an active role in reforming the nature of institutional life in America so that it is more equitable and humane for all employees and so that it is actively enriched by the diversity of humans who make up our society.

Our focus on gendered communication in present-day organizations might lead you to feel overwhelmed by the serious problems that exist. Yet there is good reason to believe we can bring about changes. For instance, in 1979 only about 100 employers provided any kind of child-care support; a decade later, well over 4,000 do ("Firms Design Benefits," 1989), and we have our first national family leave policy. Between 1987 and 1989, about 100 firms adopted some kind of elder-care assistance programs ("Firms Design Benefits," 1989). More and more organizations are experimenting with "flexitime," which allows employees to arrange schedules to accommodate both family and job responsibilities. Other changes are happening, and still more can be realized through our efforts.

For innovations to occur, we need to resist gender stereotypes in our own thinking and to challenge them in the thinking and actions of others. One of the most pressing challenges for your generation is to revise institutional gender stereotypes and communication systems that restrict the possibilities open to men and women for full lives as professionals and members of families. In short, we need to remake our institutions so that they correspond to the lives of today's men and women. By recognizing inequities that exist and the kinds of stereotypes behind them, you empower yourself to instigate changes that can improve the conditions in which we live and work.

$\mathscr{D}$iscussion Questions

1. Have you observed instances of classifying women into the four sex stereotypes identified in the text: sex object, mother, child, and iron maiden? Have you observed or experienced these in environments where you have worked? Think about how working women are represented in television shows and in movies. Are they depicted in sex-stereotypical roles?

2. How might being classified as a sex object, mother, or child affect a woman's career opportunities and effectiveness? How might the iron-maiden role influence them? What do you see as options for how women might resist being cast into these stereotypes?

3. Now, contemplate sex stereotypes of working men. Have you seen examples of men being classified as sturdy oaks, fighters, and/or breadwinners? Have you seen men classified as wimps? How do such sex stereotypes limit career opportunities and effectiveness for men? What happens to men who don't "measure up" to stereotypes of masculinity?

4. Do you agree with the chapter's claim that professionalism is generally defined by masculine standards? Is this a problem? How does defining normative behavior from the standpoint of only a particular group affect people who are not members of that group? Should professionalism be more inclusively defined to incorporate diverse styles of communication?

5. Discuss women's and men's leadership styles. If you have worked for both men and women, draw on your experience to discuss similarities and differences in female and male supervisors' expectations of employees, communication styles, and relationships with co-workers and employees. If you haven't worked for both sexes, consider male and female executives on television. How are they alike and different?

Do they use power differently? Does one sex tend to encourage more participation than the other? Do they build different kinds of connections with others in work settings?

6. The text suggests that both culturally defined feminine and masculine styles of communication can be effective in professional contexts, including in leadership roles. Do you agree or disagree? Do you think people would generally be more effective in their careers if they were skilled in communication typical of both sexes? What might you do to increase your own communication repertoire so that you are able to draw on strengths of what society defines as feminine and masculine styles?

7. Do you think organizations should accommodate families beyond what is required in the 1993 act? Specifically, discuss whether organizations should adapt their policies and practices to provide more than 12 weeks leave when employees have or adopt children. Should organizations encourage men to be more actively involved in family life? Should organizations support workers who need time off to care for parents or other dependents? Should leaves be paid?

8. Interview some people involved in careers to discover how important networks are. Do women and men professionals report they are equally welcomed into informal networks in their organizations and fields? Do they report receiving equal guidance and mentoring from more established colleagues?

9. The chapter mentions gender awareness programs that some organizations now provide to their employees. Do you think these are a good idea? Thinking about all that you have learned in this course, what would you include in a gender awareness training program for a company? What understandings of gender and communication would assist people in working together comfortably and would provide equally friendly working environments to women and men? As a class, design the content of what you think would be an effective program in gender awareness.

$\mathcal{L}$ooking Backward, Looking Forward

The cultural conversation about gender is ongoing. It is carried on in barrooms and living rooms, college classes and beauty pageants, Saturday morning cartoons and newspaper stories, and private relationships and public platforms. It is a conversation that continues and in which we all participate, with each generation adding new themes to the overall dialogue. Even though this book is ending, what you've learned about communication, gender, and culture will affect your personal future and how you shape our collective horizons. In this final chapter, I will locate gender and communication issues within a context by reviewing major changes that have occurred and choices open to us as we continue the conversation through which we constantly re-create ourselves, gender, and the social world.

▄▄ The Cultural Construction and Reconstruction of Gender

Throughout this book, we've seen that social order and meanings are created in daily messages that remind us what society regards as feminine and masculine, what it expects of women and men, and what value it bestows on each gender. We not only are receivers of cultural communication about gender, but also we send our own messages. We fortify or resist prevailing views as we enact and express our own gender and our own beliefs about what is normal, inferior, and superior.

Historically and today, Western society defines white skin, heterosexual affectional preference, and maleness as standard, while skin of color, gay and lesbian affectional preferences, and femaleness are considered inferior. These arbitrary definitions are elaborated through social practices that accord greater value to traditionally masculine behavior (assertion, independence) and lesser to traditionally feminine behavior (cooperation, interdependence), as well as more respect to conventionally masculine priorities (power, money, competition) than to typically feminine ones (relationships, feelings, harmony). We are encouraged to accept these standards by constant communication that normalizes prevailing views of gender and entices us to regard them as natural.

Yet a central theme of *Gendered Lives* is that socially constructed views of gender are not the only possible ones, nor are they necessarily the best ones. In this book, I've invited you to become an active, critical member of your society, which means to reflect on its values and to challenge those that limit human potential. We must not be lulled into believing that the views and values our culture seeks to normalize are, in fact, inevitable. Our symbolic nature allows us to question, reflect, and remake our human world and ourselves in ever new ways.

Regardless of whether you define yourself as any type of feminist and regardless of whether you embrace traditional or less conventional values, you

REMAKING OURSELVES

Freedom ... is characterized by a constantly renewed obligation to remake the Self, which designates the free being.

Sartre, J. P. (1966). *Being and nothingness: An essay in phenomenological ontology* (pp. 34–35). New York: Citadel Press.

live in a gendered society. By implication, not only are you affected by social views of masculinity and femininity, but you are part of shaping those understandings. Because each of us participates in cultural life, we affect it, including the meanings our society assigns to gender. This implies that you and others of your generation will revise cultural understandings of gender. Given the pervasive and profound impact of gender on individual and social life, this is no small responsibility. It is your capacity to revise gender and culture that we will explore in the pages that follow.

Looking Backward, Looking Forward

You have inherited opportunities and definitions of gender crafted by the second wave of feminism in the United States. My generation challenged restrictive definitions of women and men and social practices that limit the opportunities available to both sexes. We devoted much of our energy to identifying gender inequities and fighting to change economic, political, professional, and social subordination of women. The legacy of our efforts is substantial, and it has altered the educational, social, professional, and legal rights that you enjoy.

Your generation faces its own distinct issues, and you will need to define different priorities than those that inspired my generation. Framing the issues of your era is growing awareness of how intersections among communication, gender, and culture privilege some people and oppress others. All around us are inequities — some glaringly obvious and others more subtle. In shaping the future, your generation will decide how to respond to social practices that produce decisive differences in the standpoints, quality of life, and opportunities available to various groups in our culture. Dotting the contemporary cultural landscape are a number of gender controversies whose outcomes you will influence. To explore these, we'll ask what changes have been made and what issues invite our attention in the various contexts this book addresses.

Communication

Views of communication have altered considerably. Most notably, recent decades have heightened awareness of differences in how women and men generally communicate and have enlarged understanding of the distinctive strengths of women's style. As our knowledge of gender-linked communication and its effects has grown, many women have become more assertive and some men have worked to become more responsive and inclusive.

Women's communication.   As the 1992 year-end issue of *Newsweek* (Salholz et al., 1992) points out, "Women are breaking the silence" (p. 22). Anita Hill's courage in taking sexual harassment out of the closet encouraged a great many women to follow suit. No longer are women generally willing to accept harassment on the job and in schools as "just how things are done." Instead, they are using their voices to name the offense and to demand change. The Equal Employment Opportunity Commission (EEOC) reports that 10,522 people filed sexual harassment claims in 1992, a considerable rise from the 6,883 claims made in 1991 (Salholz et al., 1992, p. 22). Women are also taking strong voices on other issues, naming as government priorities support of family life, access to abortion, and education for children, particularly disadvantaged ones. Clearly many women have incorporated more vocal, less deferential forms of communication into their rhetorical repertoires.

Men's communication.   We've also seen some changes in men's communication patterns. Historically the open, collaborative style that attempts to include others has been associated with women and devalued. Men have been expected to engage in more competitive, powerful forms of rhetoric. Yet the 1992 presidential campaign turned this stereotype on its head when candidate Bill Clinton consistently relied on an interactive, conversational mode of communication. He collaborated with others, including Hillary Rodham Clinton, to build and refine his ideas. He appeared on talk shows to engage in conversations with hosts and audience members. He fomented change in the traditional format of debates, which relied on sequential speeches by individual candidates. Instead, he favored an open format that allowed him to interact directly with citizens by letting them pose questions he would answer.

Viewers' responses to this innovative debate structure were overwhelmingly positive. They felt they were listened to; they felt included in the conversation. Throughout his campaign, Bill Clinton not only used traditionally feminine forms of communication, but he also included more conventionally feminine content. He spoke of feelings and responding to people's needs, and he showed emotions about both public and personal issues. In blending assertion and responsiveness, confidence and openness, and power and sensitivity, Bill Clinton inaugurated a new image of how successful men communicate. In many ways, he challenged and changed the masculine stereotype of effective political rhetoric. In the opening months of his presidency, Bill Clinton continued to engage in a more open, inclusive, and responsive communication style than is typical of masculine speech.

Gender and communication in the future.   Looking ahead, how will women's and men's communication continue to evolve? Will there be more men like Bill Clinton who demonstrate that one can be sensitive without being weak? Will we see more models like Hillary Rodham Clinton who show us that power and success can combine with domestic commitments in women? As your generation experiments with styles of interaction that depart from the rigid dichotomies of sex stereotypes, you will redefine the range of human communication that we see as appropriate for both sexes.

Women's and Men's Movements

Another context of change in views of gender has been women's and men's movements. Here we have seen remarkable developments, and additional ones promise to emerge in the coming years.

Liberal feminism. The most pronounced changes recent movements have instigated have been achieved by liberal feminists and especially by the National Organization for Women (NOW). Prior to the second wave of feminism in this country, there was no national organization dedicated to securing rights for women. Today NOW is 27 years old, and it has accomplished major changes in the material and social conditions of women's lives. As a political voice for women, NOW has led the way on a number of pivotal issues. For instance, women today have laws that guarantee equal opportunity in education and employment. In addition, legal recourse exists for anyone who suffers gender discrimination in salary, working conditions, or advancement. With NOW's support of the pivotal *Roe* v. *Wade* case, women won the right to control their bodies and to make decisions about their reproductive health.

Issues such as these were priorities between 1960 and today because women had to have some legal, publicly recognized rights as a foundation for addressing other ways in which cultural prescriptions for gender oppress people. Changing public policies, however, is only a start in rethinking gender and the ways it affects social life. Much more needs to be done if we are to remake our world so that all members may participate fully. How will women's movements, including NOW, reconfigure themselves and their priorities to fit the future?

The future of feminism. What will be the shape and focus of women's movements in the coming decades? One important issue is whether the dominant branch of feminism will be the liberal one, as exemplified by NOW and other groups that seek to expand women's rights to participate in traditional male spheres and to enjoy traditionally male prerogatives such as fair wages. As you'll recall, a second major form of feminism is cultural, which argues that the goal is not to let women operate by male standards, but to alter the standards themselves so that our culture values and relies on qualities, interests, styles, and abilities historically ascribed to women as well as those associated with men. Cultural feminism seeks to change basic cultural structures and practices and the values underlying them so that our society esteems empowerment, cooperation, responsiveness, and community. In the future, will cultural feminism ascend and weave traditionally feminine values more fully into social life?

Valuing diversity. A second key question that movements of your generation will address is how to deal with the critique that mainstream feminism has been too focused on the issues and needs of white, middle-class women in Western societies and too unaware of issues confronting women of color in this country and globally (Davis, 1991; hooks, 1990; Spelman, 1988). Will feminism in the 1990s become more inclusive in its concerns, more sensitive to the effects of race and class in compounding gender oppression? This is a critical issue for women's movements of the future.

Reproductive rights. A third urgent issue in the years ahead is policies on reproduction. Back for a return engagement on the cultural agenda is abortion rights, which was a central concern for women in the 1960s and 1970s. In 1992, the Supreme Court modified the landmark *Roe v. Wade* case, which established women's right to abortion in the first two trimesters. Some restrictions now abridge that right, and others are being debated in courtrooms across the country. As this book goes to press, the U.S. Supreme Court just refused to hear a case in which a lower court ruled against the territory of Guam's extremely restrictive abortion guidelines. The import of this action is that the Supreme Court did not support the severe limits Guam wishes to impose on women's access to abortion. Almost simultaneously, the Court refused to hear a case challenging Mississippi's requirements for counseling and a 24-hour waiting period, thus attaching some conditions to women's options. Meanwhile, President Clinton relaxed a number of restrictions on abortion within weeks of taking office. These mixed signals from the highest court reflect wrenching discord surrounding the issue of reproductive rights. You will need to be informed on this topic and on the implications of affirming or restricting women's rights to make decisions about their bodies. Will you take the time to learn about the issues, to participate in political and legislative activities to influence decisions?

Men's movements. Let's think now about what has happened and what may develop within men's movements. Since the 1980s, we have seen a number of efforts to define issues for men — efforts that grow out of widely divergent views of masculinity. Some of the men's movements born in the last couple of decades seek to reinscribe highly traditional views of men as dominant, superior, and powerful; others argue men should become more feeling and more cooperative; and still others, such as Robert Bly's, urge men to rediscover a traditionally masculine mode of emotionality and to build deep connections with other men, especially with their fathers.

How will men's movements evolve in the years ahead? Will one of the movements we discussed earlier eclipse others to become dominant? Will still other men's movements be born? Indicative of growing interests in exploring men's concerns is the fact that in 1992 two journals premiered: *The Journal of Men's Studies*, an academic journal devoted to research and theory on men's lives and issues, was launched and already has substantial subscribers. On the popular scene, *Men's Journal* debuted, announcing its purpose as exploring the contemporary masculine psyche and issues. Will there be enough interest (and subscribers) to sustain these journals? Will more follow? Another indicator of growing interest in masculinity and men's issues is the number of books on these topics appearing in stores and libraries. According to Scott Heller (1993), there is an explosion of scholarship on men as well as the ways in which cultures shape our ideas about masculinity and how individual men embody it. Heller observes that many scholars of men and masculinity eschew Robert Bly's mythopoetic movement because it evades the real problems that define men's lives and social interaction (p. A8). Alternatives to the mythopoetic branch of men's movements are being generated as research clarifies the kinds of constraints and inequities that society's gender stereotypes impose on men.

As I write this chapter, more than 25 books on men and masculinity are just released or in production (Heller, 1993). Each one argues a certain point of view about how men and masculinity have been socially constructed, and each emphasizes particular issues as key ones facing men today. Which of these will emerge as central issues that men need to address in considering how cultural prescriptions for gender shape their lives? If you are a man, will you read these journals or other publications about men? Will you explore matters in your own life by attending workshops sponsored by various men's groups? If you are a woman, will you be as open to considering men's issues and your relation to them as many women have asked men to be about women's issues? The coming years may be a pivotal time for men if they, like second-wave feminists, come together to define their interests, needs, and priorities and to use collective efforts to identify and change gender ideologies that inhibit their participation and satisfaction in personal and public realms.

Gender in Education

Within educational contexts, we have seen some significant changes in gender and communication. At the same time, there is still much to be done if we wish to have our schools equally empowering of all students.

Reducing gender discrimination.   Most basic among changes that have transpired is that we now have laws that make it illegal to discriminate on the basis of gender. In addition, there are regulations to ensure equitable funding of

A M Y

can't imagine not having had the chance to take courses about gender and women's studies. I'm not majoring in that or anything, but I have taken about three courses, and I've really learned a lot about discrimination. Even more important to me is what I've learned about myself, like not to take femininity as a given. I've had to reflect a lot on why I am like I am and whether that's how I want to be. And I've started noticing things I wouldn't have seen before—like when my English literature course included only 2 women authors and 18 male ones. Before, I would never have even noticed this, much less questioned it. Now I do. I asked my professor if he thought only one-ninth of the authors worth studying were female. Like I say, courses in women's studies and gender have changed how I think. I guess I'm pretty lucky to have come to college after those were allowed into the curriculum. There really have been some changes.

women's and men's activities in any educational units that receive federal funding. Other changes of note include the growing number of women faculty members and the rising presence of women in formerly masculine majors such as science and in graduate and professional schools. Clearly, women are more present and active in educational contexts than they were years ago.

It's also important to note that since the early 1980s, educational researchers have called attention to subtle forms of gender discrimination that often make educational settings "chilly climates" for women. Naming taken-for-granted institutional practices that favor male students and devalue females removes these from invisibility and allows individual educators and institutions to address gender discrimination.

Another major change in the past two decades has been expansion of the curriculum to include study of gender both in its own right and as it interacts with all other areas of social life. In response to the critique of sedimented sexism in education, many curricula have been reformed to include courses that focus on or include attention to gender and women's issues. Women's studies programs exist on most campuses today, whereas they were virtually nonexistent 25 years ago. Equally important, many courses not specifically focused on gender include issues of gender, race, and class. This enhances students' opportunities to learn how gender is implicated deeply in history, sociology, psychology, literature, and other areas formerly defined as uninfluenced by gender.

Future gender issues in education. Yet, important as these developments are, educational contexts need further reform if they are to live up to the espoused ideal of equal opportunity for all students. It's evident that sexism persists when a report in the 1990s confirms that educational practices identified 10 years ago as contributing to a chilly climate are alive and well in classrooms across the country. Further evidence of continuing gender discrimination lies in the gaps between salaries of women and men faculty with equivalent experience, records, and seniority, as well as in the paucity of qualified women faculty who are promoted to the higher ranks in academic structures. Will the coming years further progress in eradicating gender discrimination in educational settings? If you continue your education, will you take a voice to speak out against educational practices that disadvantage women? If you have children, will your daughters get as much intellectual encouragement and attention as your sons? Will you be active in making this happen by, for instance, learning how candidates running for school boards stand on gender equity issues? Will you perhaps run for such a position yourself so that you may more directly work toward gender equity in education?

Gender in Media

Media are particularly visible indicators of shifting views of gender. We've seen substantial changes in how media represent women and men as well as in who controls media. In the years to come, media will continue to redraft images of gender.

Changes in women in media. Since the 1960s, we have seen substantial shifts in both the kinds of roles available to women and the number of women influencing media from behind the scenes (Lont, 1990). Linda Bloodworth-Thomason, for instance, produced "Designing Women," "Evening Shade," and "Hearts Afire," each of which portrays women in nonstereotypical roles. Diane English produces "Murphy Brown," which became emblematic of the cultural battle over women's identity when former Vice President Dan Quayle criticized her independent and nontraditional life-style. Murphy Brown, with her outspoken, ambitious style, is a far cry from Mary Tyler Moore's earlier depiction of a working woman as one who remained within supportive, deferential roles traditionally prescribed for women.

Meanwhile, a key figure in the 1992 presidential race was Mandy Grunwald, who runs the media consulting organization that orchestrated Bill Clinton's campaign. My niece, who worked directly with Mandy Grunwald, reported that the media virtuoso was extraordinarily smart, aggressive, intuitively tuned to public feelings, and supportive and empowering of co-workers. This combination of qualities, ones *Newsweek* echoed (Salholz et al., 1992, p. 19), combines attributes traditionally associated with masculinity and femininity into a person who is both effective and sensitive. The difference between the style and content of Bill Clinton's campaign and that of candidates whose strategies men designed may provide clues to how women use media to represent issues and people.

Other changes of note in media include the increase in women's music and companies like Redwood and Ladyslipper that exclusively produce music by and for women. Women artists like Mary-Chapin Carpenter, En Vogue, K. T. Oslin, Gloria Estefan, Suzie Bogguss, Tracy Chapman, and k. d. lang give voice to experiences, values, and aesthetic forms that were not characteristically represented by males or by women singing lyrics written by men from a mainstream masculine perspective. New women artists increasingly are attracting mainstream listening audiences consisting of both men and women.

Films, too, have offered us some new visions of women. In 1992, Disney produced *Aladdin*, which is the first animated feature film to have a nonwhite human hero. Rumor has it that Disney is currently working on *Pocahontas*, which will highlight a strong, autonomous female figure. One of the most controversial adult films in recent years was *Thelma and Louise*, which was a bold departure from former images of women as supportive sidekicks to men. Taking to the road on their own, Thelma and Louise defined themselves as independent of men and as entitled to respond strongly, even violently, to male assaults and devaluations of them. While many saw the very fact that such a film *could* be made and could become a popular hit as a mark of real progress in exploding images of women as dependent and passive, others note that criticism of Thelma and Louise for claiming their freedom and defending themselves against men indicates that many people still don't accept women as autonomous and active agents.

Mediated gender in the future.   What images of women and men will media issue in the future? In this area, there are a number of issues that merit the attention of your generation. Consider, first, advertising. Lana Rakow (1992) reports that ads continue to depict women and men in highly gender-stereotyped ways. Beauty and youth are still pushed as the be-all and end-all of successful womanhood (Greer, 1992; Rakow, 1992; Schwichtenberg, 1989; Wolf, 1991). In addition, ads for men in magazines such as *Esquire* continue to promote images of sturdy oaks and big wheels as the epitome of masculinity (Kervin, 1990).

As I was writing this chapter at 4:27 P.M. on January 2, 1993, a commercial interrupted the pro-football playoffs on ABC. In the commercial, three contestants in a beauty pageant were asked to answer the question, How would you save the planet? The first candidate, a serious-looking woman, responded she would focus on educating youth. The second candidate thoughtfully replied that she would concentrate on environmental concerns. The final candidate, a blonde woman whose nonverbal communication fit her into the "dumb blonde" stereotype, answered, "Planet? Which planet?" Immediately, the judges of the pageant all nodded enthusiastically that this was the winner — the best model of womanhood. The final line in the ad was, "Why ask why? Drink Bud Dry." Somehow, I lost my taste for this brew. Will you and your peers be part of reforming advertising so that it does not promote unrealistic and unhealthy images of women and men? Will you write to manufacturers when you find their ads offensive? Will you quit buying products from firms that persist in using sex-stereotypical advertising? Will you give up Bud Dry and insist that we should ask why?

Liberal and cultural feminist views of women. In the future, media are likely to provide a stage in which we observe debates between cultural and liberal wings of feminism. Bonnie Dow (1992) offered an insightful analysis of "Murphy Brown," in which she showed that Murphy exemplifies a liberal feminist version of women — someone able to operate effectively in the public sphere formerly reserved for men. But, notes Dow, Murphy does it on masculine terms. She accepts as desirable the cultural standards that have been defined by men and shows only that women too can meet those standards. The question not posed in "Murphy Brown" is whether the standards themselves are desirable. This is the focus of cultural feminism — a critique of exclusively masculine standards in cultural life. Will future programs include women who are successful on terms other than masculine ones?

As views of women become less consensual, we can expect to see competing images promoted in media. For instance, Madonna's most recent book, *Sex*, takes to new extremes her efforts to explode any stable definition of women (Schwichtenberg, 1992). She insists there is no one definition for all women and individual women need not constantly embody any single image. Certainly Madonna is a controversial figure. Whether you regard her public escapades as progressive in liberating women from restrictive definitions or as regressive in resurrecting persisting associations of women with sexuality, she is a figure to watch because she forces us to ask how we define women and whether other definitions are possible.

In stark contrast to Madonna is another visible image of women emerging in the present: Hillary Rodham Clinton. She has a professional degree and her own career, and for years she has outearned her husband. She is what Linda Bloodworth-Thomason calls a "brain trust" (Clift & Miller, 1992, p. 23). During the 1992 elections, George Bush's campaign indicted her for her lack of femininity, pointing out that she was a successful lawyer and an outspoken woman. Then-President Bush's campaign also condemned Bill Clinton as unmanly for "allowing" his wife to be an activist and scholar and for consulting her on matters of policy and judgment. Efforts to discredit Hillary Rodham Clinton as not a "real woman" and Bill Clinton as not a "real man" were not persuasive to the majority of voters, signaling greater acceptance of women and men in nontraditional roles. After the inauguration, Hillary Rodham Clinton broke decades of tradition when

HILLARY ON WOMEN

In a *Newsweek* (Clift & Miller, 1992, pp. 24–25) interview, Hillary Rodham Clinton offered some of her views on women:

> What we are going through is generational and social and global, and a large part of it has to do with the role and responsibilities of women. . . . There isn't yet any clear consensus about how we are defining ourselves, the changing roles between men and women.
>
> I think the '90s is a time where we're trying to reconcile a lot of the changes that we've lived through in the last 20 or 30 years, where we acknowledge that we have a right to have control over our own destinies, and to define ourselves as individuals; but where we also acknowledge that . . . women want to be part of relationships as well, and to be connected to something bigger than themselves as part of the kind of ongoing cycle of life.
>
> Women are always being tested. The tests go on inside the home as well as outside the home. And I think that is an extra burden that we carry to be able to fit into a workplace that is based on values and experiences that we didn't have much role in shaping. . . . And men . . . are equally confused about how to define themselves and their relation to this new world order that is coming up between the sexes.

she set up her office in the West Wing of the White House, where policy-makers work. Historically, first ladies have operated from the East Wing. As a number of commentators noted, the move makes sense, since *this* first woman is a policy-maker—and a major one. She has been labeled the "Lady Macbeth of Little Rock," the "Evita Peron of America," Bill Clinton's co-president, a brilliant scholar, a "feminist shrew," and a committed social reformer. As a highly visible symbol of changing roles of women, Hillary Rodham Clinton will be a major focus of media attention (Quinn, 1993). We need to be attentive and critical in watching how media attempt to mold our impressions of her and, by extension, all women who deviate from historically feminine roles. Whatever Hillary Rodham Clinton does and however she crafts her image will instigate widespread rethinking about women.

Gender in Personal Relationships

The cover of the first 1993 issue of *Utne* magazine asks in giant letters, CAN MEN AND WOMEN GET ALONG? SHOULD THEY EVEN TRY? With this cover story, *Utne* signals the urgency of attending to personal relations between women and men. The second wave of feminism in the United States identified, but did not resolve, many issues in close relationships between women and men. Because mainstream second-wave feminism concentrated on diminishing gender discrimination in the public sphere, less systematic effort focused on inequities in private relationships. In other words, gender issues in personal life that were subordinated in prior decades will be spotlighted in the years ahead.

Changes in gender relations.   Among the changes achieved in personal relationships during recent decades, three stand out. First, date rape and acquaintance rape have been named as crimes. This gives these acts public visibility and allows victims a socially recognized vocabulary for seeking justice for what they suffer. Second, divorce laws have been rewritten in many states so that nonfinancial investments in marriage are better recognized and accommodated in making property settlements. This is a pivotal change because it means that contributions to relationships, family life, and support of another's public career are legally recognized as having value. Third, many men and women of my generation pioneered new forms of friendship and committed romantic relationships, and we worked out more equitable partnerships with our mates than those modeled by our parents (Blumstein & Kollock, 1988; Maccoby, 1990). These three changes reflect growing awareness of gender discrimination in the private sphere, which was formerly off-limits for public and legal intervention. Yet there is much work still to be done in remaking our close relationships so that they are workable in the present era.

Addressing gender divisions.   One of the greatest urgencies facing your generation is divisions between women and men. To make women's oppression visible, discrepancies between the rights of women and the rights of men had to be articulated and changed. That, however, was only the first stage (Friedan, 1981) in the larger effort to create a truly equitable society. It is not the end point of the journey.

The problem to which Betty Friedan refers (see the box on p. 302) is the tension in heterosexual relationships in which both partners work outside of the home. Lack of social support for family life combined with inadequate personal commitments to equity in personal relationships inevitably creates frustrations and disappointments. The "second shift" we discussed earlier is an example of gender inequity in the private sphere. It is neither fair nor loving when one partner

TRANSCENDING DIVISIONS

The liberation that began with the women's movement [the second wave of feminism] isn't finished. The equality we fought for isn't livable, isn't workable, isn't comfortable.... We have somehow to transcend the polarities of the first stage.... How do we transcend the polarization between women and women and between women and men, to achieve the new human wholeness that is the promise of feminism? ... This is the personal and political business of the second stage.

Friedan, B. (1981). The second stage (pp. 40–41). New York: Summit Books.

---

in a dual-worker family expects the other to assume the majority of domestic and child-care responsibilities. While some men today are doing more inside the home than their fathers, it's still the case that only 20% of men in dual-worker relationships assume a full share of responsibilities (Hochschild, 1989). When 80% of men still do not, not enough progress has been made.

Clearly we need more generous national policies to attenuate strains in contemporary families, but public action is not the only and not a sufficient source of change. Just as important are personal commitments that individuals live out in their daily lives. You will make choices in your private relationships that belie or enact a commitment to equity. Will you enjoy the differences and similarities of friendships with women and men (Jones and Dembo, 1989; Sapadin, 1988)? What kind of family responsibilities will you assume, and what will you expect of your partner? If you are a man, will you contribute equally to cleaning, cooking, and child care, including the repetitive, less satisfying tasks of bathing, feeding, and transporting children? If you are a woman, will you be more assertive than many members of the current generation of women in insisting on equity in homelife? You will answer these questions not with statements of intent, but in daily practices through which you reinforce or reconfigure existing cultural patterns.

Will your generation find ways to overcome the divisiveness that too often poisons relationships between women and men? Recent decades have tended to portray women's interests as opposed to those of men and gains in women's opportunities as losses for men. Perhaps your generation will redefine issues so that they are not seen as win-lose. Your voice will serve to fuel or defuse divisions between women and men. Will you be part of identifying interests, goals, rights, and needs that are common to both sexes? Will you find ways to cooperate and collaborate in creating relationships that are fair and satisfying to men and women? Will you go even further and search for shared interests among other groups: European-Americans, Hispanics, Latinos and Latinas, African-Americans, Native Americans, and other peoples of color, straights, lesbians, and gays, those with education and money and those with little of either? Can we begin to discover what is common to us—the needs we share, the dreams we have—without erasing what is unique about us as individuals?

Denouncing violence. Also on your generation's agenda is further work to identify and eliminate crimes of violence, of which women are disproportionately the victims worldwide (Brownmiller, 1993; Heise, 1989; Roberts, 1983). From fraternity activities that demean and violate women to battering, incest, and rape, there is a lengthy and shameful list of crimes of violence that have too long contaminated life in our society (Pleck, 1987). Legal recognition of rape as a serious crime needs to be enlarged to include acquaintance and date rape. While there has been progress in interposing these terms into public language, cases are difficult to prosecute. In the winter of 1992, Carl Fox, the district attorney in my county, told me that juries are reluctant to convict a man of rape when a victim knew him and had been friendly with him. In short, rape is not yet defined as *any* unwanted sex. It is still considered assault by a stranger. This means that knowing a person functionally negates a woman's right to say "no" and have that right respected by our legal system.

Debate about the meaning of rape will extend to marriage. In 1993, my home state, North Carolina, will consider for a second time legislation to make unwanted sexual intercourse within marriage a crime. Currently it is a crime in only 18 states in the nation (Dew, 1992, p. 1A). As long as men have the legal right to force sex on their wives, rape is not outlawed; it is only regulated. Until the legal system recognizes marital rape as a crime, married women will not be recognized as autonomous agents with rights but will be defined as property to whom husbands may do whatever they wish. Where do you stand on this issue, and how will you communicate your beliefs to personal friends and public officials?

Gender in Institutional Settings

We have seen a number of changes in institutional policies and practices related to gender. Growing out of NOW's work in lobbying for legislation, we have some laws to protect women against discrimination in hiring, advancement, and pay. Yet the achievement of gender equity in institutional life is far from finished. While feminist efforts of the past three decades have increased women's entry into professional and public life, the majority of women have been excluded from positions of leadership and power. Laws that have diminished discrimination in hiring have had little impact on the more informal structures that govern promotion and advancement. For instance, the Pregnancy Discrimination Act, passed in 1978 with NOW's support, makes it illegal to discriminate against pregnant women. Nonetheless, working women are reporting in increasing numbers that they are discriminated against when they become pregnant. They suddenly receive a bad evaluation, after years of positive ones, or their job is filled or erased during a pregnancy leave (Noble, 1993). These and other informal forms of discrimination create grave inequities for the 85% of working women likely to become pregnant at some point in their lives. Whether through discrimination against pregnancy or other gender issues, most women in the workplace hit the glass ceiling we discussed in Chapter 10, and the power structures of government and most organizations are still dominated by white, heterosexual men.

Women's positions in institutions. As this book goes to press, signs of change are on the horizon. The 1992 elections increased the number of women in the U.S. Senate from two to six, including Carol Mosely Braun, the first African-American woman in that deliberative body. These same elections sent the first Native American to Capitol Hill. Some political and social commentators predict that women's presence in Congress and other decision-making forums will result in greater attention to human needs, especially ones of families and people marginalized in our society (Lott, 1987). In late 1992, a number of incoming women in political positions met to map out priorities. The four top ones they named were fully funding Head Start, enacting family leave legislation, securing legal abortion, and rescinding congressional representatives' current immunity to sexual harassment laws (Salholz et al., 1992, p. 22). This suggests that national debate and the policies that grow out of it may reflect the increasing number of women in decision-making roles. Will those who make policies work harder to represent the multiple people and issues in our country?

Valuing diversity in institutional life. In trades, business, education, and government we need to watch for signs of change. Increasingly, companies recognize the talents and abilities of diverse workers and see the value of including people with varied backgrounds and perspectives at all levels of organizations. As it becomes clear that organizations are likely to benefit from diversity, they are making stronger efforts to identify and dismantle subtle barriers that have limited the professional growth of women and minorities (Reskin & Roos, 1990). A dramatic instance of increasing efforts to diversify institutional power is the cabinet Bill Clinton assembled for his presidency. He broke tradition by appointing to his cabinet four blacks, three women, and two Hispanics. Not only did he include more women and minorities in the group that will work with him to run the nation, but also he appointed some to positions traditionally earmarked as white and masculine. For instance, never before has a woman been secretary of energy, chair of the Council of Economic Advisors, or attorney general. A humorous yet significant indicator of women's growing presence in government is that the Capitol was remodeled in early 1993 to add a women's restroom adjacent to the Senate floor (Salholz et al., 1992, p. 22)! In the coming years, we will see how the increased participation and status of diverse people changes organizations and national policies.

Heightened awareness of sexual harassment. Another important area in which institutional views of gender have changed and will change further is sexual harassment. When I was 20 years old, there was no name for sexual harassment (Wood, 1992b, 1993f). It existed—few women of my generation weren't sexually harassed at least once—but because it was unnamed, it was not subject to critique and change. As attorney Catherine MacKinnon (1987) points out, once "the facts that amounted to sexual harassment did not amount to sexual harassment because they were not socially recognized" (p. 106). In giving sexual harassment a name and a judgment, it came to exist socially.

Your generation will further define sexual harassment and what is done about it. In recent years, much progress has been made in creating laws and institutional policies that condemn sexual harassment and levy penalties for its commission. Yet inequities persist. Men who are sexually harassed are often ridiculed, a response that reflects cultural views that men should be strong and self-sufficient. Further, in 1991, Anita Hill was not believed by the all-male, all-white senators who interrogated her or by the majority of the public, although 1 year later that had changed—the majority of people had come to believe she was telling the truth (Salholz et al., 1992, p. 21). Next came Tailhook, the egregious sexual harassment scandal in the navy. And in 1992 and 1993, Senator Packwood of Oregon responded to a number of women's accusations that he had sexually harassed them by claiming his problems with alcohol were responsible, but he personally wasn't. Where do we draw a line regarding personal responsibility for actions?

By the time this book is published, Senator Packwood will be old news, but the business of defining sexual harassment will not be. Your generation is pivotal in translating abstract policies and laws against sexual harassment into concrete, pragmatic realities. This means, for instance, that you will need to consider not just what constitutes sexual harassment, but the ways in which those who bring charges, both men and women, are systematically devalued and dismissed (Taylor & Conrad, 1992). What can you do to ensure that victims receive fair hearings? How can you—whether you're a man or a woman—be part of creating contexts in which sexual harassment is not tolerated and people who are victimized are treated with respect?

Social support for families. Finally, the future of gender in institutional contexts includes government and business policies regarding family life. In her book *The Second Stage* (1981), Betty Friedan named the family as the new frontier for feminist efforts at change. As we saw in Chapters 7 and 10 of this book, only a minority of couples have created equitable relationships, so women, more than men, continue to do the vast majority of homemaking and caregiving (Wood, 1993c). Despite passage of the 1993 Family and Medical Leave Act, we still have no national policies that guarantee *all* workers leaves to care for newborns and newly adopted children or for partners, parents, children, or other relatives who need care. Unlike *every other* developed country in the world, the United States has not designed government and business regulations that enable women and men to be both involved professionals and responsible members of families.

This may be changing. While George Bush — and before him, Ronald Reagan — opposed profamily policies, President Clinton campaigned in favor of them, and he has actively promoted them since taking office. In the next few years, you will see articles in newspapers and magazines about this issue, and legislation to provide various levels of family support will be introduced at state and national levels. You will have a voice in deciding whether and to what extent our country adopts policies that strengthen families. In your professional life, you will have opportunities to influence what your company or field does to make it possible for people to participate responsibly in both careers and families. In influencing government and business policies regarding families, your generation will play a critical role in redesigning institutional practices that have an impact on every citizen.

Creating the Future

All of the issues we've discussed in this chapter converge to influence individual and social views of gender. Each generation has to define femininity and masculinity anew. As we move toward the 21st century, how will you and your peers redraw cultural images of men and women? Historically, efforts to change views of women and men have resulted in pitting one vision of manhood or womanhood against another. Should men be strong or sensitive? Should women be traditional homemakers or fast-track careerists? Is Hillary Rodham Clinton or Madonna the *real* modern woman? Creating polar views of women and men does little to expand options, and it promotes divisiveness. Your generation has the opportunity to lead us away from oppositional images and embrace a flexible perspective that recognizes as valid the substantial variability within each gender. You could depart from previous and existing models to craft altogether new understandings of masculinity, femininity, and the relationships possible between people.

E D W I N A

I really hope my generation does get away from images of the one way to be a man or a woman. It just doesn't make sense for all of us to be the same, when clearly we're not. I say let Madonna do her thing, and let Hillary do hers, and maybe both are okay. Why does one of them have to be not all right? Why isn't it all right to be a full-time homemaker, or a full-time working mother, or not a mother at all? Why is only one choice considered "the right one"? Well, I really hope people of my generation can put a little elastic into social views of women and men and how each should be.

Defining Masculinity and Femininity

What will you define as the crux of being a man? Will it be physical strength as in the 1800s or salary and position as it is today? Consider recent media emphasis on men as sex objects, whose value is contingent on muscles and wardrobe, and media images of men as incompetent in housework and child care. If you are a man, you might raise the salience of friendships between men and men's involvement in family life, particularly fathering, making these part of what we understand it means to be a man. Likewise, you can choose to assume an equitable share of responsibilities for relationship health and for domestic work in your private life. In refashioning masculinity, you will also need to consider the traditional relationship between violence and manhood. Like all social views, that can be changed, but only if you and others take a role in renouncing violence as part of what it means to be a man. Another aspect of masculinity that will need rethinking will become clear as an increasing number of men of your generation have partners who earn higher salaries, prestige, and public position than you. If your view of manhood remains tied to status and power, this will create enormous tension in your relationships and your identity. Through your personal and collective choices, your generation will author its own vision of manhood, one that has the potential to revise and enlarge how women and men view masculinity (Peterson, Baucom, Elliott, & Farr, 1989).

What femininity means will also be recast by you. If you are a woman, think about how you will define your identity; if you are a man, think about what you will expect and value in women. Will you work to create healthier images that do not encourage normal women to starve themselves or to seek breast surgery in order to meet cultural standards? Will you recognize women for their minds and hearts more than their bodies? You have the capacity to resist cultural images of women that oppress you and others. By embodying a different view of women in your personal identity, you become part of creating new alternatives for everyone. As women and men, you can change what it means to be either in our society — that's an exciting opportunity for influence.

Defining Differences

Growing out of what we have discussed is perhaps the most urgent challenge for your generation: enlarging recognition and respect for differences that include and go beyond those between men and women. Diversity can be a source of strength or divisiveness, and you will choose which one it comes to mean in the future. Will you appreciate a woman who bakes her own bread as well as a woman who manages multi-million-dollar accounts? Will you respect men who give up careers to be homemakers and primary parents and men who find their fulfillment in intense entrepreneurial ventures? Will you encourage your sons and daughters to be caring and strong? Understand that your real answers to these questions are not what you say, but how you live your life. There is a saying that "those who talk the talk should also walk the walk," which means we should practice what we claim to believe in. In living out answers to these questions, you will define your views of women, men, and differences.

Redefining Culture

Throughout this book, we have seen that communication, gender, and culture interact constantly to affect one another. One implication of this is that as your generation transforms social meanings of women, men, and differences, you will simultaneously influence our collective vision of who we are as a culture.

Our country has always consisted of people of varied gender identities, affectional preferences, socioeconomic classes, and races. Yet our language and the dominant cultural ideology misrepresent us as homogeneous in character. We are all supposed to be the same — or, more truthfully, to agree on a single cultural ideal that some people embody more fully than others. Within this perspective, differences are matters of better and worse, and we are encouraged to evaluate ourselves and others in terms of a single standard. Historically, of course, the white, middle-class, heterosexual male has been that standard. The quest for a single cultural ideal is the impulse behind the "melting pot" metaphor that has long reigned in North America. We have encouraged people to erase their differences and become alike — to assimilate into a single culture based on a single denominator. The painful divisions in our society suggest that the melting pot is an inappropriate ideal for us. It no longer works — if indeed it ever did.

Perhaps it is time to abandon the melting pot metaphor and inaugurate a new one that acclaims difference as valuable and desirable, one that remakes the cultural ideal to incorporate all citizens instead of trying to remake diverse citizens to fit a single, noninclusive ideal. Maybe your generation will discard the melting pot metaphor and compose one that recognizes commonality without obliterating real and valuable differences among people. To create a new vision, we must realize that we participate in a common world, yet each of us experiences it somewhat differently from standpoints shaped by intersections among gender, race, class, and affectional preference. What sort of metaphor might capture this as our national character?

In her recent and excellent history of the second wave of feminism in North America, Flora Davis (1991) uses the metaphor of a salad bowl to describe our society. Davis argues that a salad consists of many different ingredients, which retain their individual tastes, textures, and colors and at the same time contribute to a whole that is more complex, interesting, and enjoyable than the individual parts or some fusion of those parts. The Reverend Jesse Jackson offered the compelling metaphor of our nation as a family quilt made up of patches having various colors and designs. Another metaphor is that of a collage in which distinct patterns stand out in their individual integrity while simultaneously contributing to the character and complexity of the whole. If your generation is able to affirm diversity in women and men, as well as in race, class, ethnicity, and affectional preference, then you will have inaugurated a bold new theme in the cultural conversation — one that has the potential to make our society richer and more equitable for all. That is a responsibility and an opportunity that belongs to each of you.

Taking a Voice

Men and women like you will provide the leadership in the next stage of the cultural conversation about gender. You cannot avoid participation nor the responsibilities it entails. Just as speaking out against discrimination is a choice, so too is choosing silence. If you don't exercise your voice, you become complicit in the status quo. You can't avoid influence; instead, you only have the options of what influence you will exert and how you will communicate it.

Society is a human creation that we constantly remake through communication in private and public settings. Your voice will join those of others to shape the meaning of gender and the concrete realities of being men and women in the coming years. You will also influence attitudes toward diversity either by reinscribing the view that differences are divisive or by affirming them a source of individual and collective enrichment, regeneration, and growth. What gender and culture will mean in the future is up to you. In your private relationships, public interactions, professional engagements, and civic activities, you will create and communicate new visions of who we can be and how we will live.

*D*iscussion Questions

1. Based on all that you have now read and discussed in this class, what does it mean to say that gender is socially created? How does communication produce and reproduce gendered identities and expectations? How can communication be used to alter gender roles in our society?

2. The chapter identifies changing patterns in women's and men's communication. Do you see evidence of changes discussed in the chapter? Do you see additional changes in how women and men communicate and interact?

3. What do you see as the future of women's and men's movements? Do you think one branch will come to predominate in each movement? Will new kinds of movements emerge?

4. Respond to the chapter's discussion of the future of feminism. What do you see as the critical issues for women's movements and women in the next 5 to 10 years? Do you plan to be part of these, to take a voice in them?

5. What kind of evolution do you predict in men's movements during the coming decade? Do you think they will gain in popularity and visibility? What do you see as the primary issues to be addressed by contemporary men and men's movements? Do you plan to take part in these movements?

6. What do you envision as changes that will come in how media represent women, men, and relationships? Do you think emphasis on beauty and thinness in women in advertising will diminish? Will women be less depicted as silly, scatter-brained, and deferential? Will men be portrayed as less self-reliant and uninterested in relationships with others?

7. Have a class discussion about Madonna. As the chapter indicated, some people see her as liberating women from any and all cultural prescriptions by defying boundaries on her identity. Others claim Madonna's explicit and flagrant sexuality reinforces historical views of women as sex objects. What's your opinion on this? Why? Focus class discussion on understanding different perceptions of Madonna, rather than agreeing on one view.

8. At the moment, very different images of women are embodied by visible public figures like Madonna, Sister Souljah, Murphy Brown, Rigoberta Menchu, and Hillary Rodham Clinton. What do these diverse visions of women imply about cultural views of femininity? Are there equally diverse images of men embodied in public

figures? Do Bill Clinton, Denzel Washington, Phil Donahue, and the Reverend Jesse Jackson represent different models of masculinity? Do you think alternative versions of womanhood and manhood will continue to emerge, or will we as a society settle on one or two we will consider "normal" and "right"? Do you find the diversity in women and men exciting, empowering, frustrating?

9. Think about your parents' and/or stepparents' marriages and those of other relatives and folks with whom you spent a lot of time. If you commit to an enduring romantic relationship, do you plan to model it after any of these? If not, how do you want to design your committed relationships? How does what you have learned in this course affect your thinking and dreaming about your ideal relationship?

10. How can you be part of changing social attitudes and policies regarding gender? Do you plan to take a voice on public issues such as laws to ensure family leave policies for men and women who work outside the home? Do you plan to make commitments within your personal relationships that lead to greater gender equity than traditional norms for relationships have? In the places you work, will you speak out for policies that provide equitable opportunities, working environments, and rewards for women and men on the job?

11. If you could write the script, how would you define masculinity and femininity in the year 2000? Ideally, what would each gender be like—or would there not be any need for two distinct genders? If gender is a linchpin of culture, then changing gender changes culture. How would the ideals you have in mind affect the character of social life?

12. The text closes by discussing metaphors that might replace the melting pot metaphor of the United States. Do you like the alternatives suggested in the chapter: a family quilt, a salad bowl, or a collage? Can you come up with other metaphors that simultaneously represent diversity and commonality among members of our society?

$\mathcal{G}$lossary

affirmative action   Policies that go beyond equal opportunity laws in efforts to realize greater equality for all. Affirmative action assumes that *historical patterns* of discrimination against *groups* of people justify preferential treatment for members of those groups. Also, affirmative action focuses on *results,* not intent of efforts to redress inequities. Affirmative action attempts to increase the number of *qualified* members of minorities in education and the workplace, commensurate with their availability.

alternate paths model   A view of friendships that claims that masculine and feminine ways of creating and expressing closeness are distinct, yet equally valid.

androgyny   Psychological, as distinct from biological, sex typing. Androgynous people tend to identify with and enact qualities socially ascribed to both women and men.

artifacts   Personal objects that influence how we see ourselves and how we express our identities.

backlash   This is a countermovement that seeks to repudiate and contain feminism by arguing two contradictory claims:

(1) Women have never had it so good, so there is no longer any need for feminism, and (2) feminism has caused serious problems in women's lives and family relationships.

biological theory Maintains that biological characteristics of the sexes are the basis of gender differences such as ways of thinking, communicating, and feeling.

close, personal relationships Relationships that endure over an extended period of time, in which partners depend on one another and consider each other irreplaceable—they are strongly and specifically connected to each other.

cognitive development theory Claims that children participate actively in defining their genders by acting on internal motivations to be competent, which lead children to seek out models of gender that allow them to sculpt their own femininity and/or masculinity.

communication A dynamic, systemic process in which meanings are created and reflected in and through humans' interactions with symbols.

content level of meaning The literal meaning of communication. Content level meanings are the lexigraphic, formal, or informal meanings of messages.

cultural feminists A group of feminists who believe women and men differ in fundamental ways, including these: Women are more moral, nurturing, concerned about others, and committed to harmony. These allegedly womanly qualities are celebrated and were often referred to as "the cult of domesticity" in first wave feminism.

culture The structures and practices, especially communication ones, through which a culture produces and reproduces a particular social order by legitimizing certain values, expectations, meanings, and patterns of behavior.

ecofeminism Launched in 1974, this movement integrates the intellectual and political bases of feminist theorizing with ecological philosophy. The result is a movement focused on the large issue of oppression, of which the specific oppression of women is seen as a particular instance of a larger ideology that esteems violence and domination of women, children, animals, and the earth.

ego boundaries The point at which an individual stops and the rest of the world begins. Ego boundaries are an individual's sense of the line between her or his own self and others. Ego boundaries exist on a continuum from permeable (a sense of self that includes others and their issues, problems, and so on) to rigid (a sense of self more distinct from others).

equal opportunity laws Laws that prohibit discrimination on the basis of race, color, religion, sex, or national origin. Equal opportunity laws seek to protect *individual* members of groups that have been targets of discrimination, and they confine their efforts to *present* discrimination, not historical bias.

erotica Depictions of sexual activities that are agreed to and enjoyed by all parties.

essentializing The tendency to reduce any phenomenon to essential characteristics, which are generally presumed to be innate and/or unchangeable. Essentializing the sexes implies that all women are alike in basic respects, that all men are alike in basic respects, and that the two sexes are distinct from each other because of fundamental, essential qualities.

father hunger　From the mythopoetic men's movement, this concept refers to men's yearning to be close to other men and to build deep, enduring bonds with other men. The label "father hunger" is based on mythopoetic belief that most young boys have distant relationships with the primary man in their lives, the father, and the hunger for a meaningful contact with men they were deprived of in youth continues through life.

Free Men　One branch of the men's movement that seeks to restore the traditional, macho image of men by reviving competitive, independent, and rugged qualities in men.

gender　A social, symbolic construction that expresses the meanings a society confers on biological sex. Gender varies across cultures, over time within any given society, and in relation to the other gender.

gender constancy　A person's understanding, usually arising between 3 and 6 years of age, that her or his gender is relatively fixed, or unchanging.

glass ceiling　An invisible barrier that limits the advancement of women and minorities. Making up the glass ceiling are subtle and often unconscious prejudices and stereotypes that limit women's and minorities' opportunities.

goals　Statements of intention for representation of women and minorities. Goals do not require results, nor do they require any measures designed to increase the number of women and minorities hired by or admitted into institutions.

hidden curriculum　The organization, content, and teaching styles of educational institutions that reflect gender stereotypes and sustain gender inequities by marginalizing and devaluing female and minority students.

lesbian feminists　Feminists whose affectional preference is women and who define themselves as woman-identified and committed to fighting for legal rights for all woman-identified women.

liberal feminism　(also called middle-class feminism and white feminism). Liberal feminism, as distinct from cultural feminism, maintains that women and men are alike in important respects and that women should have the same economic, political, professional, and civic opportunities and rights as men. NOW is the best known organization representing liberal feminism.

male deficit model　A view of friendships that claims men are deficient in forming and participating in close relationships. According to the male deficit model, most men's ways of experiencing and expressing closeness are not simply different from those typical of women but are inferior.

male feminists　(also called profeminist men, New Age men, and sensitive men). Male feminists believe that women and men are alike in important respects and that, therefore, the sexes should enjoy the same privileges, rights, opportunities, and status in society. Male feminists join liberal women feminists in fighting for equitable treatment for women. In addition, many male feminists seek to rid themselves of what they regard as "toxic masculinity" promoted in men by socialization and to develop in themselves sensitivities and tenderness more typically socialized into women.

male generic language　Words and phrases that claim to include both women and men yet refer specifically only to men. Examples of male generic terms are *mailman*, *mankind*, and *chairman*.

monitoring The process of observing and regulating our own attitudes and behaviors. This process is possible because humans are able to reflect on themselves from the perspective of others (self-as-object).

mythopoetic movement A branch of the men's movement, headed by poet Robert Bly. Mythopoetics believe men need to rediscover their distinctively masculine modes of feeling rooted largely in myth.

nonverbal communication All elements of communication other than words themselves. Estimated to carry 65% to 93% of the total meaning of communication, nonverbal communication includes visual, vocal, environmental, and physical aspects of interaction.

paralanguage Vocal cues that accompany verbal communication, such as accent, volume, and inflection.

patriarchal Literally, "rule by the fathers." The term *patriarchy* is generally used to refer to systems of ideology and social structures and practices that were created by masculine individuals and that reflect the values, priorities, and views of men as a group.

pornography Materials that vividly depict subordination and degradation of a person; for example, sadistic assaults are presented as pleasurable. Pornographic presentations do not feature activities that involve mutual agreement and mutual benefit.

proxemics Space and the human use of space, including personal territories.

psychodynamic theory Claims that family relationships, especially ones between mother and child during the formative years of life, have a pivotal and continuing impact on the development of self, particularly gender identity.

psychological responsibility Responsibility to remember, plan, think ahead, organize, and so forth. In most heterosexual relationships, even when physical labor is divided between partners, women have greater psychological responsibility for the home and children.

quota system Rules that specify that a particular number or percentage of women and/or minorities must be admitted to schools, hired in certain positions, or promoted to certain levels in institutions.

radical feminism A branch of feminism that grew out of New Left politics and demanded the same attention to women's oppression as New Left organizations gave to racial oppression and other ideological issues. Radical feminists pioneered revolutionary communication techniques such as consciousness-raising, leaderless group discussion, and guerrilla theater.

relationship level of meaning The nonliteral meaning of communication. The relational level of meaning expresses how a speaker sees self and other and the relationship between them; in addition, it may provide cues about how to interpret the literal meaning of the message, for instance, to take it as a joke.

revalorists Feminists who focus on uncovering and valuing women and their contributions to personal, interpersonal, and cultural life.

role Social definitions of expected behaviors and the values associated with them that are internalized by individuals in the process of socialization.

self-as-object The ability to reflect on the self from the standpoint of others. Because humans are able to take others' perspectives on themselves, their views of self are necessarily social.

separatists Group of feminists who believe patriarchal culture cannot be changed or reformed and so women who find it oppressive must create and live in their own women-centered communities, separated from the culture at large.

sex A personal quality determined by biological and genetic characteristics. *Male, female, man,* and *woman* are terms that indicate sex.

social learning theory Claims that individuals learn to be masculine and feminine (among other things) by observing and imitating others and by reacting to the rewards and punishments others give in response to their imitative behaviors.

speech community A community defined by shared assumptions regarding how, when, and why to communicate as well as understandings of how to interpret others' communication.

spotlighting Highlighting the sex of a person rather than other characteristics that may be more relevant to why the person is being discussed. For example, spotlighting occurs in a headline that reads, "Woman Elected Mayor."

standpoint theory Focuses on how gender, race, class, and other social categories influence the circumstances of people's lives, especially the social positions they have and the kinds of experiences fostered within those positions.

stereotype A broad generalization about an entire class of phenomena based on some knowledge of limited aspects of certain members of the class.

structural feminists Modern version of cultural feminism in the 1800s. Structural feminists contend that women and men differ primarily because, in general, women and men have distinct experiences that foster different qualities (for instance, nurturance in women and independence in men).

symbolic interactionism Theory that claims individuals develop self-identity and an understanding of social life, values, and codes of conduct through communicative interactions with others in a society.

tactile communication Touch as a form of nonverbal communication.

territoriality An aspect of proxemics that refers to an individual's sense of personal space that we don't want others to invade.

theory A way to describe, explain, and predict relationships among phenomena.

womanists Group of feminists that define their identity and goals as reflecting both race and gender oppression. The womanist movement arose out of dissatisfaction with mainstream feminism's focus on white, middle-class women and their interests.

women's rights Movement in the middle 1800s to the 1920s that focused on gaining basic rights for women, such as the rights to vote, to pursue higher education, and to enter professions.

$\mathscr{R}$eferences

Academe. (1990, March/April). Some dynamic aspects of academic careers: The urgent need to match aspirations with compensation. Pp. 3–20.

Adams, C. (1991, April). The straight dope. *Triangle Comic Review*, p. 26.

Addington, D. W. (1968). The relationship of selected vocal characteristics to personality perceptions. *Speech Monographs, 35*, 492–503.

Adelmann, P. (1989, May). Marital myths: What we "know" hurts. *Psychology Today, 23*, 68–69.

Adler, J., with Duignan-Cabrera, A., & Gordon, J. (1991, June 24). Drums, sweat and tears. *Newsweek*, pp. 46–54.

Adler, L. L. (1991). *Women in cross-cultural perspective*. Westport, CT: Praeger.

Adler, T. (1989, June). Early sex hormone exposure studied. *APA Monitor*, p. 9.

Adler, T. (1990, January). Differences explored in gays and straights. *APA Monitor*, p. 27.

Aleguire, D. G. (1978). *Interruptions as turn-taking*. Paper presented at the International Sociological Association Ninth World Congress of Sociology, Uppsala University, Sweden.

"An all consuming passion." (1991, May 13). *Newsweek*, p. 58.

Allgeier, E. R. (1987). Coercive versus consensual sexual interactions. In V. P. Makosky (Ed.), *The G. Stanley Hall Lecture Series* (Vol. 7, pp. 7–63). Washington, DC: American Psychological Association.

Allis, S. (1990, fall). What do men really want? *Time*, pp. 80–82.

American Association of University Women (AAUW). (1991). *Short-changing girls, shortchanging America*. Washington, DC: Greenberg-Lake Analysis Group.

American Demographics. (1990, February). P. 4.

Andelin, H. (1975). *Fascinating womanhood*. New York: Bantam Books.

Anderson, E. A., & Leslie, L. A. (1991). Coping with employment and family stress: Employment arrangement and gender differences. *Sex Roles, 24,* 223–237.

Antill, J. K. (1987). Parents' beliefs and values about sex roles, sex differences, and sexuality: Their sources and implications. In P. Shaver & C. Hendrick (Eds.), *Sex and gender* (pp. 294–328). Newbury Park, CA: Sage.

Apter, T. (1990). *Altered loves: Mothers and daughters in adolescence*. New York: St. Martins.

Aries, E. (1977). Male-female interpersonal styles in all male, all female, and mixed groups. In A. Sargent (Ed.), *Beyond sex roles* (pp. 292–299). St. Paul, MN: West.

Aries, E. (1987). Gender and communication. In P. Shaver & C. Hendricks (Eds.), *Sex and gender* (pp. 149–176). Newbury Park, CA: Sage.

Aries, E. J., & Johnson, F. L. (1983). Close friendship in adulthood: Conversational content between same-sex friends. *Sex Roles, 9,* 1183–1196.

Aronson, J. (1992). Women's sense of responsibility for the care of old people: "But who else is going to do it?" *Gender and Society, 6,* 8–29.

Astin, A. W. (1977). *Four critical years: Effects of college on beliefs, attitudes and knowledge.* San Francisco, CA: Jossey-Bass.

Aukett, R., Ritchie, J., & Mill, K. (1988). Gender differences in friendship patterns. *Sex Roles, 19,* 57–66.

Austin, A. M. B., Salehi, M., & Leffler, A. (1987). Gender and developmental differences in children's conversations. *Sex Roles, 16,* 497–510.

Baird, J. E. (1976). Sex differences in group communication: A review of relevant research. *Quarterly Journal of Speech, 62,* 179–192.

Bakan, D. (1966). *The duality of human existence: Isolation and communion in Western man.* Boston, MA: Beacon Press.

Bakan, D. (1968). *Disease, pain and sacrifice.* Boston, MA: Beacon Press.

Ball, K. (1991, May 23). Family leave poses few problems, study finds. *Morning Call*, p. B23.

Balswick, J. O. (1988). *The inexpressive male.* Lexington, MA: Lexington Books.

Balswick, J. O., & Peek, C. W. (1976). The inexpressive male: A tragedy of American society. In D. Brannon & R. Brannon (Eds.), *The forty-nine percent majority: The male sex-role* (pp. 55–57). Reading, MA: Addison-Wesley.

Bandura, A., & Walters, R. H. (1963). *Social learning and personality development*. New York: Holt, Rinehart & Winston.

Bardewell, J. R., Cochran, S. W., & Walker, S. (1986). Relationship of parental education, race, and gender to sex role stereotyping in 5-year-old kindergartners. *Sex Roles, 15,* 275–281.

Baron, L., & Straus, M. A. (1989). *Four theories of rape in American society*. New Haven, CT: Yale University Press.

Barry, H., III, Bacon, M. K., & Child, I. L. (1957). A cross-cultural survey of some sex differences in socialization. *Journal of Abnormal Psychology, 55,* 327–332.

Basow, S. A. (1990). Effects of teacher expressiveness: Mediated by sex-typing? *Journal of Educational Psychology, 82,* 599–602.

Basow, S. A. (1992). *Gender: Stereotypes and roles* (3rd ed.). Pacific Grove, CA: Brooks/Cole.

Basow, S. A., & Kobrynowicz, D. (1990, August). *How much is she eating? Impressions of a female eater*. Paper presented at the meeting of the American Psychological Association, Boston, MA. (ERIC Document Reproduction Service No. ED 326 827)

Bate, B. (1988). *Communication between the sexes*. New York: Harper and Row.

Baxter, L. A. (1990). Dialectical contradictions in relational development. *Journal of Social and Personal Relationships, 7,* 143–158.

Beck, A. T. (1988). *Love is never enough*. New York: Harper and Row.

Beck, J. (1990, September 5). Calling them "balance laws" doesn't make quotas right. *Raleigh News and Observer*, p. 17A.

Becker, C. S. (1987). Friendship between women: A phenomenological study of best friends. *Journal of Phenomenological Psychology, 18,* 59–72.

Beckwith, L. (1972). Relationships between infants' social behavior and their mothers' behavior. *Child Development, 43,* 397–411.

Belenky, M. F., Clinchy, B. M., Goldberger, N. R., & Tarule, J. M. (1986). *Women's ways of knowing: The development of self, voice, and mind*. New York: Basic Books.

Bell, R. R. (1981). Friendships of women and men. *Psychology of Women Quarterly, 5,* 402–417.

Bellinger, D. C., & Gleason, J. B. (1982). Sex differences in parental directives to young children. *Sex Roles, 8,* 1123–1139.

Bem, S. (1993). *The lenses of gender: Transforming the debate on sexual inequality*. New Haven: Yale University Press.

Bem, S., & Bem, D. (1973). Does sex-biased job advertising aid and abet sex discrimination? *Journal of Applied Social Psychology, 3,* 6–18.

Bergner, R. M., & Bergner, L. L. (1990). Sexual misunderstanding: A descriptive and pragmatic formulation. *Psychotherapy, 27,* 464–467.

Bernard, J. (1972). *The future of marriage*. New York: World.

Bernard, J. (1981). The good-provider role. *American Psychologist, 36,* 1–12.

Berscheid, E., Snyder, M., & Omoto, A. M. (1989). Issues in studying close relationships. In C. Hendrick (Ed.), *Close relationships* (pp. 63–91). Newbury Park, CA: Sage.

The best in the house. (1988, October 19). *New York Times*, p. 52Y.

Bettelheim, B. (1943). Individual and mass behavior in extreme situations. *Journal of Abnormal and Social Psychology, 38*, 417–452.

Birdwhistell, R. (1970). *Kinesics and context*. Philadelphia, PA: University of Pennsylvania Press.

Bleier, R. (1986). Sex differences research: Science or belief? In R. Bleier (Ed.), *Feminist approaches to science* (pp. 147–164). New York: Pergamon Press.

Blumer, H. (1969). *Symbolic interactionism: Perspective and method*. Englewood Cliffs, NJ: Prentice-Hall.

Blumstein, P., & Kollock, P. (1988). Personal relationships. *Annual Review of Sociology, 14*, 467–490.

Blumstein, P., & Schwartz, P. (1983). *American couples: Love, sex, and money*. New York: Morrow.

Boston Women's Health Club Book Collective. (1976). *Our bodies/our selves* (2nd ed.). New York: Simon and Schuster.

Bovee, T. (1991, November 14). Women suffer pay gap bias. *Morning Call*, p. A3.

Bowen, S. P., & Wyatt, N. J. (Eds.). (1993). *Transforming visions: Feminist critiques of speech communication*. Cresskill, NJ: Hampton Press.

Boyer, P. J. (1986, February 16). TV turns to the hard-boiled male. *New York Times*, pp. H1, H29.

Bradley, P. H. (1981). The folk-linguistics of women's speech: An empirical examination. *Communication Monographs, 48*, 73–90.

Brandt, D. R. (1980). A systematic approach to the measurement of dominance in human face-to-face interaction. *Communication Quarterly, 28*, 21–43.

Brannon, R. (1987). Strange bedfellows. *Brother, 6*, 5–6.

Brannon, R., & Juni, S. (1984). A scale for measuring attitudes about masculinity. *Psychological Documents, 14*, 6–7.

Brehm, S. S. (1992). *Intimate relationships* (2nd ed.). New York: McGraw-Hill.

Bretl, D., & Cantor, J. (1988). The portrayal of men and women in U.S. commercials: A recent content analysis and trend over 15 years. *Sex Roles, 18*, 595–609.

Bridges, J. S. (1989). Sex differences in occupational values. *Sex Roles, 20*, 205–211.

Brock-Utne, B. (1989). *Feminist perspectives on peace and peace education*. New York: Pergamon Press.

Brod, H. (1987). Introduction: Themes and theses of men's studies. In H. Brod (Ed.), *The making of masculinities: The new men's studies* (pp. 1–17). Boston, MA: Allen and Unwin.

Broverman, I., Broverman, D. M., Clarkson, F. E., Rosenkrantz, P. S., & Vogel, S. R. (1970). Sex-role stereotypes and clinical judgments of mental health. *Journal of Consulting and Clinical Psychology, 34*, 1–7.

Brown, D. G. (1956). Sex-role preference in young children. *Psychological Monographs, 70*, 1–19.

Brown, J. D., & Campbell, K. (1986). Race and gender in music videos: The same beat but a different drummer. *Journal of Communication, 36,* 94–106.

Brown, J. D., Campbell, K., & Fisher, L. (1986). American adolescents and music videos: Why do they watch? *Gazette, 37,* 19–32.

Brown, J. D., Childers, K. W., Bauman, K. E., & Koch, G. G. (1990). The influence of new media and family structure on young adolescents' television and radio use. *Communication Research, 17,* 65–82.

Brownmiller, S. (1975). *Against our wills: Men, women, and rape.* New York: Simon and Schuster.

Brownmiller, S. (1993, January 4). Making female bodies the battlefield. *Newsweek,* p. 37.

Brumberg, J. J. (1988). *Fasting girls: The emergence of anorexia nervosa as a modern disease.* Cambridge, MA: Harvard University Press.

Buck, R. (1976). A test of nonverbal receiving ability: Preliminary studies. *Human Communication Research, 2,* 162–171.

Buhrke, R. A., & Fuqua, D. R. (1987). Sex differences in same- and cross-sex supportive relationships. *Sex Roles, 17,* 339–352.

Burgoon, J. K., Buller, D. B., Hale, J. L., & deTurck, M. A. (1988). Relational messages associated with nonverbal behaviors. *Human Communication Research, 10,* 351–378.

Burgoon, J. K., Buller, D. B., & Woodall, G. W. (1989). *Nonverbal communication: The unspoken dialogue.* New York: Harper and Row.

Burgoon, J. K., & Hale, J. L. (1988). Nonverbal expectancy violations: Model elaborations and application to immediacy behaviors. *Communication Monographs, 55,* 58–79.

Burns, A., & Homel, R. (1989). Gender division of tasks by parents and their children. *Psychology of Women Quarterly, 13,* 113–125.

Burton, R. V., & Whiting, J. W. M. (1961). The absent father and cross-sex identity. *Merrill-Palmer Quarterly of Behavior and Development, 7,* 85–95.

Butler, D., & Geis, F. L. (1990). Nonverbal affect responses to male and female leaders: Implications for leadership *58,* 48–59.

Byrne, D., London, S., & Reeves, K. (1968). The effects of physical attractiveness, sex, and attitude similarity in interpersonal attraction. *Journal of Personality, 36,* 259–262.

Caldera, Y. M., Huston, A. C., & O'Brien, M. (1989). Social interactions and play patterns of parents and toddlers with feminine, masculine, and neutral toys. *Child Development, 60,* 70–76.

Calderone, K. L. (1990). The influence of gender on the frequency of pain and sedative medication administered to postoperative patients. *Sex Roles, 23,* 713–725.

Caldwell, M. A., & Peplau, L. A. (1982). Sex differences in same-sex friendship. *Sex Roles, 8,* 721–732.

Campbell, K. K. (1973). The rhetoric of women's liberation: An oxymoron. *Quarterly Journal of Speech, 59,* 74–86.

Campbell, K. K. (1989a). *Man cannot speak for her: I. A critical study of early feminist rhetoric*. New York: Praeger.

Campbell, K. K. (1989b). *Man cannot speak for her: II. Key texts of the early feminists*. New York: Greenwood Press.

Campbell, K. K. (1991). Hearing women's voices. *Communication Education, 40*, 33–48.

Campbell, K. K. (Ed.). (1993). *Women public speakers in the United States: A bio-critical sourcebook*. Westport, CT: Greenwood Press.

Cancian, F. (1987). *Love in America*. Cambridge, MA: Cambridge University Press.

Cancian, F. (1989). Love and the rise of capitalism. In B. Risman & P. Schwartz (Eds.), *Gender in intimate relationships* (pp. 12–25). Belmont, CA: Wadsworth.

Cann, A., & Siegfried, W. D. (1990). Gender stereotypes and dimensions of effective leader behavior. *Sex Roles, 23*, 413–419.

Carli, L. L. (1989). Gender differences in interaction style and influence. *Journal of Personality and Social Psychology, 56*, 565–576.

Carlson, R. (1971). Sex differences in ego functioning: Exploratory studies of agency and communion, *Journal of Consulting and Clinical Psychology, 37*, 267–277.

Carter, B. (1991, May 1). Children's TV, where boys are king. *New York Times*, pp. A1, C18.

Carty, L. (1992). Black women in academia: A statement from the periphery. In H. Bannerji, L. Carty, K. Dehli, S. Heald, & K. McKenna, *Unsettling relations* (pp. 13–44). Boston, MA: South End Press.

Cassirer, E. (1978). *An essay on man*. New Haven, CT: Yale University Press.

Cazenave, N. A., & Leon, G. H. (1987). Men's work and family roles and characteristics: Race, gender, and class. In M. S. Kimmel (Ed.), *Changing men: New directions in research on men and masculinity* (pp. 244–262). Newbury Park, CA: Sage.

Chaiken, S., & Pliner, P. (1987). Women, but not men, are what they eat: The effect of meal size and gender on perceived femininity and masculinity. *Personality and Social Psychology Bulletin, 13*, 166–176.

Chase, S. (Ed.). (1991). *Defending the earth: A dialogue between Murray Bookchin & Dave Foreman*. Boston, MA: South End Press.

Cherry, L., & Lewis, M. (1978). Differential socialization of girls and boys: Implications for sex differences in language development. In N. Waterson & C. Snow (Eds.), *The development of communication* (pp. 189–197). New York: John Wiley and Sons.

Chesler, P. (1972). *Women and madness*. Garden City, NY: Doubleday.

Child care. (1992, August 10). *Fortune*, pp. 50–54.

Chodorow, N. J. (1978). *The reproduction of mothering: Psychoanalysis and the sociology of gender*. Berkeley, CA: University of California Press.

Chodorow, N. J. (1989). *Feminism and psychoanalytic theory*. New Haven, CT: Yale University Press.

Christensen, A., & Heavey, C. (1990). Gender and social structure in the demand/withdraw pattern in marital conflict. *Journal of Personality and Social Psychology, 59*, 73–81.

Clarke-Stewart, K. A. (1973). Interactions between mothers and their young children: Characteristics and consequences. *Monographs of the Society for Research in Child Development, 38*, 6–7. (Serial No. 153).

Clift, E., & Miller, M. (1992, December 28). Hillary: Behind the scenes. *Newsweek*, pp. 23–25.

Clutter, S. (1990, May 3). Gender may affect response and outrage to sex abuse. *Morning Call*, p. D14.

Coates, J. (1986). *Women, men, and language: Studies in language and linguistics*. London: Longman.

Coates, J., & Cameron, D. (1989). *Women in their speech communities: New perspectives on language and sex*. London: Longman.

Cochran, S. D., & Peplau, L. A. (1985). Value orientations in heterosexual relationships. *Psychology of Women Quarterly, 9*, 477–488.

Cohen, R. (1969). Conceptual styles, culture conflict, and nonverbal tests of intelligence. *American Anthropologist, 71*, 828–856.

Collins, P. H. (1986). Learning from the outsider within. *Social Problems, 33*, 514–532.

Condry, J., & Condry, S. (1976). Sex differences: A study of the eye of the beholder. *Child Development, 47*, 812–819.

Condry, S. M., Condry, J. C., & Pogatshnik, L. W. (1983). Sex differences: A study of the ear of the beholder. *Sex Roles, 9*, 697–704.

Cornell, D. (1991, summer). Sex discrimination law and equivalent rights. *Dissent*, pp. 400–405.

Costin, F., & Schwartz, N. (1987). Beliefs about rape and women's social roles: A four-nation study. *Journal of Interpersonal Violence, 2*, 46–56.

Courtney, A. E., & Whipple, T. W. (1983). *Sex stereotyping in advertising*. Lexington, MA: D. C. Heath.

Cowan, G., Lee, C., Levy, D., & Snyder, D. (1988). Dominance and inequality in X-rated videocassettes. *Psychology of Women Quarterly, 12*, 299–311.

Cowan, G., & O'Brien, M. (1990). Gender and survival vs. death in slasher films: A content analysis. *Sex Roles, 23*, 187–196.

Cowell, S. (1992, September/October). Work and family: The missing movement. *Democratic Left*, pp. 14–15.

Craft, C. (1988). *Too old, too ugly, and not deferential to men: An anchorwoman's courageous battle against sex discrimination*. Rockland, CA: Prima.

Crawford, M. (1988). Agreeing to differ: Feminist epistemologies and women's ways of knowing. In M. Crawford & M. Gentry (Eds.), *Gender and thought: Psychological perspectives* (pp. 128–145). New York: Springer-Verlag.

Crawford, M., & MacLeod, M. (1990). Gender in the college classroom: An assessment of the "chilly climate" for women. *Sex Roles, 23*, 101–122.

Dabbs, J. M., Jr., & Morris, R. (1990). Testosterone, social class, and antisocial behavior in a sample of 4,452 men. *Psychological Science, 1*, 209–211.

Daly, M. (1968). *The church and the second sex.* New York: Harper and Row.

Daly, M. (1973). *Beyond God the father: Toward a philosophy of women's liberation.* Boston, MA: Beacon.

Daly, M. (1978). *Gyn/ecology: The meta-ethics of radical feminism.* Boston, MA: Beacon.

Daly, M. (1992). *Outercourse: The bedazzling voyage.* San Francisco: Harper & Row.

The daughter track/trading places. (1990, July 16). *Newsweek*, pp. 48–54.

Davidson, L. R., & Duberman, L. (1982). Friendship: Communication and interactional patterns in same-sex dyads. *Sex Roles, 8,* 809–822.

Davis, D. M. (1990). Portrayals of women in prime-time network television: Some demographic characteristics. *Sex Roles, 23,* 325–332.

Davis, F. (1991). *Moving the mountain: The women's movement in America since 1960.* New York: Simon and Schuster.

Davis, S. (1990). Men as success objects and women as sex objects: A study of personal advertisements. *Sex Roles, 23,* 43–50.

Deaux, K. (1976). *The behavior of men and women.* Monterey, CA: Brooks/Cole.

Degler, C. N. (1980). *At odds: Women and the family in America from the Revolution to the present.* New York: Oxford University Press.

Delk, J. L., Madden, R. B., Livingston, M., & Ryan, T. T. (1986). Adult perceptions of the infant as a function of gender labeling and observer gender. *Sex Roles, 15,* 527–534.

DeLucia, J. L. (1987). Gender role identity and dating behavior: What is the relationship? *Sex Roles, 17,* 153–161.

Demare, D., Briere, J., & Lips, H. M. (1988). Violent pornography and self-reported likelihood of sexual aggression. *Journal of Research in Personality, 22,* 140–153.

Derlega, V. J., & Chaiken, A. L. (1976). Norms affecting self-disclosure in men and women. *Journal of Consulting and Clinical Psychology, 44,* 376–380.

Dew, J. (1992, December 19). Panel wants law on marital rape. *Raleigh News and Observer*, p. A1.

The Diagram Group. (1977). *Woman's body: An owner's manual.* New York: Bantam Books.

Diamond, I., & Orenstein, G. F. (Eds.). (1990). *Reweaving the world: The emergence of ecofeminism.* San Francisco, CA: Sierra Club Books.

Dieter, P. (1989, March). *Shooting her with video, drugs, bullets, and promises.* Paper presented at the meeting of the Association of Women in Psychology, Newport, RI.

Dobash, R. E., & Dobash, R. P. (1979). *Violence against wives: A case against the patriarchy.* New York: Free Press.

Donnerstein, E., Linz, D., & Penrod, S. (1987). *The question of pornography: Research findings and policy implications.* New York: Free Press.

Donovan, J. (1985). *Feminist theory: The intellectual traditions of American feminism.* New York: Frederick Unger.

Douglas, A. (1977). *The feminization of American culture*. New York: Knopf.

Dow, B. J. (1992). Femininity and feminism in "Murphy Brown." *Southern Journal of Communication, 57,* 143–155.

Doyle, J. A. (1989). *The male experience* (2nd ed.). Dubuque, IA: William C. Brown.

Duck, S. (1988). *Relating to others.* Chicago, IL: Dorsey.

Eagly, A. H., & Johnson, B. T. (1990). Gender and leadership style: A meta-analysis. *Psychological Bulletin, 108,* 233–256.

Eagly, A. H., & Karau, S. J. (1991). Gender and the emergence of leaders: A meta-analysis. *Journal of Personality and Social Psychology, 60,* 687–710.

Eakins, B., & Eakins, G. (1976). Verbal turn-taking and exchanges in faculty dialogue. In B. L. DuBois & I. Crouch (Eds.), *Papers in southwest English: IV. Proceedings of the conference on the sociology of the languages of American women* (pp. 53–62). San Antonio, TX: Trinity University Press.

Eakins, B. W., & Eakins, R. G. (1978). *Sex differences in human communication.* Boston, MA: Houghton Mifflin.

Eccles, J. S. (1989). Bring young women to math and science. In M. Crawford & M. Gentry (Eds.), *Gender and thought: Psychological perspectives* (pp. 36–58). New York: Springer-Verlag.

Eckman, P., Friesen, W., & Ellsworth, P. (1971). *Emotion in the human face: Guidelines for research and an integration of findings.* Elmsford, NY: Pergamon Press.

Edmondson, B. (1987, August). Reality on screen. *American Demographics, 9,* 21.

Eichenbaum, L., & Orbach, S. (1983). *Understanding women: A feminist psychoanalytic approach.* New York: Basic Books.

Eichenbaum, L., & Orbach, S. (1987). *Between women: Love, envy, and competition in women's friendships.* New York: Viking.

Eisenstock, B. (1984). Sex-role differences in children's identification with counter-stereotypical televised portrayals. *Sex Roles, 10,* 417–430.

Eldridge, N. S., & Gilbert, L. A. (1990). Correlates of relationship satisfaction in lesbian couples. *Psychology of Women Quarterly, 14,* 43–62.

Elias, M. (1992, August 3). Difference seen in brains of gay men. *USA Today,* p. 8-D.

Ellsworth, P. C., & Ludwig, L. M. (1972). Visual behavior in social interaction. *Journal of Communication, 22,* 375–403.

Ellsworth, P. C., & Ross, L. (1975). Intimacy in response to direct gaze. *Journal of Experimental Social Psychology, 11,* 592–613.

Epperson, S. E. (1988, September 16). Studies link subtle sex bias in schools with women's behavior in the workplace. *Wall Street Journal,* p. 27.

Epstein, C. F. (1968, November). Women in professional life. *Psychiatric Spectator,* n.p.

Epstein, C. F. (1981). *Women in law.* New York: Basic Books.

Epstein, C. F. (1982). *Changing perspectives and opportunities and their impact on careers and aspirations: The case of women lawyers.* Paper presented at the Annual Scientific Meeting of the Gerontological Society of America, Boston, MA.

Evans, D. (1993, March 1). The wrong examples. *Newsweek*, p. 10.

Evans, G. W., & Howard, R. B. (1973). Personal space. *Psychological Bulletin, 80*, 334–344.

Eyer, D. E. (1992). *Mother-infant bonding: A scientific fiction.* New Haven, CT: Yale University Press.

Fagot, B. I. (1978). The influence of sex of child on parental reaction to toddler behaviors. *Child Development, 49*, 459–465.

Fagot, B. I. (1981). Stereotypes versus behavioral judgments of sex differences in young children. *Sex Roles, 7*, 1093–1096.

Fagot, B. I. (1984). Teacher and peer reactions to boys' and girls' play styles. *Sex Roles, 11*, 691–702.

Fagot, B. I. (1985). A cautionary note: Parents' socialization of boys and girls. *Sex Roles, 12*, 471–476.

Fagot, B. I., Hagan, R., Leinbach, M. D., & Kronsberg, S. (1985). Differential reactions to assertive and communicative acts of toddler boys and girls. *Child Development, 56*, 1499–1505.

Fagot, B. I., & Leinbach, M. D. (1987). Socialization of sex roles within the family. In B. Carter (Ed.), *Current conceptions of sex roles and sex typing: Theory and research* (pp. 89–100). New York: Praeger.

Fagot, B. I., & Leinbach, M. D. (1989). The young child's gender schema: Environmental input, internal organiza-tion. *Child Development, 60*, 663–672.

Faludi, S. (1991). *Backlash: The undeclared war against American women.* New York: Crown.

Farrell, W. (1991, May/June). Men as success objects. *Utne Reader*, pp. 81–84.

Fasteau, M. F. (1974). *The male machine.* New York: McGraw-Hill.

Fears for careers curb paternity leaves. (1990, August 24). *Wall Street Journal*, p. B1.

Feingold, A. (1990). Gender differences in effects of physical attractiveness on romantic attraction: A comparison across five research paradigms. *Journal of Personality and Social Psychology, 59*, 981–993.

Feinman, S. (1984). A status theory of the evaluation of sex-role and age-role behavior. *Sex Roles, 10*, 445–456.

Feldman, N. S., & Brown, E. (1984, April). *Male vs. female differences in control strategies: What children learn from Saturday morning television.* Paper presented at the meeting of the Eastern Psychological Association, Baltimore, MD. (Cited in Basow, 1992.)

Feldman, R. S., & White, J. B. (1980). Detecting deception in children. *Journal of Communication, 30*, 121–128.

Ferree, M. M. (1988). *Negotiating household roles and responsibilities: Resistance, conflict and change.* Paper presented at the National Council on Family Relations, Philadelphia, PA.

Ferree, M. M., & Hall, E. J. (1990). Visual images of American society: Gender and race in introductory sociology textbooks. *Gender and Society, 4*, 500–533.

Fiebert, M. (1987). Some perspectives on the men's movement. *Men's Studies Review, 4*, 8–10.

Firms design benefits with families in mind. (1989, September 4). *Raleigh News and Observer*, pp. 1A, 4A.

Fisher, J. D., & Byrne, D. (1975). Too close for comfort: Sex differences in response to invasions of personal space. *Journal of Personal and Social Psychology, 32*, 15–21.

Fishman, P. M. (1978). Interaction: The work women do. *Social Problems, 25*, 397–406.

Fiske, S. T., Bersoff, D. N., Borgida, E., Deaux, K., & Heilman, M. E. (1991). Social science on trial: Use of sex stereotyping research in *Price Waterhouse* v. *Hopkins. American Psychologist, 46*, 1049–1060.

Flanders, L. (1990, November/December). Military women and the media. *New Directions for Women*, pp. 1, 9.

Fleming, J. (1984). *Blacks in college*. San Francisco, CA: Jossey-Bass.

Fliess, R. (1961). *Ego and body ego*. New York: International Universities Press.

Folb, E. (1985). Who's got room at the top? Issues of dominance and nondominance in intracultural communication. In L. A. Samovar & R. E. Porter (Eds.), *Intercultural communication: A reader* (4th ed., pp. 119–127). Belmont, CA: Wadsworth.

Foreit, K. G., Agor, T., Byers, J., Larue, J., Lokey, H., Palazzini, M., Patterson, M., & Smith, L. (1980). Sex bias in the newspaper treatment of male-centered and female-centered news stories. *Sex Roles, 6*, 475–480.

Fowers, B. J. (1991). His and her marriage: A multivariate study of gender and marital satisfaction. *Sex Roles, 24*, 209–221.

Fox-Genovese, E. (1991). *Feminism without illusions: A critique of individualism*. Chapel Hill, NC: University of North Carolina Press.

Frank, L. K. (1957). Tactile communication. *Genetic Psychology Monographs, 56*, 209–255.

Franzoi, S. L. (1991, August). *Gender role orientation and female body perception*. Paper presented at the meeting of the American Psychological Association, San Francisco, CA.

Franzwa, H. H. (1975). Female roles in women's magazine fiction, 1940–1970. In R. K. Unger & F. L. Denmark (Eds.), *Woman: Dependent or independent variable?* New York: Psychological Dimensions.

Fraternities raise consciousness, not hell. (1992, September 24). *Raleigh News and Observer*, pp. A1, A17.

Freedman, C. (1985). *Manhood redux: Standing up to feminism*. Brooklyn, NY: Samson Publishers.

Freiberg, P. (1991, May). Separate classes for black males? *APA Monitor*, p. 33.

French, M. (1992). *The war against women*. New York: Summit Books.

Freud, S. F. (1957). *The ego and the id* (J. Riviere, Trans.). London: Hogarth Press.

Friedan, B. (1963). *The feminine mystique*. New York: Dell.

Friedan, B. (1981). *The second stage*. New York: Summit Books.

Frieze, I. H., Parsons, J. E., Johnson, P. B., Ruble, D. N., & Zellman, G. L. (1978). *Women and sex roles: A social psychological perspective*. New York: W. W. Norton.

Frieze, I. H., & Ramsey, S. J. (1976). Nonverbal maintenance of traditional sex roles. *Journal of Social Issues, 32,* 133–141.

Frisch, H. L. (1977). Sex stereotypes in adult-infant play. *Child Development, 48,* 1671–1675.

Gabriel, S. L., & Smithson, I. (Eds.). (1990). *Gender in the classroom: Power and pedagogy.* Urbana, IL: University of Illinois Press.

Garbarino, M. (1976). *Native American heritage.* Boston, MA: Little, Brown.

Garlick, B., Dixon, S., & Allen, P. (Eds.). (1992). *Stereotypes of women in power: Historical perspectives and revisionist views.* Westport, CT: Greenwood Press.

Gary, L. E. (1987). Predicting interpersonal conflict between men and women: The case of black men. In M. S. Kimmel (Ed.), *Changing men: New directions in research on men and masculinity* (pp. 232–243). Newbury Park, CA: Sage.

Gastil, J. (1990). Generic pronouns and sexist language: The oxymoronic character of masculine generics. *Sex Roles, 23,* 629–643.

Gaylin, W. (1992). *The male ego.* New York: Viking/Penguin.

Gelles, R., & Straus, M. (1988). *Intimate violence.* New York: Simon and Schuster.

Gervasio, A. H., & Crawford, M. (1989). Social evaluations of assertiveness: A critique and speech act reformulation. *Psychology of Women Quarterly, 13,* 1–25.

Gibbs, N. (1990, fall). The dreams of youth. Women: The road ahead. *Time* [Special issue], pp. 11–14.

Gilbert, L. A., & Evans, S. L. (1985). Dimensions of same-gender student-faculty role-model relationships. *Sex Roles, 12,* 111–123.

Gilligan, C. (1982). *In a different voice: Psychological theory and women's development.* Cambridge, MA: Harvard University Press.

Gilligan, C., & Pollack, S. (1988). The vulnerable and invulnerable physician. In C. Gilligan, J. V. Ward, & J. M. Taylor, with B. Baldridge (Eds.), *Mapping the moral domain* (pp. 245–262). Cambridge, MA: Harvard University Press.

Gilligan, C., Ward, J. V., Taylor, J. M., with Bardige, B. (Eds.). (1988). *Mapping the moral domain.* Cambridge, MA: Harvard University Press.

Gilman, C. P. (1979/1915). *Herland.* New York: Harper and Row.

Gold, D., Crombie, G., & Noble, S. (1987). Relations between teachers' judgments of girls' and boys' compliance and intellectual competence. *Sex Roles, 16,* 351–358.

Goldberg, S., & Lewis, M. (1969). Play behavior in the year-old infant: Early sex differences. *Child Development, 40,* 21–31.

Goldner, V., Penn, P., Sheinberg, M., & Walker, G. (1990). Love and violence: Gender paradoxes in volatile attachments. *Family Process, 19,* 343–364.

Golub, S. (1988). A developmental perspective. In L. H. Gise (Ed.), *The premenstrual syndromes.* New York: Churchill Livingstone.

Gomberg, E. S. L. (1986). Women: Alcohol and other drugs. *Drugs and Society, 1,* 75–109.

Goodnow, J. J. (1988). Children's household work: Its nature and functions. *Psychological Bulletin, 103,* 5–26.

Gordon, L. (1976). *Woman's body, woman's right: A social history of birth control in America.* New York: Grossman.

Gordon, L. (1988). *Heros of their own lives.* New York: Viking.

Gordon, S. (1983). What's new in endocrinology? Target: Sex hormones. In M. Fooden, S. Gordon, & B. Hughley (Eds.), *Genes and gender* (Vol. IV, pp. 39–48). Staten Island, NY: Gordian Press.

Gordon, S. (1991). *Prisoners of men's dreams: Striking out for a new feminine future.* Boston, MA: Little, Brown.

Grant, L. (1985). Race-gender status, classroom interaction, and children's socialization in elementary school. In L. C. Wilkinson & C. B. Marrett (Eds.), *Gender influences in classroom interaction* (pp. 57–77). Orlando, FL: Academic Press.

Gray, H. (1986). Television and the new black man: Black male images in prime-time situation comedies. *Media, Culture, and Society, 8,* 223–242.

Greene, R., & Dalton, K. (1953). The premenstrual syndrome. *British Medical Journal, 1,* 1007–1014.

Greer, G. (1992). *The change: Women, aging, and menopause.* New York: Alfred Knopf.

Griffin, S. (1981). *Pornography and silence: Culture's revenge against nature.* New York: Harper and Row.

Groce, S. B., & Cooper, M. (1990). Just me and the boys? Women in local-level rock and roll. *Gender and Society, 4,* 220–229.

Gross, D. (1990, April 16). The gender rap. *The New Republic,* pp. 11–14.

Gross, J. (1990, September 2). Navy is urged to root out lesbians despite abilities. *New York Times,* p. A24.

Gunter, N. C., & Gunter, B. G. (1990). Domestic division of labor among working couples: Does androgyny make a difference? *Sex Roles, 14,* 355–370.

Gutmann, D. L. (1965). Women and the conception of ego strength. *Merrill-Palmer Quarterly of Behavior and Development, 11,* 229–240.

Hacker, H. M. (1951). Women as a minority group. *Social Forces, 30,* 60–69.

Halberstadt, A. G., & Saitta, M. B. (1987). Gender, nonverbal behavior, and perceived dominance: A test of the theory. *Journal of Personality and Social Psychology, 53,* 257–272.

Hale-Benson, J. E. (1986). *Black children: Their roots, culture, and learning styles* (rev. ed.). Provo, UT: Brigham Young University Press.

Hall, D., & Langellier, K. (1988). Storytelling strategies in mother-daughter communication. In B. Bate & A. Taylor (Eds.), *Women communicating: Studies of women's talk* (pp. 197–226). Norwood, NJ: Ablex.

Hall, E. T. (1959). *The silent language.* Greenwich, CT: Fawcett Publications.

Hall, E. T. (1966). *The hidden dimension.* New York: Anchor/Doubleday.

Hall, E. T. (1968). Proxemics. *Current Anthropology, 9,* 83–108.

Hall, J. A. (1978). Gender effects in decoding nonverbal cues. *Psychological Bulletin, 85,* 845–857.

Hall, J. A. (1979). Gender, gender roles, and nonverbal communication skills. In R. Rosenthal (Ed.), *Skill in nonverbal communication: Individual differences* (pp. 32–67). Cambridge, MA: Oelgeschlager, Gunn & Hain.

Hall, J. A. (1987). On explaining gender differences: The case of nonverbal communication. In P. Shaver & C. Hendricks (Eds.), *Sex and gender* (pp. 177–200). Newbury Park, CA: Sage.

Hall, J. A., & Taylor, M. C. (1985). Psychological androgyny and the masculinity × femininity interaction. *Journal of Personality and Social Psychology, 49,* 429–435.

Hall, R. M., with Sandler, B. R. (1982). *The classroom climate: A chilly one for women?* Washington, DC: Association of American Colleges, Project on the Status and Education of Women.

Hall, R. M., & Sandler, B. R. (1984). *Out of the classroom: A chilly campus climate for women.* Washington, DC: Association of American Colleges, Project on the Status and Education of Women.

Hamilton, M. C. (1988). Using masculine generics: Does generic *he* increase male bias in the user's imagery? *Sex Roles, 19,* 785–799.

Hamilton, M. C. (1991). Masculine bias in the attribution of personhood: People = male, male = people. *Psychology of Women Quarterly, 15,* 393–402.

Hanisch, C. (1970). What can be learned? A critique of the Miss America protest. In L. Tanner (Ed.), *Voices from women's liberation* (pp. 132–136). New York: Signet Classics.

Hansen, C. H., & Hansen, R. D. (1988). How rock music videos can change what is seen when boy meets girl: Priming stereotypic appraisal of social interactions. *Sex Roles, 19,* 287–316.

Harding, S. (1991). *Whose science? Whose knowledge? Thinking from women's lives.* Ithaca, NY: Cornell University Press.

Hare-Mustin, R. T., & Marecek, J. (1988). The meaning of difference: Gender theory, postmodernism, & psychology. *American Psychologist, 43,* 455–464.

Harper, L. V., & Sanders, K. M. (1975). Preschool children's use of space: Sex differences in outdoor play. *Developmental Psychology, 11,* 119.

Hartlage, L. C. (1980, March). *Identifying and programming for differences.* Paper presented at the Parent and Professional Conference on Young Children with Special Needs, Cleveland, OH.

Hartmann, E. (1991). *Boundaries in the mind: A new psychology of personality.* New York: Basic Books.

Haskell, M. (1988, May). Hollywood Madonnas. *Ms.,* pp. 84, 86, 88.

Hatcher, M. A. (1991). The corporate woman of the 1990s: Maverick or innovator? *Psychology of Women Quarterly, 15,* 251–259.

Hearn, J. (1987). *The gender of oppression: Men, masculinity and the critique of Marxism.* New York: St. Martin's Press.

Hegel, G. W. F. (1807). *Phenomenology of mind*. (J. B. Baillie, Trans.). Germany: Wurzburg & Bamburg.

Heilbrun, A. B. (1986). Androgyny as type and androgyny as behavior: Implications for gender schema in males and females. *Sex Roles, 14*, 123–139.

Heilbrun, A. B., & Han, Y. (1984). Cost-effectiveness of college achievement by androgynous men and women. *Psychological Reports, 55*, 977–978.

Heise, L. (1989, April 9). The global war against women. *World Watch*, p. 187. (Cited in French, 1992)

Helgesen, S. (1990). *The female advantage: Women's ways of leadership*. New York: Doubleday Currency.

Heller, S. (1993, February 3). Scholars debate the Marlboro Man: Examining stereotypes of masculinity. *Chronicle of Higher Education*, pp. A6–A8, A15.

Hemmer, J. D., & Kleiber, D. A. (1981). Tomboys and sissies: Androgynous children? *Sex Roles, 7*, 1205–1211.

Hendrick, C., & Hendrick, S. (1986). A theory and method of love. *Journal of Personality and Social Psychology, 50*, 392–402.

Henley, N. M. (1977). *Body politics: Power, sex and nonverbal communication*. Englewood Cliffs, NJ: Prentice-Hall.

Henley, N. M. (1989). Molehill or mountain? What we know and don't know about sex bias in language. In M. Crawford & M. Gentry (Eds.), *Gender and thought: Psychological perspectives* (pp. 59–78). New York: Springer-Verlag.

Hertz, S. H. (1977). The politics of the Welfare Mothers Movement: A case study. *Signs: Journal of Women in Culture and Society, 2*, 600–611.

Hewlett, S. (1986). *A lesser life: The myth of female liberation in America*. New York: Morrow.

Hewlett, S. (1991). *When the bough breaks: The cost of neglecting our children*. New York: Basic Books.

Hilts, P. J. (1991, September 10). Women still lag behind in medicine. *New York Times*, p. C7.

Hines, M. (1992, April 19). [Untitled report] *Health Information Communication Network, 5*, 2.

Hochschild, A. (1975). The sociology of feeling and emotion: Selected possibilities. In M. Millman & R. M. Kanter (Eds.), *Another voice* (pp. 180–307). New York: Doubleday/Anchor.

Hochschild, A. (1979). Emotion work, feeling rules, and social structure. *American Journal of Sociology, 85*, 551–595.

Hochschild, A. (1983). *The managed heart: Commercialization of human feeling*. Berkeley, CA: University of California Press.

Hochschild, A. (1989). The economy of gratitude. In D. Franks & E. D. McCarthy (Eds.), *The sociology of emotions: Original essays and research papers* (pp. 95–113). Greenwich, CT: JAI Press.

Hochschild, A., with Manchung, A. (1989). *The second shift: Working parents and the revolution at home*. New York: Viking/Penguin.

hooks, bell. (1990). Definitions of difference. In D. L. Rhode (Ed.), *Theoretical perspectives on sexual difference* (pp. 185–193). New York: Yale University Press.

Hope for working families. (1991, April 17). *Raleigh News and Observer*, p. A16.

Horovitz, B. (1989, August 10). In TV commercials, men are often the butt of the jokes. *Philadelphia Inquirer*, pp. 5b, 6b.

Howard, J. A., Blumstein, P., & Schwartz, P. (1986). Sex, power, and influence factors in intimate relationships. *Journal of Personality and Social Psychology, 51*, 102–109.

How boys and girls teach each other. (1992, October). *Working Mother*, p. 116.

Hudson, L., & Jacot, B. (1992). *The way men think*. New Haven, CT: Yale University Press.

Hughes, J. O., & Sandler, B. R. (1986). In case of sexual harassment: A guide for women students. Washington, DC: Project on the Status and Education of Women. Association of American Colleges.

Huston, A. C. (1985). The development of sex typing: Themes from recent research. *Developmental Review, 5*, 1–17.

Hyde, J. S. (1984). Children's understanding of sexist language. *Developmental Psychology, 20*, 697–706.

Hymowitz, C. (1992, October). Who earns what? *Smart Money*, 110–116.

The implant circus. (1992, February 18). *Wall Street Journal*, p. A20.

Jacklin, C. N. (1989). Female and male: Issues of gender. *American Psychologist, 44*, 127–133.

Jackson, L. A. (1983). The perception of androgyny and physical attractiveness: Two is better than one. *Personality and Social Psychology Bulletin, 9*, 405–430.

Jacobs, J. A. (1989). *Revolving doors: Sex segregation and women's careers*. Stanford, CA: Stanford University Press.

James, K. (1989). When twos are really threes: The triangular dance in couple conflict. *Australian and New Zealand Journal of Family Therapy, 10*, 179–186.

Janeway, E. (1971). *Man's world, woman's place: A study in social mythology*. New York: Dell.

Jay, R. (1969). *Javanese villagers: Social relations in rural Modjukuto*. Cambridge, MA: Harvard University Press.

Johnson, C. B., Stockdale, M. S., & Saal, F. E. (1991). Persistence of men's misperceptions of friendly cues across a variety of interpersonal encounters. *Psychology of Women Quarterly, 15*, 463–465.

Johnson, F. L. (1989). Women's culture and communication: An analytical perspective. In C. M. Lont & S. A. Friedley (Eds.), *Beyond boundaries: Sex and gender diversity in communication* (pp. 301–316). Fairfax, VA: George Mason University Press.

Jones, D. C. (1991). Friendship satisfaction and gender: An examination of sex differences in contributors to friendship satisfaction. *Journal of Social and Personal Relationships, 8*, 167–185.

Jones, G. P., & Dembo, M. H. (1989). Age and sex role differences in intimate friendships during childhood and adolescence. *Merrill-Palmer Quarterly of Behavior and Development, 35*, 445–462.

Joseph, G. I., & Lewis, J. (1981). *Common differences*. New York: Anchor.

Kahn, A. S., & Yoder, J. D. (1989). The psychology of women and conservatism: Rediscovering social change. *Psychology of Women Quarterly, 13*, 417–432.

Kanter, R. M. (1977). *Men and women of the corporation*. New York: Basic Books.

Kanter, R. M. (1983). *The change masters: Innovations for productivity in the American corporation*. New York: Simon and Schuster.

Katzenstein, M. F. (1990). Feminism within American institutions: Unobtrusive mobilization in the 1980s. *Signs: Journal of Women in Culture and Society, 16*, 27–54.

Kaye, L. W., & Applegate, J. S. (1990). Men as elder caregivers: A response to changing families. *American Journal of Orthopsychiatry, 60*, 86–95.

Keen, S. (1991). *Fire in the belly: On being a man*. New York: Bantam Books.

Keller, E. F. (1983). *A feeling for the organism: The life and work of Barbara McClintock*. New York: Freeman.

Keller, E. F. (1985). *Reflections on gender and science*. New Haven, CT: Yale University Press.

Kelly, G. P. (Ed.). (1989). *International handbook of women's education*. Westport, CT: Greenwood Press.

Kelly-Gadol, J. (1977). Did women have a renaissance? In R. Bridenthal & C. Koonz (Eds.), *Becoming visible: Women in European history* (pp. 136–164). Boston, MA: Houghton Mifflin.

Kemper, S. (1984). When to speak like a lady. *Sex Roles, 10*, 435–443.

Kervin, D. (1990). Advertising masculinity: The representation of males in *Esquire* advertisements. *Journal of Communication Inquiry, 14*, 51–70.

Kessler, S., & McKenna, W. (1978). *Gender: An ethnomethodological approach*. New York: Wiley.

Kimball, M. M. (1986). Television and sex-role attitudes. In T. M. Williams (Ed.), *The impact of television: A natural experiment in three communities* (pp. 265–301). Orlando, FL: Academic Press.

Kimbrell, A. (1991, May/June). A time for men to pull together. *Utne Reader*, pp. 66–71.

Klein, S. S. (1985). *Handbook for achieving sex equity in education*. Baltimore, MD: Johns Hopkins University Press.

Koblinsky, S. A., & Sugawara, A. I. (1984). Nonsexist curricula, sex of teacher, and children's sex-role learning. *Sex Roles, 10*, 357–367.

Koedt, A. (1973). Lesbianism and feminism. In A. Koedt, E. Levine, & A. Raphone (Eds.), *Radical feminism* (pp. 246–258). New York: Quadrangle.

Kohlberg, L. (1958). *The development of modes of thinking and moral choice in the years 10 to 16*. Unpublished doctoral dissertation, University of Chicago.

Kohlberg, L. (1966). A cognitive-developmental analysis of children's sex-role concepts and attitudes. In E. M. Maccoby (Ed.), *The development of sex differences* (pp. 82–173). Stanford, CA: Stanford University Press.

Kohn, A. (1986). *No contest: The case against competition.* Boston, MA: Houghton Mifflin.

Komarovsky, M. (1940). *The unemployed man and his family.* New York: Dryden Press.

Koss, M. P. (1990). The women's mental health research agenda: Violence against women. *American Psychologist, 45,* 374–380.

Koss, M. P., & Dinero, T. E. (1988). Predictors of sexual aggression among a national sample of male college students. In V. I. Quinsey & R. Orentky (Eds.), *Human sexual aggression* (pp. 133–147). New York: Academy of Sciences.

Koss, M. P., Dinero, T. E., Seibel, C. A., & Cox, S. L. (1988). Stranger and acquaintance rape: Are there differences in the victim's experience? *Psychology of Women Quarterly, 12,* 1–24.

Koss, M. P., Gidycz, C. J., Wisniewski, N. (1987). The scope of rape: Incidence and prevalence of sexual aggression and victimization in a national sample of higher education students. *Journal of Consulting and Clinical Psychology, 55,* 162–170.

Kramarae, C. (1981). *Women and men speaking: Frameworks for analysis.* Rowley, MA: Newbury House.

Kramarae, C., Schultz, M., & O'Barr, W. (Eds.). (1984). *Language and power.* Beverly Hills, CA: Sage.

Kramarae, C., Thorne, B., & Henley, N. (1978). Perspectives on language and communication. *Signs: Journal of Women in Culture and Society, 5,* 638–651.

Kramer, C. (1974). Women's speech: Separate but unequal? *Quarterly Journal of Speech, 60,* 14–24.

Kreps, G. L. (Ed.). (1992). *Communication and sexual harassment in the workplace.* Cresskill, NJ: Hampton Press.

Krupnick, C. G. (1985, May). Women and men in the classroom: Inequality and its remedies. *On Teaching and Learning: The Journal of the Harvard-Danforth Center for Teaching and Learning,* pp. 18–25.

Kurdek, L. A., & Schmitt, J. P. (1986a). Early development of relationship quality in heterosexual married, heterosexual cohabiting, gay, and lesbian couples. *Developmental Psychology, 22,* 305–309.

Kurdek, L. A., & Schmitt, J. P. (1986b). Interaction of sex-role self-concept with relationship quality and relationship belief in married, heterosexual cohabiting, gay, and lesbian couples. *Journal of Personality and Social Psychology, 51,* 365–370.

Kurdek, L. A., & Schmitt, J. P. (1986c). Relationship quality of partners in heterosexual married, heterosexual cohabiting, and gay and lesbian relationships. *Journal of Personality and Social Psychology, 51,* 711–720.

Kurdek, L. A., & Schmitt, J. P. (1987). Partner homogamy in married, heterosexual cohabiting, gay, and lesbian couples. *Journal of Sex Research, 23,* 212–232.

Kurtz, D. (1989). Social science perspectives on wife abuse: Current debates and future directions. *Gender and Society, 3,* 489–505.

Labov, W. (1972). *Sociolinguistic patterns.* Philadelphia, PA: University of Pennsylvania Press.

Lacher, M. R. B. (1978). On advising undergraduate women: A psychologist's advice to academic advisors. *Journal of College Student Personnel, 19,* 488–493.

LaFrance, M., & Mayo, C. (1979). A review of nonverbal behaviors of women and men. *Western Journal of Speech Communication, 43,* 96–107.

Lakoff, R. (1975). *Language and woman's place.* New York: Harper and Row.

Lamb, M. E. (1986). The changing roles of fathers. In M. E. Lamb (Ed.), *The father's role: Applied perspectives* (pp. 3–27). New York: Wiley.

Lamke, L. K. (1982). The impact of sexual orientation on self-esteem in early adolescence. *Child Development, 53,* 1530–1535.

Lang, S. S. (1991, January 20). When women drink. *Parade,* pp. 18–20.

Langer, S. K. (1953). *Feeling and form: A theory of art.* New York: Scribner's.

Langer, S. K. (1979). *Philosophy in a new key: A study in the symbolism of reason, rite and art* (3rd ed.). Cambridge, MA: Harvard University Press.

Lawson, C. (1989, June 15). Toys: Girls still apply make-up, boys still fight wars. *New York Times,* pp. C1, C10.

Lawson, C. (1993, February 16). Gender-benders. *Raleigh News and Observer,* p. E1.

Leathers, D. G. (1986). *Successful nonverbal communication: Principles and applications.* New York: Macmillan.

Lee, P. C., & Gropper, N. B. (1974). Sex-role culture and educational practice. *Harvard Educational Review, 44,* 369–407.

Lee, V. E., & Marks, H. M. (1990). Sustained effects of the single-sex secondary school experience on attitudes, behaviors, and values in college. *Journal of Educational Psychology, 82,* 578–592.

Leland, J., & Leonard, E. (1993, February 1). Back to Twiggy. *Newsweek,* pp. 64–65.

Lerner, G. (Ed.). (1972). *Black woman in white America: A documentary history.* New York: Pantheon.

Lesak, M. (1976). *Neuropsychological assessment.* New York: Oxford University Press.

Levinson, D. (1989). *Family violence in cross-cultural perspective.* Newbury Park, CA: Sage.

Levinson, R., Powell, B., & Steelman, L. C. (1986). Social location, significant others, and body image among adolescents. *Social Psychology Quarterly, 49,* 330–337.

Lewis, E. T., & McCarthy, P. R. (1988). Perceptions of self-disclosure as a function of gender-linked variables. *Sex Roles, 19,* 47–56.

Lewis, M. (1972, May). Culture and gender roles — there's no unisex in the nursery. *Psychology Today,* pp. 54–57.

Lichter, S. R., Lichter, L. S., & Rothman, S. (1986, September/October). From Lucy to Lacey: TV's dream girls. *Public Opinion,* pp. 16–19.

Lichter, S. R., Lichter, L. S., Rothman, S., & Amundson, D. (1987, July/August). Prime-time prejudice: TV's images of blacks and Hispanics. *Public Opinion,* pp. 13–16.

Lips, H. M. (1981). *Women, men, and the psychology of power.* Englewood Cliffs, NJ: Prentice-Hall/Spectrum Books.

Lisak, D., & Roth, S. (1988). Motivational factors in nonincarcerated sexually aggressive men. *Journal of Personality and Social Psychology, 55,* 795–802.

Lont, C. M. (1990). The roles assigned to females and males in non-music radio programming. *Sex Roles, 22,* 661–668.

Lott, B. (1987). *Women's lives: Themes and variations in gender learning.* Belmont, CA: Wadsworth.

Lott, B. (1989). Sexist discrimination as distancing behavior: II. Prime-time television. *Psychology of Women Quarterly, 13,* 341–355.

Luebke, B. F. (1989). Out of focus: Images of women and men in newspaper photographs. *Sex Roles, 20,* 121–133.

Lunneborg, P. W. (1990). *Women changing work.* Westport, CT: Greenwood Press.

Lynn, D. B. (1969). *Parental and sex role identification: A theoretical formulation.* Berkeley, CA: McCutchan.

Lytton, H., & Romney, D. M. (1991). Parents' differential socialization of boys and girls: A meta-analysis. *Psychological Bulletin, 109,* 267–296.

Maccoby, E. E. (1990). Gender and relationships: A developmental account. *American Psychologist, 45,* 513–520.

Maccoby, E. E., & Jacklin, C. N. (1974). *The psychology of sex differences.* Stanford, CA: Stanford University Press.

Maccoby, E. E., & Jacklin, C. N. (1987). Gender segregation in childhood. *Advances in Child Development and Behavior, 20,* 239–287.

MacKinnon, C. A. (1987). *Feminism unmodified: Discourses on life and law.* Cambridge, MA: Harvard University Press.

Mahlstedt, D. (1992). *Female survivors of dating violence and their social networks.* Working paper.

Major, B. (1980). Gender patterns in touching behavior. In C. Mayo & N. M. Henley (Eds.), *Gender and nonverbal behavior* (pp. 3–37). New York: Springer-Verlag.

Major, B., Schmidlin, A. M., & Williams, L. (1990). Gender patterns in social touch: The impact of setting and age. *Journal of Personality and Social Psychology, 58,* 634–643.

Malamuth, N. M., & Briere, J. (1986). Sexual violence in the media: Indirect effects on aggression against women. *Journal of Social Issues, 42,* 75–92.

Malandro, L. A., & Barker, L. L. (1983). *Nonverbal communication.* Reading, MA: Addison-Wesley.

Male hormone causes killer hyena cubs. (1991, May 4). *Raleigh News and Observer,* p. A3.

Malovich, N. J., & Stake, J. E. (1990). Sexual harassment on campus: Individual differences in attitudes and beliefs. *Psychology of Women Quarterly, 14,* 63–81.

Maltz, D. N., & Borker, R. (1982). A cultural approach to male-female miscommunication. In J. J. Gumpertz (Ed.), *Language and social identity* (pp. 196–216). Cambridge, UK: Cambridge University Press.

Mann, J. (1989, March 15). The demeaning "mommy track." *Washington Post*, p. C3.

Maraniss, D. (1991, June 23). Blacks see quotas working for whites. *Raleigh News and Observer*, p. B7.

Marhoefer-Dvorak, S., Resick, P., Hutter, C., & Girelli, S. (1988). Single- versus multiple-incident rape victims: A comparison of psychological reactions to rape. *Journal of Interpersonal Violence, 3*, 145–160.

Markel, N. N., Long, J. F., & Saine, T. J. (1976). Sex effects in conversational interaction: Another look at male dominance. *Human Communication Research, 2*, 356–364.

Marks, J. (1979). "On the road to find out": The role music plays in adolescent development. In C. B. Kopp (Ed.), *Becoming female: Perspectives on development* (pp. 333–362). New York: Plenum Press.

Markstrom-Adams, C. (1989). Androgyny and its relation to adolescent psychosocial well-being: A review of the literature. *Sex Roles, 21*, 325–340.

Martin, C. L. (1989). Children's use of gender-related information in making social judgments. *Developmental Psychology, 25*, 80–88.

Martyna, W. (1978). What does "he" mean — use of the generic pronoun. *Journal of Communication, 28*, 131–138.

Maslin, J. (1990, June 17). Bimbos embody retro rage. *New York Times*, pp. H13, H14.

Masse, M. A., & Rosenblum, K. (1988). Male and female created they them: The depiction of gender in the advertising of traditional women's and men's magazines. *Women's Studies International Forum, 11*, 127–144.

Mattel offers trade-in for "Teen Talk" Barbie. (1992, October 13). *Raleigh News and Observer*, p. A3.

Mazur, E. (1989). Predicting gender differences in same-sex friendships from affiliation motive and value. *Psychology of Women Quarterly, 13*, 277–291.

Mazur, E., & Olver, R. R. (1987). Intimacy and structure: Sex differences in imagery of same sex relationships. *Sex Roles, 16*, 539–558.

McCauley, C., Thangavelu, K., & Rozin, P. (1988). Sex stereotyping of occupations in relation to television representations and census facts. *Basic and Applied Social Psychology, 9*, 197–212.

McCormick, N., & Jordan, T. (1988). Thoughts that destroy intimacy: Irrational beliefs about relationships and sexuality. In W. Dryden & P. Trower (Eds.), *Developments in rational emotive therapy*. Philadelphia, PA: Open University Press.

McGowen, K. R., & Hart, L. E. (1990). Still different after all these years: Gender differences in professional identity formation. *Professional Psychology: Research and Practice, 21*, 118–223.

McHale, S. M., Bartko, W. T., Crouter, A. C., & Perry-Jenkins, M. (1990). Children's housework and psychosocial functioning: The mediating effects of parents' sex-role behaviors and attitudes. *Child Development, 61*, 1413–1426.

McHenry, S., & Small, L. L. (1989, March). Does part-time pay off? *Ms.*, pp. 83–93.

Mead, G. H. (1934). *Mind, self, and society*. Chicago, IL: University of Chicago Press.

Mead, M. (1935/1968). *Sex and temperament in three primitive societies*. New York: Dell.

Mediaworks. (1991, February 18). *Advertising Age*, p. 37.

Mehrabian, A. (1971). *Silent messages*. Belmont, CA: Wadsworth.

Mehrabian, A. (1972). *Nonverbal communication*. Chicago, IL: Aldine.

Mehrabian, A. (1981). *Silent messages: Implicit communication of emotion and attitudes* (2nd ed.). Belmont, CA: Wadsworth.

Menopause. (1992, May 25). *Newsweek*, pp. 71–80.

Mickelson, A., & Smith, S. (1992). Education and the struggle against race, class, and gender inequality. In M. Andersen & P. H. Collins (Eds.), *Race, class, and gender: An anthology* (pp. 359–376). Belmont, CA: Wadsworth.

Miller, C. L. (1987). Qualitative differences among gender-stereotyped toys: Implications for cognitive and social development. *Sex Roles, 16*, 473–487.

Miller, J. B. (1986). *Toward a new psychology of women* (2nd ed.). Boston, MA: Beacon Press.

Miller, J., Schooler, C., Kohn, M., & Miller, K. (1979). Women and work: The psychological effects of occupational conditioning. *American Journal of Sociology, 85*, 66–94.

Mills, C. J., & Bohannon, W. E. (1983). Personality, sex-role orientation, and psychological health in stereotypically masculine groups of males. *Sex Roles, 9*, 1161–1169.

Mills, K. (1988). *A place in the news: From the women's pages to the front page*. New York: Dodd, Mead.

Mintz, L. B., & Betz, N. E. (1986). Sex differences in the nature, realism, and correlates of body image. *Sex Roles, 15*, 185–195.

Mischel, W. (1966). A social learning view of sex differences in behavior. In E. E. Maccoby (Ed.), *The development of sex differences* (pp. 93–106). Stanford, CA: Stanford University Press.

Mishkind, M. E., Rodin, J., Silberstein, L. R., & Striegel-Moore, R. H. (1987). The embodiment of masculinity: Cultural, psychological, and behavioral dimensions. In M. S. Kimmel (Ed.), *Changing men: New directions in research on men and masculinity* (pp. 37–52). Newbury Park, CA: Sage.

Mitscherlich, A. (1970). *Society without the father*. New York: Schocken Books.

Modleski, T. (1982). *Loving with a vengeance: Mass-produced fantasies for women*. New York: Methuen.

Moen, P. (1991). *Disfigured images: The historical assault on Afro-American women*. Westport, CT: Greenwood Press.

Mommy tracks. (1991, November 25). *Newsweek*, pp. 48–49.

Money, J. (1986). *Venuses penuses: Sexology, sexosophy, and exigency theory*. Buffalo, NY: Prometheus.

Money, J. (1988). *Money, straight, and in-between: The sexology of erotic orientation*. New York: Oxford University Press.

Money, J., & Ehrhardt, A. (1972). *Man and woman: Boy and girl.* Baltimore, MD: Johns Hopkins University Press.

Monsour, M. (1992). Meanings of intimacy in cross- and same-sex friendships. *Journal of Social and Personal Relationships, 9,* 277–295.

Morgan, M. (1973). *The total woman.* New York: Pocket Books.

Morgan, M. (1987). Television, sex-role attitudes, and sex-role behavior. *Journal of Early Adolescence, 7,* 269–282.

Morrison, A. M., & Von Glinow, M. A. (1990). Women and minorities in management. *American Psychologist, 45,* 200–208.

Morrow, F. (1990). *Unleashing our unknown selves: An inquiry into the future of femininity and masculinity.* Westport, CT: Praeger.

Mulac, A., Wiemann, J. M., Widenmann, S. J., & Gibson, T. W. (1988). Male/female language differences and effects in same-sex and mixed-sex dyads: The gender-linked language effect. *Communication Monographs, 55,* 315–335.

Muro, M. (1989, April 23). Comment: New era of eros in advertising. *Morning Call,* pp. D1, D16.

Murrell, A. J., Frieze, I. H., & Frost, J. L. (1991). Aspiring to careers in male- and female-dominated professions: A study of black and white college women. *Psychology of Women Quarterly, 15,* 103–126.

National Commission on Working Women of Wider Opportunities for Women. (1989). *Women, work and child care.* Washington, DC: Author.

National Commission on Working Women of Wider Opportunities for Women. (1990, March). *Women and work.* Washington, DC: Author.

National Public Radio. (1992, July 23). Untitled report on parental responses to children.

Nearly half of teen girls trying to diet, survey says. (1991, November 11). *Morning Call,* p. A7.

A new court decision. (1992, September). *The Newsletter,* p. 5.

Newsprint Information Committee. (1992). *Newspaper and newsprint facts at a glance 1991–92* (33rd ed.). New York: Author.

The new traditionalist. (1988, November 17). *New York Times,* p. Y46.

Nicotera, A. M., & Cushman, D. P. (1992). Organizational ethics: A within-organization view. *Journal of Applied Communication, 4,* 437–462.

Nielsen Media Research. (1989). *'89 Nielsen report on television.* Northbrook, IL: Author.

Nigro, G. N., Hill, D. E., Gelbein, M. E., & Clark, C. L. (1988). Changes in the facial prominence of women and men over the last decade. *Psychology of Women Quarterly, 12,* 225–235.

Nikken, P., & Peeters, A. L. (1988). Children's perceptions of television reality. *Journal of Broadcasting and Electronic Media, 32,* 441–452.

Ninety percent of big firms get sex complaints. (1988, November 23). *Easton Express,* p. D9.

Noble, B. P. (1993, January 2). Bias up against pregnant workers. *Raleigh News and Observer,* pp. A1, A8.

Noller, P. (1986). Sex differences in nonverbal communication: Advantage lost or supremacy regained? *Australian Journal of Psychology, 38,* 23–32.

No sexism please, we're Webster's. (1991, June 24). *Newsweek,* p. 59.

Nussbaum, J. F. (1992). Effective teacher behaviors. *Communication Education, 41,* 167–180.

Nussbaum, M. (1992, October 18). Justice for women! *New York Review of Books,* pp. 43–48.

Oakley, A. (1974). *The sociology of housework.* London: Martin Robertson.

O'Connor, J. J. (1989, June 6). What are commercials selling to children? *New York Times,* p. 28.

O'Kelly, C. G., & Carney, L. S. (1986). *Women and men in society* (2nd ed.). Belmont, CA: Wadsworth.

Okin, S. M. (1989). *Justice, gender, and the family.* New York: Basic Books.

O'Leary, V. E. (1988). Women's relationships with women in the workplace. In B. A. Gutek, L. Larwood, & A. Stromberg (Eds.), *Women and work: An annual review* (Vol. 3, pp. 189–214). Beverly Hills, CA: Sage.

O'Leary, V. E., & Ickovics, J. R. (1991). Cracking the glass ceiling. Overcoming isolation and alienation. In U. Sekeran & F. Long (Eds.), *Pathways to excellence: New patterns for human utilization.* Beverly Hills, CA: Sage.

Olien, M. (1978). *The human myth.* New York: Harper and Row.

O'Meara, J. D. (1989). Cross-sex friendship: Four basic challenges of an ignored relationship. *Sex Roles, 21,* 525–543.

Palmer, H. T., & Lee, J. A. (1990). Female workers' acceptance in traditionally male-dominated blue-collar jobs. *Sex Roles, 22,* 607–625.

Paludi, M. A. (Ed.). (1990). *Ivory power: Sexual harassment on campus.* Albany, NY: State University of New York Press.

Paradise, L. V., & Wall, S. M. (1986). Children's perceptions of male and female principals and teachers. *Sex Roles, 14,* 1–7.

Pareles, J. (1990, October 21). The women who talk back in rap. *New York Times,* pp. H33, H36.

Parlee, M. B. (1973). The premenstrual syndrome. *Psychological Bulletin, 80,* 454–465.

Parlee, M. B. (1979, May). Conversational politics. *Psychology Today,* pp. 48–56.

Parlee, M. B. (1987). Media treatment of premenstrual syndrome. In B. E. Ginsburg & B. F. Carter (Eds.), *Premenstrual syndrome.* New York: Plenum Press.

Paul, E., & White, K. (1990). The development of intimate relationships in late adolescence. *Adolescence, 25,* 375–400.

Pearson, J. C. (1985). *Gender and communication.* Dubuque, IA: William C. Brown.

Peirce, K. (1990). A feminist theoretical perspective on the socialization of teenage girls through *Seventeen* magazine. *Sex Roles, 23,* 491–500.

Peterson, C. D., Baucom, D. H., Elliott, M. J., & Farr, P. A. (1989). The relationship between sex role identity and marital adjustment. *Sex Roles, 21,* 775–787.

Philips, S. U., Steele, S., & Tanz, C. (Eds.). (1987). *Language, gender, and sex in comparative perspective.* Cambridge, UK: Cambridge University Press.

Phillips, G. M., Gouran, D. S., Kuehn, S. A., & Wood, J. T. (1993). *Professionalism: A survival guide for beginning academics.* Cresskill, NJ: Hampton Press.

Piaget, J. (1932, 1965). *The moral judgment of the child.* New York: Free Press.

Pleck, E. (1987). *Domestic tyranny: The making of American social policy against family violence from colonial times to the present.* New York: Oxford University Press.

Pleck, J. H. (1981). *The myth of masculinity.* Cambridge, MA: MIT Press.

Pleck, J. H. (1985). *Working wives, working husbands.* Beverly Hills, CA: Sage.

Pleck, J. H. (1986). Employment and fatherhood: Issues and innovative policies. In M. E. Lamb (Ed.), *The father's role: Applied perspectives* (pp. 385–412). New York: Wiley.

Pleck, J. H. (1987). American fathering in historical perspective. In M. S. Kimmel (Ed.), *Changing men: New directions in research on men and masculinity* (pp. 83–97). Newbury Park, CA: Sage.

Pleck, J. H., & Sawyer, J. (Eds.). (1974). *Men and masculinity.* Englewood Cliffs, NJ: Prentice-Hall.

Poire, B. A., Burgoon, J. K., & Parrott, R. (1992). Status and privacy restoring communication in the workplace. *Journal of Applied Communication Research, 4,* 419–436.

Polit, D., & LaFrance, M. (1977). Sex differences in reaction to spatial invasion. *Journal of Social Psychology, 102,* 59–60.

Pomerleau, A., Bolduc, D., Malcuit, G., & Cossette, L. (1990). Pink or blue: Environmental stereotypes in the first two years of life. *Sex Roles, 22,* 359–367.

Poppen, P. J., & Segal, N. J. (1988). The influence of sex and sex role orientation on sexual coercion. *Sex Roles, 19,* 689–701.

Public Agenda Foundation. (1990). *Remedies for racial inequality: Why progress has stalled, what should be done.* Dubuque, IA: Kendall/Hunt.

Puka, B. (1990). The liberation of caring: A different voice for Gilligan's different voice. *Hypatia, 5,* 59–82.

Purcell, P., & Stewart, L. (1990). Dick and Jane in 1989. *Sex Roles, 22,* 177–185.

Quinn, S. (1993, February 15). Look out: It's superwoman. *Newsweek,* pp. 24–25.

Rakow, L. F. (1986). Rethinking gender research in communication. *Journal of Communication, 36,* 11–26.

Rakow, L. F. (1992). "Don't hate me because I'm beautiful": Feminist resistance to advertising irresistible meanings. *Southern Communication Journal, 57,* 132–141.

Raphael, R. (1988). *The men from the boys: Rites of passage in male America.* Lincoln, NE: University of Nebraska Press.

Rasmussen, J. L., & Moley, B. E. (1986). Impression formation as a function of the sex role appropriateness of linguistic behavior. *Sex Roles, 14,* 149–161.

Raspberry, W. (1990, December 13). Affirmative action is call for fairness. *Raleigh News and Observer*, p. A11.

Reisman, J. M. (1990). Intimacy in same-sex friendships. *Sex Roles, 23,* 65–82.

Researcher: Male students get more for their money in college. (1990, April 29). *Durham Morning Herald,* p. A10.

Reskin, B. F., & Roos, P. A. (1990). *Job queues, gender queues: Explaining women's inroads into male occupations.* Philadelphia, PA: Temple University Press.

Reuther, R. R. (Ed.). (1974). *Religion and sexism: Images of woman in the Jewish and Christian traditions.* New York: Simon and Schuster.

Reuther, R. R. (1975). *New woman/new earth: Sexist ideologies and human liberation.* New York: Seabury.

Reuther, R. R. (1983). *Sexism and God-talk: Toward a feminist theology.* Boston, MA: Beacon Press.

Rice, J. K., & Hemmings, A. (1988). Women's colleges and women achievers: An update. *Signs: Journal of Women in Culture and Society, 13,* 546–559.

Rich, A. (1979). *On lies, secrets and silences: Selected prose, 1966–1978.* New York: W. W. Norton.

Rich, A. (1980). Compulsory heterosexuality and lesbian existence. *Signs: Journal of Women in Culture and Society, 5,* 631–660.

Richmond-Abbott, M. (1992). *Masculine and feminine: Gender roles over the life cycle.* New York: McGraw-Hill.

Rideau, W., & Sinclair, B. (1982). Prison: The sexual jungle. In A. Scacco, Jr.

(Ed.), *Male rape* (pp. 3–29). New York: AMS Press.

Riessman, C. K. (1990). *Divorce talk: Women and men make sense of personal relationships.* New Brunswick, NJ: Rutgers University Press.

Risman, B. J. (1989). Can men mother?: Life as a single father. In B. J. Risman & P. Schwartz (Eds.), *Gender in intimate relationships* (pp. 155–164). Belmont, CA: Wadsworth.

Roberts, B. (1983). No safe place: The war against women. *Our Generation, 15,* 7–26.

Rodin, J., Silberstein, L., & Striegel-Moore, R. H. (1985). Women and weight: A normative discontent. In T. B. Sonderegger (Ed.), *Nebraska symposium on motivation 1984: Psychology and gender* (Vol. 32, pp. 267–307). Lincoln, NE: University of Nebraska Press.

Root, M. P. P. (1990). Disordered eating in women of color. *Sex Roles, 22,* 525–536.

Rose, S., & Frieze, I. H. (1989). Young singles' scripts for a first date. *Gender and Society, 3,* 258–268.

Rosenberg, M. (1979). *Conceiving the self.* New York: Basic Books.

Rosener, J. (1990, November/December). Ways women lead. *Harvard Business Review,* pp. 119–125.

Rosengrant, T. J., & McCroskey, J. C. (1975). The effect of race and sex on proxemic behavior in an interview setting. *Southern Speech Communication Journal, 40,* 408–420.

Rosenthal, R., Archer, D., DiMatteo, M. R., Koivumaki, J. H., & Rogers, P. L. (1974, September). Body talk and tone of voice: The language without words. *Psychology Today, 8,* 64–68.

Rosenthal, R., & DePaulo, B. M. (1979). Sex differences in eavesdropping on nonverbal cues. *Journal of Personality and Social Psychology, 37,* 273–285.

Rosenwasser, S. M., Lingenfelter, M., & Harrington, A. F. (1989). Nontraditional gender role portrayals on television and children's gender role perceptions. *Journal of Applied Developmental Psychology, 10,* 97–105.

Ross, S. I., & Jackson, J. M. (1991). Teachers' expectations for black males' and black females' academic achievement. *Personality and Social Psychology Bulletin, 17,* 78–82.

Rossi, A. S. (Ed.). (1974). *The feminist papers: From Adams to de Beauvoir.* New York: Bantam Books.

Rubin, J. Z., Provenzano, F. J., & Luria, Z. (1974). The eye of the beholder: Parents' views on sex of newborns. *American Journal of Orthopsychiatry, 44,* 512–519.

Rubin, L. B. (1983). *Intimate strangers: Men and women together.* New York: Harper and Row.

Rubin, L. (1985). *Just friends: The role of friendship in our lives.* New York: Harper and Row.

Ruddick, S. (1989). *Maternal thinking: Towards a politics of peace.* Boston, MA: Beacon Press.

Rusbult, C. (1987). Responses to dissatisfaction in close relationships: The exit-voice-loyalty-neglect model. In D. Perlman & S. W. Duck (Eds.), *Intimate relationships: Development, dynamics, and deterioration* (pp. 209–238). London, UK: Sage.

Russell, D. E. H. (1982). *Rape in marriage.* New York: Macmillan.

Russell, D. E. H. (Ed.). (1993). *Feminist views on pornography.* Cholchester, VT: Teachers College Press.

Ryan, M. (1979). *Womanhood in America: From colonial times to the present* (2nd ed.). New York: New Viewpoints.

Sadker, M., & Sadker, D. (1984). *The report card on sex bias.* Washington, DC: MidAtlantic Center for Sex Equity.

Sadker, M., & Sadker, D. (1986, March). Sexism in the classroom: From grade school to graduate school. *Phi Delta Kappan,* pp. 512–515.

Safilios-Rothschild, C. (1979). Sex role socialization and sex discrimination: A synthesis and critique of the literature. Washington, DC: National Institute of Education.

Sagan, C., & Druyan, A. (1992). *Shadows of forgotten ancestors.* New York: Random House.

St. Lawrence, J. S., & Joynder, D. J. (1991). The effects of sexually violent rock music on males' acceptance of violence against women. *Psychology of Women Quarterly, 15,* 49–63.

Sales, K. (1987, September 26). Ecofeminism — a new perspective. *The Nation,* pp. 302–305.

Salholz, E., with Beachy, L., Miller, S., Annin, P., Barrett, T., & Foote, D. (1992, December 28). Did America "get it"? *Newsweek,* pp. 20–22.

Sallinen-Kuparinen, A. (1992). Teacher communicator style. *Communication Education, 41,* 153–166.

Salomone, R. (1986). *Equality of education under the law.* New York: St. Martin's Press.

Saltzman, A. (1991, June 17). Trouble at the top. *U.S. News and World Report*, pp. 40–48.

Sanday, P. R. (1986). Rape and the silencing of the feminine. In S. Tomaselli & R. Porter (Eds.), *Rape* (pp. 84–101). Oxford, UK: Basil Blackwell.

Sanders, M., & Rock, M. (1988). *Waiting for prime time: The women of television news*. Urbana, IL: University of Illinois Press.

Sandler, B. R., & Hall, R. M. (1986). *The campus climate revisited: Chilly for women faculty, administrators, and graduate students*. Washington, DC: Project on the Status and Education of Women, Association of American Colleges.

Sapadin, L. A. (1988). Friendship and gender: Perspectives of professional men and women. *Journal of Social and Personal Relationships, 5*, 387–403.

Sartre, J. P. (1966). *Being and nothingness: An essay in phenomenological ontology*. New York: Citadel Press.

Saurer, M. K., & Eisler, R. M. (1990). The role of masculine gender roles stress in expressivity and social support network factors. *Sex Roles, 23*, 261–271.

Saxby, L., & Bryden, M. P. (1985). Left visual-field advantage in children for processing visual emotional stimuli. *Developmental Psychology, 21*, 253–261.

Scarf, M. (1987). *Intimate partners*. New York: Random House.

Schaef, A. W. (1981). *Women's reality*. St. Paul, MN: Winston Press.

Schneider, B. E., & Gould, M. (1987). Female sexuality: Looking back into the future. In B. B. Hess and M. M. Ferree (Eds.), *Analyzing gender: A handbook of social science research* (pp. 120–153). Newbury Park, CA: Sage.

Schneider, J., & Hacker, S. (1973). Sex role imagery and use of the generic "man" in introductory texts: A case in the sociology of sociology. *American Sociologist, 8*, 12–18.

Schroedel, J. R. (1990). Blue-collar women: Paying the price at home and on the job. In H. Y. Grossman & N. L. Chester (Eds.), *The experience and meaning of work in women's lives* (pp. 241–260). Hillsdale, NJ: Lawrence Erlbaum.

Schwartz, F. (1989, January/February). Management women and the new facts of life. *Harvard Business Review*, pp. 65–76.

Schwichtenberg, C. (1989). The "motherlode" of feminist research: Congruent paradigms in the analysis of beauty culture. In B. Dervin, L. Grossberg, B. J. O'Keefe, & E. Wartella (Eds.), *Rethinking communication* (Vol. 2, pp. 291–306). Beverly Hills, CA: Sage.

Schwichtenberg, C. (1992). Madonna's postmodern feminism: Bringing the margins to center. *Southern Communication Journal, 57*, 120–131.

Scott, R., & Tetreault, L. (1987). Attitudes of rapists and other violent offenders toward women. *Journal of Social Psychology, 124*, 375–380.

Scully, D. (1990). *Understanding sexual violence: A study of convicted rapists*. Boston, MA: Unwin Hyman.

Sedney, M. A. (1987). Development of androgyny: Parental influences. *Psychology of Women Quarterly, 11*, 311–326.

Segal, A. T., with Zellner, W. (1992, June 8). Corporate women: Progress? Sure. But the playing field is still far from level. *Business Week*, pp. 74–78.

Segel-Evans, K. (1987). Rape prevention and masculinity. In F. Abbott (Ed.), *New men, new minds: Breaking male tradition* (pp. 117–121). Freedom, CA: Crossing Press.

Seligmann, J., Joseph, N., Donovan, J. B., & Gosnell, M. (1987, July 27). The littlest dieters. *Newsweek*, p. 48.

Sexism in the schoolhouse. (1992, February 24). *Newsweek*, p. 62.

Shapiro, J., & Kroeger, L. (1991). Is life just a romantic novel? The relationship between attitudes about intimate relationships and the popular media. *American Journal of Family Therapy, 19*, 226–236.

Shapiro, L. (1990, May 28). Guns and dolls. *Newsweek*, pp. 56–65.

Sheldon, A. (1990, January). "Kings are royaler than queens": Language and socialization. *Young Children*, pp. 4–9.

Shelton, B. A. (1992). *Women, men, and time: Gender differences in paid work, housework and leisure*. Westport, CT: Greenwood Press.

Sherman, M. A., & Haas, A. (1984, June). Man to man, woman to woman. *Psychology Today*, pp. 72–73.

Sherrod, D. (1989). The influence of gender on same-sex friendships. In C. Hendrick (Ed.), *Close relationships* (pp. 164–186). Newbury Park, CA: Sage.

Siever, M. D. (1988, August). *Sexual orientation, gender, and the perils of sexual objectification*. Paper presented at the American Psychological Association, Atlanta, GA.

Sights, sounds and stereotypes. (1992, October 11). *Raleigh News and Observer*, pp. G1, G10.

Silverstein, B., Perdue, L., Peterson, B., & Kelly, E. (1986). The role of the mass media in promoting a thin standard of bodily attractiveness for women. *Sex Roles, 14*, 519–532.

Simon, R. J., & Danziger, G. (1991). *Women's movements in America: Their successes, disappointments, and aspirations*. Westport, CT: Praeger.

Slater, P. (1961). Toward a dualistic theory of identification. *Merrill-Palmer Quarterly of Behavior and Development, 7*, 113–126.

Smith, D. (1987). *The everyday world as problematic*. Boston, MA: Northeastern University Press.

Smith, J. E., Waldorf, V. A., & Trembath, D. L. (1990). "Single white male looking for thin, very attractive . . ." *Sex Roles, 23*, 675–685.

Snell, W. E., Jr., Hawkins, R. C., II, & Belk, S. S. (1988). Stereotypes about male sexuality and the use of social influence strategies in intimate relationships. *Journal of Clinical and Social Psychology, 7*, 42–48.

Snyder, T. D. (1987). *Digest of education statistics*. Washington, DC: Department of Education.

Soeken, K., & Damrosch, S. (1986). Randomized response technique: Application to research on rape. *Psychology of Women Quarterly, 10*, 119–126.

Sollie, D. L., & Fischer, J. L. (1985). Sexrole orientation, intimacy of topic, and target person differences in self-disclosure among women. *Sex Roles, 12*, 917–929.

Sommer, R. (1959). Studies in personal space. *Sociometry, 22,* 247–260.

Sommer, R. (1965). Further studies of small group ecology. *Sociometry, 28,* 337–348.

Sommer, R. (1969). *Personal space: The behavioral basis of design.* Englewood Cliffs, NJ: Prentice-Hall.

Soroka v. *Dayton Hudson Corporation* (1991, October 25). California Court of Appeals. No. A052157.

South, S. J., & Felson, R. B. (1990). The racial patterning of rape. *Social Forces, 69,* 71–93.

Spain, D. (1992). *Gendered spaces.* Chapel Hill, NC: University of North Carolina Press.

Spelman, E. V. (1988). *Inessential woman: Problems of exclusion in feminist thought.* Boston, MA: Beacon Press.

Spender, D. (1984a). *Man made language.* London: Routledge and Kegan Paul.

Spender, D. (1984b). Defining reality: A powerful tool. In C. Kramarae, M. Schultz, & W. O'Barr (Eds.), *Language and power* (pp. 195–205). Beverly Hills, CA: Sage.

Spender, D. (1989). *Invisible women: The schooling scandal.* London: Women's Press.

Spitzack, C. (1993). The spectacle of anorexia nervosa. *Text and Performance Quarterly, 13,* 1–21.

Spitzack, C., & Carter, K. (1987). Women in communication studies: A typology for revision. *Quarterly Journal of Speech, 73,* 401–423.

Stanley, J. P. (1977). Paradigmatic woman: The prostitute. In D. L. Shores & C. P. Hines (Eds.), *Papers in language*

variation (pp. 303–321). Tuscaloosa, AL: University of Alabama Press.

Statham, A. (1987). The gender model revisited: Differences in the management styles of men and women. *Sex Roles, 16,* 409–429.

Statham, A., Richardson, L., & Cook, J. A. (1991). *Gender and university teaching: A negotiated difference.* Albany, NY: State University of New York Press.

Steil, J. M., & Turetsky, B. A. (1987). Is equal better? The relationship between marital equality and psychological symptomology. In S. Oskamp (Ed.), *Applied social psychology annual* (Vol. 7, pp. 73–97). Newbury Park, CA: Sage.

Steil, J. M., & Weltman, K. (1991). Marital inequality: The importance of resources, personal attributes, and social norms on career valuing and the allocation of domestic responsibilities. *Sex Roles, 24,* 161–179.

Steinbacher, R., & Holmes, H. B. (1987). Sex choice: Survival and sisterhood. In G. Corea, R. D. Klein, J. Hanmer, H. B. Holmes, B. Hoskins, M. Kishwar, J. Raymond, R. Rowland, & R. Steinbacher (Eds.), *Man-made women: How new reproductive technologies affect women* (pp. 52–63). London: Hutchinson Press.

Steinem, G. (1990, July/August). Sex, lies, and advertising. *Ms.,* pp. 18–28.

Stern, M., & Karraker, K. H. (1989). Sex stereotyping of infants: A review of gender labeling studies. *Sex Roles, 20,* 501–522.

Stewart, L. P., Stewart, A. D., Friedley, S. A., & Cooper, P. J. (1990). *Communication between the sexes: Sex differences, and sex role stereotypes* (2nd ed.). Scottsdale, AZ: Gorsuch Scarisbrick.

Strine, M. S. (1992). Understanding how things work: Sexual harassment and academic culture. *Journal of Applied Communication Research, 4,* 391–400.

Stroman, C. A. (1989). To be young, male and black on prime-time television. *Urban Research Review, 12,* 9–10.

Study finds family changed forever. (1992, August 25). *Raleigh News and Observer,* p. A4.

Study links high testosterone to male urge for upper hand. (1991, July 17). *Raleigh News and Observer,* pp. A1, A8.

Study links men's cognitive abilities to seasonal cycles. (1991, November 11). *Raleigh News and Observer,* p. A3.

Study of black females cites role of praise. (1985, June 25). *New York Times,* p. C5.

Study reports sex bias in news organizations. (1989, April 11). *New York Times,* p. C22.

Study says women face glass walls as well as ceilings. (1992, March 3). *Wall Street Journal,* pp. B1, B2.

Suitor, J. J. (1991). Marital quality and satisfaction with the division of household labor across the family life cycle. *Journal of Marriage and the Family, 53,* 221–230.

Sullivan, H. S. (1953). *The interpersonal theory of psychiatry.* New York: W. W. Norton.

Surrey, J. L. (1983). The relational self in women: Clinical implications. In J. V. Jordan, J. L. Surrey, & A. G. Kaplan

(Speakers), *Women and empathy: Implications for psychological development and psychotherapy* (pp. 6–11). Wellesley, MA: Stone Center for Developmental Services and Studies.

Swain, S. (1989). Covert intimacy: Closeness in men's friendships. In B. J. Risman & P. Schwartz (Eds.), *Gender and intimate relationships* (pp. 71–86). Belmont, CA: Wadsworth.

Switzer, J. Y. (1990). The impact of generic word choices: An empirical investigation of age- and sex-related differences. *Sex Roles, 22,* 69–82.

Tangney, J. P., & Feshbach, S. (1988). Children's television viewing frequency: Individual differences and demographic correlates. *Personality and Social Psychology Bulletin, 14,* 145–158.

Tannen, D. (1986). *That's not what I meant! How conversational style makes or breaks relationships.* New York: Ballantine.

Tannen, D. (1990a). Gender differences in conversational coherence: Physical alignment and topical cohesion. In B. Dorval (Ed.), *Conversational organization and its development.* (Vol. XXXVIII, pp. 167–206). Norwood, NJ: Ablex.

Tannen, D. (1990b). *You just don't understand: Women and men in conversation.* New York: William Morrow.

Tannen, D. (1991, June 19). Teachers' classroom strategies should recognize that men and women use language differently. *Chronicle of Higher Education,* pp. B1, B3.

Tannen, D. (1992, October 12). The real Hillary factor. *New York Times,* p. A19.

Tavris, C. (1992). *The mismeasure of woman.* New York: Simon and Schuster.

Tavris, C., & Baumgartner, A. (1983, February). How would your life be different? *Redbook,* pp. 92–95.

Taylor, B., & Conrad, C. R. (1992). Narratives of sexual harassment: Organizational dimensions. *Journal of Applied Communication Research, 4,* 401–418.

Television Bureau of Advertising. (1990). *Media comparisons* (SRI Rep. A 9055-15). New York: Author.

Television Bureau of Advertising. (1991). *Media comparisons* (SRI Rep. A 9055-4). New York: Author.

Tetenbaum, T. J., & Pearson, J. (1989). The voices in children's literature: The impact of gender on the moral decisions of storybook characters. *Sex Roles, 20,* 381–395.

Texier, C. (1990, April 22). Have women surrendered in MTV's battle of the sexes? *New York Times,* pp. H29, H31.

Thomas, V. G. (1989). Body-image satisfaction among black women. *Journal of Social Psychology, 129,* 107–112.

Thomas, V. G., & James, M. D. (1988). Body image, dieting tendencies, and sex-role traits in urban black women. *Sex Roles, 18,* 523–529.

Thompson, E. H., Jr. (1991). The maleness of violence in dating relationships: An appraisal of stereotypes. *Sex Roles, 24,* 261–278.

Thompson, E. H., Jr., & Pleck, J. H. (1987). The structure of male role norms. In M. S. Kimmel (Ed.), *Changing men: New directions in research on men and masculinity*

(pp. 25–36). Newbury Park, CA: Sage.

Thompson, L., & Walker, A. J. (1989). Gender in families: Women and men in marriage, work, and parenthood. *Journal of Marriage and the Family, 51,* 845–871.

Thorne, B., & Henley, N. (1975). *Language and sex: Difference and dominance.* Rowley, MA: Newbury House.

Tidball, M. E. (1989). Women's colleges: Exceptional conditions, not exceptional talent, produce high achievers. In C. S. Pearson, D. L. Shavlik, & J. G. Touchton (Eds.), *Educating the majority: Women challenge tradition in higher education* (pp. 157–172). New York: American Council on Education/Macmillan.

Tierney, H. (Ed.). (1989). *Volume I: Views from the sciences.* Westport, CT: Greenwood Press.

Tierney, H. (Ed.). (1990). *Volume II: Literature, arts, and learning.* Westport, CT: Greenwood Press.

Tierney, H. (Ed.). (1991). *Volume III: History, philosophy, and religion.* Westport, CT: Greenwood Press.

Tiggemann, M., & Rothblum, E. D. (1988). Gender differences in social consequences of perceived overweight in the United States and Australia. *Sex Roles, 18,* 75–86.

Todd-Mancillas, W. (1981). Masculine generics — sexist language: A review of literature and implications for speech communication professionals. *Communication Quarterly, 29,* 107–115.

Tognoli, J. (1980). Male friendship and intimacy across the life span. *Family Relations, 29,* 273–279.

Treichler, P. A., & Kramarae, C. (1983). Women's talk in the ivory tower. *Communication Quarterly, 31,* 118–132.

Trotter, R. J. (1983, August). Baby face. *Psychology Today,* pp. 15–20.

Trouble at the top. (1991, June 17). *U.S. News and World Report,* pp. 40–48.

Tucker, L. A. (1983). Muscular strength and mental health. *Journal of Personality and Social Psychology, 45,* 1255–1360.

Ueland, B. (1992, November/December). Tell me more: On the fine art of listening. *Utne Reader,* pp. 104–109.

Unger, R., & Crawford, M. (1992). *Women and gender: A feminist psychology.* New York: McGraw-Hill.

U. S. Department of Labor, Bureau of Labor Statistics. (1991). *Employment and earnings, February 1991.* Washington, DC: U. S. Government Printing Office.

U. S. Merit Systems Protection Board. (1988). *Sexual harassment in the federal government: An update 2.* Washington, DC: Author.

The Virginia Slims Opinion Poll. (1990), pp. 79–81. (Cited in Faludi, 1991, p. 91.)

Wadsworth, A. J. (1989). The uses and effects of mass communication during childhood. In J. Nussbaum (Ed.), *Lifespan communication* (pp. 93–116). Hillsdale, NJ: Lawrence Erlbaum.

Wagenheim, J. (1990, September/October). The secret life of men. *New Age Journal,* pp. 40–45, 106–118.

Wallis, C. (1989, December 4). Onward women! *Time,* pp. 80–89.

Walsh, K. (1978). *Neuropsychology.* Edin-burg, London: Churchill Livingstone.

Wamboldt, F. S., & Reiss, D. (1989). Defining a family heritage and a new relationship identity: Two central tasks in the making of a marriage. *Family Process, 28,* 317–335.

Warme, B. D., Lundy, K. L. P., & Lundy, L. A. (Eds.). (1992). *Working part-time: Risks and opportunities.* Westport, CT: Praeger.

Warshaw, R. (1988). *I never called it rape.* New York: Harper and Row.

Warshaw, R. (1991, May 5). Ugly truths of date rape elude the screen. *New York Times,* pp. H17, H22.

Waterman, A. S., & Whitbourne, S. K. (1982). Androgyny and psychological development among college students and adults. *Journal of Personality, 50,* 121–133.

Watzlawick, P., Beavin, J., & Jackson, D. D. (1967). *Pragmatics of human communication.* New York: W. W. Norton.

Weedon, C. (1987). *Feminist practice and poststructuralist theory.* New York: Basil Blackwell.

Weiler, K. (1988). *Women teaching for change: Gender, class and power.* New Haven, CT: Yale University Press.

Weisman, L. K. (1992). *Discrimination by design: A feminist critique of the man-made environment.* Chicago: University of Chicago Press.

Weiss, L., & Lowenthal, M. F. (1975). Life course perspectives on friendships. In M. F. Lowenthal, M. Thurner, & D. Chiriboga (Eds.), *Four stages of life: A comparative study of women and men facing transitions* (pp. 48–61). San Francisco, CA: Jossey Bass.

Welch, L. B. (Ed.). (1992). *Perspectives on minority women in higher education.* Westport, CT: Praeger.

Welter, B. (1966). The cult of true womanhood: 1820–1960. *American Quarterly, 18,* 151–174.

West, C., & Zimmerman, D. H. (1983). Small insults: A study of interruptions in cross-sex conversations between unacquainted persons. In B. Thorne, C. Kramarae, & N. Henley (Eds.), *Language, gender and society* (pp. 102–117). Rowley, MA: Newbury House.

West, C., & Zimmerman, D. H. (1987). "Doing gender." *Gender and Society, 1,* 125–151.

Wheeless, V. E. (1984). A test of the theory of speech accommodation using language and gender orientation. *Women's Studies in Communication, 7,* 13–22.

Where have all the smart girls gone? (1989, April). *Psychology Today,* p. 20.

White, B. (1989). Gender differences in marital communication patterns. *Family Process, 28,* 89–106.

Whiting, B., & Edwards, C. (1973). A cross cultural analysis of sex differences in the behavior of children aged three through eleven. *Journal of Social Psychology, 91,* 171–188.

Wilkie, J. R. (1991). The decline in men's labor force participation and income and the changing structure of family economic support. *Journal of Marriage and the Family, 53,* 111–122.

Williams, D. G. (1985). Gender, masculinity-femininity, and emotional intimacy in same-sex friendship. *Sex Roles, 12,* 587–600.

Williams, J. E., & Best, D. L. (1990). *Measuring sex stereotypes: A multination study* (rev. ed.). Newbury Park, CA: Sage.

Williams, J. H. (1973). Sexual role identification and personality functioning in girls: A theory revisited. *Journal of Personality, 41,* 1–8.

Williamson, N. E. (1976). *Sons and daughters: A cross-cultural survey of parental preferences.* Beverly Hills, CA: Sage.

Willis, F. N., Jr. (1966). Initial speaking distance as a function of the speaker's relationship. *Psychonomic Science, 5,* 221–222.

Wills, T. A., Weiss, R. L., & Patterson, G. R. (1974). A behavioral analysis of the determinants of marital satisfaction. *Journal of Consulting and Clinical Psychology, 42,* 802–811.

Winch, R. F. (1962). *Identification and its familial determinants.* New York: Schocken Books.

Winstead, B. A. (1986). Sex differences in same-sex friendships. In V. J. Derlega & B. A. Winstead (Eds.), *Friendship and social interaction* (pp. 81–99). New York: Springer-Verlag.

Wise, S., & Stanley, L. (1987). *Georgie Porgie: Sexual harassment in everyday life.* New York: Pandora Press.

Witt, S. L. (1990). *The pursuit of race and gender equity in American academe.* Westport, CT: Praeger.

Wolf, N. (1991). *The beauty myth.* New York: William Morrow.

Women in media say careers hit "glass ceiling." (1988, March 2). *Easton Express,* p. A9.

Women on tv: The picture still needs some tuning, study says. (1990, October 20). *Charlotte Observer*, pp. B1, B2.

Women on Words and Images. (1972). *Dick and Jane as victims*. Princeton, NJ: Author.

Wood, J. T. (1982). Communication and relational culture: Bases for the study of human relationships. *Communication Quarterly, 30*, 75–84.

Wood, J. T. (1986). Different voices in relationship crises: An extension of Gilligan's theory. *American Behavioral Scientist, 29*, 273–301.

Wood, J. T. (1992a). *Spinning the symbolic web: Human communication and symbolic interaction*. Norwood, NJ: Ablex.

Wood, J. T. (1992b). Telling our stories: Narratives as a basis for theorizing sexual harassment. *Journal of Applied Communication Research, 4*, 349–363.

Wood, J. T. (1993a). Engendered relationships: Interaction, caring, power, and responsibility in close relationships. In S. Duck (Ed.), *Processes in close relationships: Contexts of close relationships* (Vol. 3). Beverly Hills, CA: Sage.

Wood, J. T. (1993b). Engendered identities: Shaping voice and mind through gender. In D. Vocate (Ed.), *Intrapersonal communication: Different voices, different minds*. Hillsdale, NJ: Lawrence Erlbaum.

Wood, J. T. (1993c). *Who cares: Women, care, and culture*. Carbondale, IL: Southern Illinois University Press.

Wood, J. T. (1993d). Issues facing nontraditional members of academe. In

G. M. Phillips, D. S. Gouran, S. A. Kuehn, & J. T. Wood (Eds.), *Professionalism: A survival guide for beginning academics*. Cresskill, NJ: Hampton Press.

Wood, J. T. (1993e). Gender and relationship crises: Contrasting reasons, responses, and relational orientations. In J. Ringer (Ed.), *Queer words, queer images: The (re)construction of homosexuality*. Albany, NY: New York University Press.

Wood, J. T. (1993f). Defining and studying sexual harassment as situated experience. In G. Kreps (Ed.), *Communication and sexual harassment in the workplace*. Cresskill, NJ: Hampton Press.

Wood, J. T. (1993g). Enlarging conceptual boundaries: Research in interpersonal communication. In S. Bowen & N. Wyatt (Eds.), *Transforming visions* (pp. 19–49). Cresskill, NJ: Hampton Press.

Wood, J. T. (1994, in press). Saying it makes it so: The discursive construction of sexual harassment. In S. Bingham (Ed.), *Discursive conceptualizations of sexual harassment*. Greenwood, NJ: Praeger.

Wood, J. T., & Conrad, C. R. (1983). Paradox in the experience of professional women. *Western Journal of Speech Communication, 47*, 305–322.

Wood, J. T., & Inman, C. (1993, August). In a different mode: Recognizing male modes of closeness. *Journal of Applied Communication Research*.

Wood, J. T., & Lenze, L. F. (1991a). Strategies to enhance gender sensitivity in communication education. *Communication Education, 40*, 16–21.

Wood, J. T., & Lenze, L. F. (1991b). Gender and the development of self: Inclusive pedagogy in interpersonal communication. *Women's Studies in Communication, 14,* 1–23.

Wood, W. (1987). Meta-analytic review of sex differences in group performance. *Psychological Bulletin, 102,* 53–71.

Woodman, S. (1991, May). How super are heros? *Health,* pp. 40, 49, 82.

Woody, B. (1989). Black women in the emerging services economy. *Sex Roles, 21,* 45–67.

Woody, B. (1992). *Black women in the workplace: Impacts of structural change in the economy.* Westport, CT: Greenwood Press.

Wooley, S. C., & Wooley, O. W. (1984, February). Feeling fat in a thin society. *Glamour,* pp. 198–252.

Working dads finding more flexibility on the job. (1991, June 16). *Raleigh News and Observer,* p. E6.

The wounds of words. (1992, October 12). *Newsweek,* pp. 90–91.

Wright, P. H. (1982). Men's friendships, women's friendships, and the alleged inferiority of the latter. *Sex Roles, 8,* 1–20.

Wright, P. H. (1988). Interpreting research on gender differences in friendship: A case for moderation and a plea for caution. *Journal of Social and Personal Relationships, 5,* 367–373.

Wright, P. H., & Scanlon, M. B. (1991). Gender role orientations and friendship: Some attenuation but gender differences still abound. *Sex Roles, 24,* 551–566.

Yellin, J. F. (1990). *Women and sisters: Antislavery feminists in American culture.* New Haven, CT: Yale University Press.

Young, C. (1992, October 4). Female trouble. *Washington Post,* pp. C1, C4.

Zimmerman, D. H., & West, C. (1975). Sex roles, interruptions and silences in conversation. In B. Thorne & N. Henley (Eds.), *Language and sex: Differences and dominance* (pp. 105–129). Rowley, MA: Newbury House.

Zita, J. N. (1981). Historical amnesia and the lesbian continuum. *Signs: Journal of Women in Culture and Society, 7,* 172–187.

Index